Contemporary College Reader

Contemporary College Reader

Second Edition

Joyce S. Steward
University of Wisconsin-Madison

Scott, Foresman and Company
Glenview, Illinois   Dallas, Tex.   Oakland, N.J.
Palo Alto, Calif.   Tucker, Ga.   London, England

For Chuck and Peggy
Who Share the Work and the Joy
of Writing

An Instructor's Manual is available. It may be obtained through a local Scott, Foresman representative or by writing to English Editor, College Division, Scott, Foresman and Company, 1900 E. Lake Avenue, Glenview, IL 60025.

Library of Congress Cataloging in Publication Data
Main entry under title:

Contemporary college reader.

   Includes bibliographical references and index.
   1. College readers.   2. English language—Rhetoric.
I. Steward, Joyce S.
PE1417.C652   1981   808'.0427   80-22824
ISBN 0-673-15404-1 (pbk.)

   2 3 4 5 6-KPF-85 84 83 82 81

Acknowledgments

Shana Alexander. "The Fine Art of Marital Fighting" from *Women Talking* by Shana Alexander, written originally for *Life* (1963) Time Inc. Reprinted with permission.   Maya Angelou. "A Lesson in Living." From *I Know Why the Caged Bird Sings* by Maya Angelou. Copyright © 1969 by Maya Angelou. Reprinted by permission of Random House, Inc.   James Austin. "How to Make Your Luck Work For You" by James H. Austin. Copyright © 1977 by Executive Publications. Reprinted by permission of Executive Health Reports and the author.   Russell Baker. "Ben Was Swell, but He's Out" by Russell Baker, from *The New York Times* (1965). © 1965 by The New York Times Company. Reprinted by permis-

PREFACE

Writers are readers first, and learning to write is inextricably linked to learning to read. " 'Tis the good reader that makes the good book," wrote Ralph Waldo Emerson, and the Second Edition of *Contemporary College Reader*, like the first, is intended to help students become both good readers and good writers. The selections and the accompanying study materials may be read for facts and ideas to initiate discussion and written reactions, but they should also be read for much more. Good readers will observe not only what is written, but how. And through sensitive attention to such features as choice of words and images, the form of sentences, the shape of paragraphs, and the structure of the writing as a whole, they should then become better able to make the decisions and embark on the practice necessary for success in writing.

As in the First Edition of this text, most of the selections are fairly short, and they exemplify the patterns conveniently identified as methods of development. This edition has a slightly larger number of selections, and nearly half of the fifty-one here are new, although some authors from the earlier edition are represented by different titles.

The arrangement of material in this Second Edition is the same as in the first. Because a writer's initial need is to find something to say, Chapter 1 emphasizes the importance of observation and the recording of personal experience. A writer's notebooks are both records and workbooks, a way of preserving incidents and thoughts and of providing a testing ground for experimenting with language and form. But writing does not stop with the notebook or the first draft, and while the selections in Chapter 1 suggest ways to begin, the final paired excerpts from Thoreau's *Journal* and *Walden* also illustrate the power of revision.

Chapters 2 and 3 offer examples of description and narration, not for the sake of picture and story alone but for the purpose of making a point. Included are scenes, events, and ideas for readers to relate to, as well as vivid and original ways of describing and narrating for them to observe. For instance, Andrew Ward's word picture of the changes at his neighborhood gas station will show how to find subjects in everyday life and at the same time acquaint the beginning reader with the need for careful selection of details; Maya Angelou's account of an influential friendship should both prompt readers to recall similar experiences and teach them the skillful use of dialogue.

Chapters 4 through 10 present traditional expository methods. Of course, the patterns frequently merge and blur, and most pieces of writing are not developed by one mode alone. Nevertheless, many are organized by a recognizably dominant method, and it is often easier to learn principles of organization by tackling one major purpose, one method of development, at a time. In their college and postcollege writing, students will face situations where they need to exemplify, to trace a process, to compare and contrast, to explain causes and effects, to define, and to classify and divide. The selections in all these chapters, however, do more than illustrate a pattern, for they have been carefully chosen for content that will stimulate thinking as well as for their skillful and lively writing. For instance, students should be captivated by Cousteau's pictures of the human qualities of whales and at the same time discover the care he takes in arranging those qualities in a list; they should better understand the movement of the solar system as Sir James Jeans compares it to a busy London traffic circle and also see the function of analogy in explaining the unknown.

Finally, Chapter 11 offers essays and articles written primarily to persuade. Here the writers combine various methods of development to achieve their purpose: to convince a reader to agree or even to take action. Certainly most writing is to some degree persuasive, and many selections in the text have an argumentative edge, but this chapter provides special opportunities both for reacting to issues and for examining the reasoning and strategies used in presenting them. When Norman Cousins, for instance, denounces the general ignorance about pain and drugs, he does so in writing that reveals careful handling of deductive thought, that gains power from charged language, and that utilizes effective examples—all attributes characteristic of persuasive writing.

Formulating a plan, finding a system of organization, seems to give more trouble to the developing writer than does any other part of writing. To offer help here, the chapter introductions include brief models—themes in miniature—where the principles governing each method become obvious. Again, as in the First Edition, a marginal guide provides an outline of major divisions for the initial selection in each chapter after the first.

Study questions following the selections emphasize "Content and Form" and "Special Techniques." The numerous and varied suggestions for "Generating Ideas" may be used for discussion as well as for writing assignments. Although rhetorical and grammatical features are explained when they are introduced with specific essays, the Glossary of Techniques both defines and locates those features.

It is perfectly possible to rearrange the order of chapters or selections. Chapter 1 is, however, intended as a point of departure and a way of initiating discussion about writing. Chapters 2 and 3 probably belong together, either at the beginning of a course or at the end. In the chapters that treat exposition, consideration has been given to building skills, starting with the relatively easy and moving to the increasingly complex, but other orders might be equally effective. Whatever the arrangement of material, however, it is hoped that students will enjoy the reading and find in it both ideas and methods to stimulate and improve their writing.

As with the First Edition, many friends and colleagues have contributed to the development of this book. Professor Emeritus Ednah S. Thomas of the University of Wisconsin-Madison continues to be both friend and mentor in all that I attempt. Assistant Professor Abigail McCann, my co-worker in the management of the Wisconsin writing laboratory, has helped in many ways. Mary Feirn, Judy Gurd, Sally Hansen, and Gladys Veidemanis have reacted to selections and assignments, as have several groups of students with whom I have used the book or some of the materials from it. Before work on the new edition began, numerous colleagues from other universities and colleges responded to requests for comments, suggesting "keepers and changers" among the selections. Although they did not always agree, their advice was exceedingly helpful. Ann Boehm of Ithaca College; Thomas Hemmens of Pittsburg State University; Arthur Palacas of the University of Akron; Maryann Rishel of Ithaca College; John Ruszkiewicz of the University of Texas at Austin; Marjorie Smelstor of the University of Texas at San Antonio; Adam Sorkin of Pennsylvania State University; and Joan Thron of the University of Wisconsin at Green Bay all gave valuable assistance along the way as the new edition developed. Richard Welna and Stan Stoga of Scott, Foresman and Company were the inspiration and force behind the First Edition. This second time around, Amanda Clark, Doris Donald, Victoria Stewart, Mary LaMont, and Marcia Egger-Langford helped with many editorial details, and Harriett Prentiss has been a good friend not only to the book but to me. Her wise counsel and kindly encouragement have made shaping the new edition a pleasurable process. To all of these, I am deeply grateful.

Joyce S. Steward
University of Wisconsin-Madison

CONTENTS

1

2

3

NARRATION:
Framing Events   55

Contemporary College Reader

1

OBSERVING, RECORDING, WRITING

OBSERVING

"What a great idea! Why didn't I think of it?" Have you ever read a magazine article or an informal essay and thought that you could write about the same subject? Have you ever had the same experience, made similar observations, but never thought about turning the event or opinion into a subject for writing? Or have you lamented, "I just don't have anything to write about," and let it go at that?

Good writing is closely linked to good observation. "One man walks through the world with his eyes open, another with his eyes shut; and upon this difference depends all the superiority of knowledge which one man acquires over another," says a character in Charles Kingsley's *Madam How and Lady Why*. The sources for observing are everywhere. Watch the people around you. Notice the way they work, listen to what they say, see how they interact and how they solve problems. Study the natural world. Storms and droughts, sunsets and rainbows, birds and animals and plants—all are exciting if you observe them closely. Pay attention to the mechanical world. Automobiles lined up at a gas pump, a pocket calculator, a rusty windmill rattling away on an abandoned farm—any of these might spark an idea for a writer. Or find subjects to write about in the world of arts: paintings and photographs, music and dance, films and television.

Printed material provides another source of observation, for reading enables you to gather information and to get acquainted with the thoughts and opinions of other people in other times and places. As you read, notice not only *what* writers say but also *how* they say it. Observe the pattern of their thoughts, the words they use, and the ways they put them together.

The biographies and memoirs of many professional writers attest to the value of observation. In "City Walking," essayist Edward Hoagland says, ". . . aiming to be a writer, I knew that every mile I walked, the better writer I'd be." Like the artist, the photographer, and the scientist, the writer must learn to use all five senses.

A student of the Harvard geologist and zoologist Louis Agassiz wrote the following reminiscence about learning to observe closely. Although it was written about 1875, its meaning remains the same today.

Samuel Scudder

Look Again, Look Again!

It was more than fifteen years ago that I entered the laboratory of Professor Agassiz, and told him I had enrolled my name in the Scientific School as a student of natural history. He asked me a few questions about my object in coming, my antecedents generally, the mode in which I afterwards proposed to use the knowledge I might acquire, and, finally, whether I wished to study any special branch. To the latter I replied that, while I wished to be well grounded in all departments of zoology, I purposed to devote myself specially to insects.

"When do you wish to begin?" he asked.

"Now," I replied.

This seemed to please him, and with an energetic "Very well!" he reached from a shelf a huge jar of specimens in yellow alcohol. "Take this fish," he said, "and look at it; we call it a haemulon; by and by I will ask what you have seen."

With that he left me, but in a moment returned with explicit instructions as to the care of the object entrusted to me.

"No man is fit to be a naturalist," said he, "who does not know how to take care of specimens."

I was to keep the fish before me in a tin tray, and occasionally moisten the surface with alcohol from the jar, always taking care to replace the stopper tightly. Those were not the days of ground-glass stoppers and elegantly shaped exhibition jars; all the old students will recall the huge neckless glass bottles with their leaky, wax-besmeared corks, half eaten by insects, and begrimed with cellar dust. Entomology was a cleaner science than ichthyology, but the example of the Professor, who had unhesitatingly plunged to the bottom of the jar to produce the fish, was infectious; and though this alcohol had a "very ancient and fishlike smell," I really dared not show any aversion within these sacred precincts, and treated the alcohol as though it were pure water. Still I was conscious of a passing feeling of disappointment, for gazing at a fish did not commend itself to an ardent entomologist. My friends at home, too, were annoyed when they discovered that no amount of eau-de-Cologne would drown the perfume which haunted me like a shadow.

8   In ten minutes I had seen all that could be seen in that fish, and started in search of the Professor—who had, however, left the Museum; and when I returned, after lingering over some of the odd animals stored in the upper apartment, my specimen was dry all over. I dashed the fluid over the fish as if to resuscitate the beast from a fainting fit, and looked with anxiety for a return of the normal sloppy appearance. This little excitement over, nothing was to be done but to return to a steadfast gaze at my mute companion. Half an hour passed—an hour—another hour; the fish began to look loathsome. I turned it over and around; looked it in the face—ghastly; from behind, beneath, above, sideways, at a three-quarters' view—just as ghastly. I was in despair; at an early hour I concluded that lunch was necessary; so, with infinite relief, the fish was carefully replaced in the jar, and for an hour I was free.

9   On my return, I learned that Professor Agassiz had been at the Museum, but had gone, and would not return for several hours. My fellow-students were too busy to be disturbed by continued conversation. Slowly I drew forth that hideous fish, and with a feeling of desperation again looked at it. I might not use a magnifying-glass; instruments of all kinds were interdicted. My two hands, my two eyes, and the fish: it seemed a most limited field. I pushed my finger down its throat to feel how sharp the teeth were. I began to count the scales in the different rows, until I was convinced that that was nonsense. At last a happy thought struck me—I would draw the fish; and now with surprise I began to discover new features in the creature. Just then the Professor returned.

10   "That is right," said he; "a pencil is one of the best of eyes. I am glad to notice, too, that you keep your specimen wet, and your bottle corked."

11   With these encouraging words, he added:

"Well, what is it like?" 12

He listened attentively to my brief rehearsal of the 13
structure of parts whose names were still unknown to me:
the fringed gill-arches and movable operculum; the pores
of the head, fleshy lips and lidless eyes; the lateral line, the
spinous fins and forked tail; the compressed and arched
body. When I finished, he waited as if expecting more, and
then, with an air of disappointment:

"You have not looked very carefully; why," he continued 14
more earnestly, "you haven't even seen one of the most
conspicuous features of the animal, which is as plainly
before your eyes as the fish itself; look again, look again!"
and he left me to my misery.

I was piqued; I was mortified. Still more of that wretched 15
fish! But now I set myself to my task with a will, and
discovered one new thing after another, until I saw how
just the Professor's criticism had been. The afternoon
passed quickly; and when, towards its close, the Professor
inquired:

"Do you see it yet?" 16

"No," I replied, "I am certain I do not, but I see how little 17
I saw before."

"That is next best," said he, earnestly, "but I won't hear 18
you now; put away your fish and go home; perhaps you
will be ready with a better answer in the morning. I will
examine you before you look at the fish."

This was disconcerting. Not only must I think of my fish 19
all night, studying, without the object before me, what this
unknown but most visible feature might be; but also,
without reviewing my discoveries, I must give an exact
account of them the next day. I had a bad memory; so I
walked home by Charles River in a distracted state, with
my two perplexities.

The cordial greeting from the Professor the next morning 20
was reassuring; here was a man who seemed to be quite as
anxious as I that I should see for myself what he saw.

"Do you perhaps mean," I asked, "that the fish has 21
symmetrical sides with paired organs?"

His thoroughly pleased "Of course! of course!" repaid 22
the wakeful hours of the previous night. After he had
discoursed most happily and enthusiastically—as he

always did—upon the importance of this point, I ventured to ask what I should do next.

23 "Oh, look at your fish!" he said, and left me again to my own devices. In a little more than an hour he returned, and heard my new catalogue.

24 "That is good, that is good!" he repeated; "but that is not all; go on"; and so for three long days he placed that fish before my eyes, forbidding me to look at anything else, or to use any artificial aid. "Look, look, look," was his repeated injunction.

25 This was the best entomological lesson I ever had—a lesson whose influence has extended to the details of every subsequent study; a legacy the Professor had left to me, as he has left it to many others, of inestimable value, which we could not buy, with which we cannot part.

26 A year afterward, some of us were amusing ourselves with chalking outlandish beasts on the Museum blackboard. We drew prancing starfishes; frogs in mortal combat; hydra-headed worms; stately crawfishes, standing on their tails, bearing aloft umbrellas; and grotesque fishes with gaping mouths and staring eyes. The Professor came in shortly after, and was as amused as any at our experiments. He looked at the fishes.

27 "Haemulons, every one of them," he said; "Mr.———— drew them."

28 True; and to this day, if I attempt a fish, I can draw nothing but haemulons.

29 The fourth day, a second fish of the same group was placed beside the first, and I was bidden to point out the resemblances and differences between the two; another and another followed, until the entire family lay before me, and a whole legion of jars covered the table and surrounding shelves; the odor had become a pleasant perfume; and even now, the sight of an old, six-inch, worm-eaten cork brings fragrant memories.

30 The whole group of haemulons was thus brought in review; and, whether engaged upon the dissection of the internal organs, the preparation and examination of the bony framework, or the description of the various parts, Agassiz's training in the method of observing facts and their orderly arrangement was ever accompanied by the

urgent exhortation not to be content with them.

"Facts are stupid things," he would say, "until brought   31
into connection with some general law."

At the end of eight months, it was almost with reluctance   32
that I left these friends and turned to insects; but what I had
gained by this outside experience has been of greater value
than years of later investigation in my favorite groups.

RECORDING

Get into the habit of keeping a record of your observations,
of storing them in a notebook or journal. "When found,
make a note of," says Captain Cuttle, a character in Charles
Dickens' novel *Dombey and Son*. As a student, you no doubt
have taken notes on the reading for your various courses.
Perhaps you have also jotted down memorable passages,
things that you like so well that you wish to recall them
later. But you should also get into the habit of making notes
on your experiences and on your observations of everyday
life so that these too are preserved. It is sad not to be able to
retrieve a lost idea that seemed brilliant when it flashed
across your mind, or a forgotten fact or faded memory that
you need to make a point in an argument or to illustrate a
conclusion. The best way to store your observations is to
keep a journal.

The journal habit has still another value. Just as you need
to record observations—the material for writing—you need
to practice putting thoughts on paper. Learning to write is
more like learning to ski or to play the piano than it is like
studying calculus or anthropology. Practice helps you
discover ways to improve. Writing down ideas for your
own use forces you to examine them. Putting thoughts on
paper for someone else to read forces you to evaluate not
only the content—what you say—but also the expression—how you say it. As soon as you have written a page or
two, you become the reader of the material. And you can
assess its clarity or its imprecision, its effectiveness or
ineffectiveness in conveying your thoughts and impressions.

Many writers, both past and present, comment about the

value of journal-keeping, and the journals famous writers keep are often published. The notebooks of Nathaniel Hawthorne, Virginia Woolf, Katherine Mansfield, Anaïs Nin, Flannery O'Connor, and many others reveal much about these writers' lives as well as about their practice of writing. Often the source of ideas or the triggering incident that later developed into a literary work may be discovered through reading a writer's notebooks.

In "Travelling with a Notebook" Freya Stark, a British author and photographer, tells how she writes down the causes of impressions, the particulars that will later re-evoke the original experience. The short excerpts from the journals of Henry David Thoreau are comments on the importance of the lifelong habits of journal-keeping that he started when he was twenty, a few months before his graduation from Harvard. His journals comprise thirty-nine manuscript volumes that he once referred to as his "Field Notes." Those notes were not only the direct source for much of his writing, a storehouse of experience and thoughts, but a way of practicing his craft and developing literary skills.

Freya Stark

On Travelling with a Notebook

I was walking, when the first Cyprus crisis was at its height,   1
among the narrow byways that hug the Athens Acropolis,
when three or four very small boys came round a corner
and asked me where I belonged, naming one country after
another. Having exhausted all they could think of, they
looked at me with horror when I said, *"Anglia,"* English.
The eldest reached for a stone and they all in chorus cried,
"Kyprus." Not knowing any Greek with which to argue, I
took the first historic name that came into my mind and
said, "Pericles." The classic bond held. "Themistocles"
one little boy responded, and I added "Alcibiades" for
good measure. The little group instantly adopted me and
shepherded me through all the dangers of their fellows,
just out from school. This is years ago now and I had
forgotten the episode until I happened to read the single
word *Anglia* in a notebook of that day and the whole picture
with its fierce gay little figures and the Acropolis hanging
above them came back into my mind. The notebook, with
its single word, had saved it from total oblivion.

A pen and a notebook and a reasonable amount of   2
discrimination will change a journey from a mere annual
into a perennial, its pleasures and pains renewable at will.

The keeping of a regular diary is difficult and apt in most   3
lives to be dull as it plods through good and bad at one even
pace. But the art of the notebook is selective.

One's own sensations and emotions should be left out,   4
while the *causes* that produced them are carefully identified. These are usually small concrete facts not particularly
spectacular in themselves, and a single word, as we have
seen, may recall them. In describing Venice or Athens for
instance, it is useless to record the rapture: no mere
mention can renew it: but the cause—some shimmer of
light or shadow, some splash of the flat-prowed gondola as
its crest turns a corner, or a sudden vignette, or the Greeks
reading their morning papers in the theatre of Diony-

sius—such concrete glimpses produced the delight in the first place and can recapture it in the notebook's pages. Colours, odours (good or bad), even apparently irrelevant details like the time of day, are far more evocative than a record of feelings, which represent the writer and not the scene and are, usually, a mere embarrassment in later reading.

5   I have notes for instance of the Persian tribes moving to their summer pastures under the great tombs of their kings at Naksh-i-Rustum: the tumult of goats, camels and horses, the women's black turbans, the clanking of cooking-pots tied to the saddle, and some effect of dust and distance are jotted down; and the remembrance of that wide freedom, the immensity of the background in space and time, come back automatically with the mention of the sights that caused them.

6   A painter once told me how important it is in a quick sketch that the few details one has time for should be put in with particular care; far from being less precise they should be more so, or the illusion of reality will fail. The same rule applies to notebook jottings. A painter like Edward Lear shows the same awareness in his diary as in his sketches, where the details of light and colour for which he had no time are scribbled in pencil at the side.

7   In poetry the process is fundamentally the same, but is worked out more completely with the harmony of words. The everyday traveller's notebook stops short of this process: it is intended for himself alone, it touches a chord already familiar to him, and therefore need not concern itself with the facilities of language: it is reminiscent, not creative, and can be brief and quite unreadable. With a little practice in selection, a very few lines will hold the gist of a whole day's journey; and the writing of them is much less of a labour than one would suppose.

8   You can amuse yourself too by reversing the process when you are reading. Pick out of any particular description the concrete things the author must have seen and remembered: they have an immediate and convincing authenticity. The psalmist's hills in the mirage of noon that "skip like lambs"—have we not seen them at the deserts'

edges?—or Keats's musk rose "the murmurous haunt of flies on summer eves."

From things seen and remembered the fancy soars into the abstract and wanders beyond the notebook's scope—though sometimes even there a simile or image may well be recorded: "wine-dark" one may fancy the young Homer writing, on some Aegean headland while his sight still held. No confines to the human thought have yet been recorded. But the notebook is not the patrimony only of the thinker: it is an "Open Sesame" for every holiday traveller who learns to select his adjectives carefully and pack them compactly, so that at any odd moment he may recapture the spell of his days.

Henry David Thoreau

On Keeping a Journal

1   I would fain keep a journal which should contain those thoughts and impressions which I am most liable to forget that I had; which would have in one sense the greatest remoteness, in another, the greatest nearness to me.

(January 10, 1851)

2   To set down such choice experiences that my own writings may inspire me and at last I may make wholes of parts. Certainly it is a distinct profession to rescue from oblivion and to fix the sentiments and thoughts which visit all men more or less generally, that the contemplation of the unfinished picture may suggest its harmonious completion. Associate reverently and as much as you can with your loftiest thoughts. Each thought that is welcomed and recorded is a nest egg, by the side of which more will be laid. Thoughts accidentally thrown together become a frame in which more may be developed and exhibited. Perhaps this is the main value of a habit of writing, of keeping a journal, —that so we remember our best hours and stimulate ourselves. My thoughts are my company. They have a certain individuality and separate existence, aye, personality. Having by chance recorded a few disconnected thoughts and then brought them into juxtaposition, they suggest a whole new field in which it was possible to labor and to think. Thought begat [sic] thought.

(January 22, 1852)

3   A Journal is a record of experiences and growth, not a preserve of things well done or said. I am occasionally reminded of a statement which I have made in conversation and immediately forgotten, which would read much better than what I put in my journal. It is a ripe, dry fruit of

long-past experience which falls from me easily, without giving pain or pleasure. The charm of the journal must consist in a certain greenness, though freshness, and not in maturity. Here I cannot afford to be remembering what I said or did, my scurf cast off, but what I am and aspire to become.

(January 24, 1856)

I would fain make two reports in my Journal, first the incidents and observations of to-day; and by to-morrow I review the same and record what was omitted before, which will often be the most significant and poetic part. I do not know at first what it is that charms me. The men and things of to-day are wont to lie fairer and truer in to-morrow's memory.

4

(March 27, 1857)

WRITING

Now what will you make of all this observing once you have recorded it? How will it become something significant for others to read? This is where your individuality comes in again. Just as your observations are yours alone, for no two people look at things in quite the same way, your shaping of these observations into a piece of writing is also unique.

For most people, ideas emerge when relationships become apparent, when a thread of meaning links several observations. For instance, you notice a raccoon killed on the highway, and you think, "His instincts did not adapt him to be aware of speeding cars." At the library, you go through a door that swings open automatically, and you bump a small child who has wandered away from his parents. Suddenly you have a subject for an essay on the encroachment of mechanical devices into our everyday lives. Or you find that a small fishing village you love to visit has been invaded by too many tourists, too much traffic. The experience could generate an essay contrasting the "two faces" of the town, as it once was and as it now is; or your paper might analyze the effects of the tourists on the town's economy. Someone once said that "ideas go in pairs," and such "pairing" should happen for you if you observe closely and think about your experiences.

Translating your observations into writing is largely a matter of making choices. The first choice, of course, is the decision about what to write. After that comes the choice of which details to include and which to leave out. You should choose only those materials that develop and keep the focus on your main point and purpose. But many other choices are also involved. Should your idea be expressed implicitly or explicitly? What inferences can you draw from what you have observed? Is there sufficient evidence to carry your judgments persuasively? Should you interpret facts or let them stand by themselves? These are some of the questions you must ask yourself prior to, during, and even after you write—and you must answer them to your and to your readers' satisfaction.

After deciding what to include and what to omit, you must decide on the form and style you want, and that takes practice. Most writers do not write a piece once; they write and rewrite it several times. E. B. White (see p. 86) says, "A writer does a lot of work the reader isn't conscious of, and never gets any credit." Writing is work, and doing it well brings satisfaction. Henry David Thoreau comments on this third step in the process: "No day will have been wholly misspent, if one sincere, thoughtful page has been written."

Thoreau's work illustrates the transforming of observations recorded in a notebook into writing of lasting significance. Compare the following excerpts: the first is a journal entry Thoreau made in August, 1845; the second is the expanded version of that same experience as Thoreau wrote it for *Walden*. Although that book was first published in 1854, scholars have discovered earlier manuscripts that reveal how Thoreau changed and enriched both the style and the form through several writings.

From Thoreau's *Journal*— August, 1845

After the evening train has gone by and left the world to   1
silence and to me, the whip-poor-will chants her vespers
for half an hour. And when all is still at night, the owls take
up the strain, like mourning women their ancient ululu.
Their most dismal scream is truly Ben-Jonsonian. Wise
midnight hags! It is no honest and blunt tu-whit tu-who of
the poets, but, without jesting, a most solemn graveyard
ditty,—but the mutual consolations of suicide lovers
remembering the pangs and the delights of supernal love in
the infernal groves. And yet I love to hear their wailing,
their doleful responses, trilled along the woodside,
reminding me sometimes of music and singing birds, as if it
were the dark and tearful side of music, the regrets and
sighs, that would fain be sung. The spirits, the *low* spirits
and melancholy forebodings, of fallen spirits who once in
human shape night-walked the earth and did the deeds of
darkness, now expiating with their wailing hymns,
threnodiai, their sins in the very scenery of their
transgressions. They give me a new sense of the vastness
and mystery of that nature which is the common dwelling
of us both. "Oh-o-o-o-o that I never had been bor-or-or-or-
orn!" sighs one on this side of the pond, and circles in the
restlessness of despair to some new perch in the gray oaks.
Then, "That I never had been bor-or-or-or-orn!" echoes one
on the further side, with a tremulous sincerity, and
"Bor-or-or-or-orn" comes faintly from far in the Lincoln
woods.

And then the frogs, bullfrogs; they are the more sturdy   2
spirits of ancient wine-bibbers and wassailers, still unrepentant, trying to sing a catch in their Stygian lakes. They
would fain keep up the hilarious good fellowship and all
the rules of their old round tables, but they have waxed
hoarse and solemnly grave and serious their voices,
mocking at mirth, and their wine has lost its flavor and is
only liquor to distend their paunches, and never comes
sweet intoxication to drown the memory of the past, but
mere saturation and water-logged dullness and distension.

Still the most aldermanic, with his chin upon a pad, which answers for a napkin to his drooling chaps, under the eastern shore quaffs a deep draught of the once scorned water, and passes round the cup with the ejaculation *tr-r-r-r-oonk, tr-r-r-r-oonk, tr-r-r-r-oonk!* and straightway comes over the water from some distant cove the selfsame password, where the next in seniority and girth has gulped down to his mark; and when the strain has made the circuit of the shores, then ejaculates the master of ceremonies with satisfaction *tr-r-r-r-oonk!* and each in turn repeats the sound, down to the least distended, leakiest, flabbiest paunched, that there be no mistake; and the bowl goes round again, until the sun dispels the morning mist, and only the patriarch is not under the pond, but vainly bellowing *troonk* from time to time, pausing for a reply.

From *Walden*—Chapter IV, "Sounds"

Regularly at half-past seven, in one part of the summer, 1
after the evening train had gone by, the whip-poor-wills
chanted their vespers for half an hour, sitting on a stump by
my door, or upon the ridge-pole of the house. They would
begin to sing almost with as much precision as a clock,
within five minutes of a particular time, referred to the
setting of the sun, every evening. I had a rare opportunity
to become acquainted with their habits. Sometimes I heard
four or five at once in different parts of the wood, by
accident one a bar behind another, and so near me that I
distinguished not only the cluck after each note, but often
that singular buzzing sound like a fly in a spider's web, only
proportionally louder. Sometimes one would circle round
and round me in the woods a few feet distant as if tethered
by a string, when probably I was near its eggs. They sang at
intervals throughout the night, and were again as musical
as ever just before and about dawn.

When other birds are still, the screech owls take up the 2
strain, like mourning women their ancient u-lu-lu. Their
dismal scream is truly Ben Jonsonian. Wise midnight hags!
It is no honest and blunt tu-whit tu-who of the poets, but,
without jesting, a most solemn graveyard ditty, the mutual
consolations of suicide lovers remembering the pangs and
the delights of supernal love in the infernal groves. Yet I
love to hear their wailing, their doleful responses, trilled
along the woodside; reminding me sometimes of music and
singing birds; as if it were the dark and tearful side of music,
the regrets and sighs that would fain be sung. They are the
spirits, the low spirits and melancholy forebodings, of
fallen souls that once in human shape night-walked the
earth and did the deeds of darkness, now expiating their
sins with their wailing hymns or threnodies in the scenery
of their transgressions. They give me a new sense of the
variety and capacity of that nature which is our common
dwelling. *Oh-o-o-o-o that I never had been bor-r-r-r-n!* sighs
one on this side of the pond, and circles with the
restlessness of despair to some new perch on the gray oaks.

Then—*that I never had been bor-r-r-n!* echoes another on the farther side with tremulous sincerity, and—*bor-r-r-n!* comes faintly from far in the Lincoln woods.

3   I was also serenaded by a hooting owl. Near at hand you could fancy it the most melancholy sound in Nature, as if she meant by this to stereotype and make permanent in her choir the dying moans of a human being—some poor weak relic of mortality who has left hope behind, and howls like an animal, yet with human sobs, on entering the dark valley, made more awful by a certain gurgling melodiousness,—I find myself beginning with the letters *gl* when I try to imitate it,—expressive of a mind which has reached the gelatinous, mildewy stage in the mortification of all healthy and courageous thought. It reminded me of ghouls and idiots and insane howlings. But now one answers from far woods in a strain made really melodious by distance,— *Hoo hoo hoo, hoorer hoo;* and indeed for the most part is suggested only pleasing associations, whether heard by day or night, summer or winter.

4   I rejoice that there are owls. Let them do the idiotic and maniacal hooting for men. It is a sound admirably suited to swamps and twilight woods which no day illustrates, suggesting a vast and undeveloped nature which men have not recognized. They represent the stark twilight and unsatisfied thoughts which all have. All day the sun has shone on the surface of some savage swamp, where the single spruce stands hung with usnea lichens, and small hawks circulate above, and the chickadee lisps amid the evergreens, and the partridge and rabbit skulk beneath; but now a more dismal and fitting day dawns, and a different race of creatures awakes to express the meaning of Nature there.

5   Late in the evening I heard the distant rumbling of wagons over bridges,—a sound heard farther than almost any other at night,—the baying of dogs, and sometimes again the lowing of some disconsolate cow in a distant barn-yard. In the meanwhile all the shore rang with the trump of bullfrogs, the sturdy spirits of ancient wine-bibbers and wassailers, still unrepentant, trying to sing a catch in their Stygian lake,—if the Walden nymphs will pardon the comparison, for though there are almost no weeds,

there are frogs there,—who would fain keep up the hilarious rules of their old festal tables, though their voices have waxed hoarse and solemnly grave, mocking at mirth, and the wine has lost its flavor, and become only liquor to distend their paunches, and sweet intoxication never comes to drown the memory of the past, but mere saturation and waterloggedness and distention. The most aldermanic, with his chin upon a heartleaf, which serves for a napkin to his drooling chops, under this northern shore quaffs a deep draught of the once scorned water, and passes round the cup with the ejaculation *tr-r-r-oonk, tr-r-r-oonk, tr-r-r-oonk!* and straightway comes over the water from some distant cove the same password repeated, where the next in seniority and girth has gulped down to his mark; and when this observance has made the circuit of the shores, then ejaculates the master of ceremonies, with satisfaction, *tr-r-r-oonk!* and each in his turn repeats the same down to the least distended, leakiest, and flabbiest paunched, that there be no mistake; and then the bowl goes round again and again, until the sun disperses the morning mist, and only the patriarch is not under the pond, but vainly bellowing *troonk* from time to time, and pausing for a reply.

2

DESCRIPTION:
SHAPING DETAILS

In her novel *Their Eyes Were Watching God,* Zora Neale Hurston describes a time when a group of her characters "sat around on the porch and passed around the pictures of their thoughts" for the others to see. How do you pass around the pictures of your thoughts? By describing, as specifically as you can, those people, places, things, and events that have become a part of your thought because they have been a part of your experience. Description is a part of conversation, and of almost all writing. It is a part of autobiography, and will be a part of the writing you do about yourself; it is a part of storytelling, whether the story is fictional or real. And, as you will discover from the essays in this section, it is a part of exposition, writing that explains an idea or opinion. Passages of description are found in almost all exposition, from a personal essay to a scientific explanation to an argument. The amount of description will vary. Some paragraphs and sections of essays may be purely descriptive, while in other cases description may be the primary method by which the writer conveys ideas.

Regardless of the amount of description in an essay, the writer attempts to make the reader see, feel, and hear by *showing* rather than by merely *telling*. It is through the use of specific detail and concrete language that abstract ideas and half-formed thoughts can become vividly real. By showing sense impressions and the thoughts these impressions evoke—by painting pictures in words—the writer can make a forceful comment about an experience or condition in life.

Description ranges from the *objective*, or scientific, to the *subjective*, or impressionistic. The former is factual writing in which the writer treats with detachment the subject being described. In the latter, the writer steps in not only to record observations but also to present and sometimes to comment upon the feelings and attitudes aroused by an experience or scene, showing the reader both what it was like and how the writer reacted to it. The word *ranges* is important here, since description can be more or less objective, more or less subjective.

The purpose of the objective description is different from that of the more subjective one. In a description of a solar power system for the home or in the description of the fish that Agassiz wanted to elicit from Samuel Scudder, the purpose is practical and scientific. In such cases, the describer makes an accurate record of the phenomena observed and the relationships between them. You can find many such descriptions in textbooks, in encyclopedias, in direction-giving manuals on a variety of subjects. At the other extreme, the purpose for a purely impressionistic description may be the recording of a mood or the creation of a picture whose significance you wish to share.

Most descriptive writing falls somewhere in between these two extremes. No matter where it falls, however, the qualities of good description remain the same. Effective description depends on close observation, the careful selection of details, and precise language with which to paint the picture, whether it be objective or subjective. Furthermore, through the careful arrangement of the details and language, the writer unifies the picture so that it projects a *dominant impression*.

Notice the rich details and language in this paragraph:

The fading sunlight came through chinks in the pepper trees and fluttered about upon the hard-packed earth, like a covey of yellow evening birds. The houses, though small, and almost all alike, because they were company-owned, were neat and white washed. Their porches were filled with large potted plants growing in cheerful red Hills Brothers coffee cans, or with smaller potted plants in green Del Monte peach cans. In some of the houses, the shades were drawn, for here people worked on shifts and one man's night might be his neighbor's day. A picket fence, also white washed, ran the length of the street, and each man had a private gate to his yard, weighted in such a manner with old springs and defunct batteries that it swung shut of itself and he need never give a thought to its closing. From under the pepper trees, the derricks were out of sight. It was only the smell of oil—which was taste as much as smell—the sight of an occasional sump hole at the end of a side street, and the sound of the pumps that reminded Cress where she was. The sound of the pumps filled the air, deep, rhythmical, as if the hills themselves breathed; or as if deep in the wells some kind of heart shook the earth with so strong a beat that Cress could feel it in the soles of her feet as she walked along.—Jessamyn West, *Cress Delahanty*

The author herself never intrudes, never speaks as "I." Yet she is there, selecting and arranging to produce a vivid impression of a small California oil town. She places the plants not just in "flower pots" or "coffee cans" but in "cheerful red Hills Brothers coffee cans" and "green Del Monte peach cans." She recreates the sensory experience of the "smell of oil" and the "sound of the pumps," which "Cress could feel . . . in the soles of her feet." Such sharp details, concrete words, and language that conveys vivid sense impressions are all marks of good descriptive writing.

West's paragraph is also planned to give a sense of movement—the reader moves along the streets of the town, past the houses, gradually becoming aware of the constant rhythm of the oil pumps. The arrangement of the paragraph is spatial, but other paragraphs of description may move from a general impression to the supporting details, or from the details to a general impression, stated or implied. Note the movement in this paragraph from the author's description of his boyhood:

The kitchen was the great machine that set our lives running; it whirred down a little only on Saturdays and holy days. From my mother's kitchen I gained my first picture of life as a white, overheated, starkly lit workshop redolent with Jewish cooking, crowded with women in housedresses, strewn with fashion magazines, patterns, dress material, spools of thread—and at whose center, so lashed to her machine that bolts of energy seemed to dance out of her hands and feet as she worked, my mother stamped the treadle hard against the floor, hard, hard, and silently, grimly at war, beat out the first rhythm of the world for me.—Alfred Kazin, *A Walker in the City*

Both the choice and arrangement of details in description depend largely on the writer's point of view. Some description is clearly written from a physical point of view—from a single place of observation: an open window facing out on a noisy and crowded city street, a cliff overlooking an ocean, for example. The physical point of view can shift, especially in description that involves the passing of time. When this occurs, the writer must provide clear signals to indicate that time is passing. In other cases, however, the point of view is mental rather than physical. Here the writer not only presents details impressionistically, he also describes his reactions to and feelings about the scene. The paragraph by Kazin provides a good example of this kind of point of view.

Like the point of view, the language of description can vary; but it should be chosen for the exactness of both *denotation* (the literal meaning of a word) and *connotation* (the emotional overtones and shades of meaning of a word). West's reference to "red Hills Brothers coffee cans" is literal—denotative; but she uses the connotative word *cheerful* to lend an added meaning to the phrase. A great deal of descriptive language may involve *metaphors,* which are figures of speech that imply comparisons between apparently unlike things. When Kazin calls the kitchen a "machine that set our lives running," and when he says that his mother's "bolts of energy seemed to dance out of her hands and feet," he is using metaphors to make the reader see what the scene and the activity were like.

All these devices are used by writers to lend variety, power, and color to their descriptions. The essays in this section exemplify these and other techniques for passing around the pictures of your thoughts.

John J. Rowlands

John J. Rowlands (b. 1892), son of a Canadian lumberman, began his close observations of nature as a gold prospector in upper Ontario and Quebec at the age of eighteen. After working for the United Press as a reporter and eventually as manager of its Boston office, he became Director of News Services for the Massachusetts Institute of Technology. He now lives in Cohasset, Massachusetts. Rowlands has recorded his observations of nature in two ways: with words and with camera. His book *Cache Lake Country* (1947) is based on his travels in the trackless forests of northern Canada, a region that he has photographed extensively. In the following selection from *Spindrift* (1960), subtitled "From a House by the Sea," he vividly recreates pictures with words.

Lonely Place

1

Generalization about loneliness, followed by an immediate focus on the amusement park (par. 1)

There are many kinds and varying degrees of loneliness, but the peculiar loneliness of a once-teeming place deserted and for the time forgotten can be found only in a seaside amusement resort on a cloudy Sunday afternoon in winter. Nothing but the warming sun of another spring can dispel the all-pervading sense of abandonment and desolation.

2

General impression of the area (par. 2)

Crowded with strollers on summer evenings, the broad promenade that fronts the gaudy palaces in the World of Fun and Frivolity is deserted, and dirty drifted snow lies in the sheltered niches. Across the boulevard where a milk truck scurries to more lucrative fields lies the sea and miles of empty beach on which thousands come to bask and bathe in summer. The empty life-guard towers look out to sea; their boats are gone; no human being in sight. The wind and the waves alone are moving and the only sound is the sea.

3

Initial block of specific details: the closed attractions (pars. 3–8)

The merry-go-rounds are boarded up for winter, but in a shed the saddled animals, running lions and tigers, leaping deer, prancing ponies, a sedate goat, and one giraffe, are huddled close together as if for companionship and warmth. Just along the walk the cavernous mouth of the Tunnel of Love is closed, and the echoes of summer squeals of adventure within have long since died away.

The serpentine skeleton of "The Longest, Fastest, Steepest, Most Thrilling Roller Coaster on Earth" stands black against the winter sky, its cars in canvas shrouds below. Gone is the roar and the clatter of flying wheels and the screams of clinging riders. 4

A faded poster of a sinuous dancer, with its bold promise of exotic sights within, flaps in the wind, and next door shutters hide the counter of the ring-tossing game with its prizes of paunchy pandas, garish dolls, and slender canes. And the dodger who sticks his head through a canvas curtain to taunt his customers to hit him will not be heard again until the sun is high and warm. 5

The season is closed in the shooting gallery and some of the ducks on their endless belt, a deer, and a white rabbit still lie where they fell to the midnight shots on Labor Day night. 6

Through the grimy window of the saltwater taffy counter you see the cold steel arms of the taffy puller motionless and empty-handed. Somehow that brings back memories of the prickly feeling of spun sugar on the tongue. Then suddenly for a moment—or is it just the wind?—you hear the voice of a barker calling "Hurr-ree-ee, hurr-ree-ee, hurr-ree-ee, folks! See the harem girls in the Dance of Love! Strictly for adults only." But the platform with its gaudy backdrop from which he always makes his pitch is gone. Just the wind. 7

A sign painter's portrait of The Fattest Woman in the Universe, a monstrosity on a stool, is all but obliterated by the wind and flying sand. Her hair is thin and her face is pale, but the smile still shows. 8

Area of description is widened (pars. 9–10)

9

Beyond the boulevard near the long white bathhouse the bandstand is filled with drifted snow and flying rubbish, but the winds have swept the open places clean. The stark white guide-lines on the empty parking lot lie row on slanting row like the bleaching bones of huge fish.

10

Further along where the great ferris wheel stands with its seats swathed in canvas, a sign recalls the delights of fried clams, but now the vats are dry and the corn-meal bin is empty. The gray thing that scurries under the counter is just a rat.

Recollection of past odors (par. 11)

11

Although it is near the freezing mark and the wind is rising you remember the cold satisfaction of frozen custard, "The Kind Your Mother Used To Make." And so it was, but the shop is dark and gloomy now. Gone are the smells of hot dogs, onions and hamburgers, frying fish and chips, hot popcorn and freshly roasted peanuts; and gone, too, the stench of hot exhaust gases from the cars that crawl through shimmering heat-waves on the boulevard.

Recollection of past sounds (par. 12)

12

Here in the shadows of the deserted buildings of The World of Fun and Frivolity lurks a kind of loneliness found nowhere else, the solitude of sounds of life replaced by silence. Back from an August night comes the carefree tinny music of the merry-go-rounds and the chain songs from jukeboxes in the snack bars, and through it all the persistent and persuasive voices of the barkers. You hear again the cries of children weary and bewildered, the irresponsible laughter of men and their girls, and the sharp crack of rifles in the shooting-gallery. Now only the yowling of a cat and the roar of the sea are real.

Recollection of past sights (pars. 13–14)

13

High across the front of the buildings neon tubing that glows so warmly on a summer night is a cold and glassy maze, hiding the patterns of signs that can't be read until they glow again.

The steamboat pier, a stubby finger pointing across the bay toward the city, is fenced off and posted with "No Trespassing" warnings. No sign now of the silent old men who fish from the cap-log all day long in summer. The blast of the steamer's midnight whistle, warning of the last trip back, is just another echo.

14

The wind is coming from the sea again and the drifting sand grits under your feet like sugar on a kitchen floor. It's cold and damp. Far ahead you glimpse a spot of neon-red. Its message when you reach it is "Hot Dogs." The tired-looking man nursing three weary-looking wieners on a hot plate slides up the window of his slot-in-the-wall booth. "No fish and chips this time of year," he tells you, "just dogs. Just dogs and piccalilli. No mustard."

15
Contrasting pictures of open hot-dog stand and closed stands (pars. 15–16)

The pizza-pie parlor just ahead is closed, of course, and there's nothing very hopeful in the next sign that offers a full-course shore dinner, "Chowder, clams and lobster, ice cream and watermelon" for two dollars. The place where creamy root beer once flowed from a huge cask with polished hoops has been replaced by an orange-drink fountain, but the big round globe is empty.

16

The day is getting close to darkness and the only other sign of life lies behind the headlights of a prowl car that slows down close to the curb to look you over. And with good reason. Why should anyone choose to walk The World of Fun and Frivolity on a Sunday afternoon in winter?

17
Conclusion: the only sign of life is an occasion for self-questioning (par. 17)

Discussing Content and Form

1. Point out specific details in the essay that are particularly successful in creating an atmosphere of loneliness.

2. How much of the description depends on the contrast of the winter scene to the memories of summer?

3. The number and the kind of details a writer of description gives help create the effect. How many closed attractions does Rowlands mention in paragraphs 3–8? Do you think he could achieve the same effect with fewer details? Why or why not?

4. Rowlands never appears in the description as "I," yet it is obvious that he is the observer and recorder of the entire scene. Why do you think he chose not to write in the first person? Who is the "you" referred to in paragraph 7 and in several paragraphs following that?

5. Even though the writer does not explicitly state that "I felt this way" or "I thought that way," he interprets the scene by selecting those details he wishes to include. Explain how this selection becomes a form of interpretation in the essay.

Considering Special Techniques

1. A writer usually organizes a piece of description to give it a feeling of movement, thus guiding the reader through a scene (or around an object) with some sense of order. Sometimes it seems the writer is actually pointing to the things the reader should notice. Using the marginal guides, trace the movement of the walker around the amusement park. What groupings and connections do you find among the details, even those within paragraphs?

2. Good description relies heavily upon sense impressions: seeing, hearing, tasting, touching, smelling. Writers try to convey what they sense in a way that will in turn awaken their readers' senses. In this essay, find examples of words and details that evoke each of the senses. Does one sense seem dominant? If so, which? Why is the park a particularly good subject for using a variety of sense impressions?

3. Rowlands' essay is characterized by many adjectives: "empty life-guard towers" (par. 2); "serpentine skeleton" (par. 4); "faded poster of a sinuous dancer" (par. 5). What is the effect of the multiplicity of such words? Do you occasionally find the use of these adjectives repetitious? Explain.

4. What is the effect of these concluding sentences from several of the paragraphs? Why are they placed as they are?

"The stark white guide-lines on the empty parking lot lie row on slanting row like the bleaching bones of huge fish." (par. 9)
"The gray thing that scurries under the counter is just a rat." (par. 10)
"Now only the yowling of a cat and the roar of the sea are real." (par. 12)

5. *Words to learn and use:* pervading *(par. 1);* sedate, cavernous *(par. 3);* sinuous *(par. 5);* swathed *(par. 10).*

Generating Ideas

1. *Describe an amusement park or resort area as it is during the peak season. Try to evoke the various senses by using vivid details and sensory language.*

2. *Describe a type of amusement or attraction with which you are familiar.*

3. *Describe some of the people who operate rides, stands, and various sideshows in an amusement park or at a circus. Try to give details that capture not only their appearance but also their way of living.*

4. *If you have ever visited a national park or state park in the off-season, or if you have seen some resort area when few people were present, write a paper in which your choice of details is influenced by your feelings (loneliness, contentment, sadness, etc.) about the place.*

5. *Write a paper describing your school when most of the students have left it, either late at night or during a vacation break. If you can, include some details that show the contrasts between the quiet time and the busy one: "There are no empty soft-drink bottles and discarded coffee cups around the dark and silent vending machines." If you have never seen the campus during such a time, you might write from imagination.*

Josephine W. Johnson

Josephine W. Johnson (b. 1910) is a novelist, short-story writer, poet, and essayist. Very early in her career (1935) she won a Pulitzer Prize for her novel *Now in November,* a vividly realistic story of a Missouri farm family struggling for survival during the Depression. Her other works include *Winter Orchard and Other Stories* (1935), *Jordanstown* (1937), *Paulina: The Story of an Apple-Butter Jar* (1939), *Wildwood* (1946), *The Dark Traveler* (1963), *The Sorcerer's Son and Other Stories* (1965), and *Circle of Seasons* (1974). Her collections of poetry are *Unwilling Gypsy* (1936) and *Year's End* (1937). *The Inland Island* (1969), from which the following sketch comes, is a collection of personal essays that comment on natural and human change as Johnson observes it through the year on a southern Ohio farm.

April

1 In two days the great forsythia cage, a vast mound of green wickets hung sparsely with yellow bells of flowers, the first leaves fine as a mist, has become a wild monster. Hairy, green, bushy, green-toothed and horned.

2 The birds no longer perch forming delicate Japanese paintings of the old school. They disappear. Who knows what goes on inside, now.

3 A great hare, dark and slow, huge as a domestic rabbit gone wild, lumbers out. We do not have many rabbits. Wild housecats have taken toll. One morning long ago the black wild Persian stalked beneath a bush. He moved around the house, and five minutes later the yard was strewn with limp brown bodies. Wantonly destroyed, as only one was eaten.

4 April is an assault. Too much. Too much of everything. It begins with the toothwort, a modest flower related to the turnip. There is not much to say about it except that it is pretty and uninteresting and first. Like most wild flowers, if picked and brought inside, it droops and has a weedy negligible look, reminiscent of one's own thoughts, which seem fresh, honest, sparkling, rare, when rooted still in the cool brain cave, but in the open air, picked and presented, tend to appear dusty and weak, irrelevant to the human condition of flesh, brass, and blood.

5 The hillside near the creek is covered with hepatica, a lovely flower. Hepatica, meaning the liver, is an ugly name.

The shape of the leaves does not resemble the liver at all. (What doctor finding a mass of flesh shaped like these leaves within the human would know what to do? What is this? These lovely green leaves? There is no liver here.)

The hillside is held up by clumps of flowers on hairy 6 stems. The petals lavender and white and pink and purple and sometimes a rare, pale blue. The same spot of earth, riddled with moss, snail shells, ferns, oak leaves, produces this pale rainbow. They last very little longer than a rainbow, and, returning in a day or two, one finds no flowers, only hard green pods and a crop of odd-cut leaves.

These spring pools of flowers, rising year after year in 7 the same place, are a recurring joy that never fails. It is one of the joys of living for years in the same place. This is not limited to wild land, nor to large places, but few stay long enough even on one small spot, or care enough to plant the reoccurring seed and know this seasonal miracle.

In the north pasture, the title "pasture" by courtesy 8 only now, a pool of mint rises each spring, a lavender pond filled with bees, great bumblebees, small yellow bees, and the brown furry bees like winged mice. It is filled with the humming of the bees and the spicy smell of the mint leaves (leaves rich, green, convoluted as seashells) and the pool widens into a wider pool of white pansy violets, like a foam at the far edges. The wild pansies are separate and move in the wind.

This is the view from the woodchuck's den above the 9 draw. His porch is well beaten down, paths lead to it under the raspberry hoops. Wrens sputter around on the ravine rocks and broken crockery from the old rabbit hutches. All this view is probably wasted on his stupid dogginess. Unless, like Pythagoras*, he thinks of the violet leaves as spinach. The morning sun warms his front porch, the mists over the cool stones withdraw. I think of him coming out and contemplating this fresh April world, the smell of broken mint, the violets moving in the morning breeze, the trilling sounds of wrens before the day has brought their spirits down. But in good truth he is not emerging that

---

*Greek philosopher of the sixth century B.C.; although little is known about him, many tales are told of his supernatural powers.

early, and if it is a cold day, he is not emerging at all. He is concerned about mating, if he is through hibernating, and thereafter (four weeks to be exact) the mate has two to eight blind, hairless young.

10   It was time for the fat old lady to leave in late March. Holing up with any of the creatures has about lost its charm by then. The smell of woodchuck holes on warm days drives out our old dream of dozing through winter in dark woodchuck dens.

11   An intermittent rain this morning, now ceasing. The quail are very shrill. Soggy but nervous. The woods are still bare except for the thousand limp umbrellas of the buckeyes—a low border holding up the hill. Spent time yesterday winding up the tents of caterpillars, shoving the flabby silk masses down in the earth. They squash green. Hateful. Hateful. Slashed at briars. An enormous ache in my head. A rage against my limitations.

12   This delicate shaking carpet of wild flowers! Ferns, violets, squirrel corn, bluebells, spring beauties, bloodroot leaves, wild poppies. All at once and together. And above the red trillium the red lilies of the papaws.

13   Goldfinches arrived. A mad twittering like a zoo full of canaries. Invisible. Finally saw a goldfinch separate from the gold-green tassels of the ash, the gold-green bunchy leaves. Finches seem paler close to the eye.

14   Rain and thunder this morning. Wish it would wash all the damn caterpillars away. They unwind in reels before my eyeballs at night. They look like phlegm on the trunks of the trees, clothing the branches. The very clouds look like their tents.

15   Now the sun has come out on a wet wash. The dogwood blossoms in the draw are dazzling. One drop of rain blazes up. The doves start their depressing cooing. What is the bird that keeps crying "Zooder-zeeee"? A whippoorwill last night was almost raging. Those cool, fierce calls!

16   The buckeye has yellow pyramids . . . thatches . . . stacks. The Ohio buckeye is *Aesculus glabra.* The extract from its bark will irritate the cerebro-spinal system of humans. (To what purpose and what end?) Its pollination is by bees. The horse chestnut is *Aesculus hippocastanum.* Alcohol from seeds is made, or can be made. The whole

vegetative world is full of stuff like that. Poisons galore.

Tried to clear a path to the last great oak through the 17
interlocking fiendishness of rusting barbed-wire fence and
wood soft as cardboard. Roots of Virginia creeper vines
booby-trapped the path. Old rotting tree held the old
rotting fence in place. Put down the wire clippers. Came
back and it had black walnut in its jaws—foraging in my
absence.

This curious passion to tidy, tidy, tidy, tidy— 18
lives . . . leaves . . . trees . . . emotions . . . house . . .
surface . . . weeds . . . lawns . . . minds . . . words . . .
endless sweeping, clipping, washing, arranging.

Lachesis,* the measurer, was young once, a terrible 19
young woman.

The worms are unspeakable today. 20

What is the composition of this delicate shaking carpet 21
of flowers, this blanket which the old king will tear away?
Squirrel corn, like bleeding hearts, but waxy, white-grey-
bluish; leaves fine-cut as ferns. The honey-and-hyacinth
fragrance lifts the heart. The windflower, the anemone, the
wind that opens the petals, blows the petals away. The
yellow wild poppy bursting from its prickly buds; the
shaking bells of the Greek valerian, the bluebells. Lavender
in our woods, delicate and deceptive, from *valere*, to be
strong and powerful. And from its roots a drug, calming
and carminative, also having tonic properties. Yellow trout
lilies, white lilies, purple violets, yellow violets, white
violets, and everywhere the red trillium. *Trillium sessile* and
erectum—also known as wake-robin, toadshade, birthwort,
squawroot and stinking Benjamin (and for good reason, as
one knows who hunts a dead mouse or a nasty fungus
smell and finds no source except this innocent and
brick-red flower).

In the open fields the rich, edible leaves of winter cress, 22
mustard or yellow rocket, *Barbarea vulgaris*. They are to be
eaten on St. Barbara's day, in December, when tender, but
the bitterness is too strong for most persons. Green satin
shining leaves named after an early saint, "murdered by

*One of the three Fates in Greek mythology, she measured the span of life
and presided over the future.

her pagan father for becoming Christian." She's turned the tables now. My bitterness is too strong for most persons. . . .

Discussing Content and Form

1. What is Johnson's reaction to the coming of spring? Explain your answer.

2. In what sense is April (at least in a region of seasonal changes) "an assault" (par. 4)? Which details convey the impression of an assault?

3. How do the following passages convey the feeling of sadness that sometimes accompanies the appreciation of beauty?

> *"if picked and brought inside, it [the toothwort] droops and has a weedy negligible look, reminiscent of one's own thoughts. . . ." (par. 4)*
> *"few stay long enough even on one small spot, or care enough to plant the reoccurring seed and know this seasonal miracle." (par. 7)*

4. How does the "curious passion to tidy" (par.18) relate to the coming of spring?

5. This selection is from a book which is an almanac of sorts, a personal reflection upon the changing seasons. You may notice that Johnson is not strict about keeping one kind of detail (flowers, plants, animal life, etc.) together in a single paragraph. Rather she organizes her impressions in a fashion that is almost random. Why does Johnson mix the kinds of details rather than treat all one type before turning to another? How does the lack of strict organization contribute to the effect of a personal observation?

Considering Special Techniques

1. Johnson's description abounds in metaphor—*saying one thing in terms of another, implying a comparison between two things that are actually unlike. Discuss the effectiveness of the following metaphors in particular, and examine any others you find.*

> *"forsythia cage" (par. 1)*
> *"birds . . . perch forming delicate Japanese paintings" (par. 2)*
> *"spring pools of flowers" (par. 7)*

"limp umbrellas of the buckeyes" (par. 11)
"sun has come out on a wet wash" (par. 15)
Closely related to metaphor is simile—*the explicit statement of likeness between two unlike things, using* like *or as to make the comparison. In Johnson's essay, "they [caterpillars] look like phlegm on the trunks of trees" (par. 14) and "wood soft as cardboard" (par. 17) are similes. Discuss the effectiveness of these, and examine any others you find.*

2. Johnson also relies heavily on the use of images —*words and phrases that convey sense impressions. Here is an example of each type of image:*

Sight: *"green wickets" (par. 1)*
Sound: *"trilling sound of wrens" (par. 9)*
Touch: *"they squash green" (par. 11)*
Smell: *"spicy . . . mint leaves" (par. 8)*
Taste: *"edible leaves of winter cress" (par. 22)*

Find images that fuse two or more senses. For instance, what senses are involved in "The smell of woodchuck holes on warm days drives out our old dream of dozing through winter in dark woodchuck dens" (par. 10)?

3. What is the effect of giving the botanical names for some of the flowers? Consider how the use of these names affects you as a reader and what it reveals about the writer.

4. Study the use Johnson makes of sentence fragments:
"Too much. Too much of everything." (par. 4)
"Hateful. Hateful. Slashed at briars." (par. 11)
"Rain and thunder this morning." (par. 14)
"Poisons galore." (par. 16)
Relate the use of sentence fragments to the idea that April is "an assault." Why is this technique appropriate in description, whereas it might not be in analytical exposition?

5. Words to learn and use: sparsely *(par. 1);* wantonly *(par. 3);* negligible, reminiscent *(par. 4);* convoluted *(par. 8);* phlegm *(par. 14);* pollination, vegetative *(par. 16);* fiendishness, foraging *(par. 17);* carminative, fungus *(par. 21).*

Generating Ideas

1. Many writers have described seasons, months, or shorter periods of the year in order to make a thoughtful or philosophical statement. The columnist L. E. Sissman describes November as "the unsung month," a pause between autumn and winter that "confers perspective on the more distant past and hence on the present and future." You are probably familiar with various reactions to the seasons: "I like spring—it gives a sense of starting over"; or "The world is most beautiful in autumn just before everything dies." Choose a month or season to describe. Use specific, vivid details to lead to a statement about the meaning of the time for you or for people in general.

2. If you have gardened or if you have an interest in plants, try one of these topics:

    a. In paragraph 20, Johnson says that the "worms are unspeakable today." Develop a paper about the pests that must be dealt with by gardeners.

    b. Obtain copies of a seed catalog, or of a magazine such as Better Homes and Gardens, Sunset, *etc., which offers suggestions for planting and maintaining gardens. Write a paper describing an outdoor setting you would like to create. Make your writing as objective as you can, using botanical names for the plants, for example.*

3. Observe the activities of an animal (either domesticated or wild) or of a bird for about a half hour. Write a paper describing exactly what the object of your observation did—how it moved, played, ate, slept, etc.

4. People often develop strong attachments to the land or to a particular area in which they have lived or which they have visited. If you have felt this strong pull, write an essay describing the area and the attraction it has for you.

5. Use paragraph 18 concerning the urge to "tidy, tidy, tidy" as the basis for a paper about compulsive housekeeping or lawn maintenance. Or write about "tidying" such things as lives, emotions, and minds.

Andrew Ward

Andrew Ward (b. 1946) attended Oberlin College and the Rhode Island School of Design. His short stories and essays appear regularly in a wide variety of magazines and his work has often been reprinted in anthologies. He has published two solo collections, *Fits and Starts: The Premature Memoirs of Andrew Ward* (1978) and *Bits and Pieces* (1980). Ward, who now lives in Connecticut, considers himself a humorist and says that he wants, above all, " to get a laugh and raise a smile." He certainly achieves that goal with the selection that follows, a thoughtful and picture-full essay that first appeared in *Atlantic Monthly*, a magazine for which Ward is a contributing editor.

They Also Wait Who Stand and Serve Themselves

Anyone interested in the future of American commerce should take a drive sometime to my neighborhood gas station. Not that it is or ever was much of a place to visit. Even when I first moved here, five years ago, it was shabby and forlorn: not at all like the garden spots they used to feature in the commercials, where trim, manicured men with cultivated voices tipped their visors at your window and asked what they could do for you.

Sal, the owner, was a stocky man who wore undersized, popped-button shirts, sagging trousers, and oil-spattered work shoes with broken laces. "Gas stinks" was his motto, and every gallon he pumped into his customers' cars seemed to take something out of him. "Pumping gas is for morons," he liked to say, leaning indelibly against my rear window and watching the digits fly on the pump register. "One of these days I'm gonna dump this place on a Puerto Rican, move to Florida, and get into something nice, like hero sandwiches."

He had a nameless, walleyed assistant who wore a studded denim jacket and, with his rag and squeegee, left a milky film on my windshield as my tank was filling. There was a fume-crazed, patchy German shepherd, which Sal kept chained to the air pump, and if you followed Sal into his cluttered, overheated office next to the service bays, you ran a gauntlet of hangers-on, many of them Sal's brothers and nephews, who spent their time debating the merits of the driving directions he gave the bewildered travelers who turned into his station for help.

4 "I don't know," one of them would say, pulling a bag of potato chips off the snack rack, "I think I would have put 'em onto 91, gotten 'em off at Willow, and then—Bango!—straight through to Hamden."

5 Sal guarded the rest room key jealously and handed it out with reluctance, as if something in your request had betrayed some dismal aberration. The rest room was accessible only through a little closet littered with tires, fan belts, and cases of oil cans. Inside, the bulb was busted and there were never any towels, so you had to dry your hands on toilet paper—if Sal wasn't out of toilet paper, too.

6 The soda machine never worked for anyone except Sal, who, when complaints were lodged, would give it a contemptuous kick as he trudged by, dislodging warm cans of grape soda which, when their pop-tops were flipped, gave off a fine purple spray. There was, besides the snack rack in the office, a machine that dispensed peanuts on behalf of the Sons of Garibaldi. The metal shelves along the cinderblock wall were sparsely stocked with cans of cooling system cleaner, windshield de-icer, antifreeze, and boxed head lamps and oil filters. Over the battered yellow wiper case, below the Coca Cola clock, and half hidden by a calendar from a janitorial supply concern, hung a little brass plaque from the oil company, awarded in recognition of Salvatore A. Castallano's ten-year business association.

7 I wish for the sake of nostalgia that I could say Sal was a craftsman, but I can't. I'm not even sure he was an honest man. I suspect that when business was slow he may have cheated me, but I never knew for sure because I don't know anything about cars. If I brought my Volvo in because it was behaving strangely, I knew that as far as Sal was concerned it could never be a simple matter of tightening a bolt or re-attaching a hose. "Jesus," he'd wearily exclaim after a look under the hood. "Mr. Ward, we got problems." I usually let it go at that and simply asked him when he thought he could have it repaired, because if I pressed him for details he would get all worked up. "Look, if you don't

want to take my word for it, you can go someplace else. I mean, it's a free country, you know? You got spalding on your caps, which means your dexadrometer isn't charging, and pretty soon you're gonna have hairlines in your flushing drums. You get hairlines in your flushing drums and you might as well forget it. You're driving junk."

I don't know what Sal's relationship was with the oil company. I suppose it was pretty distant. He was never what they call a "participating dealer." He never gave away steak knives or NFL tumblers or stuffed animals with his fill-ups, and never got around to taping company posters on his windows. The map rack was always empty, and the company emblem, which was supposed to rotate thirty feet above the station, had broken down long before I first laid eyes on it, and had frozen at an angle that made it hard to read from the highway.

If, outside of television, there was ever such a thing as an oil company service station inspector, he must have been appalled by the grudging service, the mad dog, the sepulchral john. When there was supposed to have been an oil shortage a few years ago, Sal's was one of the first stations to run out of gas. And several months ago, during the holiday season, the company squeezed him out for good.

I don't know whether Sal is now happily sprinkling olive oil over salami subs somewhere along the Sun Belt. I only know that one bleak January afternoon I turned into his station to find him gone. At first, as I idled by the no-lead pump, I thought the station had been shut down completely. Plywood had been nailed over the service bays, Sal's name had been painted out above the office door, and all that was left of his dog was a length of chain dangling from the air pump's vacant mast.

But when I got out of the car I spotted someone sitting in the office with his boots up on the counter, and at last caught sight of the "Self-Service Only" signs posted by the pumps. Now, I've always striven for a degree of self-sufficiency. I fix my own leaky faucets and I never let the bellboy carry my bags. But I discovered as I squinted at the instructional sticker by the nozzle that there are limits to my desire for independence. Perhaps it was the bewilderment with which I approach anything having to do with the internal combustion engine; perhaps it was my conviction that fossil fuels are hazardous; perhaps it was the expectation of service, the sense of helplessness, that twenty years of oil company advertising had engendered, but I didn't want to pump my own gas.

12   A mongrel rain began to fall upon the oil-slicked tarmac as I followed the directions spelled out next to the nozzle. But somehow I got them wrong. When I pulled the trigger on the nozzle, no gas gushed into my fuel tank, no digits flew on the gauge.

13   "Hey, buddy," a voice sounded out of a bell-shaped speaker overhead. "Flick the switch."

14   I turned toward the office and saw someone with Wild Bill Hickok hair leaning over a microphone.

15   "Right. Thanks," I answered, and turned to find the switch. There wasn't one. There was a bolt that looked a little like a switch, but it wouldn't flick.

16   "The switch," the voice crackled in the rain. "Flick the switch."

17   I waved back as if I'd finally understood, but I still couldn't figure out what he was talking about. In desperation, I stuck the nozzle back into my fuel tank and pulled the trigger. Nothing.

18   In the office I could see that the man was now angrily pulling on a slicker. "What the hell's the matter with you?" he asked, storming by me. "All you gotta do is flick the switch."

19   "I couldn't find the switch," I told him.

20   "Well, what do you call this?" he wanted to know, pointing to a little lever near the pump register.

21   "A lever," I told him.

22   "Christ," he muttered, flicking the little lever. The digits on the register suddenly formed neat rows of zeros. "All right, it's set. Now you can serve yourself," the long-haired man said, ducking back to the office.

23   As the gas gushed into my fuel tank and the fumes rose to my nostrils, I thought for a moment about my last visit to Sal's. It hadn't been any picnic: Sal claimed to have found something wrong with my punting brackets, the German shepherd snapped at my heels as I walked by, and nobody

had change for my ten. But the transaction had dimension to it: I picked up some tips about color antennas, entered into the geographical debate in the office, and bought a can of windshield wiper solvent (to fill the gap in my change). Sal's station had been a dime a dozen, but it occurred to me, as the nozzle began to balk and shudder in my hand, that gas stations of its kind were going the way of the village smithy and the corner grocer.

I got a glob of grease on my glove as I hung the nozzle back on the pump, and it took me more than a minute to satisfy myself that I had replaced the gas cap properly. I tried to whip up a feeling of accomplishment as I headed for the office, but I could not forget Sal's dictum: Pumping gas is for morons.   24

The door to the office was locked, but a sign directed me to a stainless steel teller's drawer which had been installed in the plate glass of the front window. I stood waiting for a while with my money in hand, but the long-haired man sat inside with his back to me, so at last I reached up and hesitantly knocked on the glass with my glove.   25

The man didn't hear me or had decided, in retaliation for our semantic disagreement, to ignore me for a while. I reached up to knock again, but noticed that my glove had left a greasy smear on the window. Ever my mother's son, I reflexively reached into my pocket for my handkerchief and was about to wipe the grease away when it hit me: at last the oil industry had me where it wanted me—standing in the rain and washing its windshield.   26

Discussing Content and Form

1. What is the purpose behind Ward's description of Sal and his place of business? Where and to what extent is the purpose (the general idea of the selection) stated explicitly?

2. Which details help you visualize Sal's appearance? What do you know about his personality? What is revealed by the content and manner of his speech?

3. What impression do you get of the station as it is when Sal owns and operates it? How does the new business differ (pars. 10–24)?

4. What does the writer reveal about Sal by means of the

faults Sal finds with the Volvo? ("spalding on your caps," "dexadrometer isn't charging," "hairlines in . . . flushing drums" (par. 7), "punting brackets" (par. 23).) What sort of relationship existed between Ward and Sal?

5. Point out elements that make the essay humorous. Which observations or incidents let you know that Ward is laughing at himself?

6. Why is it logical that a company "squeezed [Sal] out for good" (par. 9)? Why does Ward say of going to the old station that "the transaction had dimension to it" (par. 23)?

7. Sal's station is not like those in TV commercials, but the changed station is not like those either. How firmly do you think one can conclude that "stations [are] going the way of the village smithy and the corner grocer" (par. 23)?

Considering Special Techniques

1. By referring to specifics from the essay, comment on Ward's skill in utilizing observations to describe Sal and the station. Show that listening as well as seeing contributes to the vividness of his description.

2. Statements such as Ward makes at the beginning of paragraph 8—"I don't know what Sal's relationship was with the oil company. I suppose it was pretty distant."—indicate that he is drawing inferences from the specifics he observed. To infer is to draw a logical conclusion from evidence or from given premises. However, by making such a statement Ward implies—suggests to the reader—that Sal and the oil company probably do not get along very well. Use your dictionary and check the words infer and imply, inference and implication and be certain that you understand the distinction. From the details that Ward gives about Sal and his business, draw some further inferences of your own. For instance, you might conclude, "Sal ran a messy place and ran it his own way."

Find other inferences that Ward makes in the course of the essay. Why does he state some of them tentatively rather than certainly?

3. The use of verbal adjectives (participles, sometimes infinitives) in description often helps create a sense of movement or action. For instance, Ward shows Sal "leaning indelibly against my rear window and watching the digits fly on the pump register" (par. 2). Again he speaks of "a studded denim jacket" (par. 3) and a "fume-crazed dog." Find

other examples of verbal adjectives that help produce the effect of a motion picture rather than of a series of photographs.

4. Note these forceful verbs that carry not only action but pictures as well:
"*as [Sal] trudged by*" *(par. 6)*
"*the company squeezed him out*" *(par. 9)*
"*as I squinted at the instructional sticker*" *(par. 11)*
What would be the effect if Ward instead wrote "as Sal walked by," "the company discharged him," and "as I looked at the instructional sticker"? Find other verbs that describe as well as tell the action.

5. Writers often play with words or use a famous quotation in order to make a title memorable. Ward's title represents a reordering—a parody—of the final line from John Milton's sonnet "On His Blindness": "They also serve who only stand and wait." Discuss the appropriateness and the effectiveness of Ward's title.

6. Words to learn and use: indelibly *(par. 2);* reluctance, aberration, accessible *(par. 5);* contemptuous *(par. 6);* nostalgia *(par. 7);* sepulchral *(par. 9);* engendered *(par. 11);* retaliation, semantic, reflexively *(par. 26).*

Generating Ideas

1. Describe some person you deal with regularly: a filling station attendant, a bus driver, a checkout person or clerk in a store, a nurse or receptionist in a doctor's office, a guidance counselor or teacher. Make the person come alive for your reader by using details about appearance, personality, and manner. Employ revealing incidents as well as descriptive detail to show rather than tell what your subject is like.

2. Write a paper describing a business or business place that is being "squeezed out" or changed markedly. For instance, businesses sometimes relocate, by choice or necessity; others become obsolete; new ones start up. You might know of a once small, dusty coin shop that has had a sudden prominence because of buying silver and gold; an antique shop that is giving up because of a new highway development; a once popular restaurant located by a railway station, now abandoned. Or, describe some historically interesting business under a title such as one of these:

"Keeping Customers Happy for Over a Century"
"From Cash Drawer to Computer—Three Generations in the Same Spot"

3. *Assume that someone you know well and have observed closely is moving to another town. Write a letter introducing him or her to someone you know there. Or practice a skill that you may someday need by writing a descriptive letter of recommendation for someone real or imaginary. Make your letter specific and clear so that an employer will know the background, attitudes, special abilities, etc., of the person you recommend.*

4. *Like the hangers-on at Sal's station, many people argue over the "best way to get there from here." Andy Rooney recently suggested in his syndicated column that one good way to save gas would be to offer courses in direction-giving. In recounting some amusing mix-ups, he described the problem of disorganized and poorly marked city streets. Write a description of the streets and highways in a city or a section of a city that you know well. You may choose one where travel is easy or where it is difficult to find your way around.*

5. *Choose (from books, films, or television) a character whom you particularly admire. Describe the character vividly, including details of appearance, personality, and manner.*

George Orwell

George Orwell (1903–1950), whose real name was Eric Blair, is one of this century's best-known satirists and essayists. Born in India, educated at Eton, he served for a time with the Imperial Police in Burma and fought in the Spanish Civil War. All these experiences provided material for his writing. In *Animal Farm* (1945), a satirical fable, Orwell pointed out the shortcomings of a communistic state. In *1984* (published in 1949), he envisioned the horrors of a future totalitarian society. Uncannily, many of his predictions have been fulfilled. The British writer V.S. Pritchett called him "the conscience of his generation." His description in "Marrakech," first published in 1939, not only brings that Moroccan city vividly alive but also makes some prophetic comments about the future rise of the Third World nations.

Marrakech

As the corpse went past the flies left the restaurant table in a cloud and rushed after it, but they came back a few minutes later. 1

The little crowd of mourners—all men and boys, no women—threaded their way across the market-place between the piles of pomegranates and the taxis and the camels, wailing a short chant over and over again. What really appeals to the flies is that the corpses here are never put into coffins, they are merely wrapped in a piece of rag and carried on a rough wooden bier on the shoulders of four friends. When the friends get to the burying-ground they hack an oblong hole a foot or two deep, dump the body in it and fling over it a little of the dried-up, lumpy earth, which is like broken brick. No gravestone, no name, no identifying mark of any kind. The burying-ground is merely a huge waste of hummocky earth, like a derelict building-lot. After a month or two no one can even be certain where his own relatives are buried. 2

When you walk through a town like this—two hundred thousand inhabitants, of whom at least twenty thousand own literally nothing except the rags they stand up in—when you see how the people live, and still more easily they die, it is always difficult to believe that you are walking among human beings. All colonial empires are in reality founded upon that fact. The people all have brown 3 faces—besides, there are so many of them! Are they really the same flesh as yourself? Do they even have names? Or are they merely a kind of undifferentiated brown stuff, about as individual as bees or coral insects? They rise out of the earth, they sweat and starve for a few years, and then they sink back into the nameless mounds of the graveyard and nobody notices that they are gone. And even the graves themselves soon fade back into the soil. Sometimes, out for a walk, as you break your way through the prickly pear, you notice that it is rather bumpy underfoot, and only a certain regularity in the bumps tells you that you are walking over skeletons.

4   I was feeding one of the gazelles in the public gardens.

5   Gazelles are almost the only animals that look good to eat when they are still alive, in fact, one can hardly look at their hindquarters without thinking of mint sauce. The gazelle I was feeding seemed to know that this thought was in my mind, for though it took the piece of bread I was holding out it obviously did not like me. It nibbled rapidly at the bread, then lowered its head and tried to butt me, then took another nibble and then butted again. Probably its idea was that if it could drive me away the bread would somehow remain hanging in mid-air.

6   An Arab navvy working on the path nearby lowered his heavy hoe and sidled slowly towards us. He looked from the gazelle to the bread and from the bread to the gazelle, with a sort of quiet amazement, as though he had never seen anything quite like this before. Finally he said shyly in French:

"I could eat some of that bread."

7   I tore off a piece and he stowed it gratefully in some secret place under his rags. This man is an employee of the Municipality.

8   When you go through the Jewish quarters you gather some idea of what the medieval ghettoes were probably like. Under their Moorish rulers the Jews were only allowed to own land in certain restricted areas, and after centuries of this kind of treatment they have ceased to bother about overcrowding. Many of the streets are a good deal less than six feet wide, the houses are completely windowless, and sore-eyed children cluster everywhere in unbelievable

numbers, like clouds of flies. Down the centre of the street there is generally running a little river of urine.

In the bazaar huge families of Jews, all dressed in the long black robe and little black skull-cap, are working in dark fly-infested booths that look like caves. A carpenter sits crosslegged at a prehistoric lathe, turning chair-legs at lightning speed. He works the lathe with a bow in his right hand and guides the chisel with his left foot, and thanks to a lifetime of sitting in this position his left leg is warped out of shape. At his side his grandson, aged six, is already starting on the simpler parts of the job.

I was just passing the coppersmiths' booths when somebody noticed that I was lighting a cigarette. Instantly, from the dark holes all round, there was a frenzied rush of Jews, many of them old grandfathers with flowing grey beards, all clamouring for a cigarette. Even a blind man somewhere at the back of one of the booths heard a rumour of cigarettes and came crawling out, groping in the air with his hand. In about a minute I had used up the whole packet. None of these people, I suppose, works less than twelve hours a day, and every one of them looks on a cigarette as a more or less impossible luxury.

As the Jews live in self-contained communities they follow the same trades as the Arabs, except for agriculture. Fruit-sellers, potters, silversmiths, blacksmiths, butchers, leather-workers, tailors, water-carriers, beggars, porters— whichever way you look you see nothing but Jews. As a matter of fact there are thirteen thousand of them all living in the space of a few acres. A good job Hitler wasn't here. Perhaps he was on his way, however. You hear the usual dark rumours about the Jews, not only from the Arabs but from the poorer Europeans.

"Yes, *mon vieux*, they took my job away from me and gave it to a Jew. The Jews! They're the real rulers of this country, you know. They've got all the money. They control the banks, finance—everything."

"But," I said, "isn't it a fact that the average Jew is a labourer working for about a penny an hour?"

"Ah, that's only for show! They're all moneylenders really. They're cunning, the Jews."

In just the same way, a couple of hundred years ago,

9

10

11

12

13

14

15

poor old women used to be burned for witchcraft when they could not even work enough magic to get themselves a square meal.

16   All people who work with their hands are partly invisible, and the more important the work they do, the less visible they are. Still, a white skin is always fairly conspicuous. In northern Europe, when you see a labourer ploughing a field, you probably give him a second glance. In a hot country, anywhere south of Gibraltar or east of Suez, the chances are that you don't even see him. I have noticed this again and again. In a tropical landscape one's eye takes in everything except the human beings. It takes in the dried-up soil, the prickly pear, the palm tree and the distant mountain, but it always misses the peasant hoeing at his patch. He is the same colour as the earth, and a great deal less interesting to look at.

17   It is only because of this that the starved countries of Asia and Africa are accepted as tourist resorts. No one would think of running cheap trips to the Distressed Areas. But where the human beings have brown skins their poverty is simply not noticed. What does Morocco mean to a Frenchman? An orange-grove or a job in Government service. Or to an Englishman? Camels, castles, palm trees, Foreign Legionnaires, brass trays, and bandits. One could probably live there for years without noticing that for nine-tenths of the people the reality of life is an endless, back-breaking struggle to wring a little food out of an eroded soil.

18   Most of Morocco is so desolate that no wild animal bigger than a hare can live on it. Huge areas which were once covered with forest have turned into a treeless waste where the soil is exactly like broken-up brick. Nevertheless a good deal of it is cultivated, with frightful labour. Everything is done by hand. Long lines of women, bent double like inverted capital L's, work their way slowly across the fields, tearing up the prickly weeds with their hands, and the peasant gathering lucerne for fodder pulls it up stalk by stalk instead of reaping it, thus saving an inch or two on each stalk. The plough is a wretched wooden thing, so frail that one can easily carry it on one's shoulder, and

fitted underneath with a rough iron spike which stirs the soil to depth of about four inches. This is as much as the strength of the animals is equal to. It is usual to plough with a cow and a donkey yoked together. Two donkeys would not be quite strong enough, but on the other hand two cows would cost a little more to feed. The peasants possess no harrows, they merely plough the soil several times over in different directions, finally leaving it in rough furrows, after which the whole field has to to be shaped with hoes into small oblong patches to conserve water. Except for a day or two after the rare rainstorms there is never enough water. Along the edges of the fields channels are hacked out to a depth of thirty or forty feet to get at the tiny trickles which run through the subsoil.

Every afternoon a file of very old women passes down the road outside my house, each carrying a load of firewood. All of them are mummified with age and the sun, and all of them are tiny. It seems to be generally the case in primitive communities that the women, when they get beyond a certain age, shrink to the size of children. One day a poor old creature who could not have been more than four feet tall crept past me under a vast load of wood. I stopped her and put a five-sou piece (a little more than a farthing) into her hand. She answered with a shrill wail, almost a scream, which was partly gratitude but mainly surprise. I suppose that from her point of view, by taking any notice of her, I seemed almost to be violating a law of nature. She accepted her status as an old woman, that is to say, as a beast of burden. When a family is traveling it is quite usual to see a father and a grown-up son riding ahead on donkeys, and an old woman following on foot, carrying the baggage. [19]

But what is strange about these people is their invisibility. For several weeks, always at about the same time of day, the file of old women had hobbled past the house with their firewood, and though they had registered themselves on my eyeballs I cannot truly say that I had seen them. Firewood was passing—that was how I saw it. It was only that one day I happened to be walking behind them, and the curious up-and-down motion of a load of wood drew my attention to the human being beneath it. Then for [20] the first time I noticed the poor old earth-coloured bodies, bodies reduced to bones and leathery skin, bent double under the crushing weight. Yet I suppose I had not been five minutes on Moroccan soil before I noticed the overloading of the donkeys and was infuriated by it. There is no question that the donkeys are damnably treated. The Moroccan donkey is hardly bigger than a St. Bernard dog, it carries a load which in the British Army would be considered too much for a fifteen-hands mule, and very often its pack-saddle is not taken off its back for weeks together. But what is peculiarly pitiful is that it is the most willing creature on earth, it follows its master like a dog and does not need either bridle or halter. After a dozen years of devoted work it suddenly drops dead, whereupon its master tips it into the ditch and the village dogs have torn its guts out before it is cold.

21   This kind of thing makes one's blood boil, whereas—on the whole—the plight of the human beings does not. I am not commenting, merely pointing to a fact. People with brown skins are next door to invisible. Anyone can be sorry for the donkey with its galled back, but it is generally owing to some kind of accident if one even notices the old woman under her load of sticks.

22   As the storks flew northward the Negroes were marching southward—long, dusty columns, infantry, screwgun batteries, and then more infantry, four or five thousand men in all, winding up the road with a clumping of boots and a clatter of iron wheels.

23   They were Senegalese, the blackest Negroes in Africa, so black that sometimes it is difficult to see whereabouts on their necks the hair begins. Their splendid bodies were hidden in reach-me-down khaki uniforms, their feet squashed into boots that looked like blocks of wood, and every tin hat seemed to be a couple of sizes too small. It was very hot and the men had marched a long way. They slumped under the weight of their packs and the curiously sensitive black faces were glistening with sweat.

24   As they went past a tall, very young Negro turned and caught my eye. But the look he gave me was not in the least the kind of look you might expect. Not hostile, not

contemptuous, not sullen, not even inquisitive. It was the shy, wide-eyed Negro look, which actually is a look of profound respect. I saw how it was. This wretched boy, who is a French citizen and has therefore been dragged from the forest to scrub floors and catch syphilis in garrison towns, actually has feelings of reverence before a white skin. He has been taught that the white race are his masters, and he still believes it.

But there is one thought which every white man (and in this connection it doesn't matter twopence if he calls himself a socialist) thinks when he sees a black army marching past. "How much longer can we go on kidding these people? How long before they turn their guns in the other direction?"

It was curious, really. Every white man there had this thought stowed somewhere or other in his mind. I had it, so had the other onlookers, so had the officers on their sweating chargers and the white N.C.Os. marching in the ranks. It was a kind of secret which we all knew and were too clever to tell; only the Negroes didn't know it. And really it was like watching a flock of cattle to see the long column, a mile or two miles of armed men, flowing peacefully up the road, while the great white birds drifted over them in the opposite direction, glittering like scraps of paper.

Discussing Content and Form

1. Orwell presents his observations of Marrakech, showing in detail the scene and its people. In your own words, state the dominant impression that he creates. Although he seems to remain an observer, and to maintain objectivity, what emotions do you know that he feels? What emotional responses does he arouse in you, the reader?

2. Orwell generalizes very little, but in paragraph 3 he states, "nobody notices" the inhabitants as "human beings," and "All colonial empires are founded upon that fact." Find restatements or echoes of this theme of "nobody notices" throughout the essay, and formulate a thesis or purpose statement encompassing that as chief idea.

3. Examine the structure or arrangement of the details, noting the wider spacing between paragraphs 15 and 16 and

25

26

paragraphs 21 and 22. Using these divisions as the primary markers for an outline, state the chief topic or focus explored in each of the three sections.

4. What is the purpose for including the incident of feeding the gazelle (pars. 4–7)? of the incident concerning the cigarettes in the Jewish ghetto (par. 10)?

5. What misconception influences the treatment of Jews in the Marrakech ghetto? Why does Orwell say "A good job Hitler wasn't here. Perhaps he was on his way, however" (par. 11)? (Remember the essay was first published in 1939.)

6. Explain the irony Orwell finds in the acceptance of tourism in countries like Morocco.

7. What is the lot of women in Marrakech? Why is the plight of the donkeys more apparent than the condition of the women?

8. Explain the relationship between the details concerning the Senegalese soldier (par. 23) and the questions at the end of paragraph 25. In your own words, explain how the reaction to Orwell's pictures and questions differs now from what it might have been when the essay was first published.

Considering Special Techniques

1. What dramatic effect is created by opening with the single sentence paragraph? What mood does it set for the entire essay?

2. A writer may use words or phrases recurrently to build an idea or emotion, just as a composer repeats a series of notes in a musical phrase as a motif. Orwell might be said to introduce the motif of "Marrakech" with the sentence fragment, "No gravestone, no name, no identifying mark of any kind" (par. 2). Go through the essay and find the words and phrases that reiterate this theme.

3. Orwell shows the life of many of the natives of Marrakech to be marked by squalor, poverty and very hard labor. Use those general impressions as headings to classify the image-making details throughout the essay. Here are examples for a start:

> squalor—the flies (par. 1), "sweat and starve" (par. 3)
> poverty—"wrapped in a piece of rag" (par. 2), " 'I could eat some of that bread.' " (par. 6)
> hard work—"women, bent double like inverted capital L's,

work . . . slowly" (par. 18), "tearing up prickly weeds" (par. 18)
(Do not worry if an image seems to serve two functions.)

4. Orwell uses a number of similes, figures of speech which explain unknowns by comparing them to things that are familiar. For instance, in paragraph 2 he describes the burying ground as being "like a derelict building-lot"; in paragraph 3 the people are said to be "about as individual as bees or coral insects." Find other such stated comparisons that make the strange scene seem very real.

5. Examine Orwell's use of person or viewpoint.
   a. Although he occasionally shifts to the first person, the "I" viewpoint, he opens by writing in third person, keeping himself out of the scene entirely and focusing on his observations. Discuss the relationship of viewpoint to the impression of objectivity.
   b. Occasionally Orwell invites the reader along by shifting to second person: "When you walk through a town like this" (par. 3) and "When you go through the Jewish quarters" (par. 8) are examples. Find other uses of second person and draw some conclusions about its effectiveness.

6. Orwell's language is vivid, but he seldom uses a word that is not generally familiar. Note, however, the vividness of some of the verbs and adjectives:
   "hummocky earth" (par. 2)
   "they hack an oblong hole" (par. 2)
   "frenzied rush of Jews" (par. 10)
   "mummified with age and the sun" (par. 19)
Find other words that are particularly striking.
Note that Orwell uses English rather than American spelling for rumour, colour, and labour.

Generating Ideas

1. In "Marrakech" Orwell attempts to make readers notice conditions that are overlooked, that are "invisible." Consider some condition that you think is not given the attention that it should have: run-down housing, a dangerously congested street or crossroads, an area polluted by some factory, an abandoned city block or area that has become a hideout or target for vandals. Write a description in which you catch your readers' notice in such a way that they might want to correct or better the condition.

2. Observe a group of people at work—farmers planting a crop, construction workers at a building site, window washers at a shopping mall, migrant apple pickers, etc. Write a description of the people and their tasks, selecting details and language to convey clearly what they do, how they look, and what you feel about them.

3. Describe an American funeral, either one that you have observed or one that you have heard about. Or describe a cemetery in which there is a contrast to the "nobody notices" situation of the burial ground in "Marrakech." Another choice: if you have seen an historic graveyard or the gravesite of some famous person (Arlington National Cemetery might be an example), describe your visit to that spot and evoke the feeling you had about it for your reader.

4. If you have traveled or lived in a foreign country or city, describe the experience and the scene. Give your readers a sense of the place and its people by using vivid details and precise language rather than by generalizing. For instance, rather than saying "Streets in London are busy," picture such details as the double-decker buses, taxi cabs, people crossing Trafalgar Square, tourists watching the changing of the guard. Or describe some site (and sight) that you know through pictures or television: Times Square on New Year's Eve, the Olympic Ice Arena at Lake Placid, the Pasadena streets during the Rose Bowl parade.

5. Orwell asks "What does Morocco mean to a Frenchman? An orange-grove or a job in Government. Or to an Englishman? Camels, castles, palm trees, Foreign Legionnaires, brass trays, and bandits." Consider what you think are misimpressions or lack of understanding people have about some particular place. For instance, someone living in Boston may have the notion that no one in Iowa has a bathtub, a New Yorker may think few people in Arkansas wear shoes, and a midwesterner who has never traveled may think that Greenwich Village is populated entirely by artists.

3

NARRATION:
FRAMING EVENTS

From the beginning of civilization people have used narration to relate imaginary events, to record the happenings of their personal and collective histories, and to illustrate or explain ideas. Some of the many forms narration has taken include pictures on cave walls, the ancient Greek epics, the fiction and fact of chronicle and parable in the Old and New Testaments, and the popular fiction and biography of today. Much storytelling involves fictional events about imaginary characters told for the sake of the story itself. These stories provide a release from everyday life and increase our awareness and understanding of experiences outside our own. Frequently, however, narration serves an expository function: an actual story is told primarily in order to explain or to lead to an idea or a realization. In such writing, the story does not exist for its own sake, but instead serves the ideas the author wishes to present.

Notice how this brief narrative serves to make a point:

> The founding father of the Rockefeller dynasty illustrated how giving money away, and yourself in the process, squares with making it in the first place. John D. Rockefeller was larger than life. The advisers he hired were quick to see that the empire he controlled was creating problems for him

rather than solving them. They took him out of the line of fire by putting him into the spotlight as a giver—not a big giver, but a small one.

Back in the days when a dime meant something, Rockefeller started his own version of the March of Dimes. A shrewd and cynical adviser named Ivy Lee sold Rockefeller the idea of just giving away dimes. The old boy complied by going up and down the country posing for pictures while arbitrarily giving dimes away to youngsters as an inducement to them to save money and duplicate his own success story.

Of course, these dimes were not actually meant to do anybody any good—except Rockefeller himself. The purpose of the scheme was to show that he was a part of life—not larger than life—and to catch him in the act of doing what comes naturally to everyone—giving.—Eliot Janeway, *Musings on Money*

The author, an economist, uses this anecdote—a short narrative incident—in a book about managing money. The first sentence and the entire last paragraph make apparent the expository purpose for the narration they enclose. Together, the three paragraphs comprise a narrative essay in miniature.

In examining the place of narration in exposition, it is useful to understand the similarities between narration and description, for many of the same considerations apply to both. To be successful, both must grow out of good observation and selection from that observation. Description gives a vivid and exact picture of things as they appear; narration gives a vivid and exact picture of things as they occur. Thus narration provides a moving picture. Description involves careful arrangement in space; narration involves careful arrangement in time so that the events are in logical sequence, usually chronological. With description, the reader is asked to look; with narration, to follow. Both show rather than merely tell, but narration goes further than description to present events dramatically. Like description, narration may carry meaning by direct statement or by implication. For example, a writer, through his narrator, may announce, "Now all of this means. . . ."; or he may lead the reader to a certain conclusion by letting his ideas unfold implicitly rather than explicitly.

Much of the narration that you include in your expository writing will be autobiographical, although this kind of narration too should not be just a simple recounting of events. Rather, your personal experience should become part of the development of an essay in which you discover and interpret a meaning in those events. In the following narrative account, the writer leads up to a realization about a father-son relationship, yet he never states the point directly:

I remember the first time I cultivated corn. First, a trip across the field with Father showing me how. I walked behind him, and it all looked simple and easy. Father turned the team around at the end of the row and told me to take over. I looped the lines around my back, grabbed the handles, and yelled, "Get up!"

The horses jerked forward. The moist earth flew out to cover the young plants. The shovels hit a rock, and the handles were torn from my hands.

"Whoa!" Father yelled.

We went back and uncovered the plants.

"Look," Father said, "It's not a race. The only way a horse knows how fast you want him to go is by how you talk to him. You yelled. That means get out and go. Now, try again. Speak soft and easy."

I tried again. The team moved slowly along the row. Father walked behind, now and then saying "gee" or "haw" to the horses. I needed more hands. The handles vibrated and jerked like something alive as the feel of the land came up through them. I didn't dare let go to pull the horses right or left with the lines. I tried Father's "gee" and "haw" and again found that how I spoke was as important as what I said. I needed more eyes, too. I had to keep looking at the row up ahead and keep looking straight down at the same time to guide the shovels close to the plants. I also needed an eye in the back of my head to see how Father was reacting.

At the end of that first row, with the cultivator close against the woven wire fence, I breathed a sigh of relief and tried to turn the horses around onto another row. The horses couldn't seem to turn. I looked at Father. He was smiling. "You're going to have to back up a little. You've got the end of the tongue stuck through the fence."

When I finally got turned around, Father laid a hand on

my shoulder. "You're on your own." He walked back toward the house. I watched him go. He never looked back to see how I was doing. That was important.—Ben Logan, *The Land Remembers*

In writing narration for expository purposes, you should keep several points in mind. First, select details carefully, giving just enough of the right kind to make your point. Becoming intrigued with telling the story for its own sake leads to the inclusion of too much detail or to digressions. With such overtelling, the point may be diminished or even lost. Of course, selection must be aimed at evoking interest, perhaps even at creating the same kind of suspense as the fiction writer does. Even the briefest anecdote or narrative illustration should be lively and vivid. The details should help the reader identify with the characters and action, thereby sustaining interest and carrying the message at the same time.

Another important consideration is the choice of the point of view. Eliot Janeway tells his anecdote about Rockefeller without intruding himself, without using the first person *I*. Ben Logan, on the other hand, is writing about his own experience, and so he uses the first person. The first kind of viewpoint is most appropriate to objective and straightforward narration, while the second is best suited to subjective and impressionistic stories. Whatever the form or length of the narration, however, the important thing is to maintain a consistent viewpoint in telling the story.

Probably the most important point in narration is to arrange events in clear order, giving sufficient links to guide the reader through the action. One kind of link, or transition, is the word or phrase that indicates time. For instance, Ben Logan connects events with such phrases as "I remember the first time" and "At the end of that first row." A second "time link" can be found in the sequence of verbs: "I walked" and "it all looked" and "Father turned" set the time in the first paragraph, and after that all the events are recounted in the same past tense. The indicators of time and the sequence of verbs keep the events in order, whether the action is set in the past, the present, or the future.

Selecting details, maintaining a consistent point of view, and providing links to keep the sequence clear should lead to effective narration. But as with other types of writing, narration depends ultimately upon experience and observation. They are the source of material for creating the moving pictures that both illustrate and carry your ideas.

Maya Angelou

Maya Angelou (b. 1928) spent part of her early years in Stamps, Arkansas, with her grandmother, the "Momma" of the selection that follows. She has told the story of her childhood and her struggles to achieve success as a dancer, singer, actress, producer, and writer in three lively accounts: *I Know Why the Caged Bird Sings* (1970), *Gather Together in My Name* (1974), and *Singin' and Swingin' and Gettin' Merry Like Christmas* (1976). She has also published two volumes of poetry and a screenplay, *Georgia, Georgia* (1972). In the 1960s, Angelou acted as Northern Coordinator for the Southern Christian Leadership Conference organized by Dr. Martin Luther King, Jr., and in 1976 she was named Woman of the Year in Communications. "A Lesson in Living" (editor's title) comes from *I Know Why the Caged Bird Sings*. Here Angelou recalls one of the early influences that helped shape her career.

A Lesson in Living

Establishment of scene, followed by anticipatory statement (par. 1)

1   For nearly a year, I sopped around the house, the Store, the school and the church, like an old biscuit, dirty and inedible. Then I met, or rather got to know, the lady who threw me my first life line.

Details of Mrs. Flowers' appearance and actions (pars. 2–5)

2   Mrs. Bertha Flowers was the aristocrat of Black Stamps. She had the grace of control to appear warm in the coldest weather, and on the Arkansas summer days it seemed she had a private breeze which swirled around, cooling her. She was thin without the taut look of wiry people, and her printed voile dresses and flowered hats were as right for her as denim overalls for a farmer. She was our side's answer to the richest white woman in town.

3   Her skin was a rich black that would have peeled like a plum if snagged, but then no one would have thought of getting close enough to Mrs. Flowers to ruffle her dress, let alone snag her skin. She didn't encourage familiarity. She wore gloves too.

4   I don't think I ever saw Mrs. Flowers laugh, but she smiled often. A slow widening of her

thin black lips to show even, small white teeth, then the slow effortless closing. When she chose to smile on me, I always wanted to thank her. The action was so graceful and inclusively benign.

She was one of the few gentlewomen I have ever known, and has remained throughout my life the measure of what a human being can be.

Momma had a strange relationship with her. Most often when she passed on the road in front of the Store, she spoke to Momma in that soft yet carrying voice, "Good day, Mrs. Henderson." Momma responded with "How you, Sister Flowers?"

Mrs. Flowers didn't belong to our church, nor was she Momma's familiar. Why on earth did she insist on calling her Sister Flowers? Shame made me want to hide my face. Mrs. Flowers deserved better than to be called Sister. Then, Momma left out the verb. Why not ask, "How *are* you, *Mrs*. Flowers?" With the unbalanced passion of the young, I hated her for showing her ignorance to Mrs. Flowers. It didn't occur to me for many years that they were as alike as sisters, separated only by formal education.

Although I was upset, neither of the women was in the least shaken by what I thought an unceremonious greeting. Mrs. Flowers would continue her easy gait up the hill to her little bungalow, and Momma kept on shelling peas or doing whatever had brought her to the front porch.

Occasionally, though, Mrs. Flowers would drift off the road and down to the Store and Momma would say to me, "Sister, you go on and play." As I left I would hear the beginning of an intimate conversation. Momma persistently using the wrong verb, or none at all.

"Brother and Sister Wilcox is sho'ly the meanest—" "Is," Momma? "Is"? Oh, please,

5

6
Her relationship with
Momma (pars. 6–10)

7

8

9

10

not "is," Momma, for two or more. But they talked, and from the side of the building where I waited for the ground to open up and swallow me, I heard the soft-voiced Mrs. Flowers and the textured voice of my grandmother merging and melting. They were interrupted from time to time by giggles that must have come from Mrs. Flowers (Momma never giggled in her life). Then she was gone.

Mrs. Flowers is likened to fictional and film characters (pars. 11–13)

11 She appealed to me because she was like people I had never met personally. Like women in English novels who walked the moors (whatever they were) with their loyal dogs racing at a respectful distance. Like the women who sat in front of roaring fireplaces, drinking tea incessantly from silver trays full of scones and crumpets. Women who walked over the "heath" and read morocco-bound books and had two last names divided by a hyphen. It would be safe to say that she made me proud to be Negro, just by being herself.

12 She acted just as refined as whitefolks in the movies and books and she was more beautiful, for none of them could have come near that warm color without looking gray by comparison.

13 It was fortunate that I never saw her in the company of powhitefolks. For since they tend to think of their whiteness as an evenizer, I'm certain that I would have had to hear her spoken to commonly as Bertha, and my image of her would have been shattered like the unmendable Humpty-Dumpty.

First part of the narrative: events leading up to the visit (pars. 14–31)

14 One summer afternoon, sweet-milk fresh in my memory, she stopped at the Store to buy provisions. Another Negro woman of her health and age would have been expected to carry the paper sacks home in one hand, but Momma said, "Sister Flowers, I'll send Bailey up to your house with these things."

She smiled that slow dragging smile, "Thank you, Mrs. Henderson. I'd prefer Marguerite, though." My name was beautiful when she said it. "I've been meaning to talk to her, anyway." They gave each other age-group looks.

Momma said, "Well, that's all right then. Sister, go and change your dress. You going to Sister Flowers's."

The chifforobe was a maze. What on earth did one put on to go to Mrs. Flowers' house? I knew I shouldn't put on a Sunday dress. It might be sacrilegious. Certainly not a house dress, since I was already wearing a fresh one. I chose a school dress, naturally. It was formal without suggesting that going to Mrs. Flowers' house was equivalent to attending church.

I trusted myself back into the Store.

"Now, don't you look nice." I had chosen the right thing, for once.

"Mrs. Henderson, you make most of the children's clothes, don't you?"

"Yes, ma'am. Sure do. Store-bought clothes ain't hardly worth the thread it take to stitch them."

"I'll say you do a lovely job, though, so neat. That dress looks professional."

Momma was enjoying the seldom-received compliments. Since everyone we knew (except Mrs. Flowers, of course) could sew competently, praise was rarely handed out for the commonly practiced craft.

"I try, with the help of the Lord, Sister Flowers, to finish the inside just like I does the outside. Come here, Sister."

I had buttoned up the collar and tied the belt, apronlike, in back. Momma told me to turn around. With one hand she pulled the strings and the belt fell free at both sides of my waist. Then her large hands were at my neck,

15
The invitation (pars. 15–16)

16

17
The choice of a dress (pars. 17–18)

18

19
Discussion of the dress (pars. 19–31)
20

21

22

23

24

25

opening the button loops. I was terrified. What was happening?

26   "Take it off, Sister." She had her hands on the hem of the dress.

27   "I don't need to see the inside, Mrs. Henderson, I can tell . . ." But the dress was over my head and my arms were stuck in the sleeves. Momma said, "That'll do. See here, Sister Flowers, I French-seams around the armholes." Through the cloth film, I saw the shadow approach. "That makes it last longer. Children these days would bust out of sheet-metal clothes. They so rough."

28   "That is a very good job, Mrs. Henderson. You should be proud. You can put your dress back on, Marguerite."

29   "No ma'am. Pride is a sin. And 'cording to the Good Book, it goeth before a fall."

30   "That's right. So the Bible says. It's a good thing to keep in mind."

31   I wouldn't look at either of them. Momma hadn't thought that taking off my dress in front of Mrs. Flowers would kill me stone dead. If I had refused, she would have thought I was trying to be "womanish" and might have remembered St. Louis. Mrs. Flowers had known that I would be embarrassed and that was even worse. I picked up the groceries and went out to wait in the hot sunshine. It would be fitting if I got a sunstroke and died before they came outside. Just dropped dead on the slanting porch.

32   There was a little path beside the rocky road, and Mrs. Flowers walked in front swinging her arms and picking her way over the stones.

33   She said, without turning her head, to me, "I hear you're doing very good school work, Marguerite, but that it's all written. The teachers report that they have trouble getting you to talk in class." We passed the triangular farm on our left and the path widened to allow

Second part of narrative: events during walk to Mrs. Flowers' house (pars. 32–39)

us to walk together. I hung back in the separate unasked and unanswerable questions.

"Come and walk along with me, Marguerite." I couldn't have refused even if I wanted to. She pronounced my name so nicely. Or more correctly, she spoke each word with such clarity that I was certain a foreigner who didn't understand English could have understood her.

34
Discussion of
language (pars.
34–37)

"Now no one is going to make you talk—possibly no one can. But bear in mind, language is man's way of communicating with his fellow man and it is language alone which separates him from the lower animals." That was a totally new idea to me, and I would need time to think about it.

35

"Your grandmother says you read a lot. Every chance you get. That's good, but not good enough. Words mean more than what is set down on paper. It takes the human voice to infuse them with the shades of deeper meaning."

36

I memorized the part about the human voice infusing words. It seemed so valid and poetic.

37

She said she was going to give me some books and that I not only must read them, I must read them aloud. She suggested that I try to make a sentence sound in as many different ways as possible.

38
Promise of books
(pars. 38–39)

"I'll accept no excuse if you return a book to me that has been badly handled." My imagination boggled at the punishment I would deserve if in fact I did abuse a book of Mrs. Flowers'. Death would be too kind and brief.

39

The odors in the house surprised me. Somehow I had never connected Mrs. Flowers with food or eating or any other common experience of common people. There must have been an outhouse, too, but my mind never recorded it.

40
Third part of narrative:
arrival and events at
Mrs. Flowers' house
(pars. 40–46)

41   The sweet scent of vanilla had met us as she opened the door.

42   "I made tea cookies this morning. You see, I had planned to invite you for cookies and lemonade so we could have this little chat. The lemonade is in the icebox."

43   It followed that Mrs. Flowers would have ice on an ordinary day, when most families in our town bought ice late on Saturdays only a few times during the summer to be used in wooden ice-cream freezers.

44   She took the bags from me and disappeared through the kitchen door. I looked around the room that I had never in my wildest fantasies imagined I would see. Browned photographs leered or threatened from the walls and the white, freshly done curtains pushed against themselves and against the wind. I wanted to gobble up the room entire and take it to Bailey, who would help me analyze and enjoy it.

45   "Have a seat, Marguerite. Over there by the table." She carried a platter covered with a tea towel. Although she warned that she hadn't tried her hand at baking sweets for some time, I was certain that like everything else about her the cookies would be perfect.

46   They were flat round wafers, slightly browned on the edges and butter-yellow in the center. With the cold lemonade they were sufficient for childhood's lifelong diet. Remembering my manners, I took nice little lady-like bites off the edges. She said she had made them expressly for me and that she had a few in the kitchen that I could take home to my brother. So I jammed one whole cake in my mouth and the rough crumbs scratched the insides of my jaws, and if I hadn't had to swallow, it would have been a dream come true.

As I ate she began the first of what we later called "my lessons in living." She said that I must always be intolerant of ignorance but understanding of illiteracy. That some people, unable to go to school, were more educated and even more intelligent than college professors. She encouraged me to listen carefully to what country people called mother wit. That in those homely sayings was couched the collective wisdom of generations.

47
Fourth part of narrative: Mrs. Flowers' "lesson in living" (pars 47–53)

When I finished the cookies she brushed off the table and brought a thick, small book from the bookcase. I had read *A Tale of Two Cities* and found it up to my standards as a romantic novel. She opened the first page and I heard poetry for the first time in my life.

48

"It was the best of times and the worst of times. . . ." Her voice slid in and curved down through and over the words. She was nearly singing. I wanted to look at the pages. Were they the same that I had read? Or were there notes, music, lined on the pages, as in a hymn book? Her sounds began cascading gently. I knew from listening to a thousand preachers that she was nearing the end of her reading, and I hadn't really heard, heard to understand, a single word.

49

"How do you like that?"

50

It occurred to me that she expected a response. The sweet vanilla flavor was still on my tongue and her reading was a wonder in my ears. I had to speak.

51

I said, "Yes, ma'am." It was the least I could do, but it was the most also.

52

"There's one more thing. Take this book of poems and memorize one for me. Next time you pay me a visit, I want you to recite."

53

I have tried often to search behind the sophistication of years for the enchantment I so easily found in those gifts. The essence

54
Summary of the significance of the visit (par. 54)

escapes but its aura remains. To be allowed, no, invited, into the private lives of strangers, and to share their joys and fears, was a chance to exchange the Southern bitter wormwood for a cup of mead with Beowulf or a hot cup of tea and milk with Oliver Twist. When I said aloud, "It is a far, far better thing that I do, than I have ever done . . ." tears of love filled my eyes at my selflessness.

55

Final part of narrative: the return home and various reactions to the visit (pars. 55–59)

On that first day, I ran down the hill and into the road (few cars ever came along it) and had the good sense to stop running before I reached the Store.

56

I was liked, and what a difference it made. I was respected not as Mrs. Henderson's grandchild or Bailey's sister but for just being Marguerite Johnson.

57

Childhood's logic never asks to be proved (all conclusions are absolute). I didn't question why Mrs. Flowers had singled me out for attention, nor did it occur to me that Momma might have asked her to give me a little talking to. All I cared about was that she had made tea cookies for *me* and read to *me* from her favorite book. It was enough to prove that she liked me.

58

Momma and Bailey were waiting inside the Store. He said, "My, what did she give you?" He had seen the books, but I held the paper sack with his cookies in my arms shielded by the poems.

59

Momma said, "Sister, I know you acted like a little lady. That do my heart good to see settled people take to you all. I'm trying my best, the Lord knows, but these days . . ." Her voice trailed off. "Go on in and change your dress."

Discussing Content and Form

1. What in the narrative explains Angelou's statement that Mrs. Flowers "threw" her a "life line"?

2. Which details reveal Mrs. Flowers' qualities as a gentlewoman?

3. We sometimes speak of adults as "role models" for children or young people. In what ways was Mrs. Flowers a model for Angelou?

4. Why was Angelou embarrassed over Momma's behavior with Mrs. Flowers? How is that embarrassment epitomized in Angelou's correction of Momma's grammar (par. 10)?

5. In light of Angelou's fame as an actress and writer, explain the significance of Mrs. Flowers' admonition about speaking well: "Words mean more than what is set down on paper" (par. 36). Do you agree that it is important to be "intolerant of ignorance but understanding of illiteracy" (par. 47)? Why or why not?

6. How important were books to the writer when she was a child?

7. This selection is not a short story but an auto-biographical account that culminates in a significant point. Nevertheless, it is blocked out in a series of scenes or incidents just as short stories frequently are. Note how the incidents fit together. How does the writer catch and build interest? How does she resolve the tensions built up throughout the account?

8. Angelou's narrative involves persons comparable to characters in fiction. It is less important that these people are real than that they seem real. Which details make the persons in the narration seem lifelike? How does the writer make you feel about Momma, Mrs. Flowers, and herself?

Considering Special Techniques

1. Characters from fiction and persons from biography and autobiography are presented not only through the writer's direct comments but also through their actions, their speech, and the comments of other characters. Show how Angelou uses each of these methods in her presentation of Mrs.

Flowers and Momma. Show how the same methods paint a picture of Angelou herself.

  a. Why does speech play an important part in revealing the personalities of the people in the selection?

  b. Point out two or three incidents that are particularly revealing of character. You might begin with paragraphs 25-31, the examination of the dress. What does this incident contribute to our understanding of the three persons involved?

  c. What do the details concerning books reveal about Mrs. Flowers and her young guest?

2. What makes the dialogue in the selection effective? How does the writer distinguish between her grandmother and Mrs. Flowers? (Consider both grammatical patterns and word choice.) What does the dialogue between the two women reveal about their relationship? Why does Angelou say, "It didn't occur to me for many years that they were as alike as sisters, separated only by formal education" (par. 7)?

3. Angelou makes effective use of similes (stated comparisons) and metaphors (implied comparisons). Make a list of the similes and metaphors that you find particularly vivid. You might begin with these:

  "I sopped around the house . . . like an old biscuit, dirty and inedible." (par. 1)

  "One summer afternoon, sweet-milk fresh in my memory. . . ." (par. 14)

4. Paragraph 47 lists the "lessons in living" through the use of several phrases constructed according to the same pattern. In the second sentence, "She said that" establishes the pattern. How do the two sentence fragments, both beginning with that, fit the pattern of the second sentence? Why do you think Angelou chose to express her ideas in two fragments rather than in full sentences?

Generating Ideas

1. Write a paper telling about a meeting or a series of meetings with someone who has been an influence in your life. Or relate a sequence of events that led to some "lesson in living."

2. Explain why role models are important to young people. Although you may find incidents helpful in developing your explanation, you need not write narration.

3. *Dialogue is one of the best methods for revealing one's thoughts and feelings. Imagine or draw from real life two persons who are concerned with similar things, ideas, events, etc., but who have different perspectives about them. Write a narrative in which they meet and talk about their beliefs. Here are a few examples:*

> *A trucker and a tourist talk about the use of their C.B. radios.*
>
> *A salesperson and a prospective buyer talk about a new car.*
>
> *A person with a great deal of formal education and one with little discuss the value (or the lack of it) of a college degree.*
>
> *A social worker who has no children and a mother who has several talk about day-care centers.*

4. *Write a short autobiographical narrative telling of some embarrassment that you have suffered. Try to make your experience as vivid as Angelou does her feelings about her grandmother's grammar and about being told to show Mrs. Flowers the seams in her dress.*

Tom Wolfe

Tom Wolfe (b. 1931) has written extensively on many public figures and
pop trends in contemporary American society. He holds a Ph.D. in
American Studies from Yale and was for a time a reporter for the
Washington Post and a reporter and magazine writer for the *New York
Herald Tribune*. Since 1968, he has been a contributing editor for *New York*
magazine. In 1965 he gained attention with his collection of trendsetting
articles entitled *The Kandy-Kolored Tangerine-Flake Streamline Baby*. Since
then he has published *The Electric Kool-Aid Acid Test* (1968) and three
other volumes of essays: *The Pump House Gang* (1968), *Radical Chic and
Mau-Mauing the Flak Catchers* (1970), and *Mauve Gloves & Madmen,
Clutter & Vine* (1976). He analyzed the trends he and others set in *The New
Journalism* (1973) and attacked contemporary art in *The Painted Word*
(1975). *The Right Stuff* (1979) is a lively and detailed account of the lives of
the astronauts.

"The Frisbee Ion" is from an article entitled "The Intelligent Co-ed's
Guide to America," a commentary on what Wolfe calls the "O'Hare
philosophers." These are intellectuals who Wolfe contends spend their time
at O'Hare Airport in Chicago, waiting for planes to fly them to profitable
speaking engagements on college campuses where they preach their
gloom-and-doom philosophies.

The Frisbee Ion

1   If you happen to attend a conference at which whole
contingents of the O'Hare philosophers assemble, you can
get the message in all its varieties in a short time. Picture, if
you will, a university on the Great Plains . . . a new
Student Activities Center the color of butter-almond ice
cream . . . a huge interior space with tracks in the floor,
along which janitors in green twill pull Expando-Flex
accordion walls to create meeting rooms of any size. The
conference is about to begin. The students come surging in
like hormones. You've heard of rosy cheeks? They *have*
them! Here they come, rosy-cheeked, laughing, with
Shasta and 7-Up pumping through their veins, talking
chipsy, flashing weatherproof smiles, bursting out of their
down-filled Squaw Valley jackets and their blue jeans—
looking, all of them, boys and girls, Jocks & Buds & Freaks,
as if they spent the day hang-gliding and then made a
Miller commercial at dusk and are now going to taper off
with a little Culture before returning to the co-ed dorm.

They grow quiet. The conference begins. The keynote speaker, a historian wearing a calfskin jacket and hair like Felix Mendelssohn's, informs them that the United States is "a leaden, life-denying society."

Over the next thirty-six hours, other O'Hare regulars fill in the rest: 2

Sixty families control one-half the private wealth of 3 America, and 200 corporations own two-thirds of the means of production. "A small group of nameless, faceless men" who avoid publicity the way a werewolf avoids the dawn now dominates American life. In America a man's home is not his castle but merely "a gigantic listening device with a mortgage"—a reference to eavesdropping by the FBI and the CIA. America's foreign policy has been and continues to be based upon war, assassination, bribery, genocide, and the sabotage of democratic governments. "The new McCarthyism" (Joe's, not Gene's) is already upon us. Following a brief charade of free speech, the "gagging of the press" has resumed. Racism in America has not diminished; it is merely more subtle now. The gulf between rich and poor widens daily, creating "permanent ghetto-colonial populations." The decline in economic growth is causing a crisis in capitalism, which will lead shortly to authoritarian rule and to a new America in which everyone waits, in horror, for the knock on the door in the dead of the night, the descent of the knout on the nape of the neck—

How other people attending this conference felt by now, 4 I didn't dare ask. As for myself, I was beginning to feel like Job or Miss Cunégonde. What further devastations or humiliations could possibly be in store, short of the sacking of Kansas City? It was in that frame of mind that I attended the final panel discussion, which was entitled "The United States in the Year 2000."

The prognosis was not good, as you can imagine. But I 5 was totally unprepared for the astounding news brought by an ecologist.

"I'm not sure I want to be alive in the year 2000," he said, 6 although he certainly looked lively enough at the moment.

He was about thirty-eight, and he wore a Madras plaid cotton jacket and a Disco Magenta turtleneck jersey.

7   It seemed that recent studies showed that, due to the rape of the atmosphere by aerosol spray users, by 2000 a certain ion would no longer be coming our way from the sun. I can't remember which one . . . the aluminum ion, the magnesium ion, the neon ion, the gadolinium ion, the calcium ion . . . the calcium ion perhaps; in any event, it was crucial for the formation of bones, and by 2000 it would be no more. Could such a thing be? Somehow this went beyond any of the horrors I was already imagining. I began free-associating. . . . Suddenly I could see Lexington Avenue, near where I live in Manhattan. The presence of the storm troopers was the least of it. It was the look of ordinary citizens that was so horrible. Their bones were going. They were dissolving. Women who had once been clicking and clogging down the Avenue up on five-inch platform soles, with their pants seams smartly cleaving their declivities, were now mere denim & patent-leather blobs . . . oozing and inching and suppurating along the sidewalk like amoebas or ticks. . . . A cabdriver puts his arm out the window . . . and it just dribbles down the yellow door like hot Mazola. . . . A blind news dealer tries to give change to a notions buyer for Bloomingdale's, and their fingers run together like fettucine over a stack of *New York Posts*. . . . It's horrible . . . it's obscene . . . it's the end.—

8   I was so dazed, I was no longer wondering what the assembled students thought of all this. But just at that moment one of them raised his hand. He was a tall boy with a lot of curly hair and a Fu Manchu moustache.

9   "Yes?" said the ecologist.

10   "There's one thing I can't understand," said the boy.

11   "What's that?" said the ecologist.

12   "Well," said the boy. "I'm a senior, and for four years we've been told by people like yourself and the other gentlemen that everything's in terrible shape, and it's all going to hell, and I'm willing to take your word for it, because you're all experts in your field. But around here, at this school, for the past four years, the biggest problem, as

far as I can see, has been finding a parking place near the campus."

Dead silence. The panelists looked at this poor turkey to 13 try to size him up. Was he trying to be funny? Or was this the native bray of the heartland? The ecologist struck a note of forbearance as he said:

"I'm sure that's true, and that illustrates one of the 14 biggest difficulties we have in making realistic assessments. A university like this, after all, is a middle-class institution, and middle-class life is calculated precisely to create a screen—"

"I understand all that," said the boy. "What I want to 15 know is—how old are you, usually, when it all hits you?"

And suddenly the situation became clear. The kid was no 16 wiseacre! He was genuinely perplexed! . . . For four years he had been squinting at the horizon . . . looking for the grim horrors which he knew—on faith—to be all around him . . . and had been utterly unable to find them . . . and now he was afraid they might descend on him all at once when he least expected it. He might be walking down the street in Omaha one day, minding his own business, when—whop! whop! whop! whop!—War! Fascism! Repression! Corruption!—they'd squash him like bowling balls rolling off a roof!

Who was that lost lad? What was his name? Without 17 knowing it, he was playing the xylophone in a boneyard. He was the unique new creature of the 1970s. He was Candide in reverse. Candide and Miss Cunégonde, one will recall, are taught by an all-knowing savant, Dr. Pangloss. He keeps assuring them that this is "the best of all possible worlds," and they believe him implicitly—even though their lives are one catastrophe after another. Now something much weirder was happening. The Jocks & Buds & Freaks of the heartland have their all-knowing savants of O'Hare, who keep warning them that this is "the worst of all possible worlds," and they know it must be true—and yet life keeps getting easier, sunnier, happier . . . *Frisbee!*

How can such things be? 18

Discussing Content and Form

1. What point does Wolfe want to make in his narration? Is his point stated explicitly or is it merely implied? Explain.

2. Describe the kind of reader Wolfe is trying to reach. Give reasons for your view.

3. Based on your experience, how accurate do you find Wolfe's description of the student audience?

4. What is your reaction to the problems discussed by the speakers? Which problem do you consider the most urgent and real? Can most of them be solved? Explain.

5. Is Wolfe in agreement with the "O'Hare philosophers" or with the student questioner? Support your answer by referring to the essay.

6. In paragraph 17, Wolfe compares the situation of the student to that of the hero of Candide, a philosophical novel by Voltaire, published in 1759. Explain how irony functions in both situations. To what extent is the student's situation humorous? Is it also sad? Explain.

7. What is the significance of the title "The Frisbee Ion"? Of using the word Frisbee at the end of paragraph 17?

Considering Special Techniques

1. To what extent does the vividness of the descriptive and narrative sections in this selection depend upon the use of specific details? How much does the quantity of detail contribute to its overall effect?

2. What is the function of the single sentence that comprises paragraph 2? Identify the two-fold function of paragraph 8. How does this paragraph contribute to the organization, and what does it reveal about Wolfe's attitude toward his subject?

3. Wolfe frequently uses the dash, and he also uses three dots (four at the ends of sentences) as punctuation marks to separate phrases or even sentences. What does this kind of punctuation contribute to the movement of the narrative? What special effect is achieved by the punctuation in paragraph 16?

4. The first three paragraphs of the narrative are in the present tense ("The conference is about to begin." "The decline in economic growth is causing. . . ."). In paragraph 4,

Wolfe shifts to the past tense. Account for his use of the two tenses. Is the shift logical? Why or why not?

5. Wolfe is a master of the precise phrase and comparison, and he often gives a humorous and vivid twist to his descriptions by using fresh and colorful images. Discuss the effect of the following phrases in particular, and find others that are equally effective:

"a new Student Activities Center the color of butter-almond ice cream" (par. 1)

"students come surging in like hormones" (par. 1)

"with Shasta and 7-Up pumping through their veins" (par. 1)

"fingers run together like fettucine" (par. 7)

Generating Ideas

1. Write a narrative about a lecturer's visit to your campus. If you can, include several outstanding incidents as part of your paper. You might discuss the content of the lecture, describe student reactions, and record any questions and answers that were exchanged. Or, imagine yourself a guest lecturer, and write a narrative about your visit. Try to give vivid impressions of the campus, the students, and the reception given you.

2. If you have ever had a question misinterpreted by the person to whom it was directed, recount what happened. Here are some titles that may suggest an approach:

"A Question I Should Not Have Asked"

"No Questions, Please"

"Why Parents (Teachers) Refuse to Answer"

"Asked Out of Innocence"

"Answers by the Experts"

3. Write a paper about one of the catastrophes that so-called experts predict will befall the world in the next fifty years or so. Give reasons for believing or not believing in the prediction and its consequences. Here are some suggestions:

The depletion of fossil fuels

Thermonuclear war

A new Ice Age

The destruction of the earth's ozone layer from aerosol sprays

Worldwide starvation

Or narrate an event which has brought home to you the

possible truth of such predictions. For example, if you have experienced heavy smog over a city, you might write about your realization of pollution. If you have been through a power failure, you might write about "the day the energy gives out."

4. Using narration, present your own view of what life will be like in the year 2000.

5. Although the essay contains many examples of future catastrophes, it concludes with the idea that "life keeps getting easier, sunnier, happier" (par. 17). Create a dialogue or interview between two persons (real or imaginary) who hold these opposing views.

Nora Ephron

Nora Ephron (b. 1941) was educated at Wellesley and Briarcliffe and began her writing career as a reporter for the *New York Post*. Since 1968, she has been a free-lance writer, contributing numerous articles to such magazines as *Newsweek, New York,* and *Esquire*. Her writing, which is often humorous and satirical, and always penetratingly insightful, is chiefly about women. Her collections of essays are *Wallflower at the Orgy* (1970), *Crazy Salad* (1975), and *Scribble, Scribble* (1978). In "The Hurled Ashtray" (from *Crazy Salad*), she presents in narrative form some of the confusion that she and other women feel about their relationship to men.

The Hurled Ashtray

I once heard a swell story about Gary Cooper. The person I heard the story from did this terrific Gary Cooper imitation, and it may be that when I tell you the story (which I am about to), it will lose something in print. It may lose everything, in fact. But enough. The story was that Gary Cooper was in a London restaurant at a large table of friends. He was sitting in a low chair, with his back to the rest of the room, so no one in the restaurant even knew that he was tall, much less that he was Gary Cooper. Across the way was a group of Teddy boys (this episode took place long long ago, you see), and they were all misbehaving and making nasty remarks about a woman at Cooper's table. Cooper turned around to give them his best mean-and-threatening stare, but they went right on. Finally he got up, very very slowly, so slowly that it took almost a minute for him to go from this short person in a low chair to a ten-foot-tall man with Gary Cooper's head on top of his shoulders. He loped over to the table of Teddy boys, looked down at them, and said, "Wouldja mind sayin' that agin?" The men were utterly cowed and left the restaurant shortly thereafter.

Well, you had to be there.

I thought of Gary Cooper and his way with words the other day. Longingly. Because in the mail, from an editor of *New York* magazine, came an excerpt from a book by Michael Korda called *Male Chauvinism: How It Works* (Random House). I have no idea whether Korda's book is any good at all, but the excerpt was fascinating, a sort of reverse-twist update on Francis Macomber, as well as a pathetic contrast to the Gary Cooper story. It seems that Korda, his wife, and another woman were having dinner in a London restaurant recently. Across the way was a table of drunks doing sensitive things like sniggering and leering and throwing bread balls at Mrs. Korda, who is a looker. Her back was to them, and she refused to acknowledge their presence, instead apparently choosing to let the flying bread balls bounce off her back onto the floor. Then, one of the men sent over a waiter with a silver tray. On it was a printed card, the kind you can buy in novelty shops, which read: "I want to sleep with you! Tick off your favorite love position from the list below, and return this card with your telephone number. . . ." Korda tore up the card before his wife could even see it, and then, consumed with rage, he picked up an ashtray and threw it at the man who had sent the card. A fracas ensued, and before long, Korda, his wife, and their woman friend were out on the street. Mrs. Korda was furious.

4   "If you ever do that again," she screamed, "I'll leave you! Do you think I couldn't have handled that, or ignored it? Did I ask you to come to my defense against some poor stupid drunk? You didn't even think, you just reacted like a male chauvinist. You leapt up to defend *your* woman, *your* honor, you made me seem cheap and foolish and powerless. . . . God Almighty, can't you see it was none of your business! Can't you understand how it makes me feel? I don't mind being hassled by some drunk, I can take that, but to be treated like a chattel, to be robbed of any right to decide for myself whether I'd been insulted, or how badly, to have you react for me because I'm *your* woman . . . that's really sickening, it's like being a slave." Korda repeats the story (his wife's diatribe is even longer in the original version) and then, in a *mea culpa* that is only too reminiscent of the sort that used to appear in 1960s books by white liberals about blacks, he concludes that his wife is doubtless right, that men do tend to treat women merely as appendages of themselves.

5   Before printing the article, *New York* asked several couples—including my husband and me—what our

reaction was to what happened, and what we would have done under the circumstances. My initial reaction to the entire business was that no one ever sends me notes like that in restaurants. I sent that off to the editor, but a few days later I got to thinking about the story, and it began to seem to me that the episode just might be a distillation of everything that has happened to men and women as a result of the women's movement, and if not that, at least a way to write about etiquette after the revolution, and if not that, nothing at all. Pulled as I was by these three possibilities, I told the story over dinner to four friends and asked for their reaction. The first, a man, said that he thought Mrs. Korda was completely right. The second, a woman, said she thought Korda's behavior was totally understandable. The third, a man, said that both parties had behaved badly. The fourth, my friend Martha, said it was the second most boring thing she had ever heard, the most boring being a story I had just told her about a fight my college roommate had with a cabdriver at Kennedy Airport.

In any case, before any serious discussion of the incident   6
of the hurled ashtray, I would like to raise some questions for which I have no answers. I raise them simply because if that story were fed into a computer, the only possible response it could make is We Do Not Have Sufficient Information To Make An Evaluation. For example:

Do the Kordas have a good marriage?   7

Was the heat working in their London hotel room the   8
night of the fracas?

Was it raining out?   9

What did the second woman at the table look like? Was   10
she as pretty as Mrs. Korda? Was she ugly? Was part of Michael Korda's reaction—and his desire to assert possession of his wife—the result of the possibility that he suspected the drunks thought he was with someone funny-looking?

What kind of a tacky restaurant is it where a waiter   11
delivers a dirty message on a silver tray?

What about a woman who ignores flying bread balls?   12
Wasn't her husband justified in thinking she would be no more interested in novelty cards?

13   Did Michael Korda pay the check before or after throwing the ashtray? Did he tip the standard 15 percent?

14   Since the incident occurs in London, a city notorious for its rampant homoerotic behavior, and since the table of drunks was all male, isn't it possible that the printed card was in fact intended not for Mrs. Korda but for Michael? In which case how should we now view his response, if at all?

15   There might be those who would raise questions about the ashtray itself: was it a big, heavy ashtray, these people might ask, or a dinky little round one? Was it glass or was it plastic? These questions are irrelevant.

16   In the absence of answers to any of the above, I would nonetheless like to offer some random musings. First, I think it is absurd for Mrs. Korda to think that she and she alone was involved in the incident. Yes, it might have been nice had her husband consulted her; and yes, it would have been even nicer had he turned out to be Gary Cooper, or failing that, Dave DeBusschere, or even Howard Cosell—anyone but this suave flinger of ashtrays he turned out to be. But the fact remains that the men at the table *were* insulting Korda, and disturbing his dinner, as well as hers. Their insult was childish and Korda's reaction was ludicrous, but Mrs. Korda matched them all by reducing a complicated and rather interesting emotional situation to a tedious set of movement platitudes.

17   Beyond that—and the Kordas quite aside, because God Almighty (as Mrs. Korda might put it) knows what it is they are into—I wonder whether there is any response a man could make in that situation which would not disappoint a feminist. Yes, I want to be treated as an equal and not as an appendage or possession or spare rib, but I also want to be taken care of. Isn't any man sitting at a table with someone like me damned whatever he does? If the drunks in question are simply fools, conventioneers with funny paper hats, I suppose that a possible reaction would be utter cool. But if they were truly insulting and disturbing, some response does seem called for. Some wild and permanent gesture of size. But on whose part? And what should it consist of? And how tall do you have to be to bring it off? And where is the point that a mild show of strength

becomes crude macho vulgarity; where does reserve veer off into passivity?

Like almost every other question in this column, I have   18
no positive answer. But I think that if I ever found myself in a similar situation, and if it was truly demeaning, I would prefer that my husband handle it. My husband informs me, after some consideration, that the Gary Cooper approach would not work. But he could, for example, call over the captain and complain discreetly, perhaps even ask that our table be moved. He could hire a band of aging Teddy boys to find out where the drunks were staying and short-sheet all their beds. Or—and I think I prefer this—he could produce, from his jacket pocket, a printed card from a novelty shop reading: "I'm terribly sorry, but as you can see by looking at our dinner companion, my wife and I have other plans."

I'm going out to have those cards made up right now.   19

Discussing Content and Form

1. What is the relationship between the two narrative incidents with which Ephron opens her essay? What is her purpose in telling the two stories?

2. In what sense is paragraph 5 a third narrative incident in which the author is involved?

3. What are your reactions to the story about Gary Cooper? To the incident involving the Kordas? How do your reactions differ from those of the people to whom Ephron told the story (par. 5)?

4. Account for the reaction of Mrs. Korda. Do her actions indicate that she is a feminist? Do you agree or disagree that she reduced the situation to "a tedious set of movement platitudes" (par. 16)?

5. What do Ephron's comments indicate about her views of the male/female roles in the stories? What does she mean by the statement that "the episode just might be a distillation of everything that has happened to men and women as a result of the women's movement" (par. 5)? To what extent do you think Ephron is serious? Explain.

Considering Special Techniques

1. A relevant and often amusing anecdote is frequently used as an opener for essays or articles. Comment on the effectiveness of the narrative techniques that Ephron uses. For instance, does she make the events of the stories dramatic? Does she interest you in the people involved as well as in the events? Is the dialogue true to life? Explain.

2. Give your opinions of the tone and language of the essay. Make a list of terms that seem effective here but that might not be suitable in more formal writing. You might begin with "swell," "terrific," and "utterly" in paragraph 1.

3. What is the effect of the one-sentence paragraph (2), "Well, you had to be there"?

4. Why does the writer resort to so many unanswered questions? What is the relationship of the repetition of questions to the main idea of the essay?

5. The allusions in this informal narrative are to actual people or to fictional characters that you probably can identify. For instance, Francis Macomber (par. 3) is the title character of an Ernest Hemingway short story. Macomber is killed by his wife while on an African safari; the author leaves it up to the reader to decide whether or not the shooting is accidental. Identify Dave DeBusschere and Howard Cosell (par. 16). How do you think they might have acted in Korda's position?

6. Other terms to explain: Teddy boys (par. 1); chattel, diatribe, mea culpa (par. 4); rampant homoerotic behavior (par. 14).

Generating Ideas

1. Take a stand favoring one of the opinions or actions presented in the essay, and write a paper explaining your views to a friend. These titles might help:
"I Agree, Mrs. Korda!"
"Throw It Harder, Mike!"
"Good Going, Gary Cooper!"
"Like Nora's Friend, I Think It Boring"

2. Recount an embarrassing incident you have observed, and draw some conclusions about what it is like to be placed in such an awkward situation. Or narrate an incident involving a public display of temper or bad manners; then draw your

conclusions about such behavior. You might employ either a serious or humorous tone.

3. If you are a woman, relate an incident in which you felt that you were treated as an insignificant object by a man. If you are a man, write a narrative about circumstances that forced you, against your better judgment, to display masculine aggressiveness.

4. Write a paper dealing with one of these problems raised in the essay:

> *"some response does seem called for. . . . But on whose part?" (par. 17)*
>
> *"I wonder whether there is any response a man could make in that situation which would not disappoint a feminist." (par. 17)*
>
> *"where is the point that a mild show of strength becomes crude macho vulgarity; where does reserve veer off into passivity?" (par. 17)*

E. B. White

E. B. White (b. 1899) is one of America's finest prose stylists. He is known for his essays, editorials, and columns; he has also written verse. He revised and enlarged *The Elements of Style,* by his college professor William Strunk, Jr., a best-selling book for writers. Many readers, too, know and love his children's classics, *Stuart Little* (1945) and *Charlotte's Web* (1952). His essay collections include *Is Sex Necessary?* (with James Thurber, 1929), *One Man's Meat* (1942), *The Second Tree from the Corner* (1953), and *The Points of My Compass* (1962). In 1976 a collection of White's letters appeared, giving him what he describes as an "entirely different kind of exposure." Even the letters that White wrote as a very young boy reveal his gift for handling words, and the letters as a whole reveal the charm and humor that readers have appreciated in the essays.

For many years both White and his wife, Katharine Sergeant White, a *New Yorker* editor, were associated with that magazine. In 1938 they left Manhattan to live in their farmhouse on the coast of Maine, where White continues to live since his wife's death in 1977. Some of White's best-known essays are based on his observations of life in the country. "Once More to the Lake" links his own boyhood summers in Maine with the experience of watching his son enjoy the same scene.

Once More to the Lake
August 1941

1 One summer, along about 1904, my father rented a camp on a lake in Maine and took us all there for the month of August. We all got ringworm from some kittens and had to rub Pond's Extract on our arms and legs night and morning, and my father rolled over in a canoe with all his clothes on; but outside of that the vacation was a success and from then on none of us ever thought there was any place in the world like that lake in Maine. We returned summer after summer—always on August 1st for one month. I have since become a salt-water man, but sometimes in summer there are days when the restlessness of the tides and the fearful cold of the sea water and the incessant wind which blows across the afternoon and into the evening make me wish for the placidity of a lake in the woods. A few weeks ago this feeling got so strong I bought myself a couple of bass hooks and a spinner and returned to the lake where we used to go, for a week's fishing and to revisit old haunts.

I took along my son, who had never had any fresh water   2
up his nose and who had seen lily pads only from train
windows. On the journey over to the lake I began to
wonder what it would be like. I wondered how time would
have marred this unique, this holy spot—the coves and
streams, the hills that the sun set behind, the camps and the
paths behind the camps. I was sure the tarred road would
have found it out and I wondered in what other ways it
would be desolated. It is strange how much you can
remember about places like that once you allow your mind
to return into the grooves which lead back. You remember
one thing, and that suddenly reminds you of another thing.
I guess I remembered clearest of all the early mornings,
when the lake was cool and motionless, remembered how
the bedroom smelled of the lumber it was made of and of
the wet woods whose scent entered through the screen.
The partitions in the camp were thin and did not extend
clear to the top of the rooms, and as I was always the first up
I would dress softly so as not to wake the others, and sneak
out into the sweet outdoors and start out in the canoe,
keeping close along the shore in the long shadows of the
pines. I remembered being very careful never to rub my
paddle against the gunwale for fear of disturbing the
stillness of the cathedral.

The lake had never been what you would call a wild lake.   3
There were cottages sprinkled around the shores, and it
was in farming country although the shores of the lake
were quite heavily wooded. Some of the cottages were
owned by nearby farmers, and you would live at the shore
and eat your meals at the farmhouse. That's what our
family did. But although it wasn't wild, it was a fairly large
and undisturbed lake and there were places in it which, to a
child at least, seemed infinitely remote and primeval.

I was right about the tar: it led to within half a mile of the   4
shore. But when I got back there, with my boy, and we
settled into a camp near a farmhouse and into the kind of
summertime I had known, I could tell that it was going to be
pretty much the same as it had been before—I knew it,
lying in bed the first morning, smelling the bedroom, and
hearing the boy sneak quietly out and go off along the shore
in a boat. I began to sustain the illusion that he was I, and

therefore, by simple transposition, that I was my father. This sensation persisted, kept cropping up all the time we were there. It was not an entirely new feeling, but in this setting it grew much stronger. I seemed to be living a dual existence. I would be in the middle of some simple act, I would be picking up a bait box or laying down a table fork, or I would be saying something, and suddenly it would be not I but my father who was saying the words or making the gesture. It gave me a creepy sensation.

5 We went fishing the first morning. I felt the same damp moss covering the worms in the bait can, and saw the dragonfly alight on the tip of my rod as it hovered a few inches from the surface of the water. It was the arrival of this fly that convinced me beyond any doubt that everything was as it always had been, that the years were a mirage and there had been no years. The small waves were the same, chucking the rowboat under the chin as we fished at anchor, and the boat was the same boat, the same color green and the ribs broken in the same places, and under the floor-boards the same fresh-water leavings and débris—the dead helgramite, the wisps of moss, the rusty discarded fishhook, the dried blood from yesterday's catch. We stared silently at the tips of our rods, at the dragonflies that came and went. I lowered the tip of mine into the water, tentatively, pensively dislodging the fly, which darted two feet away, poised, darted two feet back, and came to rest again a little farther up the rod. There had been no years between the ducking of this dragonfly and the other one—the one that was part of memory. I looked at the boy, who was silently watching his fly, and it was my hands that held his rod, my eyes watching. I felt dizzy and didn't know which rod I was at the end of.

6 We caught two bass, hauling them in briskly as though they were mackerel, pulling them over the side of the boat in a businesslike manner without any landing net, and stunning them with a blow on the back of the head. When we got back for a swim before lunch, the lake was exactly where we had left it, the same number of inches from the dock, and there was only the merest suggestion of a breeze. This seemed an utterly enchanted sea, this lake you could leave to its own devices for a few hours and come back to,

and find that it had not stirred, this constant and trustworthy body of water. In the shallows, the dark, water-soaked sticks and twigs, smooth and old, were undulating in clusters on the bottom against the clean ribbed sand, and the track of the mussel was plain. A school of minnows swam by, each minnow with its small individual shadow, doubling the attendance, so clear and sharp in the sunlight. Some of the other campers were in swimming, along the shore, one of them with a cake of soap, and the water felt thin and clear and unsubstantial. Over the years there had been this person with the cake of soap, this cultist, and here he was. There had been no years.

Up to the farmhouse to dinner through the teeming, dusty field, the road under our sneakers was only a two-track road. The middle track was missing, the one with the marks of the hooves and the splotches of dried, flaky manure. There had always been three tracks to choose from in choosing which track to walk in; now the choice was narrowed down to two. For a moment I missed terribly the middle alternative. But the way led past the tennis court, and something about the way it lay there in the sun reassured me; the tape had loosened along the backline, the alleys were green with plantains and other weeds, and the net (installed in June and removed in September) sagged in the dry noon, and the whole place steamed with midday heat and hunger and emptiness. There was a choice of pie for dessert, and one was blueberry and one was apple, and the waitresses were the same country girls, there having been no passage of time, only the illusion of it as in a dropped curtain—the waitresses were still fifteen; their hair had been washed, that was the only difference—they had been to the movies and seen the pretty girls with the clean hair.

Summertime, oh summertime, pattern of life indelible, the fade-proof lake, the woods unshatterable, the pasture with the sweetfern and the juniper forever and ever, summer without end; this was the background, and the life along the shore was the design, the cottages with their innocent and tranquil design, their tiny docks with the flagpole and the American flag floating against the white clouds in the blue sky, the little paths over the roots of the trees leading from camp to camp and the paths leading back to the outhouses and the can of lime for sprinkling, and at the souvenir counters at the store the miniature birch-bark canoes and the post cards that showed things looking a little better than they looked. This was the American family at play, escaping the city heat, wondering whether the newcomers in the camp at the head of the cove were "common" or "nice," wondering whether it was true that the people who drove up for Sunday dinner at the farmhouse were turned away because there wasn't enough chicken.

9   It seemed to me, as I kept remembering all this, that those times and those summers had been infinitely precious and worth saving. There had been jollity and peace and goodness. The arriving (at the beginning of August) had been so big a business in itself, at the railway station the farm wagon drawn up, the first smell of the pine-laden air, the first glimpse of the smiling farmer, and the great importance of the trunks and your father's enormous authority in such matters, and the feel of the wagon under you for the long ten-mile haul, and at the top of the last long hill catching the first view of the lake after eleven months of not seeing this cherished body of water. The shouts and cries of the other campers when they saw you, and the trunks to be unpacked, to give up their rich burden. (Arriving was less exciting nowadays, when you sneaked up in your car and parked it under a tree near the camp and took out the bags and in five minutes it was all over, no fuss, no loud wonderful fuss about trunks.)

10   Peace and goodness and jollity. The only thing that was wrong now, really, was the sound of the place, an unfamiliar nervous sound of the outboard motors. This was the note that jarred, the one thing that would sometimes break the illusion and set the years moving. In those other summertimes all motors were inboard; and when they were at a little distance, the noise they made was a sedative, an ingredient of summer sleep. They were one-cylinder and two-cylinder engines, and some were make-and-break and some were jump-spark, but they all made a sleepy sound across the lake. The one-lungers throbbed and

fluttered, and the twin-cylinder ones purred and purred, and that was a quiet sound too. But now the campers all had outboards. In the daytime, in the hot mornings, these motors made a petulant, irritable sound; at night, in the still evening when the afterglow lit the water, they whined about one's ears like mosquitoes. My boy loved our rented outboard, and his great desire was to achieve single-handed mastery over it, and authority, and he soon learned the trick of choking it a little (but not too much), and the adjustment of the needle valve. Watching him I would remember the things you could do with the old one-cylinder engine with the heavy flywheel, how you could have it eating out of your hand if you got really close to it spiritually. Motor boats in those days didn't have clutches, and you would make a landing by shutting off the motor at the proper time and coasting in with a dead rudder. But there was a way of reversing them, if you learned the trick, by cutting the switch and putting it on again exactly on the final dying revolution of the flywheel, so that it would kick back against compression and begin reversing. Approaching a dock in a strong following breeze, it was difficult to slow up sufficiently by the ordinary coasting method, and if a boy felt he had complete mastery over his motor, he was tempted to keep it running beyond its time and then reverse it a few feet from the dock. It took a cool nerve, because if you threw the switch a twentieth of a second too soon you would catch the flywheel when it still had speed enough to go up past center, and the boat would leap ahead, charging bull-fashion at the dock.

We had a good week at the camp. The bass were biting well and the sun shone endlessly, day after day. We would be tired at night and lie down in the accumulated heat of the little bedrooms after the long hot day and the breeze would stir almost imperceptibly outside and the smell of the swamp drift in through the rusty screens. Sleep would come easily and in the morning the red squirrel would be on the roof, tapping out his gay routine. I kept remembering everything, lying in bed in the mornings—the small steamboat that had a long rounded stern like the lip of a Ubangi, and how quietly she ran on the moonlight sails, when the older boys played their mandolins and the girls sang and we ate doughnuts dipped in sugar, and how sweet the music was on the water in the shining night, and what it had felt like to think about girls then. After breakfast we would go up to the store and the things were in the same place—the minnows in a bottle, the plugs and spinners disarranged and pawed over by the youngsters from the boys' camp, the fig newtons and the Beeman's gum. Outside, the road was tarred and cars stood in front of the store. Inside, all was just as it had always been, except there was more Coca-Cola and not so much Moxie and root beer and birch beer and sarsaparilla. We would walk out with a bottle of pop apiece and sometimes the pop would backfire up our noses and hurt. We explored the streams, quietly, where the turtles slid off the sunny logs and dug their way into the soft bottom; and we lay on the town wharf and fed worms to the tame bass. Everywhere we went I had trouble making out which was I, the one walking at my side, the one walking in my pants.

12   One afternoon while we were there at that lake a thunderstorm came up. It was like the revival of an old melodrama that I had seen long ago with childish awe. The second-act climax of the drama of the electrical disturbance over a lake in America had not changed in any important respect. This was the big scene, still the big scene. The whole thing was familiar, the first feeling of oppression and heat and a general air around camp of not wanting to go very far away. In midafternoon (it was all the same) a curious darkening of the sky, and a lull in everything that had made life tick; and then the way the boats suddenly swung the other way at their moorings with the coming of a breeze out of the new quarter, and the premonitory rumble. Then the kettle drum, then the snare, then the bass drum and cymbals, then crackling light against the dark, and the gods grinning and licking their chops in the hills. Afterward the calm, the rain steadily rustling in the calm lake, the return of light and hope and spirits, and the campers running out in joy and relief to go swimming in the rain, their bright cries perpetuating the deathless joke about how they were getting simply drenched, and the children screaming with delight at the new sensation of bathing in the rain, and the joke about getting drenched

linking the generations in a strong indestructible chain. And the comedian who waded in carrying an umbrella.

When the others went swimming my son said he was going in too. He pulled his dripping trunks from the line where they had hung all through the shower, and wrung them out. Languidly, and with no thought of going in, I watched him, his hard little body, skinny and bare, saw him wince slightly as he pulled up around his vitals the small, soggy, icy garment. As he buckled the swollen belt suddenly my groin felt the chill of death. 13

Discussing Content and Form

1. In what sense are the first three paragraphs an introduction to the point made in paragraph 4: "I began to sustain the illusion that he was I, and therefore, by simple transposition, that I was my father"?

2. In the essay, White narrates in order to convey a central idea, to make a point not only about his experience but also about human experience in general. State his point in your own words. How does it relate to White's feeling of "transposition" expressed in paragraph 4? In succeeding paragraphs, find sentences that restate this idea. What special force does the last paragraph contribute?

3. White describes the lake as a "holy spot" and tells of his worries that it "would be desolated" (par. 2). Do you think he is sorry that he returned? Support your answer by referring to the essay.

4. White finds that fishing and swimming are unchanged, that the lake is still "enchanted" (par. 6), but that the middle track is "missing" from the road (par. 7). What is the significance of the change in the road? Why does White regret the loss of the "middle alternative"? What essential difference between nature and human beings is emphasized throughout the essay?

5. White says, "It seemed to me . . . that those times and those summers had been infinitely precious and worth saving" (par. 9). Do you think his son will feel the same way about the trip to the lake? Explain.

Considering Special Techniques

1. Most of White's paragraphs are tightly organized clusters of sentences that develop a single topic. Treating the first three paragraphs as the introduction, determine the general topic for each paragraph that follows.

2. Analyze the method of organization for paragraphs 10 and 12.

    a. What use is made of contrast in paragraph 10? Note the linking phrases such as "In those other summertimes" and "But now the campers." Find other examples of such phrases in the essay.

    b. Read the introduction to Chapter 7 on analogy and explain how the comparison of the thunderstorm to a drama organizes paragraph 12. In what ways does a storm resemble a play?

3. White's writing furnishes many examples of what is sometimes called the cumulative sentence. Such sentences are made up of a main clause, or base, with an accumulation of modifying phrases added to enrich and enlarge the meaning and to make it more specific. The following sentence from paragraph 6 has three additions, each enlarging the idea expressed in the main clause:

"We caught two bass,
    hauling them in briskly as though they were mackerel,
    pulling them over the side of the boat in a businesslike manner without any landing net,
    and stunning them with a blow on the back of the head."

In another cumulative sentence (par. 6), note how the added phrases tell something more about the school of minnows:

"A school of minnows swam by,
    each minnow with its small individual shadow,
    doubling the attendance,
    so clear and sharp in the sunlight."

Find other sentences in the essay where the details are added cumulatively to give increasingly specific information. Make an analysis of the first sentence of paragraph 8.

4. In paragraph 11, White shifts the form of the verbs from the simple past to the progressive form with the modal would: "We would be tired"; "the breeze would stir"; "Sleep would come." Why does he make this shift only in this paragraph?

5. Why does the writer change the order of the second sentence in paragraph 9 and use it as the opener for paragraph 10?

6. Explain the effect produced by these words and phrases: "a salt-water man" (par. 1); "the stillness of the cathedral" (par. 2); "this person with the cake of soap, this cultist" (par. 6); "the American family at play" (par. 8); "nervous sound of the outboard motors" (par. 10).

Generating Ideas

1. Choose one of these subjects for an essay based on your experience or on that of others whom you know:
   A visit to a place where you once lived
   A storm and its effects on a town, resort area, etc.
   A change in a family, in customs, or in a particular locale
   A childhood journey or visit you made with an adult

2. Write an essay about the "American family at play" as you know it. Use narrative incidents to illustrate your points. For example, if you think that families seldom take vacations nowadays, you will want to gather evidence to support your view.

3. White says the lake was "to a child . . . enchantment." Write of some spot or some experience that holds enchantment for you, trying to recreate in narration and description the emotional attachment you feel for the place.

4. Write a narrative about the visit to the lake as it might have appeared to White's son.

Wallace Stegner

Wallace Stegner (b. 1909) lives in Los Altos, California. He is Professor
Emeritus at Stanford University, where he taught and directed a center for
creative writing. After undergraduate work at the University of Utah,
Stegner earned his M.A. and Ph.D. degrees at the University of Iowa,
where he later taught for a time in the English Department. He has
published widely, both fiction and nonfiction. In 1972 he won the Pulitzer
Prize in Fiction for *Angle of Repose*, and in 1977, the National Book Award
in Fiction for *The Spectator Bird*. Among his best known books are *Wolf
Willow* (1962), *The Gathering of Zion* (1967), and *The Uneasy Chair: A
Biography of Bernard De Voto* (1975). Stegner has always set his students a
stellar example, for he has published countless short stories, articles, and
essays. "The Town Dump," a descriptive narrative of his boyhood in the
Canadian West, is one of the most often reprinted of his essays.

The Town Dump

1   The town dump of Whitemud, Saskatchewan, could only
have been a few years old when I knew it, for the village
was born in 1913 and I left there in 1919. But I remember the
dump better than I remember most things in that town,
better than I remember most of the people. I spent more
time with it, for one thing; it had more poetry and
excitement in it than people did.

2   It lay in the southeast corner of town, in a section that
was full of adventure for me. Just there the Whitemud River
left the hills, bent a little south, and started its long traverse
across the prairie and the international boundary to join the
Milk. For all I knew, it might have been on its way to join
the Alph: simply, before my eyes, it disappeared into
strangeness and wonder.

3   Also, where it passed below the dumpground, it ran
through willowed bottoms that were a favorite campsite for
passing teamsters, gypsies, sometimes Indians. The very
straw scattered around those strangers' campfires, the
manure of their teams and saddle horses, were hot with
adventurous possibilities.

4   It was as an extension, a living suburb, as it were, of the
dumpground that we most valued those camps. We
scoured them for artifacts of their migrant tenants as if they
were archeological sites full of the secrets of ancient

civilizations. I remember toting around for weeks the broken cheek strap of a bridle. Somehow or other its buckle looked as if it had been fashioned in a far place, a place where they could only be exciting, and where they made a habit of plating the metal with some valuable alloy, probably silver. In places where the silver was worn away the buckle underneath shone dull yellow: probably gold.

It seemed that excitement liked that end of town better than our end. Once old Mrs. Gustafson, deeply religious and a little raddled in the head, went over there with a buckboard full of trash, and as she was driving home along the river she looked and saw a spent catfish, washed in from Cypress Lake or some other part of the watershed, floating on the yellow water. He was two feet long, his whiskers hung down, his fins and tail were limp. He was a kind of fish no one had seen in the Whitemud in the three or four years of the town's life, and a kind that none of us children had ever seen anywhere. Mrs. Gustafson had never seen one like him either; she perceived at once that he was the devil, and she whipped up the team and reported him at Hoffman's elevator.

We could hear her screeching as we legged it for the river to see for ourselves. Sure enough, there he was. He looked very tired, and he made no great effort to get away as we pushed out a half-sunken rowboat from below the flume, submerged it under him, and brought him ashore. When he died three days later we experimentally fed him to two half-wild cats, but they seemed to suffer no ill effects.

At the same end of town the irrigation flume crossed the river. It always seemed to me giddily high when I hung my chin over its plank edge and looked down, but it probably walked no more than twenty feet above the water on its spidery legs. Ordinarily in summer it carried about six or eight inches of smooth water, and under the glassy hurrying of the little boxed stream the planks were coated with deep sun-warmed moss as slick as frogs' eggs. A boy could sit in the flume with the water walling up against his back, and grab a cross brace above him, and pull, shooting himself sledlike ahead until he could reach the next brace for another pull and slide, and so on across the river in four scoots.

8   After ten minutes in the flume, he would come out wearing a dozen or more limber black leeches, and could sit in the green shade where darning needles flashed blue, and dragonflies hummed and darted and stopped, and skaters dimpled slack and eddy with their delicate transitory footprints, and there stretch the leeches out one by one while their sucking ends clung and clung, until at last, stretched far out, they let go with a tiny wet *puk* and snapped together like rubber bands. The smell of the river and the flume and the clay cutbanks and the bars of that part of the river was the smell of wolf willow.

9   But nothing in that end of town was as good as the dumpground that scattered along a little runoff coulee dipping down toward the river from the south bench. Through a historical process that went back, probably, to the roots of community sanitation and distaste for eyesores, but that in law dated from the Unincorporated Towns Ordinance of the territorial government, passed in 1888, the dump was one of the very first community enterprises, almost our town's first institution.

10   More than that, it contained relics of every individual who had ever lived there, and of every phase of the town's history.

11   The bedsprings on which the town's first child was begotten might be there; the skeleton of a boy's pet colt; two or three volumes of Shakespeare bought in haste and error from a peddler, later loaned in carelessness, soaked with water and chemicals in a house fire, and finally thrown out to flap their stained eloquence in the prairie wind.

12   Broken dishes, rusty tinware, spoons that had been used to mix paint; once a box of percussion caps, sign and symbol of the carelessness that most of those people felt about all matters of personal and public safety. We put them on the railroad tracks and were anonymously denounced in the *Enterprise*. There were also old iron, old brass, for which we hunted assiduously, by night conning junkmen's catalogues and the pages of the *Enterprise* to find how much wartime value there might be in the geared insides of clocks or in a pound of tea lead carefully wrapped in a ball whose weight astonished and delighted us. Sometimes the unimaginable outside world reached in and

laid a finger on us. I recall that, aged more than seven, I wrote a St. Louis junk house asking if they preferred their tea lead and tinfoil wrapped in balls, or whether they would prefer it pressed flat in sheets, and I got back a typewritten letter in a window envelope instructing me that they would be happy to have it in any way that was convenient for me. They added that they valued my business and were mine very truly. Dazed, I carried the windowed grandeur around in my pocket until I wore it out, and for months I saved the letter as a souvenir of the wondering time when something strange and distinguishing singled me out.

We hunted old bottles in the dump, bottles caked with   13
dirt and filth, half-buried, full of cobwebs, and we washed them out at the horse trough by the elevator, putting in a handful of shot along with the water to knock the dirt loose; and when we had shaken them until our arms were tired, we hauled them off in somebody's coaster wagon and turned them in at Bill Anderson's poolhall, where the smell of lemon pop was so sweet on the dark pool-hall air that I am sometimes awakened by it in the night, even yet.

Smashed wheels of wagons and buggies, tangles of   14
rusty barbed wire, the collapsed perambulator that the French wife of one of the town's doctors had once pushed proudly up the planked sidewalks and along ditchbank paths. A welter of foul-smelling feathers and coyote-scattered carrion which was all that remained of somebody's dream of a chicken ranch. The chickens had all got some mysterious pip at the same time, and died as one, and the dream lay out there with the rest of the town's history to rustle to the empty sky at the border of the hills.

There was melted glass in curious forms, and the   15
half-melted office safe left from the burning of Bill Day's hotel. On very lucky days we might find a piece of the lead casing that had enclosed the town's first telephone system. The casing was just the right size for rings, and so soft it could be whittled with a jackknife. It was a material that might have made artists of us. If we had been Indians of fifty years before, that bright soft metal would have enlisted our maximum patience and craft and come out as ring and medal and amulet inscribed with the symbols of our

observed world. Perhaps there were too many ready-made alternatives in the local drug, hardware, and general stores; perhaps our feeble artistic response was a measure of the insufficiency of the challenge we felt. In any case I do not remember that we did any more with the metal than to shape it into crude seal rings with our initials or pierced hearts carved in them; and these, though they served a purpose in juvenile courtship, stopped something short of art.

16   The dump held very little wood, for in that country anything burnable was burned. But it had plenty of old iron, furniture, papers, mattresses that were the delight of field mice, and jugs and demijohns that were sometimes their bane, for they crawled into the necks and drowned in the rain water or redeye that was inside.

17   If the history of our town was not exactly written, it was at least hinted at, in the dump. I think I had a pretty sound notion even at eight or nine of how significant was that first institution of our forming Canadian civilization. For rummaging through its foul purlieus I found relics of my own life tossed out there to rot or blow away.

18   The volumes of Shakespeare belonged to a set that my father had bought before I was born. It had been carried through successive moves from town to town in the Dakotas, and from Dakota to Seattle, and from Seattle to Bellingham, and Bellingham to Redmond, and from Redmond back to Iowa, and from there to Saskatchewan. Then, stained in a stranger's house fire, these volumes had suffered from a house-cleaning impulse and been thrown away for me to stumble upon in the dump. One of the Cratchet girls had borrowed them, a hatchet-faced, thin, eager transplanted Cockney girl with a frenzy, almost a hysteria, for reading. And yet somehow, through her hands, they found the dump, to become a symbol of how much was lost, how much thrown aside, how much carelessly or of necessity given up, in the making of a new country. We had so few books that I was familiar with them all, had handled them, looked at their pictures, perhaps even read them. They were the lares and penates, part of the skimpy impedimenta of household Gods we had brought with us into Latium. Finding those three thrown

away was a little like finding my own name on a gravestone.

And yet not the blow that something else was, 19
something that impressed me even more with the dump's close reflection of the town's intimate life. The colt whose picked skeleton lay out there was mine. He had been incurably crippled when dogs chased our mare, Daisy, the morning after she foaled. I had labored for months to make him well; had fed him by hand, curried him, exercised him, adjusted the iron braces that I had talked my father into having made. And I had not known that he would have to be destroyed. One weekend I turned him over to the foreman of one of the ranches, presumably so that he could be cared for. A few days later I found his skinned body, with the braces still on his crippled front legs, lying on the dump.

Not even that, I think, cured me of going there, though 20
our parents all forbade us on pain of cholera or worse to do so. For this was the kitchen midden of all the civilization we knew; it gave us the most tantalizing glimpses into our lives as well as those of our neighbors. It gave us an aesthetic distance from which to know ourselves.

The dump was our poetry and our history. We took it 21
home with us by the wagonload, bringing back into town the things the town had used and thrown away. Some little part of what we gathered, mainly bottles, we managed to bring back to usefulness, but most of our gleanings we left lying around barn or attic or cellar until in some renewed fury of spring cleanup our families carted them off to the dump again, to be rescued and briefly treasured by some other boy with schemes for making them useful. Occasionally something we really valued with a passion was snatched from us in horror and returned at once. This happened to the head of a white mountain goat, somebody's trophy from old times and the far Rocky Mountains, that I brought home one day in transports of delight. My mother took one look and discovered that his beard was full of moths.

I remember that goat; I regret him yet. Poetry is seldom 22
useful, but always memorable. I think I learned more from the town dump than I learned from school; more about

people, more about how life is lived, not elsewhere but here, not in other times but now. If I were a sociologist anxious to study the life of any community, I would go very early to its refuse piles. For a community may be as well judged by what it throws away—what it has to throw away and what it chooses to—as by any other evidence. For whole civilizations we have sometimes no more of the poetry and little more of the history than this.

Discussing Content and Form

1. The first sentence in paragraph 21 —"The dump was our poetry and our history"—is a key statement for this essay. Point out several details and incidents that represent the poetry of the dump and several that reveal the history of the community.

2. Stegner lived in the town of the dump as a young boy, but he writes about it as a mature man. Which statements that he makes show the insight of maturity? Explain the meaning of his assertion that the dump gave "an aesthetic distance from which to know ourselves" (par. 20); then explain how time also gives the writer an aesthetic distance.

3. The short narrative about Mrs. Gustafson may at first thought seem to be somewhat unrelated to the development of the essay. Use Stegner's statement that the dump "had poetry and excitement in it" (par. 1) to explain why he included this little story.

4. What do you know about the boy Stegner's nature and personality? Which details give you those insights?

5. In what sense is the dump the town's "first institution" as Stegner twice says that it is (pars. 9 and 17)? He mentions only one other institution—the school in paragraph 22. Why does he feel that he learned more from the dump than from the school?

6. The plan of Stegner's essay is very clear, with blocks of paragraphs or single paragraphs, functioning clearly in well-planned order.
   a. Decide how many paragraphs are actually introductory; then decide where Stegner starts to wrap up for the conclusion.
   b. Determine the various subsections: for instance, the story of Mrs. Gustafson is told in paragraphs 5 and 6;

the boyhood adventure in the flume comprises
paragraphs 7 and 8. What is the special function of
the single sentence paragraph 10?

Considering Special Techniques

1. Keeping in mind that description moves in space and
that narrative follows a time sequence, go through the essay
and determine which paragraphs describe the dump and
which narrate Stegner's experience. Looking back over the
other selections in this section, show that the writers of
personal essays often, naturally and purposefully, fuse the
two methods.

2. Consider the degree of specificity in the details that
Stegner uses. For instance, he names the town, gives dates,
names some of the townspeople. Show that these details
function both to give Stegner's personal history and to give
the history of the town.

3. Some of the language of the essay might be labeled
colloquial or regional. What is the effect of such words as
"toting" (par. 4), "raddled" (par. 5), "scoots" (par. 7),
"kitchen midden" (par. 20)?

4. Find examples of Stegner's use of literary allusion. For
instance, the "Alph" (par. 2) is the mysterious and imaginary
river in Coleridge's poem, "Kubla Khan." Use your dictionary
to explain the "lares and penates" referred to in paragraph
18. What is the effect of mixing these allusions and the
literary language with the dialect words?

5. Words to learn and use: artifacts, archeological (par. 4);
transitory (par. 8); eloquence (par. 11); assiduously (par. 12);
perambulator, welter (par. 14); amulet (par. 15); demijohns
(par. 16); purlieus (par. 17); impedimenta (par. 18); aesthetic
(par. 20).

Generating Ideas

1. Dumps today are quite different from that of Stegner's
Canadian town. Describe a current system or systems of
waste disposal. You might consider details such as
bulldozers burying the refuse from a city, restrictive fencing of
the area so that no one will be injured, etc. Or you might
describe an auto salvage yard and show how that type of
dump reveals history.

2. Write a paper showing that what we throw away reveals a lot about us, or one showing that what we keep makes a similar revelation. For instance, today it is actually more costly to repair small electrical appliances than to buy new ones. You might narrow the focus to show only that what an individual (either yourself or someone you know) discards or collects is revealing of personality, or you might write about society more generally.

3. Stegner tells the story of a boyish prank in paragraph 12: "We put [the percussion caps] on the railroad tracks and were anonymously denounced in the Enterprise." Write a narrative about an escapade in which you and your friends were involved. Any denunciation or punishment you experienced might make a dramatic conclusion.

4. Stegner relates at some length the poignant loss of the colt, and again mentions the disappointment when his mother made him give up the goat's head. Write a paper about one or more of your childhood disappointments, being sure to include specific details that will show your sense of loss.

5. Clearing out an attic, an old house, or a business place might be somewhat like Stegner's experience in visiting the dump because there you could find remnants that reflect the people who made the collection. Write a descriptive-narrative paper about such a project in order to give your reader insight into not only the situation but also the history of the place and people involved. Or write a narrative about moving or a garage sale and the problems of getting rid of collections, useful or useless.

4

EXAMPLE: ORGANIZING SPECIFICS

From experience and observation come the factual materials or examples that enable you to *show* rather than merely *tell* your reader what you mean. The difference between showing and telling is often the difference between writing that convinces and writing that merely presents generalizations which may or may not be convincing. Many people can make the same general statement in much the same words, but using personal observations gives writing the stamp of individuality and makes it ring true at the same time.

This chapter opens with a paragraph of generalization which needs some concrete support. That paragraph tells; this paragraph shows. Let us assume that you have in mind a generalization about the unusual stunts people perform on mountains. The following paragraph states this generalization, then lists many examples which give it powerful support:

> Mountains have always presented a stage for the offbeat and the record breaker. Longs Peak in the Rockies was in 1927 the scene of a summit marriage; three years later came the ascent by a five-year-old girl. The next year Francis W. Chamberlain got to the top on one leg and crutches, while in 1934 a marathon race up Mount Washington was held between

three one-legged men. More conventional races have been run on scores of mountains from California's Mount Shasta to Scotland's Ben Nevis, where the speed of the locals has been pitted against visitors. A Japanese has skied down Fuji at 105 miles an hour, needing a parachute to bring him to a halt. On Yosemite's El Capitan, Rick Sylvester went one better, skiing down the summit slabs and parachute-jumping the remaining 1,000 meters. According to *The Alpine Journal,* he felt that climbs he had made on the peak "no longer represented 'true adventure' as far as he was concerned, because they did not contain 'a large element of the unknown.' He therefore decided to undertake this sensational exploit, which perhaps has more in common with the circus than mountaineering, largely for the elements of uncertainty involved."
—Ronald W. Clark, *Men, Myths, and Mountains*

This paragraph represents a very simple kind of organization, one that is frequently used in arranging examples. The opening sentence contains the controlling generalization for the paragraph. Such a sentence is sometimes called the *topic sentence,* and it frequently appears at the beginning of a paragraph. The next two sentences each contain two examples, but the fourth sentence makes another general statement, one that is a little less general than that made by the first sentence. After that come two more examples: the first (about the Japanese skier) occupies one sentence, and the second (about Rick Sylvester) is expanded to fill the remainder of the paragraph. You can see that the writer has not only offered a great deal of specific support with the examples but he has also arranged those examples to build to the one he treats most fully, thus giving the paragraph both sufficient development and an emphatic conclusion.

Of course, the writer might have put his generalization in some position other than the first. And he might have used fewer examples or more, depending upon how many he thought would be both interesting and convincing. A fairly good rule of thumb in this kind of writing is to use about two-thirds to three-fourths of the space for examples and about one-fourth for generalizing, but there are no definite restrictions. In some single paragraphs, the general statement may not appear at all, but rather it may be implied. Whether explicit or implicit, the generalization is the point the writer wishes to convey by means of the examples.

We sometimes speak of the expanded example as an illustration, and in this paragraph the writer uses one such illustration from his personal experience to arrive at a statement about a word that he considers overused:

> In *The New Yorker*, a few years ago, I described the rather haphazard way in which I first came to use the term "the Establishment," and tried to explain why it has made such an antic journey into the languages of I do not know how many countries. (A German scholar has told me that the correct translation of the word into German would contain at least seven syllables.) Not a day now passes when the phrase is not shouted, or whispered, back to me; and I have long since ceased to inquire what people mean by it. It seems to me now to have little or no meaning, and I rarely use it any longer.—Henry Fairlie, "The Language of Politics," *The Atlantic*

In long articles and essays, examples and illustrations may cover several paragraphs, all of them developing a section of general introduction or leading to one or more paragraphs of conclusion. And, of course, in such writing the sections developed by examples are usually combined with those developed by other methods. Frequently, however, the use of either short examples or longer illustrations dominates an entire selection. This is the primary method employed in the four essays in this chapter. Also, the development of an entire paper around illustrative details that support a generaiization is often required in the essay questions given on tests: "Cite several examples of legal measures that have been used to control pollution of the Great Lakes"; "From the fiction we have studied, choose and discuss several examples of women who were forced by society to marry."

Whether the development by examples is long or short, "pure" or mixed with other methods, the same considerations apply. First, choose examples to fit both the purpose of the writing and the readers for whom it is intended. In writing about air pollution, for instance, it would not be suitable to introduce an example involving an oil spill in the Atlantic Ocean. The topic that is to be discussed sets limits around the choice of examples and rules out those that are marginally related. Similarly, in writing a letter to a newspaper about the dangers of pollution, you should include examples that are drawn from everyday life rather than from technical areas that would be suitable in a report for scientists. An example of the drainage problems at a local dump would serve the first audience, while examples dealing with the types and amounts of chemicals flowing into the Great Lakes might be more useful for the second.

Another major consideration—already mentioned in analyzing the paragraph about mountain climbing—is that of arrangement. When using several examples, you have to decide upon an order for placing them. At times a random or "the way things come to mind" order can be effective. (On pp. 272–73, notice how Louis Untermeyer uses randomly placed examples to define metaphor.) However, if you are writing about dictators throughout the last two centuries of history, you might choose a chronological order, or perhaps an order of "least to most successful." If you want to give examples of the equipment needed to set up a home workshop, you could arrange the items in the order of the most essential to the least essential. If you want to discuss inexpensive vacations, you might begin with either the most or least costly trip of the group. Careful arrangement not only gives coherence to the paragraph or paper, thereby making it easy for the reader to follow, but it also allows for natural transition. In the paper on vacations, you could begin with an introductory phrase such as "The least expensive" and proceed to "The most costly but still relatively cheap," thus connecting the examples so smoothly that the reader hardly notices these linking devices.

Many old books on writing stipulated a "2–3–4–1" climactic arrangement for examples, suggesting that the second most interesting item be placed first and the best saved until last. (The numbers could, of course, be extended in the middle.) That rule seems rather rigid; but it might be worth using as a point of departure when you cannot decide on a more natural arrangement, especially for longer papers developed by a series of examples. Of one thing you can be sure with any arrangement: if the examples are suited to your purpose and interesting in themselves, they will both support your generalizations and provide the liveliness that is part of a vigorous style.

Noel Perrin

Noel Perrin (b. 1927), a Professor of English at Dartmouth College in New Hampshire, lives on a farm near Thetford Center, Vermont. He holds degrees from Williams College, Duke University, and Cambridge University in England. His essays, many of them philosophical glimpses of country living, have appeared in *Vermont Life, Country Journal, New York,* the *New Yorker,* and the *New York Times.* His books include *A Passport Secretly Green* (1961), *Dr. Bowdler's Legacy* (1969), *Amateur Sugar Maker* (1972), *Vermont in All Weathers* (1973), *First Person Rural* (1978), and *Giving up the Gun* (1979). "The Wooden Bucket Principle" comes from *First Person Rural,* a charming volume of essays that Perrin says "are all concerned with country-ish things."

The Wooden Bucket Principle

April 28, 1963

To the Editors: *The New Yorker*

1

Situation prompting the "letter" (par. 1)

Dear Sirs:

Under the heading 'Incidental Intelligence (Is Nothing Sacred? Division)' you lately reported that some Vermont farmers are using plastic bags rather than wooden buckets to catch the sap from maple trees. This is true, though plastic tubes which eliminate the need to catch the sap at all (they run it directly from inside the tree down to the sugarhouse) are more popular still. But that's not what I'm writing you about.

2

First example: misconception about maple sugaring (par. 2)

I am unable to decide whether you really believe that maple producers, in Vermont or out of it, were using wooden buckets until the plastic apparatus came along. Since wooden buckets started to go out not long after the Civil War ('I like tin,' said the Secretary of the Vermont Board of Agriculture in 1886), and since they had pretty well disappeared, even on hill farms such as mine, by about 1910, it seems improbable. On the other hand, city people plainly haven't been following the development of sugaring at all closely. For example, every spring your magazine publishes one or two cartoons showing some farmer gathering sap from buckets of the wrong shape, without covers, hung too high on what look to be beech trees, or possibly box elders. Most farmers do still hang buckets (they're made of galvanized steel, with peaked lids to keep the snow out), and we mostly still boil down over wood fires, rather than oil fires, but we never tap box elders. If you can swallow those cartoons, I don't suppose you have much trouble believing in the wooden buckets.

Actually, I don't seriously blame either you or your cartoonists. I think there's something I shall henceforth call the Wooden Bucket Principle at work here. By this I mean a tendency to imagine almost anything in the country as simpler and more primitive and kind of nicer than it really is. Picture calendars are the most familiar example. Every time I see a calendar decorated with a color photograph of a New England village, I look, and I'm never disappointed. There's the little village, nestled among the hills. There's the white church. There the majestic maples. What about the filling station? It's been cropped. There are never gas stations in pictures of New England villages. Those big orange school buses don't generally get into such pictures either, nor does the town shed, with a couple of modern road scrapers lying around out front.

I also find the Wooden Bucket Principle operating in the books we have begun to buy for my daughter, who is nearing two. Some of these are books written and published in the United States in the last couple of years: animal A B C's, I-Can-Do-This-or-That books, and so forth. Supposedly they are both about and for contemporary American children. Yet I was

3
Proposal of "Wooden Bucket Principle"

Second example: picture calendars

Sub-examples: series of errors in calendars (par. 3)

4
Third example: misimpressions of chickens in children's books (par. 4)

reading from one just tonight which showed a little girl saying, 'Pick. Pick. Pick. I'm a little chick.' Behind her are five chicks, about a dozen hens, and two roosters, all wandering freely about in front of a quite charming henhouse, picking for corn. Real American chickens, of course, do no such thing, even as chicks. They neither wander nor pick. Instead they spend their time, in lots of ten thousand or a hundred thousand, locked in battery houses, never walking an inch. The cages are too small. I think their feed has Aureomycin in it.

5
Fourth example: discrepancy in dairy methods (par. 5)

There's a similar discrepancy in a slightly more advanced book my daughter has. This one shows a slightly older girl helping to drive in some cows. Not yet in Vermont, maybe, but on most modern dairy farms there's no place to drive cows in from. The modern dairy cow, under the dry-lot system, lives her full life in a concrete enclosure, receiving her feed—alfalfa, mostly—from an overhead conveyor. A little girl would just get in the way on a drylot. Besides, she'd fall and skin her knees on the concrete.

6
Fifth example: misunderstanding about beef cattle (par. 6)

I understand that in California the same method is being used for beef cattle. (One of its advantages is that permanent indoor life gives steers paler flesh. The meat thus has more room to darken, once it's cut up and put on display in a supermarket. This is handy in reducing the need to put out fresh packages.) Yet for all my daughter will learn from her books, all the cows in California hang around in the sunlight, tanned and healthy, just like the surfers.

7
Sixth example: false representation of work on bridge (par. 7)

As a matter of fact, the Wooden Bucket Principle isn't simply a country thing. I come to New York fairly often, and I've seen it in use by the Port of New York Authority. A couple of summers ago, while the second level of the

George Washington Bridge was being built, the Authority started handing out explanatory leaflets at the toll booths. I have several. I well remember getting the first. It made the customary apology for the delay and gave the customary explanation that it was for my future safety and convenience. It also showed an artist's rendering of the work in hand. The bridge was in the background, looking very handsome, but somehow only three lanes wide. The foreground was taken up with sketches of two genial-looking workmen, busy widening the New Jersey approaches. They were using for this purpose a shovel and a pickax, respectively. I had only to look out the car window to see the scene in actuality: the eight lanes of traffic streaming across, the earth-movers and giant power shovels roaring about on the Jersey approaches. There wasn't a workman in sight except dimly, inside some fifty-ton piece of equipment. (I suppose bridgebuilders' flesh is paler these days, too.)

I have no idea where all this is going to end. I may still be writing letters to you when your whole magazine is put together by plastic tubes. On the other hand, I may by then have gotten into a wooden sap bucket and pulled down the lid.

8
Conclusion:
humorous prediction
(par. 8)

Discussing Content and Form

1. What common misconception stimulates Perrin to offer his Wooden Bucket Principle? Find the sentence that explains the principle. Why do you think Perrin offers the explanation after he presents the first illustration of it?

2. Characterize the person, the voice, *that you sense behind the essay. What humor is inherent in the situation of the Vermont farmer who writes to the editors of the* New Yorker *to "set them straight"?*

3. Discuss the point that Perrin makes about the lack of knowledge behind the writing of children's books. If you can, give examples of such misconceptions (or deceptions) that you have found in books or articles, either those for children or for adults.

    a. Why do writers perpetuate such misconceptions? Do you feel that their action is intentional or does it come from ignorance? (Recall that Perrin says that he does not know whether the New Yorker editors "really believe" what they represent.)

    b. Why do makers of picture calendars present scenes that perpetuate false ideas? Support your answers as fully as you can.

    c. Is there any harm in the false impressions Perrin describes? If you think there is not, when might there be harm in such lack of knowledge?

4. The marginal guides divide the essay into sections. Explain how the number of example-illustrations relates to the paragraph divisions.

Considering Special Techniques

1. Introductions—the opening paragraph or paragraphs —usually fulfill three major requirements: a) they state or predict the subject, b) they clarify the purpose for the writing or the situation which prompts it, and c) they catch the reader's interest.

    a. How does the letter format either directly or indirectly help Perrin meet these requirements?

    b. How does the use of the letter set the tone? contribute to humor?

    c. Did you expect a signature at the end? What features in the final paragraph let you know that Perrin is still addressing the New Yorker editors of the letter opening?

2. Perrin twice announces that he is structuring by example: "For example" (par. 2) and "Picture calendars are the most familiar example" (par. 3). Point out the words with which he marks each of the other examples and show how these indicating words contribute to coherence.

3. Repeating a sentence pattern, balancing one sentence with another, often is a way of listing a number of examples. How many examples of the "principle" does Perrin find in the picture calendars (par. 3)? How does the sentence structure suggest that he is counting or ticking off the errors?

4. Perrin writes his essay in first person—using "I" to offer his thoughts and the details of his experience. In many essays the second person is used to refer to the reader, to address people (or a person) in general: "You will find. . . ." "You might think. . . ." will seem, for instance, to include you as reader in a group that the writer is addressing. How does Perrin's use of second person differ from this more common use? What is your position as reader of his letter?

Generating Ideas

1. Write a single paragraph (for more practice, write two single paragraphs) developed by examples. Use as your model paragraph 3 from "The Wooden Bucket Principle" with its itemizing of the misrepresentations in picture calendars or the paragraph about record-breaking feats of mountain climbing (pp. 105–6). Set up your topic sentence and then arrange your support. Here are some suggestions for starters, but you can think of others:

> Bloopers encountered in the morning paper or in a school magazine
> Television ads that repel instead of sell
> Television ads that appeal through some particular method—for instance, through use of children
> Olympic athletes you admire
> Singing groups currently popular
> Individual performers (any kind) currently popular
> Hobbies that "pay off"
> Best sellers—current, past
> Some "must reads"—both greats and nongreats
> Ways to beat the gas crunch
> Cars that get good mileage
> Community leaders

Then take one of your paragraphs and expand at least some of the examples by adding explanatory material about them, thus developing a short essay from your single practice paragraph.

2. Write a letter to a magazine or a newspaper that you read at least fairly regularly. Express your likes or dislikes concerning some part of that periodical. Cite examples to support your commendation or criticism. For instance, you might write praising several articles on youth in your city, or citing several editorials that you think have misrepresented some current issue.

3. *Write a paper in which you give several examples to show that people in general or a particular group of people are prone to one of these practices:*

    Thinking the worst will happen
    Suspecting the intentions of others
    Finding fault
    Stereotyping of some group—athletes, teachers, neighbors' children, etc.
    Regarding the unknown with suspicion
    Thinking everyone other than themselves lucky
    Thinking life better in another place (time)
    Regarding "business" (or some particular business) as greedy or grasping

Add others as you wish. You might treat your subject humorously or seriously. For instance, you might write humorously to show that college students often think that things will be easier once they are out of school and through with studying; or you might treat seriously the tendency of older people to declare that "things were better" when they were young.

4. *Like Perrin, develop a theory and apply it by examples in an essay using one of these titles:*

    "The Demand to Keep Up with the Times"
    "Some Old Ways Were Better"
    "New Words for Old Ideas"
    "Everything Frozen" (quick foods)
    "Drive-in and Drop-off"

5. *Write a paper giving examples of misunderstandings or misconceptions you or your friends have held about life in another place. For instance, people living in the North sometimes encounter several surprises when they first visit the South, and vice versa; New Yorkers may be surprised to find that most Iowa farms have many modern conveniences; or as a student at a large university you might have discovered that a small college offers a variety of courses and cultural opportunities. If you wish, use letter form: "Dear_____: You and I certainly were wrong in our idea that. . . . Since coming here I have discovered. . . ."*

Charles Kuralt

Charles Kuralt (b. 1934) is best known for his CBS Television news feature "On the Road." Kuralt began his career in journalism with the *Charlotte* (N.C.) *News,* where he worked as a reporter from 1955 to 1957. He has been with CBS since 1957. Over the years, he has earned three major awards: the Ernie Pyle Memorial Award in 1956, and both the George Foster Peabody and Emmy Awards for broadcasting in 1969. He is the author of *To the Top of the World* (1968) and of many articles derived from his work as a roving reporter whose chief interest is Americans and Americana. "The Great American Barbe-Queue" (editor's title) was published in 1976 as part of Kuralt's observation on the occasion of the national bicentennial.

The Great American Barbe-Queue

An old refrigerator shelf was all you really needed.   1

That was your grill. You laid it on a circle of stones   2 surrounding a bare spot on the lawn in the North Carolina backyard of my youth, started a charcoal fire under it, unwrapped a sirloin from the A&P, iced down a few bottles of beer in the wheelbarrow, and invited the neighbors over. After supper you sat talking quietly in the dusk until the mosquitoes got too bad. Contentment was within the grasp of anybody with an old refrigerator shelf.

I should have known something was going wrong when   3 I came home from college to find that my own father had built a brick fireplace in the backyard, with a chimney. The neighbors admired it and set out to exceed it. That was twenty years ago.

You, too, have noticed, I assume, how it all turned out.   4 In this summer of our celebration, the electrical hum of the three-speed spit is heard in the land. It is revolving majestically over a four-wheel, gas-fired, smoke-controlled Adjustable Grid Patio Grill with a copper hood and a warming oven. The chef is wearing an apron with a funny saying on it. He is frowning over his *caneton rôti aux pêches flambées,* trying to decide whether the sauce needs more Madeira. Contentment is not his.

5   For many years I have been traveling around America mooching meals from friends where possible and observing the decline of suburban serenity. I think the outdoor cooking machine has a lot to do with it. If we are ever going to win back our innocence, we have to rediscover the refrigerator shelf.

6   The pleasure of outdoor cooking used to be the simplicity of it. This is the ancestral secret of generations of American males that is in danger of being lost: *nothing you can do to a steak cooked outdoors can ruin it.*

7   A man (outdoor cooks are invariably men, for atavistic reasons having to do, I imagine, with knives and fire and ego) can thoughtfully marinate his steak for hours in a mixture of his own invention—wine vinegar, soy sauce, secret herbs, and tequila; then patiently wait for the coals to reach just the right color and temperature; then quickly sear the steak on both sides to contain its juices; then cook it by feel and by experience; he can do all these things—*or not*—and be certain of triumphant approval. "Good steak, George." "You cooked it just right, Daddy." They will say the same if he unwraps it half frozen, drops it on the grill, and remembers to pause in his drinking to turn it once.

8   But let this same man begin to believe himself a chef, acquire, in his pride, an outdoor cooking machine, and attempt dishes having to do with delicate sauces or, worse, flaming swords, and we would all be better off staying indoors. Indoors, Daddy disdains to help with the cooking. It is not cooking he loves; it is his machine.

9   There is still some good outdoor cooking going on in this country, but none of it needs machinery, and none of it comes from Escoffier.

10   The first meal that comes to mind as I ruminate happily through my own recent memories of outdoor eating is a clambake last summer in Maine. Here is the authentic recipe for a clambake: dig a big hole in a beach. If you have a Maine beach to dig your hole in, so much the better, but any beach will do. Line the hole with rocks. Build a big fire on the rocks and take a swim. When the fire is all gone, cover the hot rocks with seaweed. Add some potatoes just as they came from the ground; some corn just as it came from the stalk; then lobsters, then clams, then another layer of

seaweed. Cover the whole thing with a tarp and go for another swim. Dinner will be ready in an hour. It will make you very happy. No machine can make a clambake.

If there is a next-best thing to a Maine clambake, it is a 11
Mississippi fish fry. I have a friend in Mississippi who is trying to keep Yankees from finding out that beneath the slimy hide of the catfish is concealed the flakiest, most delicate of all gifts from sea, stream, or farm pond. He is trying to keep it secret because there are not enough catfish to go around. I know he is my friend because he took me to a fish fry. You dip your catfish in seasoned flour, then in eggs, then in cornmeal, then into a bubbling pot of fat—that's all. Catfish fry happiest when accompanied in the pot by hush puppies. Hush puppies are cornmeal, flour, salt, baking powder, chopped onion, and ham fat, with enough beer worked in to hold them together. A few Baptists use water instead of beer. A fish fry is wonderful, with either wet or dry hush puppies.

Clambakes and fish fries are for fun. I went on a cattle 12
roundup in West Texas this spring and found another brand of outdoor cooking that survives by necessity. Camp cooks are still much honored. They live by the principle that anything that can't be cooked in a heavy black iron skillet over live coals isn't worth eating. Any of the good ones, given a campsite and one hour, can supply from one of those skillets beans, chili, stew, coffee, and even bread baked over the hot coals with additional coals heaped on the skillet lid. It is simple fare, always delicious, and more welcome to a hungry cowhand than anything Paul Bocuse ever created for jaded palates of the Continent.

I know some trout fishermen on the Upper Peninsula of 13
Michigan who meet frequently at streamside to tell lies, play cribbage, and occasionally persuade some young brook trout that a fanciful floating speck of fur and feathers is actually a mayfly. They succeed often enough to eat well. Their specialty is mushrooms, grilled until their caps fill up with juices, served with a little salt, and washed down with bourbon out of an old tin cup. This is a meal I remember with reverence—mushrooms and bourbon—noble in its simplicity.

14   From *barbe to queue*, the French said, to describe the
roasting of a whole hog, from whiskers to tail. And thereby
started an argument. Barbecue is one of those things
Americans can't agree on, like nuclear power or Ronald
Reagan. Midwesterners, to whom barbecue is any roasted
meat with ketchup on it, think Midwestern barbecue is
best. The best barbecue comes from a genius I know in
Lexington, N.C., who merely anoints his hog with salt,
pepper, garlic, sage, and a mysterious sauce, wraps it in
burlap, buries it in coals, covers it with earth, and serves it
in precious shreds hours later with hot corn bread and
Brunswick stew. It's simple, he says.

15   There are Southerners transplanted to New York who
achieve almost the same result working with a hibachi on
an apartment balcony. They know enough not to get too
fancy with their barbecue sauce, whether swabbing it on a
whole hog with a new broom in Lexington, N.C., or
touching up a little pork tenderloin with a watercolor brush
twenty-three floors above Lexington Avenue.

16   North, South, East, or West, cooking outdoors is a
healing and a renewal for those smart enough to keep it
simple. Hot dogs and hamburgers, than which nothing is
more boring when cooked in the kitchen, become magical
delights when grilled outdoors and eaten with your back
against an oak tree. Spareribs, sausages, lamb chops, or
chicken wings smoked indolently over a section of old
stovepipe become greater than they are. Just being
outdoors, it is truly said, enhances the flavor of just about
everything, but it's not just that. *Is* there a better way of
cooking fish than sautéing it, freshly caught, in butter, over
a campfire? I have never discovered it. All you need is a fire,
a fork, and a frying pan.

17   What you don't need is a machine.

18   But I know I am too late. You probably already have one.
This is how far the al fresco escalation has gone: a man of
my acquaintance, grown rueful and contemplative over the
bigger and better outdoor cooking machines of his
neighbors, watching their parties grow in size and
sophistication, recently came upon a description of an Arab
barbecue. A chicken, it seems, is stuffed into the stomach of
a lamb, the lamb into the stomach of a cow, and the cow

into the stomach of a camel. Roasting takes three days.

He's thinking about it. He says there's a machine at the   19
hardware store that would do the job, but he can't find a
camel in Scarsdale.

Discussing Content and Form

*1. Although Kuralt states his central message or meaning
more than once, he makes it most explicit in paragraph 16:
"cooking outdoors is a healing and a renewal for those smart
enough to keep it simple."*

   *a. Find the phrases and sentences scattered throughout
   the essay that state this point in other ways.*

   *b. Discuss ways in which Kuralt's message might be
   applied to other things besides cooking. Find hints in
   the essay that suggest this wider application.*

*2. In paragraph 9 Kuralt introduces (and predicts) the
series of examples that will support his idea that old ways
were better.*

   *a. How many examples does he then give? Is the
   number sufficient to justify his conclusion? Explain.*

   *b. Relate the paragraph divisions to the series of
   examples.*

*3. Why does Kuralt say that "outdoor cooks are invariably
men . . ." (par. 7)? To what extent do you accept his
statement that "nothing you can do to a steak cooked
outdoors can ruin it" (par. 6)?*

*4. What is the function of each of the single-sentence
paragraphs—numbers 1, 9, and 17?*

Considering Special Techniques

*1. Like "The Wooden Bucket Principle," this essay is writ-
ten in the first person and the writer as "I" addresses a "you."*

   *a. Explain how the "you" addressed by Kuralt differs
   from that addressed by Perrin in the preceding
   essay. In which group are you as reader included?*

   *b. If writing is to be clear, shifts in person or viewpoint
   must be handled carefully and these shifts must
   seem logical. At times Kuralt shifts from "I" to the
   general first person: "our celebration" (par. 4), "If we
   are ever going to win . . ." (par. 5). Explain the
   reason behind these shifts and any others that you
   find.*

2. *Point out elements, other than the use of the second and first person pronouns, that make Kuralt's style conversational.*

3. *Point out instances of Kuralt's humorous jabs at the American preoccupation with French cooking. What does this "put-down" contribute to the tone? Use the dictionary to check the accuracy of his information on the origins of the word barbecue (par. 14).*

4. *Writers often establish their credentials for speaking on a subject, thereby suggesting to their readers that they know enough to express opinions and ideas. Where does Kuralt let you know that he speaks from first-hand observation? Why is this technique important?*

5. *Words to learn and use:* atavistic, marinate *(par. 7);* indolently *(par. 16);* al fresco, escalation, rueful *(par. 18).*

Generating Ideas

1. *An observer of American life has jested that in our modern homes the bathrooms have moved indoors and the kitchens have moved out. Point out other examples of ironic changes, and use these to comment on the relationship between old and new life-styles. You might consider windows that do not open, fireplaces that do not provide heat, etc.*

2. *Write a paper in which you show how several modern conveniences contribute to greater personal health and safety.*

3. *Kuralt says that "Barbecue is one of those things Americans can't agree on. . . ." Using examples, comment on the widely differing opinions Americans hold on a variety of subjects. Make your paper either serious or humorous, but be sure to state your main idea clearly. For instance, you might assert that disagreement is one of the great rights of a democratic society, or that our disagreements involve only small issues and that we agree on the big ones.*

4. *Kuralt defends American cooking. Choose another type of culinary art as a subject for an essay that contains many examples. For instance, you might discuss the pleasures of Chinese cooking, or the current vogue in health foods.*

5. *Write an essay about the modern fascination with machines or gadgets, developing your views by the use of examples. Try a title such as:*
    "Americans Will Buy Anything"
    "New Wind-Ups for Grown-Ups"
    "TV Plays Games"

Studs Terkel

[Louis] Studs Terkel (b. 1912) grew up in Chicago and received bachelor's and law degrees from the University of Chicago. Never formally practicing law, Terkel has been at various times a playwright, actor, columnist, and radio-talk-show host. Out of his experiences in radio have come the ideas for *Division Street: America* (1966), *Hard Times: An Oral History of the Great Depression in America* (1970), and *Working: People Talk About What They Do All Day and How They Feel About What They Do* (1974), collections of taped interviews with people talking about various facets of their lives. In *Talking to Myself: A Memoir of My Times* (1977), Terkel uses the same method to reveal his own thoughts on a variety of subjects. In "Here Am I, a Worker," he selects several people he included in *Working* and organizes their comments to make his point.

Here Am I, a Worker

In our society (it's the only one I've experienced, so I cannot speak for any other) the razor of necessity cuts close. You must make a buck to survive the day. You must work to make a buck. The job is often a chore, rarely a delight. No matter how demeaning the task, no matter how it dulls the senses or breaks the spirit, one *must* work or else. Lately there has been a questioning of this "work ethic," especially by the young. Strangely enough, it has touched off profound grievances in others, hitherto silent and anonymous.

Unexpected precincts are being heard from in a show of discontent by blue collar and white. Communiqués are alarming concerning absenteeism in auto plants. On the evening bus the tense, pinched faces of young file clerks and elderly secretaries tell us more than we care to know. On the expressways middle-management men pose without grace behind their wheels, as they flee city and job.

In all, there is more than a slight ache. And there dangles the impertinent question: Ought there not be another increment, earned though not yet received, to one's daily work—an acknowledgment of a man's *being*?

Steve Hamilton is a professional baseball player. At 37 he has come to the end of his career as a major-league pitcher. "I've never been a big star. I've done about as good as I can with the equipment I have. I played with Mickey Mantle and with Willie Mays. People always recognize them. But for someone to recognize me, it really made me feel good. I think everybody gets a kick out of feeling special."

5   Mike Fitzgerald was born the same year as Hamilton. He is a laborer in a steel mill. "I feel like the guys who built the pyramids. Somebody built 'em. Somebody built the Empire State Building, too. There's hard work behind it. I would like to see a building, say The Empire State, with a foot-wide strip from top to bottom and the name of every bricklayer on it, the name of every electrician. So when a guy walked by, he could take his son and say, 'See, that's me over there on the 45th floor. I put that steel beam in.' Picasso can point to a painting. I think I've done harder work than Picasso, and what can I point to? Everybody should have something to point to."

6   Sharon Atkins is 24 years old. She's been to college and acridly observes: "The first myth that blew up in my face is that a college education will get you a worthwhile job." For the last two years she's been a receptionist at an advertising agency. "I didn't look at myself as 'just a dumb broad' at the front desk, who took phone calls and messages. I thought I was something else. The office taught me differently."

7   Among her contemporaries there is no such rejection; job and status have no meaning. Blue collar or white, teacher or cabbie, her friends judge her and themselves by their beingness. Nora Watson, a young journalist, recounts a party game, Who Are You? Older people respond with their job titles: "I'm a copy writer," "I'm an accountant." The young say, "I'm me, my name is so-and-so."

8   Harry Stallings, 27, is a spot welder on the assembly line at an auto plant. "They'll give better care to that machine than they will to you. If it breaks down, there's somebody out there to fix it right away. If I break down, I'm just pushed over to the other side till another man takes my place. The only thing the company has in mind is to keep that line running. A man would be more eager to do a better job if he were given proper respect and the time to do it."

9   You would think that Ralph Grayson, a 25-year-old black, has it made. He supervises twenty people in the audit department of a large bank. Yet he is singularly discontented. "You're like a foreman on an assembly line.

Or like a technician sitting in a computer room watching the machinery. It's good for a person who enjoys that kind of job, who can dominate somebody else's life. I'm not too wrapped up in seeing a woman, 50 years old—white, incidentally—get thrown off her job because she can't cut it like the younger ones.

"I told management she was a kind and gentle person. They said, 'We're not interested in your personal feelings. Document it up.' They look over my appraisal and say: 'We'll give her about five months to shape up or ship out.' "

The hunger persists, obstinately, for pride in a man's work. Conditions may be horrendous, tensions high, and humiliations frequent, yet Paul Dietch finds his small triumphs. He drives his own truck, interstate, as a steel hauler. "Every load is a challenge. I have problems in the morning with heartburn. I can't eat. Once I off-load, the pressure is gone. Then I can eat anything. I accomplished something."

Yolanda Leif graphically describes the trials of a waitress in a quality restaurant. They are compounded by her refusal to be demeaned. Yet pride in her skills helps her through the night. "When I put the plate down, you don't hear a sound. When I pick up a glass, I want it to be just right. When someone says, 'How come you're just a waitress?' I say, 'Don't you think you deserve being served by me?' "

Peggy Terry has her own sense of pride and beauty. Her jobs have varied with geography, climate, and the ever-felt pinch of circumstance. "What I hated worst was being a waitress, the way you're treated. One guy said, 'You don't have to smile, I'm gonna give you a tip anyway.' I said, 'Keep it, I wasn't smiling for a tip.' Tipping should be done away with. It's like throwing a dog a bone. It makes you feel small."

Ballplayer. Laborer. Receptionist. Assembly-line worker. Truck driver. Bank official. Waitress. What with the computer and all manner of automation, add scores of hundreds of new occupations and, thus, new heroes and antiheroes to Walt Whitman's old anthem. The sound, though, is no longer melodious. The desperation is unquiet.

15   Perhaps Nora Watson has put her finger on it. She reflects on her father's work. He was a fundamentalist preacher, with whom she had been profoundly at odds.

16   "Whatever, he was, he was. It was his calling, his vocation. He saw himself as a core resource of the community. He liked his work, even though his family barely survived, because that was what he was supposed to be doing. His work was his life. He himself was not separate and apart from his calling. I think this is what all of us are looking for, a calling, not just a job. Most of us, like the assembly-line worker, have jobs that are too small for our spirit. Jobs are not big enough for people."

17   Does it take another, less competitive, less buck-oriented society to make one match the other?

Discussing Content and Form

1. The introduction to this chapter stated that a general guideline to follow in developing a paper around examples is to use about two-thirds to three-fourths of the space for examples and about one-fourth for general statements. Is three-fourths of this essay devoted to examples? Where does Terkel provide introductory, interpretive, and concluding materials?

2. Why do you think Terkel includes so many examples? Would he be able to make his point with less proof? Why or why not? What examples, if any, do you think he could have omitted?

3. What effect is gained by naming the workers specifically? By quoting them directly?

4. In a selection such as this, not only the number but also the range of the examples is important. What age groups and backgrounds do Terkel's examples represent? What kinds of workers does he overlook? In answering, you might refer to the list that begins paragraph 14.

5. Beginning with paragraph 4, what is the basis for most of the paragraph divisions? Why does the pattern of organization, once it is established, require few transitional phrases to connect the paragraphs?

6. What does Terkel mean when he says that Sharon Atkins' contemporaries, people obviously in their early twenties, "judge her and themselves by their beingness" rather than by more traditional standards (par. 7)? What difference does he point out between the way younger and older generations view their jobs? How does he account for the difference?

7. What attitudes are exemplified in the two waitresses, Yolanda Leif and Peggy Terry? Why might tipping be called demeaning?

Considering Special Techniques

1. Mike Fitzgerald, the steelworker, compares his work to that of Pablo Picasso, a well-known artist whose large metal sculpture is an attraction in Chicago, where Terkel lives. What special dimension does this comparison add to the picture of Fitzgerald?

2. A complex and subtle kind of comparison comes in the form of an allusion in paragraph 14, where Terkel says that "scores of hundreds of new occupations" should be added to "Walt Whitman's old anthem."

   a. In alluding to a literary work, a writer expects a reader to be familiar enough with it to see the relevance of the allusion. Read Walt Whitman's poem (the "old anthem") "I Hear America Singing," and compare the mood of the workers Whitman pictures to that of the people Terkel mentions.

   b. Although relevant allusions are forceful and economical, they can also serve to limit the audience a writer hopes to reach. What is your feeling when you recognize an allusion? What feeling do you have when you fail to recognize such a reference?

3. Discuss the level of language in this selection. Comment on whether the essay is marred or enhanced by clichés such as these: "Unexpected precincts are being heard from" (par. 2); "has it made" (par. 9); "she can't cut it" (par. 9); "shape up or ship out" (par. 10); "puts her finger on it" (par. 15).

4. Words to learn and use: increment (par. 3); acridly (par. 6); horrendous (par. 11); demeaned (par. 12).

Generating Ideas

1. *Consider Terkel's charge that America is a "buck-oriented society" and that the sound of its workers "is no longer melodious." Write a paper in which you cite examples of your own to prove or disprove this assertion.*

2. *Terkel says that American workers were once happy, or happier than they are now. Drawing on American social history for examples, write a paper proving or disproving this assumption.*

3. *Think of someone you know whose beliefs and life-style are similar to those of Nora Watson's father (par. 16). Develop a paper around that person's job and his or her feeling about the work. You might use one of Watson's lines or phrases for a title:*

> *"Jobs Are Not Big Enough"*
> *"Looking for a Calling"*
> *"Not Just a Job"*

Or make such a line as "His work was his life" your controlling generalization.

4. *Terkel says that the young judge people by their "beingness," and that they care less than older people about what a person does for a living. Use your experience to discuss the validity of this statement. Have you ever known young people who ask questions such as, "What does your father do?"*

5. *Terkel says that the "hunger persists, obstinately, for pride in a man's work" (par. 11). Project yourself into the future, and write a paper about the kind of job in which you feel you might have pride and happiness.*

Joan Didion

Joan Didion (b. 1934) is both a novelist and essayist. From 1956 to 1963, she was an associate editor for *Vogue* magazine; she now lives and writes in her native California. Her best-known novels are *Play It As It Lays* (1970) and *A Book of Common Prayer* (1976). Her essay collection *Slouching Toward Bethlehem* (1968) is the source for "Marrying Absurd." In 1979, she published a second book of essays, *The White Album.* Much of Didion's writing is aimed at revealing the troubled individuals whom she observes in the flamboyant and sophisticated world of southern California.

Marrying Absurd

To be married in Las Vegas, Clark County, Nevada, a bride   1
must swear that she is eighteen or has parental permission and a bridegroom that he is twenty-one or has parental permission. Someone must put up five dollars for the license. (On Sundays and holidays, fifteen dollars. The Clark County Courthouse issues marriage licenses at any time of the day or night except between noon and one in the afternoon, between eight and nine in the evening, and between four and five in the morning.) Nothing else is required. The State of Nevada, alone among these United States, demands neither a premarital blood test nor a waiting period before or after the issuance of a marriage license. Driving in across the Mojave from Los Angeles, one sees the signs way out on the desert, looming up from that moonscape of rattlesnakes and mesquite, even before the Las Vegas lights appear like a mirage on the horizon: "GETTING MARRIED? Free License Information First Strip Exit." Perhaps the Las Vegas wedding industry achieved its peak operational efficiency between 9:00 P.M. and midnight of August 26, 1965, an otherwise unremarkable Thursday which happened to be, by Presidential order, the last day on which anyone could improve his draft status merely by getting married. One hundred and seventy-one couples were pronounced man and wife in the name of Clark County and the State of Nevada that night, sixty-seven of them by a single justice of the peace, Mr. James A. Brennan. Mr. Brennan did one wedding at the Dunes and the other

sixty-six in his office, and charged each couple eight dollars. One bride lent her veil to six others. "I got it down from five to three minutes," Mr. Brennan said later of his feat. "I could've married them *en masse*, but they're people, not cattle. People expect more when they get married."

2   What people who get married in Las Vegas actually do expect—what, in the largest sense, their "expectations" are—strikes one as a curious and self-contradictory business. Las Vegas is the most extreme and allegorical of American settlements, bizarre and beautiful in its venality and in its devotion to immediate gratification, a place the tone of which is set by mobsters and call girls and ladies' room attendants with amyl nitrite poppers in their uniform pockets. Almost everyone notes that there is no "time" in Las Vegas, no night and no day and no past and no future (no Las Vegas casino, however, has taken the obliteration of the ordinary time sense quite so far as Harold's Club in Reno, which for a while issued, at odd intervals in the day and night, mimeographed "bulletins" carrying news from the world outside); neither is there any logical sense of where one is. One is standing on a highway in the middle of a vast hostile desert looking at an eighty-foot sign which blinks "STARDUST" or "CAESAR'S PALACE." Yes, but what does that explain? This geographical implausibility reinforces the sense that what happens there has no connection with "real" life; Nevada cities like Reno and Carson are ranch towns, Western towns, places behind which there is some historical imperative. But Las Vegas seems to exist only in the eye of the beholder. All of which makes it an extraordinarily stimulating and interesting place, but an odd one in which to want to wear a candlelight satin Priscilla of Boston wedding dress with Chantilly lace insets, tapered sleeves and a detachable modified train.

3   And yet the Las Vegas wedding business seems to appeal to precisely that impulse. "Sincere and Dignified Since 1954," one wedding chapel advertises. There are nineteen such wedding chapels in Las Vegas, intensely competitive, each offering better, faster, and, by implication, more sincere services than the next: Our Photos Best Anywhere, Your Wedding on A Phonograph Record, Candlelight with Your Ceremony, Honeymoon Accommodations, Free

Transportation from Your Motel to Courthouse to Chapel and Return to Motel, Religious or Civil Ceremonies, Dressing Rooms, Flowers, Rings, Announcements, Witnesses Available, and Ample Parking. All of these services, like most others in Las Vegas (sauna baths, payroll-check cashing, chinchilla coats for sale or rent) are offered twenty-four hours a day, seven days a week, presumably on the premise that marriage, like craps, is a game to be played when the table seems hot.

But what strikes one most about the Strip chapels, with their wishing wells and stained-glass paper windows and their artificial bouvardia, is that so much of their business is by no means a matter of simple convenience, of late-night liaisons between show girls and baby Crosbys. Of course there is some of that. (One night about eleven o'clock in Las Vegas I watched a bride in an orange mini-dress and masses of flame-colored hair stumble from a Strip chapel on the arm of her bridegroom, who looked the part of the expendable nephew in movies like *Miami Syndicate.* "I gotta get the kids," the bride whimpered. "I gotta pick up the sitter, I gotta get to the midnight show." "What you gotta get," the bridegroom said, opening the door of a Cadillac Coupe de Ville and watching her crumple on the seat, "is sober.") But Las Vegas seems to offer something other than "convenience"; it is merchandising "niceness," the facsimile of proper ritual, to children who do not know how else to find it, how to make the arrangements, how to do it "right." All day and evening long on the Strip, one sees actual wedding parties, waiting under the harsh lights at a crosswalk, standing uneasily in the parking lot of the Frontier while the photographer hired by The Little Church of the West ("Wedding Place of the Stars") certifies the occasion, takes the picture: the bride in a veil and white satin pumps, the bridegroom usually in a white dinner jacket, and even an attendant or two, a sister or a best friend in hot-pink *peau de soie,* a flirtation veil, a carnation nosegay. "When I Fall in Love It Will Be Forever," the organist plays, and then a few bars of Lohengrin. The mother cries; the stepfather, awkward in his role, invites the chapel hostess to join them for a drink at the Sands. The hostess declines with a professional smile; she has already transferred her

4

interest to the group waiting outside. One bride out, another in, and again the sign goes up on the chapel door: "One moment please—Wedding."

5   I sat next to one such wedding party in a Strip restaurant the last time I was in Las Vegas. The marriage had just taken place; the bride still wore her dress, the mother her corsage. A bored waiter poured out a few swallows of pink champagne ("on the house") for everyone but the bride, who was too young to be served. "You'll need something with more kick than that," the bride's father said with heavy jocularity to his new son-in-law; the ritual jokes about the wedding night had a certain Panglossian character, since the bride was clearly several months pregnant. Another round of pink champagne, this time not on the house, and the bride began to cry. "It was just as nice," she sobbed, "as I hoped and dreamed it would be."

Discussing Content and Form

1. What is Didion's purpose in this selection? Her essay is a form of satire, *which presents human evil and foolishness as subjects for ridicule and laughter. Like other satirists, she intends to effect some change, at least in the reader's attitudes toward the behavior being presented. Does she expect to change the actions of the objects of her satire? Explain.*

2. Didion never explicitly states the main point of her essay. What special significance, then, has the title of the selection?

3. Make at least a rough count of the examples of absurd marrying. Explain why Didion provides as many examples as she does.

4. Which details illustrate both the artificiality of Las Vegas and its bizarre role as a marriage mecca? Look closely at paragraph 2 in particular.

    a. In this paragraph, Didion generalizes about the city as "the most extreme and allegorical of American settlements, bizarre and beautiful." Yet even in the same sentence she adds examples to show the contradictions. What conclusions can you make about her style from the proportion of general statements and specific examples in this paragraph alone?

    b. Why does Didion call the city "allegorical"?

      c. *What is meant by the statement that "Las Vegas*
         seems to exist only in the eye of the beholder"? By
         the statement that it has no "historical imperative"?

    5. Which of the examples do you find amusing? How
would you characterize the type of humor in the selection? To
what kind of reader would Didion's brand of humor appeal?

    6. Do you find the final example (par. 5) poignant or
ridiculous? Explain your reaction.

    7. Today there are more unconventional attitudes toward
marriage than there were ten years ago when this article was
written. Didion says that in Las Vegas "marriage, like craps,
is a game to be played when the table seems hot." Discuss
this statement, considering whether this idea may have
spread to the rest of the country from this bizarre center for
"marrying absurd."

Considering Special Techniques

    1. Although paragraphs do not always contain a stated
topic sentence, the sentences in a paragraph usually center
on a single point or idea.
      a. *Find or state the central point in each of the five*
         paragraphs in this essay.
      b. *After stating these points, discuss their relationship to*
         an apparent outline or plan. Is the organization as
         random as one might at first think? Explain.

    2. What special force is achieved by citing statistics (par.
1)? By giving place names (par. 2)? By including the
advertisements (par. 3)?

    3. Most of the references Didion makes are to actual
people or instances. Identify, if you can, "Priscilla of Boston"
(par. 2) and "baby Crosbys" (par. 4). Paragraph 5 contains
an allusion to Dr. Pangloss, the elderly pedantic tutor in
Voltaire's satiric novel Candide *(1759). Pangloss is an*
incurable optimist who constantly reassures Candide and
others that the world is beautiful despite many terrible
misfortunes. How does this knowledge enrich the meaning of
the reference?

    4. One ingredient of satire is verbal irony—*the use of words*
and phrases that, at first glance, seem inappropriate to the
subject being considered. For instance, Didion satirizes Las
Vegas by applying the terminology of business to what is

usually a sacred and personal event: "the Las Vegas wedding industry achieved its peak operational efficiency . . ." (par. 1). Find other examples of verbal irony in the essay. What is the resulting tone?

5. *Words to learn and use:* venality, obliteration, implausibility *(par. 2);* liaisons *(par. 4);* jocularity *(par. 5).*

Generating Ideas

1. Satire ranges from the bitter exposure of human evil to the light and humorous revelation of weaknesses or follies. Write a short critical analysis (a single paragraph will do) in which you place Didion's satire where you think it falls along this spectrum. If you wish, mention other satiric writing that you find harsher or lighter as a way of supporting your judgment.

2. Choose some aspect of human behavior as a subject for a satirical paper. Shape your essay around several specific examples. Here are some possible subjects: overeating or any compulsive habit involving food; habitual cleaning or collecting; constant talking on the telephone.

3. Write a satire on some problem in an area or part of the country that you know; use as many specific examples as you can. Some suggestions: the traffic in a large city; the dullness of a small town; the artificiality of a suburb. Or you might gently poke fun at people's preoccupation with the climate: "Moving to Florida to escape the winter means coping with bugs and heat"; "If you go outdoors in Seattle, use a snorkel." The last two topics probably require a lighter touch, since these conditions really are not subject to the satirist's desire for change.

4. Didion speaks of the Las Vegas "devotion to immediate gratification" (par. 2). Consider the pursuit of gratification as you have observed it, and write a paper (satiric or serious) on that subject. Here are a few titles that may suggest approaches:

"Promises, Promises"
"Bingo! The Lottery! The TV Giveaway Shows!"
"Cattle, Not People?" (see par. 1)
"I Want It Now!"
"A's, B's, or Drops"

Jacques-Yves Cousteau

Jacques-Yves Cousteau (b. 1910) is a widely-known French marine explorer, filmmaker, and writer. He shares his research in marine biology, botany, and ecology through best-selling books and award-winning documentary films. Skin divers around the world are indebted to him for his inventions and developments of such technological innovations as a one-man jet-propelled submarine and of Conshelf I, II, and III, the first manned undersea colonies. Cousteau's personal life is a story of triumphs. A sickly boy, he was warned against strenuous physical activity, but his determination and precocious flair for engineering led him to inventing marine equipment when he was only eleven years of age. He was educated at the Collège Stanislas in Paris and at the École Navala in Brest. After serving as a lieutenant in the French navy, he entered the school of naval aviation.

Cousteau made his first underwater films in 1942 and 1945, and produced the first color film ever taken at a depth of 150 feet. His books include *The Silent World,* with Frederic Dumas (1953), *The Living Sea,* with James Dugan (1963), *World Without Sun* (1965), and a series published since 1970 for which his collaborator was his son Philippe: *The Shark: Splendid Savage of the Sea; Life and Death of a Coral Sea; Diving for Sunken Treasure; The Whale: Mighty Monarch of the Sea; Octopus and Squid: The Soft Intelligence; Three Adventures: Galapagos, Titicaca, The Blue Holes; Diving Companions: Sea Lion, Elephant Seal, Walrus;* and *Dolphins.* A twenty-volume encyclopedia designed for the general public, *The Ocean World of Jacques Cousteau,* is published in England. The filmed documentary *World Without Sun* won Cousteau an Academy Award in 1964 and his spectacular television programs, some of them the result of an expedition to Antarctica in 1972, regularly attract 35-40 million viewers. Cousteau has homes in Paris and Monaco, but he prefers to live aboard the *Calypso,* the yacht from which he conducts much of his research.

Jonah's Complaint

I sight humpbacks! Despite the flurry of excitement that follows my radio signal to Philippe, I can focus on little but the breathtaking sight of these giants gliding effortlessly on their way from warm waters toward rich arctic feeding grounds. Their long flippers stretch out like graceful wings. From time to time, slender columns of vapor rise from their blowholes up into the blue sky.

The sight of Philippe's tiny fishing boat, the tiny men on board, and the mammoth humpbacks nearby leaves me speechless. I am struck by the impossible gulf that separates them—the whales cavorting in a sea around a boat that is smaller than they, the men clustering on that boat like ants adrift on a plank. Words from *Paradise Lost* edge into my mind:

> There Leviathan,
> Hugest of living creatures, on the deep
> Stretch'd like a promontory sleeps or swims,
> And seems a moving land, and at his gills
> Draws in, and at his trunk spouts out a sea.

3   Up in the helicopter, I suddenly shudder. It occurs to me that somewhere other men in similar flying machines are using my technique to direct ships fitted with rocket launchers toward playful giant whales. These hunters track their prey not to a feeding ground but to a bloodbath.

4   Our research expeditions since that trip four years ago have been discouraging. Weeks of fruitless searching for whale species are proof enough that the experts are right. They say that the humpback, the right, the bowhead, the gray, and the blue whales are being pushed toward the threshold of extinction. The remaining four species of the nine great whales—sperm, fin, sei, and Bryde's—are steadily diminishing. What is true of coral and of all other forms of marine life is also true of whales. We are no sooner able to approach them, to admire them, to observe them, than we realize that they are in danger of becoming extinct.

5   Yet the slaughterers push on. Old whaling techniques will hardly do in a sea nearly bereft of whales; so fleets rely on space-age technology to help them sweep the oceans for surviving mammals. Sonar and exploding harpoons have replaced the simpler weapons of more romantic times. Floating factories oversee the metamorphosis from whale carcass to whale product in half an hour.

6   Soon the whalers will overcatch themselves right out of the whaling industry. Why? When the catch becomes too small for their bother, they will have made enough money to scrap their fleets with little remorse.

7   By bringing an end to the whaling era, the world outside the whaling industry has little to lose—little but "seafood platters" for cats. And there is much to gain. These remarkable creatures have kept secrets man would do well to uncover. They can dive to inky depths without risking

caisson disease, the deadly ailment human divers call the bends. They can go without breathing for an hour and a half. They can communicate with one another and are able to identify one another by voice. And they play a vital role in balancing the ecosystem.

It is difficult to explain a man's reactions to his first sight 8 of a whale underwater. The feeling is one of stupefaction at the size of the animal. A whale can weigh in excess of 100 tons. Its dimensions go beyond man's experience with life forms. On this point all our divers agree: the first sight of a whale underwater is terrifying.

The more experiences the *Calypso* has had with whales, 9 however, the less terrifying—and the more intriguing— these leviathans have become.

Diving is perhaps one of their more stupendous feats. 10 The sperm whale is the undoubted master, the only whale that can dive 4,000 feet down—or more. As he prepares to penetrate the depths, he jackknifes with an utter grace— especially in his tail movements, which seem desultory and almost casual. His grace, however, is deceptive; the power in that tail is the estimated equivalent of that of a 500-horsepower engine.

A more flashy display of a whale's abilities is a stunt 11 called breaching, or spyhopping. The whale leaps completely from the water, at a take-off speed of about 30 knots. He does a half roll in midair and falls back, hitting the water with the thunderous clap of massive flesh against water. The reasons that whales perform this showy trick remain unknown. It could be a sexual rite. One oceanographer I know believes that breaching aids digestion—that whales jump to help the food go down.

Perhaps the most mystifying of the habits peculiar to 12 whales is their "singing." Humpback whales are the most renowned for a wide range of tones, and whole herds often join together in "songs" composed of complete sequences, which, repeated, can last for hours. Some evenings, we listened to the humpbacks starting to make a few sounds, like musicians tuning their instruments. Then, one by one, they began to sing. Underwater canyons made the sounds echo, and it seemed as though we were in a cathedral listening to the faithful alternating verses of a psalm.

13   One of the most "human" qualities of the whale is its intense devotion to other whales, which is best displayed by the relationship between a mother whale and her calf.

14   The mother's first task is to lift her baby to the surface for its first breath. She continues this careful attention to his breathing when she nurses him, all the while cradling the baby in her flippers to keep his head above the surface.

15   Mothers punish their offspring as well. Once, a crew member on board our ship saw a calf rub against the hull. The mother went after the calf, pushed it far away from the ship, and then struck it several times with her flippers. Never again, that baby was taught, should it confuse a ship with its mother's stomach.

16   This sort of concern is typical not only of the relationship between mother and calf but also of the relations between members of the whole herd. When a huge sperm whale rammed into our hull one day, the chirping of the herd suddenly became frantic. Whales emerged from everywhere, rushing to the side of the stricken whale to support it at the surface.

17   Whales are affectionate as well as protective—they love to nuzzle one another, especially as a prelude to mating. Humpbacks actually embrace with their flippers. More than once, flirtatious female whales have rubbed even against our divers. The most touching of our experiences came one day as we were filming. A mother whale and her calf were swimming directly toward Bernard Delemotte, chief diver on our ship. Bernard passed between them with his camera—and the mother gently pulled back a flipper so as not to harm him.

18   I am touched by a certain sadness, then, when I leaf through volumes of ancient folklore. Rising from the pages are images of monsters from the deep, overturning ships and attacking men. I know that it has been the other way around in real life.

Discussing Content and Form

1. In your own words, state what you think is the purpose *behind this selection. Then state its message. Put both statements into single sentences.*

2. *Explain why the short narrative incident (an* anecdote) *makes an effective beginning. How does the use of a personal experience affect you as a reader?*

3. *Why is the scientific information in paragraph 4 important to Cousteau's discussion? Point out other examples of the author's use of scientific knowledge.*

4. *How many examples does Cousteau use to develop paragraph 7?*
   a. *What sentence structure does he use to present each of these examples?*
   b. *Why do you think he puts the whale's role "in balancing the ecosystem" last?*

5. *Paragraph 9 serves as a head or introduction for a series of examples.*
   a. *How many examples build on that introduction? Analyze and explain the relationship of these examples to the division into paragraphs.*
   b. *What quality in the whales is the unifying topic for paragraphs 13–17?*

6. *Discuss your reaction to the article, accounting for your response as specifically as you can. You might consider especially the appeal of the whale's "human" qualities.*

Considering Special Techniques

1. *What does the quotation (par. 2) from English poet John Milton (1608-1674) contribute to the effect of Cousteau's article? What does including such a literary citation tell you about Cousteau himself?*
   a. *Explain the link between that quotation and the reference to ancient folklore in paragraph 18.*
   b. *How do the references to the historical importance of the whale affect the feeling about possible destruction of the species?*

2. *Titles sometimes have a way of organizing the essay and of giving meaning or poignance. Explain the significance of Cousteau's title.*

3. *Find examples of Cousteau's use of specialized terminology, e.g., "caisson disease" (par. 7). How does he make clear the meanings of such terms? What effect do these terms have on the style of the selection?*

4. The whale is especially interesting as a mammal which has many human characteristics. Point out the words and details by which Cousteau builds the picture of "humanness." Here are two examples: "Mothers punish their offspring" (par. 15); "flirtatious female whales" (par. 17).

5. Note the repetition of images through which Cousteau makes especially vivid the destruction of the whale:

"These hunters track their prey not to a feeding ground but to a bloodbath." (par. 3)

". . . slaughterers push on" (par. 5)

"Floating factories oversee the metamorphosis from whale carcass to whale product. . . ." (par. 5)

" 'seafood platters' for cats" (par. 7)

Find other such vivid images and discuss their importance to the impact of the essay.

6. As you read, you should stop now and then to notice a particularly well-turned sentence. For instance, study this one from paragraph 2:

"I am struck by the impossible gulf that separates them—the whales cavorting in a sea around a boat that is smaller than they, the men clustering on that boat like ants adrift on a plank."

Account for the use of the dash. Which two elements are parallel and why? Explain grammatically "smaller than they." What figure of speech is the phrase "like ants adrift on a plank"?

7. Words to learn and use: cavorting (par. 2); leviathan (par. 2, others); bereft, metamorphosis (par. 5); stupefaction (par. 8); desultory (par. 10); mystifying (par. 12).

Generating Ideas

1. Stories and legends, pictures and museum displays depicting the life of huge creatures such as whales are always fascinating. Write a paper about this fascination, using as examples the various huge creatures, imaginary or real, that have especially interested you.

2. The Book of Jonah in the Old Testament has been described by Ernest Sutherland Bates (editor of The Bible Designed to Be Read as Living Literature) as "The most ridiculously misunderstood of all the works in the Bible." Read the tale itself (it was probably written in the third century) and then from reading or conversation discover

some of the possible interpretations given it. Write a paper using examples of those various interpretations that have arisen from the conflict between fundamentalists and skeptics.

3. Possibly next to Jonah, the most famous whale story of all time is Herman Melville's epic Moby Dick. *Read the chapters in which the crew of the Pequod first sights whales—the end of Chapter XLVII ("The Mat-Maker") and Chapter XLVIII ("The First Lowering"). Write a paper relating the feelings of excitement Melville describes to those of Cousteau in paragraphs 1–3.*

4. From reading other writing by Jacques Cousteau or from acquaintance with television programs about his work, discuss what he has done to popularize oceanography. Develop your paper by using specific examples of Cousteau's many contributions.

5. Write a paper discussing international, national, or local laws on fishing and hunting, citing examples of practices or restrictions that you think are beneficial or ill-advised.

6. Write a paper in which you give examples of several endangered species to show that such wildlife should be preserved. Or advocate consideration of one species by citing examples of its special qualities. You can obtain material from the U.S. Department of the Interior or from almost any library. For instance, Threatened Wildlife of the United States, *published by the Department of the Interior (1973) describes the federal program for endangered fish and wildlife. James A. Cox in* The Endangered Ones *(Crown Publishers, 1975) writes that since 1600 "120 forms of mammals and 150 forms of birds have traveled the road to extinction." Of these he says about one-fourth vanished by natural causes. His book lists many of the currently endangered species.*

7. Write a paper or give a report on the American Cetacean Society and its sponsorship of "whale watching" trips off the coast of California. You will find that this group has developed a new kind of tourist industry. Or, do some research and trace some of the laws regarding whaling.

8. Using examples of various wildlife stamps or other publicity methods, show how the public is made conscious of the need for wildlife protection.

5

PROCESS ANALYSIS:
TRACING THE STEPS

The first chapter of this book is an explanation of a process. It briefly traces the three important steps to follow in producing a paper: observing to get ideas and materials, recording to preserve and to see relationships, and writing and rewriting to achieve the desired product. Explanations of other processes are similar to the procedure illustrated in that chapter—narrating or tracing from start to finish how something is done, how something is made, or how something occurred.

The process or operation may be mental or physical—for instance, explaining the steps to follow in solving a math problem or giving instructions for learning to water-ski. The subject might be a phenomenon of physical growth or an event in history—how a potato develops or how a labor union organized and achieved power. Instruction manuals and recipes explain "how to do something"; these are examples of what may be called the *direction-giving process.* Explaining a scientific process—a minute-by-minute account of the eruption of a geyser—and historical tracing— the steps taken in preparation for D-day—tell "how something happens or happened"; these are examples of what may be called the *information-giving process.*

Process explanation may be very simple, as it is in this short set of instructions:

Greens: pick, wash, and boil in water with piece of fat meat until tender, cooking slowly. Or parboil them. Take out of water and put in frying pan with grease. Fry five minutes with a little salt. Pick more greens than you think you need, as they shrink. Serve with vinegar or dill pickles, or cook and season as you would spinach. When greens are older, cook in two waters, throwing cooking water away.—*Foxfire 2*

At other times direction-giving can be very complex and lengthy. The chapter in *Foxfire 2* on making a wagon wheel runs to several pages and includes diagrams and pictures. But the same principles of composition apply in both cases: the order of steps must be clear, usually starting at the beginning and proceeding chronologically; and the information offered must be sufficient to make the process clear to the intended audience. For instance, if you do not know the meaning of *greens* or *parboil,* you might not understand the recipe from *Foxfire 2.*

The same principles apply also to keeping the process clear when you are giving information about a scientific or historical event or change. The writer of this paragraph traces the relationship of the bicycle to the growing independence of women:

The widening of the physical world for women which these changed conditions involve did not really begin before 1890. Some years earlier, as we have seen, games were introduced into the more advanced girls' schools, but it was not until the early nineties that the idea that grown-up women could move about freely was at all generally accepted; and the emancipating agent in this reform was the bicycle. The women who first began to ride upon this queer machine were thought to be incredibly venturous, and most people also thought them shocking. In the very early days, indeed, when only men's bicycles were made, the enormity of riding at all was intensified by the fact that it had to be done in Bloomers, and the bold pioneers were freely hooted in the streets. After a time adaptations of the machine were made, so that the voluminous skirts of the period could be heaped up and stowed away, and a perfectly ladylike appearance maintained. The prejudice did not at once diminish, but the achievement was considered worth the persecution, and women persevered. They found in it not only what was then thought to be the exquisite pleasure of rapid motion, but also very great practical convenience. They were no longer prisoners in their own houses; they could spin off, if they chose, as far as six or seven miles away; they could go to the nearest town to do their shopping, and they could visit their friends, and be no longer dependent for these joys upon the convenience of the rest of the family, but only upon their own muscles. It was a wonderful change, and one which was rapidly appreciated by all sorts of women who had no conscious sympathy with the Women's Movement at all. No doubt it was this emancipating tendency which caused the opposition to be so acute; certainly it was the reason why a deliberate propaganda in favour of the innovation made its appearance, and a little flock of quaint pamphlets urging women to "conquer the world on wheels" remains to bear witness to this vital social change.—Ray Strachey (Mrs. Rachel Conn Strachey), *"The Cause"*

Notice that the connecting phrases in the explanation are, like those in narration, *time* phrases: "did not really begin before 1890," "Some years earlier," "but it was not until," "in the very early days," "After a time" are linking phrases indicating an orderly time sequence. As in narration, the sequence of verbs also sets the time and must be kept clear. But while these technical features are the same for narration and process, the purpose of process is less to tell a story than to trace and explain the events which are the subject.

Another difference sometimes marks the process paper, distinguishing it from the usual expository essay. The purpose in tracing or in giving directions does not require that you have in mind a *thesis* or controlling idea. This difference is important to remember because in writing other kinds of essays, you often need to formulate a thesis. If a writing assignment calls for tracing a process, it is often more logical to formulate a very general purpose statement and let that be a guide in building your paper. Among the selections in this chapter, you will discover some for which you probably cannot state a central meaning. Rather, the writers have fulfilled their purpose merely by tracing or by giving directions. But all such generalizations about writing apply only at times. The essay by John Stewart Collis (p.

157), for instance, combines the observation of a natural process with a thesis. Furthermore, in his essay and in others, you will find that process, like the other ways of organizing writing, is not necessarily used in isolation but is intermingled with other methods of development.

L. Rust Hills

L. Rust Hills (b. 1924) is a free-lance writer who was formerly fiction editor of *Esquire* and the *Saturday Evening Post*. Hills is a graduate of the U.S. Merchant Marine Academy and he also holds degrees from Wesleyan University in Connecticut. He has been editor and co-editor of several volumes of essays and articles and a regular contributor to *Saturday Review* and the *New Yorker*. "How to Be Kindly" comes from his collection of personal essays entitled *How to Do Things Right, The Revelations of a Fussy Man,* published in 1972. There his treatment of subjects familiar to everyone is sometimes lightly satiric, sometimes semiserious, but always direct and memorable.

How to Be Kindly

Conflict between virtue of kindliness and trait of fussiness (par. 1)

1 A fussy man is at a disadvantage in his family not because of his vices, but because of his virtues. Kindliness is generally reckoned to be the foremost familial virtue, and it seems to be in some sort of psychological-philosophical conflict with fussiness. Occasionally in literature you'll find some figure who combines the two—I think of Aunt Betsy Trotwell in *David Copperfield* and what's her name, Aunt Sally or Aunt Polly, in *Huck Finn*—but I suppose it scarcely needs pointing out that each of these is an *aunt*, not the man of the house, and their kindliness is concealed anyway under what used to be known as "a gruff exterior," something no one goes for these days.

Suggestion of orderly approach to the subject (par. 2)

2 Sloppiness and kindliness, however, seem to go hand-in-hand, to have one of those awful "natural" affinities, like sloth and melancholy. Your tidiness, they'll tell you, is just a manifestation of your hostility toward others. But if we take an orderly approach to this matter, I think we can out-fox them.

Distinction between innate and acquired virtue (kindliness) (par. 3)

3 We will assume, to begin with, that there are two kinds of kindliness: innate and acquired. And thus there are two ways to be kindly: naturally kindly and—uh—the opposite. Now

it is clear that the second kind of kindliness is far superior to the first kind. There is very little credit in being innately kindly: if that's just the way you are, it wouldn't be *right* for you to get any credit for it. But a person who *forces* himself to be kindly deserves all the credit in the world. A new, learned, acquired virtue is always far shinier and better than a dull old natural one. Our Lord repeatedly says how much dearer to him is the reformed man than the one who's just naturally good. Acquired kindliness, then, is really the only kind worth having.

The first step toward becoming kindly is to *appear* kindly. You should smile sweetly a lot, more or less all the time, but especially when the children spill or anything like that. Practice your sweet smile when you're alone, in the bathroom mirror, say; and if you're sure you're alone, practice saying soothing and reassuring things like "There, there," or "Oh, don't worry about *that*," or "That's *per*fectly all right," or "How could you help it? It certainly wasn't *your* fault!" Actually, I suppose it might not be a bad idea to leave the bathroom door slightly ajar, so the family can overhear you practicing saying kind things like these—that way they'll realize how hard you're trying to be able to put up with the things they do.

What's important is to learn to say kind things so they sound really natural. If, when your wife serves your dinner, you are going to try to say something enthusiastic like, "What have I done to deserve this!?" then you've got to get the tone and emphasis exactly right or she'll misunderstand you. Apparently that's where a lot of being kindly is, in the inflection rather than the words. They tell me, for instance, that saying "How could *you* help it?" actually has something of an *un*kindly tone. At any rate, you have to be constantly on guard:

4
First step: practice in appearing kindly (par. 4)

5
Second step (or subdivision of first): saying kind things (par. 5)

people, children especially, are always on the alert for any note of sarcasm in your voice. You know how suspicious children always are.

6   Everyone knows that the way you act sooner or later becomes the way you are. If you *act* kindly long enough, surely you'll really *become* kindly. My wife tells me it's harder than that, but I'm convinced that it can be done. Besides, even if you can't actually manage to become kindly, people may sort of let down their guard and begin thinking of you that way. Then when you *do* get angry, they feel they've done something so terrible that they've made even kindly you lose your temper; then they feel awful about it, and you've got them where you want them.

Conclusion: resulting success, genuine or assumed (par. 6)

Discussing Content and Form

1. On the surface, this selection seems to be simple instruction in the process of attaining kindliness. What subtle comment on human nature does the writer make in giving that instruction?

2. Examine the premise on which Hills bases his discussion of kindliness:

    a. Comment on his assumption that readers will agree that "kindliness is generally reckoned to be . . . [a] virtue."

    b. Comment on the "natural affinities" he sets up in paragraph 2.

3. Hills deliberately confuses Betsey Trotwood's name and pretends to be uncertain about Aunt Polly's. Look up these characters if you do not know them and explain how they disprove his statement that fussiness and kindliness do not go together.

4. Why must Hills dismiss "innate" kindliness and deal with only the "acquired"? Why is acquired kindliness superior?

5. Hills says "The first step . . . is to appear *kindly," and then he goes on to offer suggestions about how to achieve that appearance. Is learning "to say kind things" a second step, or another division of the first? Explain.*

6. Discuss the statement about tone and emphasis (par. 5). To what extent is how you say something as important or more important than what you say? Does your experience lead you to agree? Why or why not?

7. What cause/effect relationship does Hills set up in the last paragraph? What rationale does he give for saying that it is sufficient to appear kindly if you cannot actually achieve this virtue? Do you find his reasoning acceptable? Why or why not?

Considering Special Techniques

1. The opening sentence of this selection uses antithesis, a rhetorical device involving the balance of ideas one against the other in sentences such as the first one: "not because of his vices, but because of his virtues." Find other examples of Hills' use of words in pairs to show the opposition or balance between ideas. In what way could you say such playing of one thing against another is really the controlling purpose in his entire set of instructions?

2. Discover the writer behind the essay, the voice of the speaker. Which words indicate that Hills is speaking as a psychologist-philosopher? Find words that carry a tone of intimacy, of chattiness. To what extent is Hills intending to be taken seriously? What statements or words seem to you to be humorous?

3. Note the connecting words that Hills uses to lead a reader with him in the rather entangled reasoning of paragraph 3:
"We will assume, to begin with . . . "
"And thus . . ."
"Now it is clear that . . ."
"But a person . . ."
"Acquired kindliness, then, . . ."

4. What is the effect of referring to "Our Lord" in paragraph 3? Consider the value of the "God is on our side" argument in general. Why does it often work?

5. Words to learn and use: familial (par. 1); affinities, sloth, melancholy, manifestation (par. 2); innate (par. 3); inflection (par. 5).

Generating Ideas

1. Write a paper (put it in letter form if you wish) explaining to a friend the ways to acquire some special quality of character or behavior: for example, how to develop confidence, how to become a good conversationalist, how to become a leader, or how to become better organized or more disciplined in work habits. Or you might write practical suggestions on a subject such as saving money, choosing some product wisely, or learning some particular skill.

2. Try a reverse of the instructional process in another form by writing a paper telling how you acquired some quality or habit, or how you mastered some technique or skill. Here are a few suggestions:

"How I Learned Not to Put Off Until Tomorrow"
"The Slow Growth to Becoming a Sailor"
"Team Play—Some Experiences along the Way"
"Three Meals That Failed, One That Won"

3. Choose a character in literature who exemplifies the attainment of a quality you admire. For instance, Pip in Great Expectations *learns humility and appreciation;* Huck in The Adventures of Huckleberry Finn *learns tolerance and love for his companion, Jim; the narrator in* Surfacing *goes back into the world of her early home to discover something about herself and her roots. Write a paper tracing the development, the growth or unfolding, of that character.*

4. After some discussion about qualities that are often considered antithetical, write a paper answering one of these questions:

How can a person be both smart and popular?
How can a person be both efficient and relaxed?
How can a football player be an A student?
Add any others that you think of.

Robert Hendrickson

Robert Hendrickson (b. 1933) is a free-lance writer who has written over a thousand articles, stories, and poems for literary quarterlies and general magazines. His writing shows careful research into everyday subjects that previously have not had much written about them. In *The Great American Chewing Gum Book*, he recounts the history of an industry and a habit, tracing gum chewing from the time when the Indians taught early New England settlers the uses for spruce gum to the rise of today's giant gum manufacturers. "Civilization's First Chewing Gum Maker," a selection from that book, traces the early and colorful development of the spruce gum industry.

Civilization's First Chewing Gum Maker

The man who started America and all peoplekind chewing gum on a grand scale was named John Curtis, a former seaman born in Bradford, Maine. In our best rags-to-riches tradition, he and his son John Bacon Curtis prepared the world's first commercial chewing gum in one of his wife's large pots on a Franklin stove in the small kitchen of their little Bangor home. It was the younger Curtis, a $5 a month swamper who cleared underbrush and blocked out roads through the woods, who first saw the possibilities for manufacturing spruce gum. His father, a cautious man, doubted that anyone would buy it and only after his family's prodding did he agree to make the first batch in the spring of 1848. From the beginning John B. handled the selling end of the business, while his father manned and managed the production line.

Sales were hard to come by at first. John B. walked the streets of Portland, Maine, two full days talking spruce gum before he convinced a storekeeper to stock the family product. The gum quickly sold itself, but business was slow for the first few years, hardly enough to support a family, and young Curtis went on the road as a peddler, selling his spruce gum, patent medicines and whatever else he could take on. "Give a man all you can for his money, while making a fair profit yourself" was his motto, and he drove his team and cart throughout New England practicing what he pitched. He was so successful ("I was on the road while the other fellow was in bed") that he made the transition from peddler to commercial traveler, journeying all over the country selling his gum, which he carried with him, and as the representative of Eastern business houses. Indeed, some historians think John B. Curtis may have been one of America's first drummers, and he certainly traveled the West in advance of the railroads, using steamboat, canal boat, stage, horse, Shank's mare—whatever transportation he could get. "Many times I walked beside the stage with a rail on my shoulder, ready to help pry it out of the mud," he once said. "I passed hundreds of nights camping out with only a blanket for a covering and the ground for a bed. Did object to the rattlesnakes sometimes. It didn't pay to have them get too familiar . . ."

3   All for the glory of gum. The efforts of the young optimistic Curtis, who could have served as a model for William Wrigley, Jr., in the future, introduced spruce gum to thousands of new customers. The product was made with great care. "State of Maine Pure Spruce Gum" wasn't sold fresh-picked, but was roughly refined first. Curtis and his son threw the raw gobs of gum, bark and all, into a big black kettle and boiled it into about the consistency of thick molasses, skimming the bark and other impurities as they rose to the surface. At this point, they may have added some lard or grease, or pitch and sap from other trees to the mix, and possibly even a little sugar (none of these would change the taste of spruce gum much, but would merely increase the volume and make the mixture thicker). For "State of Maine *Pure* Spruce Gum," however, no adulterants at all were added. The mixture was simply stirred until it became thicker and then poured out on a slab, where, while still hot, it was rolled out in a sheet about a ¼-inch thick and then chopped into pinkish pieces a ½-inch wide and ¾-inch long. These in turn were dipped in cornstarch, wrapped in tissue paper and sold as "State of Maine Pure Spruce Gum," about 20 pieces to the wooden box.

4   At two chaws for a penny (later a penny apiece) Curtis' spruce gum became a resounding success and he couldn't turn out his gum fast enough. He and his son advertised for more raw gum, which they bought in great quantities from

lumberjacks, trappers, farmers, and a new breed of woodsmen who devoted themselves entirely to gum gathering in season and brought big bags of gum down to Bangor. The little Curtis Company grew so successful that Curtis was able to move into Portland in 1850 to get closer to big city markets like Boston. There the younger Curtis invented a number of machines for making gum that formed the basis for the gum-making process in chewing gum plants everywhere. Other brands were added to the Curtis line: Yankee Spruce, American Flag, Trunk Spruce, and 200 Lump Spruce, the last a more natural-looking gum, though nearly all the brands were identical in flavor. One of these gums, C.C.C. (no one knows why it was so named, unless it simply meant Curtis Chewing Gum Company), was popular throughout America and the *Portland City Guide* notes that it "started the tireless wagging of stenographer's jaws throughout the world." Curtis made enough money to take on over 200 employees, who turned out nearly 1,800 boxes of spruce gum every day. Once he wrote a check for $35,000 worth (ten tons) of raw spruce gum—a record that has never been topped. In 1852 he erected the three-story Curtis Chewing Gum Factory, which, to quote the *Portland City Guide* again, was the first chewing gum factory in the world. Curtis & Son (the company kept its original name even after John Curtis died in 1869, aged 69) thrived until the early part of this century when it was acquired by the Sen-Sen Chiclet Company, which in turn merged with the American Chicle Company. The younger Curtis died in 1897, aged 70, a very wealthy man indeed.

Oddly enough, neither John Curtis nor his son ever patented their machines or their process for making spruce gum; they probably thought it was all too obvious. Hosts of imitations soon appeared on the market and they too sold well. Only in Maine, however, did the new firms rise up, mostly in the lower half of the state; other New Englanders appeared content just to gather their own spruce gum from the woods. Latecomers included the Maine Gum Company, the B. C. Oglivie Gum Company, Roudlett Brothers, Garceau and Thistle, The Happy Day Gum Company, and, naturally, the Hiawatha Gum Company.

6   One notable competitor was John Davis, who set up a
small factory in Portland in 1850. Davis is said to have
improved on his father's rudimentary attempts to prepare
and market spruce gum and, but for a little luck, his father
might have been the first man in history to manufacture
chewing gum. Davis' business possibly survived until the
late 1930's; at least a man by the name of Harry Davis was
running the Eastern Gum Company at that time, employing some 20 gum gatherers, buying about 30,000 pounds of
rough gum annually, and shipping his finished product out
on the Monson-Maine Slate Company narrow gauge
railroad, the only commercial line in New England. His was
a fairly complex manufacturing operation, too, though on a
much smaller scale than the Curtis firm's. But Davis found
his market shrinking with each passing year; a lot of work
was required for very small profits. Indeed, there were very
few spruce gum manufacturers remaining toward the
beginning of World War II. Except for workers at the Shaker
Colony at Sabbath Day Lake, Maine, and perhaps a small
firm in Canada, Davis seems to be the only maker of spruce
gum left in the world at the time. In fact, if another Mainer
hadn't stepped in to fill his shoes when he retired, the art of
spruce gum making might have been lost forever.

7   Spruce gum offers a good example of how popular
tastes change. So many people were chewing the gum in
the nineteenth century that according to Maine Forest
Service records, the annual harvest of raw gum was
estimated at over 150 tons and valued at $300,000,
furnishing employment to hundreds. And these are very
conservative figures; other writers put the yearly crude
gum yield at closer to 1,500 tons. Gum chewing spread
rapidly across nineteenth century America, long before
chicle came on the scene. "There are the spruce gum-
chewers, all backlotters; and vulgar," an early sermonizer
despaired. "The careful observer cannot fail to note the
prevalency of spruce gum chewing, and gum is universally
chewed down East," a Maine newspaper pointed out a
century later.

8   Today, only one spruce gum manufacturer remains in
America, or in the world for that matter. He is the genial
Gerald F. Carr who lives in Portland, but does his gumming

in Five Islands, Maine, which is near Bath. Carr, a Mainer from birth (60 years ago), is a railroad man "from way back," but has been making gum on the side since 1937, when he took over the C. A. McMahan Company owned by his wife's Canadian grandfather.

Discussing Content and Form

1. Is the focus of this selection on the chewing gum maker or on the development of the gum business? Explain.

2. What qualities made John B. Curtis a good business-man? In what ways is his story the typical American success chronicle? What is meant by the statement that Curtis "could have served as a model for William Wrigley, Jr."?

3. Which details concerning the gum business surprised you? Compare the names given the early brands with those of today's chewing gum. Which do you think more colorful? Why?

4. Divide the essay into sections tracing three separate but interlocking processes: the career of John B. Curtis, the history of the Curtis company, and the manufacturing of spruce gum. Which sections are historical process? Which explain a physical process?

5. Which details help portray life as it was in late nineteenth-century America?

Considering Special Techniques

1. Point out several connectives that indicate the passing of time, for example, "From the beginning" (par.1) and "At this point" (par. 3). Why are such connectives important in explaining a process?

2. Several of the informal words in this selection are now seldom used, although they are probably clear from the context. Explain drummers and Shank's mare (par. 2). In New England villages the better homes were often built around a green or square; what then would you take backlotters (par. 7) to mean? What is the stylistic effect of these and other words such as gobs (par. 3), chaws (par. 4), and chewing (par. 7)?

3. Explain the play on words in paragraph 2: "he drove his team and cart throughout New England practicing what he pitched."

4. Writers often let a character reveal himself with a few well-chosen quotations. What is the effect of quoting Curtis' motto and his description of his travels (par. 2)? What does his understatement (the minimizing or playing down of something serious) about the rattlesnakes reveal about Curtis' sense of humor: "It didn't pay to have them get too familiar" (par. 2)?

5. Although this selection is packed with factual detail, it is lively reading. In your opinion, what are some of the characteristics that make it lively?

Generating Ideas

1. Trace the development of some venture in which you have been involved or about which you have a good deal of information, e.g., a small business, a club, a special project, a musical group, etc. Who had the original idea for the venture? How did it start? How long did you keep it going? What success or influence did it have? Make your paper factual but lively, and keep the explanations and steps clear.

2. Write a short history of someone you know who has been very successful in a career or some venture. Take into consideration the beginning of the endeavor and follow its progress step by step. (Do not, however, write a straight narration of the person's life.)

3. Explain how something is manufactured or made, using as your example the process explained in paragraph 3.

4. Several ideas or phrases in this selection might prompt papers that are organized by patterns other than process. Write a short paper explaining why the "rags-to-riches" tradition has such appeal for Americans. Or write a paper about your reaction to gum-chewing or about an unusual experience you may have had with chewing gum.

John Stewart Collis

John Stewart Collis (b. 1900) is of Irish ancestry and was educated at
Rugby and Oxford. He lives now in Ewell, Surrey. He has written
biographies of George Bernard Shaw, Leo Tolstoy, and Christopher
Columbus, but his best-known work is based on his observations of
nature. Among the titles are *An Irishman's England* (1937), *The Triumph of
the Tree* (1950), *The Moving Waters* (1955), and *The Worm Forgives the
Plough* (1973), from which the following essay is taken. The lowly potato
may seem an unlikely subject, but Collis proves that there is much to
say—both serious and humorous—about the process of its growth.

The Potato

I am anxious to say a word about the potato. . . . We sing   1
the flower, we sing the leaf: we seldom sing the seed, the
root, the tuber. Indeed the potato enters literature with no
very marked success. True, William Cobbett abused it, and
Lord Byron made it interesting by rhyming it with Plato;
but for the most part it enters politics more easily and has
done more to divide England from Ireland than Cromwell
himself.

Yet if we praise the potato we praise ourselves, for it is   2
an extreme example of artificiality. "The earth, in order that
she might urge us to labour, the supreme law of life," says
Fabre, "has been but a harsh stepmother. For the nestling
bird she provides abundant food; to us she offers only the
fruit of the Bramble and the Blackthorn." Not everyone
realizes this, he said. Some people even imagine that the
grape is today just like that from which Noah obtained the
juice that made him drunk; that the cauliflower, merely
with the idea of being pleasant, has of its own accord
evolved its creamy-white head; that turnips and carrots,
being keenly interested in human affairs, have always of
their own motion done their best for man; and that the
potato, since the world was young, wishing to please us,
has gone through its curious performance. The truth is far
otherwise. They were all uneatable at first: it is we who
have forced them to become what they now are. "In its
native countries," says Fabre, "on the mountains of Chili
and Peru, the Potato, in its wild state, is a meagre tubercle,

about the size of a Hazel-nut. Man extends the hospitality of his garden to this sorry weed; he plants it in nourishing soil, tends it, waters it, and makes it fruitful with the sweat of his brow. And there, from year to year, the Potato thrives and prospers; it gains in size and nourishing properties, finally becoming a farinaceous tuber the size of our two fists."

3   During my first year in the agricultural world I decided to have a good look at the potato and carefully watch its operations. I had never done this before. In fact I had little idea how potatoes actually arrive. With me it is always a question of either knowing a thing or not knowing it, of knowing it from A to Z or not at all; the man who knows a little about everything, from A to B, is incomprehensible to me. Thus I could approach the potato with the clear head of ignorance.

4   I took one in my hand and offered it my attention. It looked like a smooth stone; a shapeless shape; so dull in appearance that I found it hard to look at it without thinking of something else. I took a knife and cut it in two. It had white flesh extremely like an apple. But it had nothing in the middle, no seed-box, no seeds. How then can it produce more of itself? Well, the season had now come to put it down into the earth. So we planted them into the prepared field, at a distance of one foot from each other—plenty of space in which laboratory they could carry out any work they desired.

5   In about a fortnight's time I decided to dig up one and see if anything had happened. The first I came to had not changed in appearance at all. From the second, however, two white objects, about the length of a worm, were protruding. On a human face, I reflected, such protuberances would have seemed like some dreadful disease. One of them looked like a little white mouse trying to get out. I covered up these phenomena again and left them to it, wondering what they would do next.

6   After a few weeks I again visited this earthly laboratory to see how things were getting on. I found that the protuberances had become much longer and had curled round at their ends—now white snakes coming out of the humble solid. They had curly heads like purplish knots,

and some of these knots had half opened into a series of green ears. And now there was another addition: at the place where these stems, as we may now call them, came out of the potato, a network had been set up, of string, as it were, connecting the outfit with the soil. These, the roots, went downwards seeking the darkness of the earth, while every stem rose up to seek the light. But as yet there was no indication where or how new potatoes could appear.

During these early weeks the surface of the field   7
showed no sign that anything was going on underneath. Later the whole brown surface began to change into rows of green—the light-seeking stalks had risen into the air and unfurled their leaves. As the weeks passed, and the months, these little green bushes grew in size and complexity until in late July they were all flowering—and a very pretty field it then looked. As all flowers have fruit, so had these—potato fruits, of course. But not the ones we eat.

Even after the green rows had appeared above-board   8
and I made a further examination below I still did not see where the crop of potatoes was going to come from. Eventually the problem cleared itself up. I found them forming at the end of the network of roots. A few of the roots began to swell at their extremity—first about the size of a bird's egg, then a baby's shoe, getting larger and larger until some of them were four times the size of the original potato planted in the ground. And here we come to the curious thing about potatoes. The substance which grows at the end of the root is not itself a root. It is a *branch*. It is not a root, the botanists say, because roots do not bear buds and do not bear leaves, while this, the potato, does have buds and does have leaves (in the shape of scales). It is a subterranean branch, swollen and misshapen, storing up food for its buds; and botanists, no longer having the courage to call it a branch, call it a tuber. So when we plant a potato we are not planting a seed, we are not planting a root; we are planting a branch from whose gateways, called "eyes," roots reach down and stalks reach up.

To complete the circle, what happens to the original   9
potato? It conforms to the rule of eternal return by virtue of which the invisible becomes visible, and the visible takes on invisibility. It darkens, it softens, it becomes a squashy

brown mash, and finally is seen no more. I used to enjoy taking it up in my hand when I saw it lying on the ground looking like an old leather purse. It had performed a remarkable act. Now its work was done. All the virtue had gone out of it. It had given its life to the green stalks above and the tubers below. Here I seemed to see a familiar sight in nature; many things coming from one thing, much from little, even something out of nothing. This is what we seem to see. Yet it is not so. True, the original potato started the business going, sending down those roots and sending up those stalks; but they in their turn built the building. The earth is not a solid; it is chiefly gas. The air is not thin; it is massed with food. Those roots sucked gases from the earth, those leaves sucked gases from the sky, and the result was the visible, hard, concrete potato. When we eat a potato we eat the earth, and we eat the sky. It is the law of nature that all things are all things. That which does not appear to exist today is tomorrow hewn down and cast into the oven. Nature carries on by taking in her own washing. That is Nature's economy, contrary to political economy; so that he who cries "Wolf! Wolf!" is numbered amongst the infidels. "A mouse," said Walt Whitman, "is enough to stagger sextillions of infidels." Or a potato. What is an infidel? One who lacks faith. What creates faith? A miracle. How then can there be a faithless man found in the world? Because many men have cut off the nervous communication between the eye and the brain. In the madness of blindness they are at the mercy of intellectual nay-sayers, theorists, theologians, and other enemies of God. But it doesn't matter; in spite of them, faith is reborn whenever anyone chooses to take a good look at anything—even a potato.

Discussing Content and Form

1. *Ostensibly, much of this essay is devoted to observing and tracing a physical process: the growth "operations" of the potato. But Collis also conveys a more general message through the recording of his observations.*

    a. *How does paragraph 1 indicate that Collis is writing with a broader purpose than tracing physical growth?*

  b. *Paragraph 9 is an explicit and fully developed philosophical statement. In which sentence (or sentences) is Collis' key idea or thesis most clearly presented?*
  c. *Find other sentences that are in themselves memorable messages.*
  d. *We are accustomed to comments on the miracles of nature. What special force is gained by observing these miracles in "even a potato"? How does Collis relate his message to Walt Whitman's statement about the mouse (par. 9)?*

2. *Collis says that the potato "enters literature with no very marked success" (par. 1). In what way is his essay an answer to writers who have ignored or "abused" the lowly or ugly in nature in favor of praising its more beautiful creations?*

3. *The Irish potato famine (1846 and 1847) and the invasion of Ireland by the Puritan leader Oliver Cromwell in 1649 both caused great strife between Ireland and England. How does Collis' allusion to these events (par. 1) give another kind of significance to the potato?*

4. *The quotations in paragraph 2 are from Jean Henri Fabre (1823-1911), a French naturalist who wrote a ten-volume work on insect life. What, according to Fabre and Collis, is man's relationship to nature? Is there a conflict between their view as it is expressed here and the belief that nature is better left alone? Explain.*

5. *Discuss Collis' statement that he wants to know something from "A through Z" or not at all. You might compare Collis' methods of observation to those of Samuel Scudder in his study of the fish (p. 3). Construct an argument in favor of the opposite view: knowing "a little about everything, from A to B."*

Considering Special Techniques

1. *Collis frequently uses the semicolon for a variety of stylistic effects. In order to see how he uses it to separate balanced elements, look at the fourth sentence in paragraph 2 (beginning "Some people even imagine. . . .") and at two sentences from paragraph 9: "The earth is not a solid; it is chiefly gas. The air is not thin; it is massed with food." Check a handbook of grammar for the rules governing the use of the semicolon, and explain why it is effective punctuation in these*

examples. What, for instance, would be the effect achieved by separating the various elements into shorter sentences?

2. Notice how Collis uses the dash, often a troublesome mark of punctuation. (Note especially paragraph 7.) What effects does Collis achieve from such use of the dash?

3. Paragraphs 4 through 8 trace the growth process of the potato. List the connecting words in these paragraphs, both those that link paragraphs and those that link sentences within the paragraphs. How many of these words are "time" words that indicate sequence? Which ones might indicate the presence of cause-and-effect relationships (see pp. 232–35)? Why are such links especially important in tracing a process?

4. Collis employs a question-and-answer pattern both at the beginning of paragraph 9 and again near the end of the essay. What is the effect of this technique? Note also that the questions at the end of paragraph 9 are answered with phrases. What is the effect of these short answers?

5. The concluding phrase"—even a potato" serves as a reminder of the opening of the essay. Explain the force of the word even in this position.

6. Words to learn and use: tubercle, farinaceous (par. 2); incomprehensible (par. 3); subterranean (par. 8); infidels (par. 9).

Generating Ideas

1. Many writers and thinkers, among them Thoreau (p. 15) and Annie Dillard (p. 218), have responded to the profound beauty of nature with an affirmation and a sense of wonder about the eternal. Collis, on the other hand, arrives at the same belief from observing the lowly potato. Consider some phenomenon of nature that has seemed to you miraculous or wonderful and write a short paper explaining your reactions. If you can, trace the process by which you arrived at your conclusions.

2. If you are a gardener, write a paper tracing the physical process involved in either the growth of one plant or the growth of an entire garden. For instance, if you have observed a "spider plant," you might explain its "multiplication" process. Or you might write a "how-to" paper in which you give directions for cultivating a particular kind of plant or for planting a garden.

3. Do some research into Irish history and write a paper tracing the influence of the potato on the economy of Ireland. Or choose another foodstuff that has been economically or politically important to a nation and explain the process by which it became influential. For instance, you might look into the recent grain embargo. Your paper may, of course, involve both the tracing and the explanation of causes and results.

4. Many agricultural processes provide substance for interesting papers. Here are a few suggestions, some of which may lead to topics of your own devising:

The process of reforestation (limit to one place, one type)
Protection of the fisheries
Checking erosion through contour plowing
Problems in waste disposal
The selective cutting of trees
Planned farming of the seas
The renewal of tired soils
Harvesting a specific crop

5. Choose some industrial process as a subject for analysis. Here are a few titles that may serve as the basis for your paper:

"From Wheat into Flour: A Visit to a Modern Mill"
"The Modern Refinery—Oil for a Mechanized World"
"On the Set—Making a Movie"
"The Garment Factory—10,000 Blue Jeans a Day"
"A Visit to a Brewery"

Aldo Leopold

Aldo Leopold (1887–1948), a leading conservationist, began his career with the United States Forest Service in 1909. He later became Associate Director of the Federal Forest Products Laboratory in Madison, Wisconsin, and he was an adviser on conservation to the United Nations when he died while fighting a grass fire near his Wisconsin farm. The author of two books and numerous articles on game management and forestry, Leopold collected several of his essays, which he called "delights and dilemmas," in *Sand County Almanac* (1949). His superb nature writing is often compared to that of Thoreau and John Muir, and Leopold's words from the introduction to that book express a philosophy that all three held in common: "We abuse the land because we regard it as a commodity belonging to us. When we see land as a community to which we belong, we may begin to use it with love and respect." "The Biography of an Oak" (editor's title) is from the February section of the *Almanac*.

The Biography of an Oak

1 We mourned the loss of the old tree, but knew that a dozen of its progeny standing straight and stalwart on the sands had already taken over its job of wood-making.

2 We let the dead veteran season for a year in the sun it could no longer use, and then on a crisp winter's day we laid a newly filed saw to its bastioned base. Fragrant little chips of history spewed from the saw cut, and accumulated on the snow before each kneeling sawyer. We sensed that these two piles of sawdust were something more than wood: that they were the integrated transect of a century; that our saw was biting its way, stroke by stroke, decade by decade, into the chronology of a lifetime, written in concentric annual rings of good oak.

3 It took only a dozen pulls of the saw to transect the few years of our ownership, during which we had learned to love and cherish this farm. Abruptly we began to cut the years of our predecessor the bootlegger, who hated this farm, skinned it of residual fertility, burned its farmhouse, threw it back into the lap of the County (with delinquent taxes to boot), and then disappeared among the landless anonymities of the Great Depression. Yet the oak had laid down good wood for him; his sawdust was as fragrant, as

sound, and as pink as our own. An oak is no respecter of persons.

The reign of the bootlegger ended sometime during the dust-bowl drouths of 1936, 1934, 1933, and 1930. Oak smoke from his still and peat from burning marshlands must have clouded the sun in those years, and alphabetical conservation was abroad in the land, but the sawdust shows no change.   4

Rest! cries the chief sawyer, and we pause for breath.   5

Now our saw bites into the 1920's, the Babbittian* decade when everything grew bigger and better in heedlessness and arrogance—until 1929, when stock markets crumpled. If the oak heard them fall, its wood gives no sign. Nor did it heed the Legislature's several protestations of love for trees: a National Forest and a forest-crop law in 1927, a great refuge on the Upper Mississippi bottomlands in 1924, and a new forest policy in 1921. Neither did it notice the demise of the state's last marten in 1925, nor the arrival of its first starling in 1923.   6

In March 1922, the 'Big Sleet' tore the neighboring elms limb from limb, but there is no sign of damage to our tree. What is a ton of ice, more or less, to a good oak?   7

Rest! cries the chief sawyer, and we pause for breath.   8

Now the saw bites into 1910–20, the decade of the drainage dream, when steam shovels sucked dry the marshes of central Wisconsin to make farms, and made ash-heaps instead. Our marsh escaped, not because of any caution or forbearance among engineers, but because the river floods in each April, and did so with a vengeance—perhaps a defensive vengeance—in the years 1913–16. The oak laid on wood just the same, even in 1915, when the Supreme Court abolished the state forests and Governor Phillip pontificated that 'state forestry is not a good business proposition.' (It did not occur to the Governor that there might be more than one definition of what is good, and even of what is business. It did not occur to him that while the courts were   9

*A reference to Sinclair Lewis' novel, *Babbitt*, which reflected life in the 1920s.

writing one definition of goodness in the law books, fires were writing quite another one on the face of the land. Perhaps, to be a governor, one must be free from doubt on such matters.)

10   While forestry receded during this decade, game conservation advanced. In 1916 pheasants became successfully established in Waukesha County; in 1915 a federal law prohibited spring shooting; in 1913 a state game farm was started; in 1912 a 'buck law' protected female deer; in 1911 an epidemic of refuges spread over the state. 'Refuge' became a holy word, but the oak took no heed.

11   Rest! cries the chief sawyer, and we pause for breath.

12   Now we cut 1910, when a great university president published a book on conservation, a great sawfly epidemic killed millions of tamaracks, a great drouth burned the pineries, and a great dredge drained Horicon Marsh.

13   We cut 1909, when smelt were first planted in the Great Lakes, and when a wet summer induced the Legislature to cut the forest-fire appropriations.

14   We cut 1908, a dry year when the forests burned fiercely, and Wisconsin parted with its last cougar.

15   We cut 1907, when a wandering lynx, looking in the wrong direction for the promised land, ended his career among the farms of Dane County.

16   We cut 1906, when the first state forester took office, and fires burned 17,000 acres in these sand counties; we cut 1905 when a great flight of goshawks came out of the North and ate up the local grouse (they no doubt perched in this tree to eat some of mine). We cut 1902–3, a winter of bitter cold; 1901, which brought the most intense drouth on record (rainfall only 17 inches); 1900, a centennial year of hope, of prayer, and the usual annual ring of oak.

17   Rest! cries the chief sawyer, and we pause for breath.

18   Now our saw bites into the 1890's, called gay by those whose eyes turn cityward rather than landward. We cut 1899, when the last passenger pigeon collided with a charge of shot near Babcock, two counties to the north; we cut 1898 when a dry fall, followed by a snowless winter, froze the

soil seven feet deep and killed the apple trees; 1897, another drouth year, when another forestry commission came into being; 1896, when 25,000 prairie chickens were shipped to market from the village of Spooner alone; 1895, another year of fires; 1894, another drouth year; and 1893, the year of 'The Bluebird Storm,' when a March blizzard reduced the migrating bluebirds to near-zero. (The first bluebirds always alighted in this oak, but in the middle 'nineties it must have gone without.) We cut 1892, another year of fires; 1891, a low in the grouse cycle; and 1890, the year of the Babcock Milk Tester, which enabled Governor Heil to boast, half a century later, that Wisconsin is America's Dairyland. The motor licenses which now parade that boast were then not foreseen, even by Professor Babcock.

It was likewise in 1890 that the largest pine rafts in   19 history slipped down the Wisconsin River in full view of my oak, to build an empire of red barns for the cows of the prairie states. Thus it is that good pine now stands between the cow and the blizzard, just as good oak stands between the blizzard and me.

Rest! cries the chief sawyer, and we pause for breath.   20

Now our saw bites into the 1880's; into 1889, a drouth year   21 in which Arbor Day was first proclaimed; into 1887, when Wisconsin appointed its first game wardens; into 1886, when the College of Agriculture held its first short course for farmers; into 1885, preceded by a winter 'of unprecedented length and severity'; into 1883, when Dean W. H. Henry reported that the spring flowers at Madison bloomed 13 days later than average; into 1882, the year Lake Mendota opened a month late following the historic 'Big Snow' and bitter cold of 1881–2.

It was likewise in 1881 that the Wisconsin Agricultural   22 Society debated the question, 'How do you account for the second growth of black oak timber that has sprung up all over the country in the last thirty years?' My oak was one of these. One debater claimed spontaneous generation, another claimed regurgitation of acorns by southbound pigeons.

Rest! cries the chief sawyer, and we pause for breath.   23

24   Now our saw bites the 1870's, the decade of Wisconsin's carousal in wheat. Monday morning came in 1879, when chinch bugs, grubs, rust, and soil exhaustion finally convinced Wisconsin farmers that they could not compete with the virgin prairies further west in the game of wheating land to death. I suspect that this farm played its share in the game, and that the sand blow just north of my oak had its origin in over-wheating.

25   This same year of 1879 saw the first planting of carp in Wisconsin, and also the first arrival of quack-grass as a stowaway from Europe. On 27 October 1879, six migrating prairie chickens perched on the rooftree of the German Methodist Church in Madison, and took a look at the growing city. On 8 November the markets at Madison were reported to be glutted with ducks at 10 cents each.

26   In 1878 a deer hunter from Sauk Rapids remarked prophetically, 'The hunters promise to outnumber the deer.'

27   On 10 September 1877, two brothers, shooting Muskego Lake, bagged 210 blue-winged teal in one day.

28   In 1876 came the wettest year of record; the rainfall piled up 50 inches. Prairie chickens declined, perhaps owing to hard rains.

29   In 1875 four hunters killed 153 prairie chickens at York Prairie, one county to the eastward. In the same year the U.S. Fish Commission planted Atlantic salmon in Devil's Lake, 10 miles south of my oak.

30   In 1874 the first factory-made barbed wire was stapled to oak trees; I hope no such artifacts are buried in the oak now under saw!

31   In 1873 one Chicago firm received and marketed 25,000 prairie chickens. The Chicago trade collectively bought 600,000 at $3.25 per dozen.

32   In 1872 the last wild Wisconsin turkey was killed, two counties to the southwest.

33   It is appropriate that the decade ending the pioneer carousal in wheat should likewise have ended the pioneer carousal in pigeon blood. In 1871, within a 50-mile triangle spreading northwestward from my oak, 136 million pigeons are estimated to have nested, and some may have

nested in it, for it was then a thrifty sapling 20 feet tall. Pigeon hunters by scores plied their trade with net and gun, club and salt lick, and trainloads of prospective pigeon pie moved southward and eastward toward the cities. It was the last big nesting in Wisconsin, and nearly the last in any state.

This same year 1871 brought other evidence of the march of empire: the Peshtigo Fire, which cleared a couple of counties of trees and soil, and the Chicago Fire, said to have started from the protesting kick of a cow. 34

In 1870 the meadow mice had already staged their march of empire; they ate up the young orchards of the young state, and then died. They did not eat my oak, whose bark was already too tough and thick for mice. 35

It was likewise in 1870 that a market gunner boasted in the *American Sportsman* of killing 6000 ducks in one season near Chicago. 36

Rest! cries the chief sawyer, and we pause for breath. 37

Our saw now cuts the 1860's, when thousands died to settle the question: Is the man-man community lightly to be dismembered? They settled it, but they did not see, nor do we yet see, that the same question applies to the man-land community. 38

This decade was not without its gropings toward the larger issue. In 1867 Increase A. Lapham induced the State Horticultural Society to offer prizes for forest plantations. In 1866 the last native Wisconsin elk was killed. The saw now severs 1865, the pith-year of our oak. In that year John Muir offered to buy from his brother, who then owned the home farm thirty miles east of my oak, a sanctuary for the wildflowers that had gladdened his youth. His brother declined to part with the land, but he could not suppress the idea: 1865 still stands in Wisconsin history as the birthyear of mercy for things natural, wild, and free. 39

We have cut the core. Our saw now reverses its orientation in history; we cut backward across the years, and outward toward the far side of the stump. At last there is a tremor in the great trunk; the saw-kerf suddenly widens; the saw is quickly pulled as the sawyers spring 40 backward to safety; all hands cry 'Timber!'; my oak leans, groans, and crashes with earth-shaking thunder, to lie prostrate across the emigrant road that gave it birth.

Discussing Content and Form

1. Perhaps you have heard someone make a comment such as this: "That old tree has seen a great deal of life." What in Leopold's tracing of the growth of the dead oak makes his version of that comment particularly dramatic?

2. Point out some of the events in the life of the oak that you can identify; point out others that you have not heard about. Explain why it makes little difference whether you can recognize every event or not.

3. Group some of the specifics that Leopold mentions. Where does he tell you about the prior owners of his farm? Which events does he use to characterize the 1930s? Which let you know that conservation was his major interest? Why does he place so much stress on weather? What type of political or legislative acts seem most important to Leopold as he cuts through the oak?

4. Who do you think is "the chief sawyer"? Explain his function in the cutting operation. In what sense does he have a function in the essay as well as in the cutting of the oak?

5. If you can remember first learning to count backwards, use that recollection as the springboard for discussing the effect of presenting a process in reverse rather than from beginning to end. Explain the line "Our saw now reverses its orientation in history; we cut backward across the years, and outward toward the far side of the stump" (par. 40).

Considering Special Techniques

1. In writing an essay of any length, a writer must decide how best to block it out, what major divisions to make in the material. Why do you think Leopold chose to make the decades his major divisions? What is the effect achieved by subdividing only some sections year by year?

2. A writer must keep verb tenses in clear relationship to show past and present. For the most part, Leopold uses past tense: "We mourned the loss" (par. 1), "It took only a dozen pulls" (par. 3), "The reign of the bootlegger ended" (par. 4). But with paragraph 5 at the end of the first decade, he places a statement in present tense, and thereafter he marks the opening and closing of each section with echo phrases in the present: "Rest, cries the chief sawyer, and we pause . . ." (par. 5); "Now our saw bites . . ." (par. 6).

    a. What is the effect achieved by the shift to present tense in these statements?

    b. Why is the tense shift logical?

    c. Explain the shift to present tense in paragraph 40. What is the effect of closing the cutting in the present?

3. What is the effect achieved by the exact repetition of the closing sentences that make up paragraphs 5, 8, 11, 17, 20, 23, and 37?

    a. Beginning with paragraph 6, point out the variations in the patterns of the opening sentences that announce the decades.

    b. Why do you think Leopold used repetition in the closing sentences but only echoes in the openers?

4. Point out details and words that make this essay very objective. Point out elements that are personal and subjective.

5. Much of the development within each block of paragraphs is by example, sometimes arranged as a list of events from the decade. How do paragraph divisions and parallel (or nearly parallel) structures give the effect of time passing?

6. Words to learn and use: progeny, stalwart (par. 1); bastioned, sawyer, transect, concentric (par. 2); residual, anonymities (par. 3); demise (par. 6); pontificated (par. 9); migrating (par. 18); regurgitation (par. 22); artifacts (par. 30); carousal (par. 33); orientation (par. 40).

Generating Ideas

1. If you have ever been involved with a group in some task such as cutting a tree, write a paper explaining the procedure. For instance, you and other students may have edited and assembled a yearbook, built a float, or promoted sales for a club or athletic event. Or you may have been part of a paint or construction crew, served on a volunteer fire fighting unit, or participated in planting or harvesting some agricultural product. Be sure you explain step by step the activity you choose as your subject.

2. At several points Leopold refers to legislation that

affected wildlife and conservation in his state. Choose some issue (current or past) and write a paper tracing the policies and legislation that have affected that issue. For instance, you might write about laws regulating child labor or immigration, or those setting hours and safety measures for mines and mills.

3. If you are enrolled in economics or sociology courses, write a paper tracing some development in one of those fields. You might examine statistics of production and price changes for a particular commodity, or trace the development of a social program such as the school lunch, housing for the elderly, food stamps or some other type of welfare.

4. Almost everyone has heard some "old-timer" recount events of an earlier era. Use those stories that you have heard, either first-hand or second-hand, for specifics in a tracing paper. Here are some possible subjects: the struggle of an immigrant grandfather who moved from job to job before finding a permanent home, the series of setbacks that plagued grandparents during the Depression, the several Christmases spent away from home in military service.

5. Few subjects are as interesting for tracing as the development of the motion picture industry. Choose an aspect of film making as a subject for a paper telling of the changes and improvements in that particular technique or area. Or read one of the many books that have been written about the making of a movie and write a summary-paper condensing the events in your own words. Eleanor Coppola's Notes is one such book; she tells of the making of Apocalypse Now.

Or choose another industry that has had great growth or change:

"From Model-T to the Pinto"
"Skiing on Barrel Staves Is Not Skiing on Heads"
"From Wood Stoves to Gas and Back Again"

These titles are meant to suggest merely, for you can think of many similar subjects.

6. If you are interested in art, write a paper tracing the process of making pottery, of producing a lithograph, of preparing a canvas for painting with oils, etc. Or trace the problems and procedure for hanging an exhibit in a gallery.

7. Write a paper tracing from beginning to end some scientific experiment that you have done or observed in a laboratory.

COMPARISON AND CONTRAST:
SEEING SIMILARITIES AND DIFFERENCES

"The drought today is like that of 1936, but this year's is even worse because of the lack of snow last winter." "The United States and Great Britain finance medical care differently." "Learning to cook and learning to play the piano were alike for me in that my mother taught me both, but they differed—I hated one and liked the other."

You constantly compare and contrast, finding likenesses and differences between two (or more) objects, persons, events, or ideas. Comparing (the one word is often used to cover both actions since there is usually no reason for comparing unless some contrast is involved) is often the basis for clarifying thought and making judgments, and for explaining choices and reaching conclusions. Whether you use comparison and contrast in speech or in writing, the same principles apply: you must use things that are logically comparable, and you must make the similarities and differences clear and comprehensible. The comparison should have a purpose. That is, it should be employed to sustain a thesis or lead to a point that you wish to make, and the choice and arrangement of the elements to be compared should fulfill that purpose.

Notice how this paragraph of comparison and contrast leads to a point:

> By comparison with the deep involvement of women in living, men appear to be only superficially engaged. Compare the love of a male for a female with the love of the female for the male. It is the difference between a rivulet and a great deep ocean. . . . Women love the human race; men behave as if they were, on the whole, hostile to it. Men act as if they haven't been adequately loved, as if they had been frustrated and rendered hostile. Becoming aggressive, they say that aggressiveness is natural, and that women are inferior because they tend to be gentle and unaggressive! But it is precisely in the capacity to love, in their cooperativeness rather than aggressiveness, that the superiority of women to men is demonstrated; for whether it be natural to be loving and cooperative or not, as far as the human species is concerned, its evolutionary destiny, its very survival, are more closely tied to the capacity for love and cooperation than to any other.—Ashley Montagu, *The Natural Superiority of Women*

Montagu uses the word *compare* in its broad sense, for he actually mentions only contrasts between the male and female capacities for love. His paragraph follows the *point-by-point* method of structuring comparison and contrast. That is, he treats the subjects or items that he is placing side by side according to their points of difference, thus achieving a "ping-pong" effect. In the paragraph, note these *points* of comparison:

1. Females and males differ in their capacity for loving each other. (This view is further illustrated by another type of comparison, the analogy of rivulet to ocean. This device is explained more fully in Chapter 7.)

2. Female love for the human race contrasts with male hostility toward it.

3. Men's hostility and aggressiveness contrast with women's gentleness and unaggressiveness.

After presenting the three points of difference in a back-and-forth pattern, Montagu generalizes that female love is superior and that the destiny of the "human species" is "closely tied to the capacity for love."

Here is an example of a second type of comparison:

> Columbus was a discoverer and not an explorer. The crucial distinction between these two roles we can see in the origins of our English words. The etymology of the word "discover" is obvious. Its primary meaning is to uncover, or to disclose to view. The discoverer, then, is a *finder*. He shows us what he already knew was there. Columbus set out to "discover," to find, the westward oceanic route to Asia. Of course he knew the ocean, and he knew of Asia. He set out to find the way. The word "explore" has quite different connotations. Appropriately, too, it has a disputed etymology. Some say it comes from *ex* (out) and *plorare* (to cry out), on the analogy of "deplore." The better view appears to be that it comes from *ex* (out) and *plorare* (from *pluere*, to flow). Either etymology reminds us that the explorer is one who surprises (and so makes people cry out) or one who makes new knowledge flow out.—Daniel Boorstin, *The Exploring Spirit*

You will see at once that this paragraph has a different structure. After his initial sentence, which signals the fact that the paragraph contains contrasting elements, Boorstin explains the etymology of *discover*. Then, almost precisely mid-paragraph, he moves on to explain the contrasting etymology of *explore*. This method of organizing is called the *unit* system of comparison: the topics, rather than the points about them, become the basis for the structure.

It may be convenient to describe the point-by-point and the unit systems with outlines. Assume that the items to be compared are A and B, and that the points of likeness or difference are 1, 2, 3, and 4.

Point-by-Point
1. A/B
2. A/B
3. A/B
4. A/B

Unit

A.

    1

    2

    3

    4

B.

    1

    2

    3

    4

Actually many long comparison papers use both methods of organizing. This paragraph by Boorstin immediately follows the one contrasting the words *discoverer* and *explorer:*

> The discoverer simply uncovers, but the explorer opens. The discoverer concludes a search; he is a finder. The explorer begins a search; he is a seeker. And he opens the way for other seekers. The discoverer is the expert at what is known to be there. The explorer is willing to take chances. He is the adventurer who risks *un*certain paths to the *un*known. Every age is inclined to give its laurels to the discoverers, those who finally arrive at the long-thought-inaccessible known destination. But posterity—the whole human community—owes its laurels to the happener-upon dark continents of the earth and of the mind. The courageous wanderer in worlds never known to be there is the explorer.

Here again is the ping-pong effect; the sentences bounce back and forth, clarifying the points of difference that lead to a conclusion. As a writer you must, of course, decide which of the methods of organization to use. While there are no hard-and-fast rules about which is better, these considerations should be kept in mind:

1. Choose the pattern that best suits your purpose, that allows you to support or to lead to the overall statement you will make on the basis of the comparison.

2. If points of difference or likeness should stand out, probably the point-by-point system is preferable. If the two topics themselves are of major interest, the unit method may be the better choice.

3. The point-by-point system may require more care in organization, but the unit system may become repetitive or tend to break the piece of writing into two nearly unrelated parts. With either structure, be coherent. Establish smooth relationships between all of the elements.

Just as comparison and contrast structures vary in purpose so they vary in complexity and length. When the items compared are more numerous or when both similarities and differences are considered, as is frequently the case in long papers, the structure is, of course, more complex. Notice how the writer of this paragraph brings together many items to show similarities and differences among various kinds of people.

On a recent morning, when I was running late because of an emergency, I noticed in my waiting room a back-up of patients. Among them were an Irish nun and a bearded Hasidic rabbi, an affluent Wasp businessman and a young black man who lived in one of Harlem's poorer neighborhoods. Now, *there* was a diversity of cultures, right in that room; yet it would have been a mistake to assume that all of these people needed to be treated entirely differently. The Irish nun, raised in a convent, and the Orthodox rabbi, who grew up in Hungary, had a number of problems in common. Both, for instance, suffered from a marked obsession with perfectionism, and from obsessive doubts about their own characters and abilities. The white corporation executive and the black ghetto youth both had an inclination to deny their symptoms and to minimize the need for treatment; and I knew that if I didn't exercise proper care (or even if I did!), there was a higher-than-average risk that they would drop out of therapy prematurely. My last two patients that morning, as it happened, were both teen-age black girls from poor families—but oh, so different. One was from a rural Southern family; the other was a New York City native. One held rigidly puritanical views about sex, while the other was relaxed and easy-going in her sexual attitudes. They came from different universes in some respects; yet the fact that they were both black in today's United States did of course influence the development of both their personalities in a variety of ways.—Ari Kiev, "Is Psychiatry a White-Middle-Class Invention?" *Saturday Review*

The particulars of this comparison are the basis on which Kiev generalizes in his next paragraph: "In sum, then, one must be aware of both the similarities and the differences and always of the uniqueness of each individual." In the selections that follow, you will once again discover the interlocking relationships between the specific and the general, but in comparison and contrast the generalization involves two or more subjects, two or more sets of specifics, side by side.

Peter F. Drucker

Peter F. Drucker (b. 1909) is a writer, economic consultant, and Clarke
Professor of Social Science and Management at the Claremont Graduate
School in Claremont, California. His distinguished career in international
business and at several universities has been recognized by nine honorary
degrees as well as many other honors. He has written some fifteen
well-known books and countless essays and articles for such publications
as *Harper's, Wall Street Journal, New York Times,* and *Public Interest.* His
autobiography, *The Adventures of a Bystander* (1979), tells a fascinating
story of growing up in a scientific and intellectual family in old Vienna.
He analyzes some of the tragic effects of World War I on his native
country, and tells of coming to America before the Hitler regime destroyed
much of the culture of Austria. "Teaching and Learning" (editor's title),
from that book, pays tribute to two teachers who inspired him to a lifetime
of scholarship.

Teaching and Learning

There is the teacher who has a gift in his keeping. And there is the pedagogue who knows how to program learning in the student. Teachers are born, and the born teacher can then improve and become better. But pedagogues have a method that can be learned, probably by almost everybody. Indeed, the "born" teacher can become a great teacher most easily by adding to his gift the method of the pedagogue. Then he will also become a universal teacher, able to teach large groups and small groups, beginners and the "master class."

1
Necessity for skills of
both teacher and
pedagogue (par.1)

Miss Sophy had charisma; Miss Elsa had method. Miss Sophy gave enlightenment; Miss Elsa gave skills. Miss Sophy conveyed vision, Miss Elsa guided learning. Miss Sophy was a teacher, Miss Elsa was a pedagogue. This distinction would not have surprised Socrates, or indeed any of the ancient Greeks. Socrates is traditionally called a great teacher. He himself would have resented this as an insult. He never spoke of himself as a teacher.

2
Comparison/contrast
of Miss Sophy
(teacher) and Miss
Elsa (pedagogue)
(par. 2)

Socrates as example
of teacher-pedagogue

He was a "pedagogue"—a guide to the learner. The Socratic method is not a teaching method, it is a *learning* method. It is programmed learning. Indeed Socrates' criticism of the Sophists was precisely that they emphasized teaching and that they believed that one teaches a subject. This he thought idle and vanity. The teacher teaches learning; the student learns the subject. Learning is fruitful; teaching is pretentious and a fraud. And it was for this that the Oracle at Delphi called him the "wisest man in Greece." For almost 2,000 years, however, the Sophists have ruled—the ones who promise to be able to teach teaching. Their ultimate triumph is the blind belief of American higher education that the Ph.D., or advanced specialized subject knowledge, is the right (indeed the only) preparation for teaching. But the Sophists have ruled only in the West. Other civilizations never accepted the Western, the Sophist, idea of the teacher. The Indian word for teacher is "guru" and a guru clearly is not made but born. He has an authority which is not that of the college course, but of the spirit. Similarly, the Japanese Sensei is a "master" rather than a teacher. But in the Western tradition, we have focused on teaching as a skill and forgotten what Socrates knew: teaching is a gift, learning is a skill.

Western idea of teacher contrasted to Indian-Japanese definitions

3

Current research on learning compared to Socrates' knowledge (par. 3)

It is only in this century that we are rediscovering what Socrates knew. We are doing so because we have done more serious work and research on learning in the last 100 years than has ever been done before. We have rediscovered that learning is built into every one of us. We have rediscovered that the human being—and all living beings—are "learning organisms" who are "programmed" to learn. We do not yet know as much about learning, as a result of a century of research, as Miss Elsa perceived. But we know that what she knew and did are right and available to practically everyone.

For 2,000 years or so, since the days of Socrates, we have debated whether teaching and learning are "cognitive" or "behavioral." It is a sham battle. Teaching and learning are both. But they are also something else: they are passion. Teachers start out with passion. Pedagogues acquire it as they become intoxicated with the enlightenment of the student. For the smile of learning on the student's face is more addictive than any drug or narcotic. It is this passion that prevents that deadly and deadening disease of the classroom, the boredom of the teacher—the one condition that absolutely inhibits both teaching and learning. Teaching and learning are the Platonic Eros, the Eros of the *Symposium*. There is in each of us Plato's Winged Horse, the noble steed which seeks the mate it can only find through teaching or learning. For the teacher, the passion is inside him or her; for the pedagogue, the passion is inside the student. But teaching and learning are always passion, passion one is born with or passion to which one becomes addicted.

4
"Passion" as requirement for teacher and pedagogue, for teaching and learning (par. 4)

Discussing Content and Form

1. Explain the distinction that Drucker makes between two kinds of teachers. How do Miss Sophy and Miss Elsa exemplify the two types? How does the difference between them relate to the contrast between teaching and learning—the overall subject of the selection?

2. Drucker might easily have "taken sides" by expressing a preference for one teacher over the other. Why is he careful not to do so? In spite of Socrates' reference to himself as a "pedagogue," does he represent Miss Sophy, Miss Elsa, or both? Support your answer.

3. Explain in your own words the difference between

teaching a "subject" and teaching "learning." What distinction does Drucker make between the American attitude and that of non-Western civilizations? Why is he skeptical of measuring of education in terms of "specialized subject knowledge" and degrees (par. 2)?

4. Look up the terms and explain the conflict between "cognitive" and "behavioral" views of education. On what basis can Drucker say that "teaching and learning are both" (par. 4)?

5. Although this selection seems at first glance to emphasize contrasts, the differences analyzed are solidly based on similarities, and the subjects for comparison and contrast must be items or ideas that are essentially comparable.

   a. What is the quality that links Miss Sophy and Miss Elsa? In what way are they comparable to Socrates?

   b. What is the commonality between teaching and learning? How is this commonality important to Drucker's final point?

6. In paragraph 4 Drucker refers to the Symposium, the dialogue in which Plato proclaims that the greatest love (Eros) is the love of wisdom. (The winged horse is apparently Pegasus of Greek myth; he was caught and tamed by a bridle provided by Athena, the goddess of wisdom.) Discuss the point that learning can be—or should be—a "passion." Explain how learning can become "addictive."

Considering Special Techniques

1. Writers almost always reinforce their general statements by means of specific examples. Analyze paragraph 1 for the back and forth movement between the contrasting generalizations; then explain how the structure of paragraph 2 follows the pattern of paragraph 1. To what part of paragraph 1 does the longer development concerning Socrates correspond?

2. Comparisons and contrasts are often expressed in carefully balanced sentences. Note such balance in the sentences from paragraph 1: "There is the teacher. . . . And there is the pedagogue. . . ."

   a. Go through the selection and find other uses of such paired or balanced sentences to carry contrasting pictures or ideas.

b. Note that Drucker divides or punctuates some of these sentences in different ways. Point out and account for these variations.

c. Some teachers frown if students use "And" and "But" as sentence openers in the way that Drucker does. On what basis would you defend the practice here?

3. The shape or structure of a single paragraph or of a short essay may sometimes be like a funnel, with all that goes before brought into focus in the final point. In what ways does the structure of this selection fit the funnel pattern?

4. An effective ending should grow out of the preceding material but not merely repeat what has already been said. Show how Drucker's first and final paragraphs relate without repetition. How do they contain or enclose the whole?

5. Several words and phrases in the selection occur frequently in discussions of education and psychology.

a. Explain "the Socratic method" (par. 2).

b. What is the original meaning of the word "Sophists" (par. 2)? Use your dictionary to explain derivatives such as sophistry, sophism, sophistic, sophistically, and sophisticate. How has the meaning of sophisticate (sophisticated, sophistication) changed with time?

c. Make a list of the derivatives from other words related to education: pedagogue (par. 1); cognitive and behavioral (par. 4).

d. Why do you think Drucker uses quotation marks around many of the words related to education? Would you call any of these words jargon? Explain.

Generating Ideas

1. Write a paper comparing or contrasting (or both) two or more teachers who have shaped your attitudes toward learning. You might, for instance, write about two teachers who led you to learn in spite of their quite different methods; or about a teacher who discouraged you and one who inspired you to want to learn more. Be sure to draw some conclusions from the comparison you make.

2. Writing a comparative evaluation may be a way of

clarifying an issue or a means of making a decision. Try one of these activities for structuring a thoughtful comparison paper:

    a. Write a comparative analysis of the advantages and disadvantages of two majors or two career choices that you are considering. You might, of course, treat the subject very objectively, or you might include some evaluation of your feelings about the fields you discuss.

    b. Assume you have been accepted by at least two colleges or universities; write a comparison of the two in order to arrive at a decision.

    c. Or try one of these educational choices as a subject:

        A music student must decide between a conservatory and a college music department.

        An art student must decide whether to enroll in a school of design or major in art at a liberal arts college.

        An athlete must decide between two schools that have offered him athletic scholarships.

        A student must decide whether to work during the school year or borrow money and concentrate on studying.

   3. Drucker admired both Miss Sophy and Miss Elsa, but for somewhat different qualities. Choose one of the following pairs and write a paper comparing and contrasting the things you admire in them:

        Two characters from fiction

        Two television personalities (newscasters, interviewers, comedians)

        Two athletes

        Two music groups or single performers

        Two political figures

Use your comparison of admirable qualities to draw some conclusions about the field your subjects are in; for instance, you might write about two candidates for public office in order to show what you value in political leadership.

   4. Everyone must constantly make choices. "Shall I fly or drive to get to my destination?" "Shall I take a pleasant job in a summer camp or shall I stay home and work in a factory where I can earn more money?" "Shall I live in a dorm or in an apartment during this school year?" Write a paper of comparison and contrast to show how you made some significant choice. If you can, draw some conclusions about

the ways in which we make comparisons in order to arrive at decisions.

5. Choose one of these subjects for a comparison paper or devise some similar subject of your own:
Science/humanities
Radio/television
Country living/city living
Health foods/ordinary foods
Dog/cat (as pets)
Farm/factory (as place to work)
Truck/rail transportation
Downhill/cross country skiing
Letter writing/long distance telephoning (in personal life or business)
Eating out/eating at home
Boutique/department store (as places for shopping)

6. You have probably felt passion for learning at some time or in some courses but not in others. Write a paper about the contrasting situations and your contrasting feelings. A title like one of these might be suitable:
"My Love/Hate Relationship with School"
"Eager Once, Discouraged Twice"
"Open a Book—Bang It Shut"
"Learning: Love It or Leave It"

William Zinsser

William Zinsser (b. 1922) was educated at Princeton and began his career
in 1946 as a feature writer with the *New York Herald Tribune*. He served
there as drama critic and editorial writer until 1959, when he left to do
free-lance writing. *Seen Any Good Movies Lately?*, a collection of his
reviews, was published in 1958, and his articles and essays have appeared
in many periodicals. Other books include *Pop Goes America* (1966) and *The
Lunacy Boom* (1970). *On Writing Well*, first published in 1976 and now in
its second edition, grew out of a course in nonfiction writing that Zinsser
taught at Yale. The following essay, from that book, demonstrates the
freshness of style and control of material that he encourages in his
students.

The Transaction

1   Several years ago a school in Connecticut held "a day
devoted to the arts," and I was asked if I would come and
talk about writing as a vocation. When I arrived I found that
a second speaker had been invited—Dr. Brock (as I'll call
him), a surgeon who had recently begun to write and had
sold some stories to national magazines. He was going to
talk about writing as an avocation. That made us a panel,
and we sat down to face a crowd of student newspaper
editors and reporters, English teachers and parents, all
eager to learn the secrets of our glamorous work.

2   Dr. Brock was dressed in a bright red jacket, looking
vaguely Bohemian, as authors are supposed to look, and
the first question went to him. What was it like to be a
writer?

3   He said it was tremendous fun. Coming home from an
arduous day at the hospital, he would go straight to his
yellow pad and write his tensions away. The words just
flowed. It was easy.

4   I then said that writing wasn't easy and it wasn't fun. It
was hard and lonely, and the words seldom just flowed.

5   Next Dr. Brock was asked if it was important to rewrite.
Absolutely not, he said. "Let it all hang out," and whatever

form the sentences take will reflect the writer at his most natural.

I then said that rewriting is the essence of writing. I pointed out that professional writers rewrite their sentences repeatedly and then rewrite what they have rewritten. I mentioned that E. B. White and James Thurber were known to rewrite their pieces eight or nine times. 6

"What do you do on days when it isn't going well?" Dr. Brock was asked. He said he just stopped writing and put the work aside for a day when it would go better. 7

I then said that the professional writer must establish a daily schedule and stick to it. I said that writing is a craft, not an art, and that the man who runs away from his craft because he lacks inspiration is fooling himself. He is also going broke. 8

"What if you're feeling depressed or unhappy?" a student asked. "Won't that affect your writing?" 9

Probably it will, Dr. Brock replied. Go fishing. Take a walk. 10

Probably it won't, I said. If your job is to write every day, you learn to do it like any other job. 11

A student asked if we found it useful to circulate in the literary world. Dr. Brock said that he was greatly enjoying his new life as a man of letters, and he told several luxurious stories of being taken to lunch by his publisher and his agent at Manhattan restaurants where writers and editors gather. I said that professional writers are solitary drones who seldom see other writers. 12

"Do you put symbolism in your writing?" a student asked me. 13

"Not if I can help it," I replied. I have an unbroken record of missing the deeper meaning in any story, play or movie, and as for dance and mime I have never had even a remote notion of what is being conveyed. 14

"I *love* symbols!" Dr. Brock exclaimed, and he described with gusto the joys of weaving them through his work. 15

So the morning went, and it was a revelation to all of us. At the end Dr. Brock told me he was enormously interested in my answers—it had never occurred to him that writing could be hard. I told him I was just as interested in *his* 16 answers—it had never occurred to me that writing could be easy. (Maybe I should take up surgery on the side.)

17   As for the students, anyone might think that we left them bewildered. But in fact we probably gave them a broader glimpse of the writing process than if only one of us had talked. For of course there isn't any "right" way to do such intensely personal work. There are all kinds of writers and all kinds of methods, and any method that helps somebody to say what he wants to say is the right method for him.

18   Some people write by day, others by night. Some people need silence, others turn on the radio. Some write by hand, some by typewriter, some by talking into a tape recorder. Some people write their first draft in one long burst and then revise; others can't write the second paragraph until they have fiddled endlessly with the first.

19   But all of them are vulnerable and all of them are tense. They are driven by a compulsion to put some part of themselves on paper, and yet they don't just write what comes naturally. They sit down to commit an act of literature, and the self who emerges on paper is a far stiffer person than the one who sat down. The problem is to find the real man or woman behind all the tension.

20   For ultimately the product that any writer has to sell is not his subject, but who he is. I often find myself reading with interest about a topic that I never thought would interest me—some unusual scientific quest, for instance. What holds me is the enthusiasm of the writer for his field. How was he drawn into it? What emotional baggage did he bring along? How did it change his life? It is not necessary to want to spend a year alone at Walden Pond to become deeply involved with a man who did.

21   This is the personal transaction that is at the heart of good nonfiction writing. Out of it come two of the most important qualities that the writer should strive for: humanity and warmth. Good writing has an aliveness that keeps the reader reading from one paragraph to the next, and it's not a question of gimmicks to "personalize" the author. It's a question of using the English language in a way that will achieve the greatest strength and the least clutter.

Can such principles be taught? Maybe not. But most of   22
them can be learned.

Discussing Content and Form

1. List the points of difference in the two attitudes toward
writing that are presented in this selection. Judging from your
experience, with which of the two do you agree?

2. How significant is it that Brock talks "about writing as an
avocation" (par. 1), while Zinsser speaks as one who writes
as a vocation?

3. What is the main point that Zinsser wants to make by
presenting the opposing views about writing? How can a
student learn the best way to write when there is little
agreement concerning the process?

4. Does Zinsser succeed in involving you in a "personal
transaction" with this essay? If so, try to account for your
reactions.

5. What does Zinsser mean by "the personal transaction
that is at the heart of good nonfiction writing" (par. 21)? What
does he consider the most important qualities in good writing,
no matter how it is achieved? Compare the qualities of writing
you admire to those Zinsser mentions.

Considering Special Techniques

1. The section of dialogue (pars. 2–15) is arranged in a
point-by-point structure, with the "he said" and then the "I
said" speeches tapping out the points in rapid order.
Comment on the effectiveness of this arrangement. Why do
you think Zinsser chose it over the unit pattern of presenting
all of Brock's views first, then his own?

2. Examine paragraphs 18 and 19 as smaller units of
comparison and contrast.
   a. In paragraph 18, how do the sentences and the
   paragraph pattern present the point-by-point
   organization in miniature?
   b. What is the function of paragraph 19? How does the
   writer change the sentence patterns in this paragraph
   to suggest likenesses rather than contrasts?

3. In paragraph 21, Zinsser says that "Good writing has an
aliveness." Point out qualities in his style that you think
contribute to liveliness. Do the short paragraphs have this

*effect? What is contributed by sentence openers such as
"But" (pars. 17, 19, and 22), and "For" (par. 17), which you
sometimes are told to reserve for mid-sentence connectives?*

*4. Zinsser refers to three writers represented elsewhere in
this book: E. B. White and James Thurber (par. 6) and (by
allusion) Henry David Thoreau (par. 20). From your reading of
these writers, determine what techniques they use that might
cause Zinsser to admire them.*

Generating Ideas

*1. Write an analysis of your writing process. You might
trace the procedure you followed in producing your last
paper, or you might explain your customary way of tackling a
composition. From your preliminary analysis, you should
become more aware of how you write, and such insights
should help you arrive at some conclusions for your paper.*

*2. Try the dialogue method of presenting contrasting
viewpoints. Here are some subjects that you might have two
real or imaginary debaters differ about:*

  *Pop versus classical music; country versus rock
  music
  American versus imported cars; small versus large
  cars
  The merits of a book and the merits of a film made
  from the book (Alex Haley's* Roots *is an example.)
  Two similar resorts or amusement centers (for
  instance, Disneyland in California and Disneyworld in
  Florida)
  The small town versus the city as a place to live; or
  inner city versus suburb
  Winter versus summer vacations
  Television versus radio as providers of good
  day-to-day news reporting*

*It may help in getting started to imagine the situation of the
speakers. For instance, a student who drives a Volkswagen
and his father who drives a large Buick might discuss the
merits of their automobiles. Look back at Zinsser's first
paragraph and notice how he sets the stage for the dialogue
of differences that ensues.*

*3. Zinsser says that a "personal transaction . . . is at the
heart of good nonfiction writing." Choose some piece of
nonfiction (an article, essay, biography, etc.) that engaged*

you fully and discuss the personal transaction that you felt with its author. What did you know of the person behind the work? How did he or she impress you? Would you like to know that author better or read more of his or her writing? These questions and those that Zinsser asks in paragraph 20 may help you get started.

    4. Try setting up a comparison and contrast paper regarding the ways people study:

        Studying with the radio on or off
        Studying in the library or alone in a room
        Reviewing with others for a test or cramming alone
        Studying late at night or early in the morning
        Preparing for a next class or test right after the
        assignment is made or just before the time it is due
Arrive at some conclusions for yourself, or, if you wish, make the paper an "advice for others" essay similar to Zinsser's notions about writing.

Joan Baum

Joan Baum, an Associate Professor of English at York College of the City University of New York, has a special interest in interdisciplinary studies. She has published articles in *Science News, Harvard Magazine, College English, New York Times Book Review,* and *Technology Review,* a publication of the Massachusetts Institute of Technology. She is at work on a book on the cultural history of algebraic terms, with particular attention to Omar Khayyam, the Persian philosopher-poet. The essay reprinted here, which first appeared in *The Chronicle of Higher Education,* is good evidence of her unusual combination of interests and talents.

The Reciprocity of Words and Numbers

1   Both mathematics and writing are deliberate, self-conscious acts. They share a sense of discipline. The ordering of words on a sheet of ruled paper, or of numbers in an equation, belongs to a common process of "composition": the putting of parts in their proper places.

2   To write an essay or to solve an algebraic problem, a student must define key terms, must understand guidelines for ordering terms in a series, and must strive for uniformity of order and tone. Factoring a quadratic equation and developing a paragraph both require consistent procedures toward the end of working out the main idea. Indeed, math and writing require such similar skills, in many respects, that the two otherwise disparate fields could reinforce each other—particularly in teaching.

3   Take, for example, the numeral 2, an Arabic symbol. The numeral can be used in several different math functions. Students readily see that 2 is part of a counting system, as in $3 + 2 = 5$. They also can see that 2 can be a negative integer, -2, as in $-2 + 3 = 1$. They accept 2 as a power, as an exponent: 3 to the second power is 9. And they see that 2 can also be the square root of 4 or the cube root of 8. Students will also accept the statement that 2 is a prime number. They recognize that the square of $(2X)$ is not the same as $2(X)$ squared. In short, they understand that punctuation—parentheses, brackets, value signs, and

function signals—are essential to reading, writing, and understanding mathematics.

But they rarely take advantage of a similar kind of flexibility in prose. They do not see that they can change verbs into nouns, past participles into adjectives, and the active voice into the passive voice to provide different emphasis. While they recognize that multiplication is really just fast addition, they tend to balk at cutting their own prose for conciseness and speed. Where they would not tolerate an incomplete comparison such as $X>$ (X is greater . . .) without "than Y," or entertain the contradiction $Y>X>Y$ ("X is greater than and less than Y"), they will argue over the right to say "more or less." They know that they can combine only like terms in math and that they must keep different logical developments distinct, but in English classes they tend to ignore injunctions against mixing metaphors, using constructions that are not parallel, or allowing ambiguity in technical exposition. In most cases they don't even recognize their mistakes in common sense. They see that algebra is a world of choice as well as one of rules—that $(a + b)c$ may be written as $ac + bc$—but they seem reluctant to acknowledge the benefits of transposing sentences so that forms can follow function.

A reciprocal relationship between mathematics and English might make a difference.

I began to see the potential for such mutual benefit a year ago when I enrolled in a freshman algebra course. Now, well along in courses in calculus and trig, I feel certain about those advantages, not only for the students but for myself. My original aim had been to study the subject matter of math, but I soon saw purpose in studying its forms and style. I began to watch myself as a student and started to gain a deeper understanding of some of the problems faced by my beginning students.

I had some suspicions early on in the algebra class that difficulties with English might be the source of much of the students' troubles in math. Those suspicions were confirmed when our algebra class first encountered problem-solving in English sentences. After weeks with exponential functions and radicands, completing the square and rooting out real, rational, and imaginary numbers; after hacking through secants, midpoints, and slopes, the class enjoyed the appearance of familiar language. Here were problems without Greek symbols and signs, material drawn from the real world. Here was English. Comparatively easy stuff:

8   "An observer on the fourth floor of a building determines that the angle of depression of the foot of a building across the street is 39 degrees, and that the angle of elevation of the top of the same building is 49 degrees. If the street is 70 feet wide, find the height of the building."

9   It seemed a simple enough problem. Draw a picture, pick the right trigonometric function, and work out the arithmetic. But what emerged was absurd: versions that only Mondrian could love—lines and boxes everywhere. Depression, not only of angle, was acute, and the explanations in our text presented in prose did not help.

10   The difficulty, as many teachers of math already know, is not with technical diction, but with ordinary words. "Hypotenuse" doesn't scare anyone, or "logarithm" or "sine." Most students will memorize most of what they are taught, anyway. It is, rather, the simplest parts of speech that cause the greatest grief—prepositions and conjunctions ("up," "if," "and," "or," "but," "to," "of")—little words that express logical relationship. Knowing how to do syllogisms and avoid logical fallacies is no guarantee that one can read examples in trig. For many students, this difficulty came as a surprise.

11   They began to see that words passed over quickly in general prose had to be carefully defined in math ("parallel," "coincident," "perpendicular"). And that compound or complex sentence constructions, ordinarily ignored, had to be clearly parsed in order to locate the logical categories, such as comparisons and contrasts, cause and effect. The class was driven finally to study simple structures and words—at my behest, in the math class. Then I went on a diction binge in my English class, where many of my freshman students were also my peers in math.

12   We looked up "algebra," "zero," "Pythagorean," gathering little bits of cultural history, some surprisingly

bizarre. With more time, we might have seen tapes from Jacob Bronowski's *The Ascent of Man* or have read chapters from Isaac Asimov's *On Numbers*. The class Aristoteleans were delighted to learn about the motto over Plato's academy door: "Let no one ignorant of mathematics enter here." The humanities majors were pleased to find that mathematicians had style and tone. And I was happy to discover another way of teaching freshman composition. The English teacher can join what S.A.T.'s and placement exams have put asunder.

There should be practical benefit, then, in presenting 13 math to students in English classes and English to freshmen in math. Students who are disposed to major in the sciences could strengthen their appreciation of writing if they were taught to recognize the syntactic features of all discourse. And students who elect to concentrate in the humanities could sharpen their semantic and logical skills by working from mathematics problems expressed in English but originally drawn from symbols, the metalanguage of math. Those with mathematical ability would recognize that prose, not formulae, should be their major concern, and those with mathematical deficiencies or fear might be tutored effectively if they were in a section of freshman English that unofficially introduced the language and the forms of math. Ideally, the freshman English sequence should be a year's course, with the first term devoted to exposition, where math could be introduced.

In college mathematics textbooks the answers are often 14 in the back of the book because it's not getting there that counts, but how you arrive. The corollary for the teacher of English is to stress drafts and revision rather than "right" answers. The English teacher can present controlled exercises in ordering ideas, beginning with the necessity of putting a topic sentence (whether overt or implied) into what mathematicians call "standard form." In English this means urging students to begin expository or persuasive essays with a positive statement—for the same reasons that it is easier to work with positive numbers in math than with their negative reciprocals (which is a guideline, not a hard-and-fast rule). If the teacher of English feels insecure at any point, he can call in a colleague in math to help with the comparisons, and if the teacher of math feels frustrated when his students can't read, he can call in the teacher of English to present specific lessons on certain basic skills.

15   Most students who take composition must also take math, and it seems inefficient for the freshman year to separate the basic requirements. Science majors, despite their disposition to deal essentially with formulae and fact, must also evaluate what they analyze, and also must invent. The intellectual and personal rewards of their studying composition would be eminently practical. And the rewards for humanities majors studying math would be ideal.

16   Too often, as proponents and critics in the two-cultures debate continue to point out, attempts at crossing the disciplinary divide are made mainly by those in the sciences and the technologies. Those in the humanities, with some exceptions in philosophy and history, tend to hang back. Fewer English majors think of studying math than math majors come over to study writing and literature. And few teachers point the way.

17   But here is Lionel Trilling, writing in 1972:
"[The] exclusion of most of us from the mode of thought which is habitually said to be the characteristic achievement of the modern age is bound to be experienced as a wound given to our intellectual self-esteem. About this humiliation, we all agree to be silent, but can we doubt that it has its consequences, that it introduces into the life of the mind a significant element of dubiety and alienation which must be taken into account in any estimate that is made of the present fortunes of mind?"

18   If the basics of reading, writing, and math have a common foundation that English teachers with no special training in math can be helped to see and to use, there may be reason to hope not only that students will fare better in all the basic skills, but that the sciences and the humanities, though different in subject matters, forms, and styles, may be perceived as part of the same culture.

Discussing Content and Form

1. What is Joan Baum trying to make teachers aware of? Find several places where she states her purpose explicitly.
   a. Is she directing her comments chiefly to English teachers or to math teachers? Defend your answer.
   b. How does her last paragraph extend or broaden the group she addresses?

2. What three things does Baum say that writing an essay and solving an algebraic problem have in common?
   a. Point out how she uses these three requirements as the basis for the three main divisions in structuring her comparison.
   b. Decide whether her essay is structured according to the point-by-point or unit method of comparison and explain your answer.

3. Baum points out that "the square of (2X) is not the same as 2(X) squared" (par. 3). You have probably heard jokes about misreading punctuation. For instance, explain how the meaning of this sentence differs if you enclose the "who" clause in commas:

   "Students who want A's study hard."

   Discuss other instances that show the importance of symbols in math and of punctuation in sentences. Why is it often easier to see the importance of such signals in working with numbers than with words?

4. Discuss Baum's statement that "In college mathematics textbooks the answers are often in the back of the book because it's not getting there that counts, but how you arrive" (par. 14). What does she think about the relative importance of the ability to solve a problem and the luck to arrive at the right answer?

5. What does Baum suggest that the English teacher should do to give the same kind of practice math students get from solving several similar problems? What is your reaction to carrying that idea into practice in your English classes?

6. Among signs math students typically must master are > and < , + and − , = , and the term given. Think of several ways to express each of these same concepts in language. What does this variety of word choice suggest about the comparable power of language and mathematics to show relationships between ideas?

7. What does the personal experience Baum cites in paragraphs 6 through 12 contribute to her argument that math and English are reciprocal?

Considering Special Techniques

1. Explain and discuss some of the techniques in writing that Baum says students ignore or fail to recognize:
"cutting . . . prose for conciseness and speed" (par. 4)
"mixing metaphors, using constructions that are not parallel, or allowing ambiguity in technical exposition" (par. 4)
"the simplest parts of speech . . . cause the greatest grief—prepositions and conjunctions ("up," "if," "and," "or," "but," "to," "of")—little words that express logical relationship" (par. 10)
beginning "expository or persuasive essays with a positive statement" (par. 14)

2. Baum's chief purpose is to point out similarities, not differences, between mathematics and writing.
   a. Analyze the sentences in the first two paragraphs to discover (1) the number of likenesses she lists, and (2) the balanced sentence structure that indicates these likenesses.
   b. What is the essential comparison made in paragraph 3? What is that in paragraph 4? How do the paragraph divisions correspond with Baum's outline of points about similarities between math and composition?

3. Show that the single sentence statement in paragraph 5 serves a dual purpose:
   a. How does it link—looking both back and forward?
   b. To what extent is it a thesis for the essay?

4. In paragraph 12 Baum makes several references to philosophers who have linked math and English.
   a. Explain any of the allusions that you know, or look up others and discuss the value of her references to these names.
   b. How does the quotation from the late Lionel Trilling (a philosopher and literary critic) relate to Baum's own conclusion in paragraph 18?

5. The methods of development do not occur in "pure"
state; that is, a writer may use one method predominately but
intersperse paragraphs that function in different ways, assume
different patterns. Analyze paragraph 13 to discover how
many benefits Baum suggests might be achieved by
presenting math to students in English classes.

6. Words to learn and use: disparate (par. 2); ambiguity,
transposing (par. 4); exponent(ial), radicands, secant,
midpoints, slopes (par. 7); hypotenuse, logarithm, sine (par.
10); asunder (par. 12); syntactic, discourse, semantic,
metalanguage (par. 13); corollary (par. 14); proponents (par.
16); dubiety (par. 17).

Generating Ideas

1. Write a paper in which you contrast those situations that
bear out the statement "it's not getting there that counts, but
how you arrive" (par. 14) with other situations in which it is
extremely important that you "get there."

2. Another comment about "getting there" is the familiar,
"It's not that you win or lose, but how you play the game."
Write a paper comparing and contrasting attitudes toward this
statement. You might consider points in favor of winning over
merely playing well, or vice versa.

3. Compare (contrast—one or both) your experiences in
mathematics and English. Or compare and contrast your
experiences in two other subjects—for instance, French and
English, history and English, biology and psychology, etc. You
might deal with the actual learning or simply make some
comparisons between the two courses.

4. Choose a pair of skills that you have acquired—for
instance, learning to swim and learning to drive. Compare
and contrast your experiences with the two by using a
point-by-point structure. You might start with the initial fears
you felt about each, move on to methods by which you
overcame the fear, then to the exhilaration of achievement.

5. Someone has said, "Science helps us live, and the
humanities help us live well." "The two-cultures debate" over
the "disciplinary divide" between sciences and humanities is
a frequent subject for both oral and written discussion. Write
a paper comparing the values derived from studies in both

areas; or, if you wish, take a stand that one area is more vital than the other and show values in contrast.

6. Read an essay or published speech that deals with "two cultures"—science and technology on the one hand, humanities on the other. (Many of the books and articles by C. P. Snow deal with the two cultures, or you might look up some of the writings of Jacob Bronowski, mentioned in Baum's paragraph 12.) Write a paper evaluating the points made about both areas of knowledge, analyzing or comparing and contrasting as seems appropriate.

7. If you have an interest in mathematics and music, you can easily write a paper showing the parallels between these two fields; or if you have knowledge of only one of them, check on the parallels, do some reading or interviewing to discover some of the similarities to use in developing a short paper.

Or write a paper explaining why several great scientists (some of them mathematicians) are also musicians. Here again you will need to utilize specific points of comparison between the two kinds of thinking and skill. Consider such figures as Schweitzer and Einstein, or go back into the history of Greece and discover the role of music in the thinking of Pythagoras.

Russell Baker

Russell Baker (b. 1925) was educated at Johns Hopkins University and began his career in journalism with the *Baltimore Sun*. In 1954 he became a member of the Washington bureau of the *New York Times*, and out of that experience came his first two books: *Washington: City on the Potomac* (1958) and *An American in Washington* (1961). Since 1962 he has written the popular *Times* column "The Observer" three times each week, and he has also contributed to almost every major magazine in the nation. His ironic and humorous commentaries are in the tradition of an earlier American newspaperman, Benjamin Franklin, who was the inspiration for "Ben Was Swell, but He's Out." This essay, contrasting the values of Franklin's time with those of today, is included in the collection *All Things Considered* (1965). Baker followed the Franklin tradition again by calling another of his collections *Poor Russell's Almanac* (1972).

Ben Was Swell, but He's Out

Old saws are wearing out. Take the case of "The devil finds   1
work for idle hands to do." As recently as fifteen years ago
when a mother caught a son loafing around the pornography rack at the corner drugstore, she could take him by the
ear and lead him home to wash the windows, with the
perfectly satisfactory explanation that "The devil finds
work for idle hands to do."

Nowadays, the world is different. With the march of   2
automation, idleness is becoming the national occupation
and sociologists will speak sternly to mothers who oppose
it. Since ever-expanding idleness is the goal of the
American economy, it is unpatriotic to mention it in the
same breath with Beelzebub.

The goal now is to rehabilitate idleness, and the first   3
step in every rehabilitation program is a name change.
During World War I, when Germany became the enemy,
the Hunnish sauerkraut was restored to respectability by
being renamed "liberty cabbage." In the same way, ugly
satanic old idleness is now rechristened "leisure."

Leisure sounds ever so much more decent than   4
idleness. It sounds like something that the uptown set
might go in for enthusiastically. Idleness was an evil to be
fought by placing such weapons as window-washing rags
and lawnmowers in the hands of the indolent young.

Leisure is merely another typical American problem to be solved by a nexus of committees, study groups and Congressional investigation.

5   Now, if a boy loafs around the pornography rack, it is merely because he has a "leisure-time problem." The solution is not to put him to work—the machines have most of the jobs well in hand—but to encourage him to take up the oboe or start a bee colony. In this way, we say, he uses his leisure "creatively."

6   The notion of creative leisure is mostly nonsense, of course. The sin that a boy may stumble into by keeping company with oboe players or going to bee-keepers' conventions is considerable, especially if his interest in oboes or bees is only a substitute for loafing around the drugstore.

7   The American economic system must, nevertheless, be justified. And so, if a boy follows the oboe path to sin, his parents are no longer permitted to blame it all on Satan; instead, the parents are indicted for failing to find a creative solution to the leisure-time problem.

8   There are many other pieces of ancient wisdom that have turned obsolete under the bizarre new American prosperity. Take "A penny saved is a penny earned." Sound enough in Franklin's day perhaps, but clearly subversive in 1965.

9   The first economic duty of every citizen today is to consume. To keep the economy booming we must consume with our cash, consume with our credit cards, consume with our charge accounts and then go to the bank to borrow the means to consume again.

10   It is obvious that if people began acting on the theory that "A penny saved is a penny earned," production would fall, unemployment would rise, salaries would be cut and the country would stagnate. Nowadays, the homily should read, "A penny spent is not good enough."

11   Then there is the collapse of "A stitch in time saves nine." To maintain even the present unsatisfactory level of employment, it is absolutely imperative that we never settle for the timely one-stitch job when a bit of dallying can make work for nine additional stitchers.

12   As we have seen in too many industries, the nine

stitchers thrown out of work either go on relief—which reduces the timely stitcher's take-home pay—or turn in desperation to braining the smug stitch-in-time takers for their entire pay envelopes. In this type of economy, the canny stitcher takes his stitch too late.

And, of course, there is old "Early to bed and early to rise makes a man healthy, wealthy and wise." Taken literally, this advice would now be disastrous.   13

In the first place, rising early would immediately raise the leisure-time problem to unmanageable proportions. The safest of all leisure-time activities is sleep, and the fellow who rolls out at cock's crow to work on his oboe is going to be thoroughly sated with leisure by breakfast time.   14

What's more, early rising tends to make a man reflect on the absurdity of his life. In this mood, he may very well realize that his way of life is insane and decide to change it by saving a penny, thereby triggering an economic catastrophe.   15

Very likely he will go to the office feeling energetic and healthy and, before he can stop himself, take a stitch in time, thus causing unemployment, raising his taxes and increasing crime. "Early to bed and early to rise" has had its day.   16

So, apparently, has Benjamin Franklin.   17

Discussing Content and Form

1. How many "old saws" does Baker consider in contrasting "then" and "now"? How many of the adages are familiar to you?

2. Baker first uses the word economy *in paragraph 2. Show that the relationship to the American economy is the "common denominator" that links all the sayings. On the basis of that link, what is the wider implication of the essay, the subject other than that stated in the first paragraph?*

3. In what ways does Baker say that "ever-expanding idleness" is a sociological problem? An economic one?

4. How many paragraphs are devoted to the first application of saying to practice? How many to each of the sayings that follow? Why does Baker devote more space to the first "old saw" than he does to subsequent ones?

*5. Point out several terms Baker uses to refer to the devil.
Explain what he means by saying that "parents are no longer
permitted to blame . . . Satan" (par. 7). How are parents
"indicted for failing to find a creative solution to the
leisure-time problem"?*

*6. Why is Baker's phrase "rehabilitate idleness" ironic?
Why is the notion of "creative leisure" fundamentally ironic?
Find other ironic phrases in the essay and explain the basis
for their irony.*

Considering Special Techniques

*1. As illustrated in his use of various names for the devil,
Baker achieves variety in his style by employing synonyms or
using slight changes in diction* (name change, renamed, *and*
rechristened *in par. 3*; unpatriotic *in par. 2 and* subversive *in
par. 8). Find other examples of synonomous words and
phrases that Baker uses to lend variety to his style.*

*2. Baker occasionally repeats words to give special force
to an idea. Note, for instance, the use of* consume *in
paragraph 9. Find other examples of such intentional
repetition. Does the repetition ever lead to exaggeration?
Explain.*

*3. Baker comments on the way we change words to make
a disagreeable idea more pleasant and acceptable. Such
changes (for example, the use of* sanitation worker *instead of*
garbage-man) *are called* euphemisms. *What are the
implications of Baker's replacing* idleness *or* sin *with*
leisure-time problem? *How does his point about changes in
language reflect the overall pattern of contrasting "then" and
"now"?*

*4. Baker makes references to Benjamin Franklin in the title
and in the last sentence. How, then, does the entire essay
relate to Franklin? In what ways does Baker use the title and
the ending to make his point and to give the essay unity?*

*5. Some of the single sentences are miniature patterns of
comparison or contrast. For instance, "Sound enough in
Franklin's day perhaps, but clearly subversive in 1965" (par.
8) is such a sentence. Find other balanced sentences that
present this pattern of "then" and "now."*

6. Words to learn and use: indolent, nexus (par. 4);
indicted *(par. 7);* obsolete, bizarre *(par. 8);* homily *(par. 10);*
imperative *(par. 11);* canny *(par. 12);* sated *(par. 14).*

Generating Ideas

1. Write a comparison and contrast paper explaining the recreative, as opposed to the wasteful or foolish, use of leisure time. Or compare and contrast the ways you spend your leisure time with the ways enjoyed by someone you know, perhaps someone from another generation. Here are some titles that may help you get started:

"But I Thought It Would Be Fun"
"Play Today, Pay Tomorrow"
"Never Dull—Until I Got Tired"
"Our Games and Theirs"
"A New Name for an Old Game"
"Boring to Some—Delight for Others"
"Two Saturday Nights"

2. Discuss Baker's idea that we are committed to idleness in order to boost the economy. Use any rhetorical method you wish.

3. Select several old sayings that you consider obsolete and write a paper comparing their original and their present-day applications. Or choose several other old sayings and show that they are as valid today as they once were. In developing the paper you might show how their application differs even though the "truth" still stands. For instance, "A stitch in time" referred to the literal stitching of a garment to prevent its unraveling. Today it has applications other than the literal.

4. Is the work ethic obsolete as Baker suggests? Are we headed for trouble if we disregard it? Take any stand you wish as to the value of work and support your views with appropriate examples.

5. A famous cartoon by J.N. Darling ("Ding") pictures several successful leaders beside a boy idling on a street corner; the caption reads, "They didn't get that way hanging around the corner drugstore." Write a paper about various places where people "hang around" or loaf; if you can, draw some comparisons between such hangouts. Treat the subject seriously or satirically, as you wish.

John Muir

John Muir (1838-1914) is sometimes called "The Father of the National Park System." He was born in Scotland, but his family soon migrated to Wisconsin, where they pioneered on a farm. Leaving the University of Wisconsin because of trouble with his eyes, Muir began his extensive travels to many of this country's wilderness areas, where he closely observed nature and wildlife. He became especially attracted to California's Yosemite region, which he wrote about in several books and which he helped establish as a national park in 1890.

Muir was a great admirer of Henry David Thoreau (see Chapter 1), although his writing style was shaped more by the English classics and the Bible. His best-known books include *My First Summer in the Sierra* (1911), *The Yosemite* (1912), *Stickeen* (a novel, 1909), and autobiographical and personal writings such as *Story of My Boyhood and Youth* (1913) and *Letters to a Friend* (1915). In "Shadow Lake," taken from *The Mountains of California* (1894), Muir contrasts the mountain region as he first saw it and as it later became. His message is still that of conservationists today.

Shadow Lake

1   The color-beauty about Shadow Lake during the Indian summer is much richer than one could hope to find in so young and so glacial a wilderness. Almost every leaf is tinted then, and the goldenrods are in bloom; but most of the color is given by the ripe grasses, willows, and aspens. At the foot of the lake you stand in a trembling aspen grove, every leaf painted like a butterfly, and away to right and left round the shores sweeps a curving ribbon of meadow, red and brown dotted with pale yellow, shading off here and there into hazy purple. The walls, too, are dashed with bits of bright color that gleam out on the neutral granite gray. But neither the walls, nor the margin meadow, nor yet the gay, fluttering grove in which you stand, nor the lake itself, flashing with spangles, can long hold your attention; for at the head of the lake there is a gorgeous mass of orange-yellow, belonging to the main aspen belt of the basin, which seems the very fountain whence all the color below it had flowed, and here your eye is filled and fixed. This glorious mass is about thirty feet high, and extends across the basin nearly from wall to wall. Rich bosses of willow flame in front of it, and from the base of these the

brown meadow comes forward to the water's edge, the whole being relieved against the unyielding green of the coniferae, while thick sun-gold is poured over all.

During these blessed color-days no cloud darkens the sky, the winds are gentle, and the landscape rests, hushed everywhere, and indescribably impressive. A few ducks are usually seen sailing on the lake, apparently more for pleasure than anything else, and the ouzels at the head of the rapids sing always; while robins, grosbeaks, and the Douglas squirrels are busy in the groves, making delightful company, and intensifying the feeling of grateful sequestration without ruffling the deep, hushed calm and peace. 2

This autumnal mellowness usually lasts until the end of November. Then come days of quite another kind. The winter clouds grow, and bloom, and shed their starry crystals on every leaf and rock, and all the colors vanish like a sunset. The deer gather and hasten down their well-known trails, fearful of being snow-bound. Storm succeeds storm, heaping snow on the cliffs and meadows, and bending the slender pines to the ground in wide arches, one over the other, clustering and interlacing like lodged wheat. Avalanches rush and boom from the shelving heights, piling immense heaps upon the frozen lake, and all the summer glory is buried and lost. Yet in the midst of this hearty winter the sun shines warm at times, calling the Douglas squirrel to frisk in the snowy pines and seek out his hidden stores; and the weather is never so severe as to drive away the grouse and little nut-hatches and chickadees. 3

Toward May, the lake begins to open. The hot sun sends down innumerable streams over the cliffs, streaking them round and round with foam. The snow slowly vanishes, and the meadows show tintings of green. Then spring comes on apace; flowers and flies enrich the air and the sod, and the deer come back to the upper groves like birds to an old nest. 4

I first discovered this charming lake in the autumn of 1872, while on my way to the glaciers at the head of the river. It was rejoicing then in its gayest colors, untrodden, hidden in the glorious wildness like unmined gold. Year after year I walked its shores without discovering any other 5 trace of humanity than the remains of an Indian camp-fire, and the thigh-bones of a deer that had been broken to get at the marrow. It lies out of the regular ways of Indians, who love to hunt in more accessible fields adjacent to trails. Their knowledge of deer-haunts had probably enticed them here some hunger-time when they wished to make sure of a feast; for hunting in this lake-hollow is like hunting in a fenced park. I had told the beauty of Shadow Lake only to a few friends, fearing it might come to be trampled and "improved" like Yosemite. On my last visit, as I was sauntering along the shore on the strip of sand between the water and sod, reading the tracks of the wild animals that live here, I was startled by a human track, which I at once saw belonged to some shepherd; for each step was turned out 35° or 40° from the general course pursued, and was also run over in an uncertain sprawling fashion at the heel, while a row of round dots on the right indicated the staff that shepherds carry. None but a shepherd could make such a track, and after tracing it a few minutes I began to fear that he might be seeking pasturage; for what else could he be seeking? Returning from the glaciers shortly afterward, my worst fears were realized. A trail had been made down the mountain-side from the north, and all the gardens and meadows were destroyed by a horde of hoofed locusts, as if swept by a fire. The money-changers were in the temple.

Discussing Content and Form

1. Although this selection opens with four paragraphs of description, Muir has a broader message. State this purpose in your own words. At what point do you actually realize that purpose? How do the descriptive paragraphs contribute to the overall idea?

2. Muir's description provides verbal "paintings" of three seasons at Shadow Lake. Why did he omit the fourth season? Why is the amount of space given to the descriptions of winter and spring considerably less than that given to the description of autumn?

3. Point out the qualities that make Muir's description very exact.

    a. How many words relate specifically to colors? How

do these help you visualize the scene? Find other
words that merely suggest color, e.g., "every leaf is
tinted" (par. 1).
  b. What is the effect of naming specific birds and
  animals?
  c. Which words evoke impressions of sound?
  d. In what way could Muir's writing be called scientific?

4. While the first four paragraphs compare and contrast the
three seasons, the final paragraph introduces a new pattern
of comparison. What exactly is this pattern? Why do you think
Muir uses it here?

Considering Special Techniques

1. Although Muir only implies a thesis, the meaning of his
essay becomes clear by his use of allusion in the two final
sentences. Even if you do not know the references, you
probably get his point. In what ways has Muir prepared you
for the concept of Shadow Lake as a region destroyed by a
horde of locusts and as a temple full of money-changers?
Check the following biblical references more fully. The plague
of the locusts was sent upon the Egyptian Pharaoh as a sign
that God demanded the release of the imprisoned people of
Israel (Exod. 10:4-5). And the story of Christ's eviction of the
money-changers is found in several of the Gospels: ". . . and
Jesus went into the temple, and began to cast out them that
sold and bought in the temple, and overthrew the tables of
the money-changers" (Mark 11:15). What does the use of
these allusions reveal about Muir's background and reading?

2. Muir's essay outlines easily, with the first four
paragraphs of comparison preparing for the final pattern that
leads to the meaning. The initial phrases in the first four
paragraphs signal the comparison pattern: "The color-beauty"
(par. 1) prepares for "During these blessed color-days" (par.
2); "This autumnal mellowness usually lasts" and "Then
come days" (par. 3); "Toward May" (par. 4). Which words or
phrases mark the pattern or division in the final paragraph?
Why are such links helpful in following the arrangement of the
paragraph?

3. Why does Muir call the green of the coniferae
"unyielding" (par. 1)? What is meant by a "feeling of grateful
sequestration" (par. 2)?

4. Point out examples of metaphor (an implied comparison
that says one thing in terms of another), e.g., "a curving

ribbon of meadow" (par. 1). Find examples of stated comparisons or similes, *e.g., "interlacing like lodged wheat" (par. 3). What do these figures of speech add to the quality of the description?*

5. Muir uses many cumulative sentences, *in which details are added to the main clause in order to enlarge and enrich the meaning, e.g., "Storm succeeds storm, heaping snow on the cliffs and meadows, and bending the slender pines to the ground in wide arches, one over the other, clustering and interlacing like lodged wheat" (par. 3). Find other examples of this cumulative pattern.*

Generating Ideas

1. Choose a scene that you once found particularly lovely but that has, like Shadow Lake, changed when you revisited it. Or choose a spot that was once attractive but that has since been made more beautiful. Write a short paper comparing either kind of place "then" and "now."

2. Muir was one of the founders of our national park system; but many people now think that the development of our national parks has led to masses of careless visitors, to the over-building of highways, and to the eventual desecration of the areas. Write a paper in which you explain the two viewpoints—the pro and con of developing large park and recreation areas. You may take a definite stand or merely explain the differing views.

3. Write a paper comparing the ways that a driver of a truck-camper and a hiker (or bicycler) might view a park or wilderness area. If you wish, assume the identity of both persons, using the "I" viewpoint to give the personal reactions of each.

4. If you have seen an area that has been quarried or strip-mined, describe what it might have looked like "before" and how it looks "after." Or read about some of the conflicts that have occurred in the western United States over grazing rights and write a paper comparing the attitudes of conservationists and ranchers. Some titles like these may get you started:

"We Have to Have the Coal"
"Keep Out the Hoofed Locusts"
"Dams and the Damned—Water Rights and Industrial Change"

7

ANALOGY: DISCOVERING LIKENESSES

"Compare the love of a male for a female with the love of the female for the male. It is the difference between a rivulet and a great deep ocean." These sentences from Ashley Montagu's paragraph about love (p. 174) involve another type of comparison known as analogy. In comparing the two kinds of love, Montagu draws an analogy between male love and a rivulet and between female love and an ocean, thus making the difference, as he perceives it, impressive. You may find this comparison vivid or helpful, or you may find it somewhat overdrawn; either way you react, the writer's purpose is the same: to illumine one thing by referring to it in terms of another. Donald Davidson, in his *American Composition and Rhetoric*, says that analogy "is . . . stating a possible or imagined likeness between two things" and that it "enables the reader to visualize and through visualization to understand."

Analogy is based on metaphor, and is sometimes referred to as extended metaphor. Metaphor too describes one thing in terms of another: "the tree of life," "a family tree," "the flower of love." We call some event "the final chapter." Or we say of someone who is pretending, "He's just playacting." But when we develop the metaphor further, not just to give a momentary picture but to clarify more fully, we use analogy as Shakespeare does in this famous passage from *As You Like It:*

> All the world's a stage.
> And all the men and women merely players,
> They have their exits and their entrances;
> And one man in his time plays many parts,
> His acts being seven ages.

In these lines the idea that life is fleeting and that men and women play temporary scenes is clarified by means of analogy. The comparison is not employed in order to make apparent the similarities and differences between two objects or ideas, but rather to explain something new or difficult (often an abstract idea) by showing its likeness to something familiar (often something concrete). The purpose of analogy is to make one-half of the comparison clear by using the other half. If it is apt, if it rings true and is fresh, analogy makes the ideas memorable as well as clear. Notice how the following analogy helps you both visualize and understand the values the writer places on ancient literature:

> In these old books the stucco has long since crumbled away, and we read what was sculptured in the granite. They are rude and massive in their proportions, rather than smooth and delicate in their finish. The workers in stone polish only their chimney ornaments, but their pyramids are roughly done. There is a soberness in a rough aspect, as of unhewn granite, which addresses a depth in us, but a polished surface hits only the ball of the eye. The true finish is the work of time, and the use to which a thing is put. The elements are still polishing the pyramids. Art may varnish and gild, but it can do no more. A work of genius is rough-hewn from the first, because it anticipates the lapse of time, and has an ingrained polish, which still appears when fragments are broken off, an essential quality of its substance. Its beauty is at the same time its strength, and it breaks with a lustre.
>
> The great poem must have the stamp of greatness as well as its essence. The reader easily goes within the shallowest contemporary poetry, and informs it with all the life and promise of the day, as the pilgrim goes within the temple, and hears the faintest strains of the worshipers; but it will have to

speak to posterity, traversing these deserts, through the ruins of its outmost walls, by the grandeur and beauty of its proportions.—Henry David Thoreau, *A Week on the Concord and Merrimack Rivers*

This analogy—describing great books as lasting architectural achievements, built of granite and growing increasingly beautiful with use and time—fulfills another requirement suggested by Donald Davidson: "Analogy is a resemblance that may be reasoned from, so that from the likeness in certain respects we may infer that other and deeper relations exist." Thoreau is defining, through his analogy, the qualities that he considers permanent in literature. And his words undoubtedly have made many readers "reason from" the analogy to speculate about these qualities.

Because analogy is memorable and thought-provoking, you will find it at the beginnings and at the ends of many essays. In both places the analogy serves a special purpose—to start the thinking and to continue it. Here is a striking analogy used as the opener for an article on the debate over genetic engineering:

> The rules of the game have not changed for upwards of three billion years: every living creature is dealt a genetic hand, the best stay in for another round. Five years ago in California a few biochemists learned how to stack the deck. They contrived a method for mixing, at will, genes from any two organisms on the planet. Genes cause a creature to be like its relatives and unlike anything else. They say, in a universal chemical language, "Wings, not feet; brown feathers, not blue; quack, not warble"; or "orange fruit, not yellow; pungent, not bland; round, not elongated."—William Bennett and Joel Gurin, "Science That Frightens Scientists," *The Atlantic*

Analogy may be subtle, a mere suggestion, allowing you as reader to fill in some of the comparison for yourself. Or it may be direct and obvious. Either way, it must seem suitable—all of the "parts" of the comparison as it is extended or developed must seem to fit. If they do not fit, the analogy becomes forced or strained. Two cautions:

analogies that are obvious or overworked may seem trite—for instance, comparing a family of various uncles, aunts, and cousins to a branching tree. But sometimes trying for an unusual or fresh analogy leads to one that may seem farfetched or artificial. For instance, comparing a group of children to many kinds of wild flowers might become rather ridiculous and funny, rather than apt or effective. Somewhere between the extremes of the obvious or hackneyed and the artificial or strained lies the happy analogy that rings true.

Sir James Jeans

Sir James Jeans (1877-1946) was a British physicist, mathematician, and philosopher. He was educated at Trinity College, Cambridge, where he later lectured, and he was awarded honorary degrees from universities in all parts of the world. From 1905 until 1909, Sir James was a professor of applied mathematics at Princeton University, and for a time after 1923 he returned to the United States to do research at Mount Wilson Observatory in California. His honors for pioneering work in astronomy and physics were innumerable; he developed the kinetic theory of gases and worked on various aspects of radiation. He is unusual among eminent scientists, for he wrote not only many learned books but many popular ones. H. L. Mencken once wrote that Sir James had the "gift for making the most difficult of scientific concepts understandable," and his books are still read and used for examples of lucidity in style. Even though his theory of the origin of the solar system is debatable, the clarity of his explanation of solar traffic is worth study and imitation. This selection comes from *The Stars in Their Courses*, published in 1931.

A View of the Solar System

Because of the way it came into existence, the solar system has only one-way traffic—like Piccadilly Circus. The traffic nearest the centre moves fastest; that further out more slowly, while that at the extreme edge merely crawls—at least by comparison with the fast traffic near the centre. It is true that even the furthest and slowest of the planets covers nearly three miles every second, which is about 200 times the speed of an express train, but this is a mere crawl in astronomy. The planets Mercury and Venus, which constitute the fast traffic near the centre, move, the former ten and the latter seven, times as fast. We shall find the reason for all this later; at present we are merely concerned with the facts.

1
Analogy of movement in solar system to one-way traffic in Piccadilly Circus (par.1)

Before we leave Piccadilly Circus, it should be understood that we cannot represent the solar system by putting up a statue of Eros in the middle to represent the sun, and letting

2
Analogy of size in solar system to objects in Piccadilly (par. 2)

nine taxicabs gyrate round it to represent the nine planets. The statue is far too big to represent the sun, and the taxicabs are enormously too big to represent planets. If we want to make a model to scale, we must take a very tiny object, such as a pea, to represent the sun. On the same scale the nine planets will be small seeds, grains of sand and specks of dust. Even so, Piccadilly Circus is only just big enough to contain the orbit of Pluto, the outermost planet of all. Think of a pea and nine tiny seeds, grains of sand and specks of dust in Piccadilly Circus, and we see that the solar system consists mainly of empty space. It is easy to understand why the planets look such tiny objects in the sky.

3

Analogy carried
further to explain
difference (par. 3)

Yet the solar system is very crowded compared with most of space. If a pea and nine smaller objects in Piccadilly Circus represent the sun and planets, the nearest of the stars will be represented by a small seed somewhere near Birmingham—all in between is empty space. Again we see how isolated the solar system is in space.

Discussing Content and Form

1. You probably are not familiar with London's Piccadilly Circus, but imagine it as similar to some traffic circle or a city square with a green or a public building at its center. How, then, does the analogy help you visualize and better understand the solar system?

2. The divisions of the analogy function to suggest various correspondences in the solar system.
   a. What image do you get of the movement and speed of the stars in their courses?
   b. Point out two comparisons that suggest size.
   c. Which details suggest emptiness, space?

3. Eros, the statue in the center of Piccadilly, is the Greek god of love. Why is it suitable to relate the sun to this central statue?

4. Look at the sky on a clear night and discuss the images evoked by Sir James' analogy. He mentions only one planet; name as many of the others as you can.

Considering Special Techniques

1. In effective analogy, one part must be familiar in order to make the unfamiliar or unknown clear by comparison. The familiar is called the "base" or "vehicle," while the unknown to which meaning is extended is the "tenor." Here Piccadilly Circus is the vehicle, the solar system the tenor. Find the other items that Sir James uses as bases in explaining the stars, their size, etc.

2. To determine the clarity and effectiveness of Sir James' analogy, try constructing a diagram of the solar system in terms of a traffic circle.

3. Although Sir James Jeans was both philosopher and scientist, he often wrote in language for lay readers. What in both vocabulary and the analogy itself tells you that this passage was intended for a general audience?

Generating Ideas

1. Write a paragraph or two in which you use an analogy to explain one of these natural phenomena:
    A sunrise or sunset
    An eclipse (of either sun or moon)
    The tides
    The action of a spring or geyser
    A tornado or hurricane
    A volcano or an earthquake
    The creation of a river bed or delta

2. Jacob Bronowski has written, "Man has only one means to discovery, and that is to find likenesses between things." Explain how you have learned something through becoming aware of a similarity. For instance, you might have come to understand political machinations better by thinking of a political party as a team engaged in a competitive sport, assigning various figures different positions of offense or defense. The analogy, of course, is only a start for your paper, not its entirety, and that is usually the way analogy is employed—it becomes merely a means to a more developed discussion of your ideas.

Annie Dillard

Annie Dillard (b. 1945) now lives in the Pacific Northwest, but when she wrote *Pilgrim at Tinker Creek* (1974), she lived in the Roanoke Valley of Virginia, the area she describes vividly in that Pulitzer Prize-winning book. She has since then published a collection of poems, *Tickets for a Prayer Wheel* (1975), and another book of philosophical-descriptive prose, *Holy the Firm* (1977). "Hidden Pennies" (editor's title) is taken from "Sight into Insight," a section of *Pilgrim at Tinker Creek* that first appeared in *Harper's* magazine, to which Dillard is a contributing editor. The selection is marked by the sensitive love for nature which characterizes all of Dillard's writing.

Hidden Pennies

1   When I was six or seven years old, growing up in Pittsburgh, I used to take a precious penny of my own and hide it for someone else to find. It was a curious compulsion; sadly, I've never been seized by it since. For some reason I always "hid" the penny along the same stretch of sidewalk up the street. I'd cradle it at the roots of a maple, say, or in a hole left by a chipped-off piece of sidewalk. Then I'd take a piece of chalk and, starting at either end of the block, draw huge arrows leading up to the penny from both directions. After I learned to write I labeled the arrows "SURPRISE AHEAD" or "MONEY THIS WAY." I was greatly excited, during all this arrow-drawing, at the thought of the first lucky passerby who would receive in this way, regardless of merit, a free gift from the universe. But I never lurked about. I'd go straight home and not give the matter another thought, until, some months later, I would be gripped by the impulse to hide another penny.

2   There are lots of things to see, unwrapped gifts and free surprises. The world is fairly studded and strewn with pennies cast broadside from a generous hand. But—and this is the point—who gets excited by a mere penny? If you follow one arrow, if you crouch motionless on a bank to watch a tremulous ripple thrill on the water, and are rewarded by the sight of a muskrat kit paddling from its den, will you count that sight a chip of copper only, and go your rueful way? It is very dire poverty indeed for a man to be so malnourished and fatigued that he won't stoop to

pick up a penny. But if you cultivate a healthy poverty and simplicity, so that finding a penny will make your day, then, since the world is in fact planted in pennies, you have with your poverty bought a lifetime of days. What you see is what you get.

Unfortunately, nature is very much a now-you-see-it, now-you-don't affair. A fish flashes, then dissolves in the water before my eyes like so much salt. Deer apparently ascend bodily into heaven; the brightest oriole fades into leaves. These disappearances stun me into stillness and concentration; they say of nature that it conceals with a grand nonchalance, and they say of vision that it is a deliberate gift, the revelation of a dancer who for my eyes only flings away her seven veils.

For nature does reveal as well as conceal: now-you-don't-see-it, now-you-do. For a week this September migrating red-winged blackbirds were feeding heavily down by Tinker Creek at the back of the house. One day I went out to investigate the racket; I walked up to a tree, an Osage orange, and a hundred birds flew away. They simply materialized out of the tree. I saw a tree, then a whisk of color, then a tree again. I walked closer and another hundred blackbirds took flight. Not a branch, not a twig budged: the birds were apparently weightless as well as invisible. Or, it was as if the leaves of the Osage orange had been freed from a spell in the form of red-winged blackbirds; they flew from the tree, caught my eye in the sky, and vanished. When I looked again at the tree, the leaves had reassembled as if nothing had happened. Finally I walked directly to the trunk of the tree and a final hundred, the real diehards, appeared, spread, and vanished. How could so many hide in the tree without my seeing them? The Osage orange, unruffled, looked just as it had looked from the house, when three hundred red-winged blackbirds cried from its crown. I looked upstream where they flew, and they were gone. Searching, I couldn't spot one. I wandered upstream to force them to play their hand, but they'd crossed the creek and scattered. One show to a customer. These appearances catch at my throat; they are the free gifts, the bright coppers at the roots of trees.

3

4

Discussing Content and Form

1. The thesis of the selection is stated clearly in the first two sentences of paragraph 2. Find restatements of the same generalization. Why does Dillard restate the generalization throughout the four paragraphs?

2. List several specific details that illustrate the thesis.
    a. How many of these details are linked to the "penny" by the suggestion of color?
    b. How many of the details illustrate the quality of "flashing" or suddenness of appearance?

3. Dillard uses several symbolic or figurative phrases; discuss the meaning of these:
    "The world is fairly studded and strewn with pennies cast broadside from a generous hand." (par. 2)
    "But if you cultivate a healthy poverty and simplicity . . . finding a penny will make your day." (par. 2)

4. How can poverty buy "a lifetime of days" (par. 2)? What is ironic about making great purchases with small coins?

5. What impression do you get of Dillard from this selection? Which words or details give you that impression?

Considering Special Techniques

1. Point out several examples of the repetition of words or ideas in the selection, e.g., "gift" and "gifts." How does such repetition aid in achieving coherence?

2. What special value has the opening narrative as an attention-getter? What does the incident make you feel about the writer?

3. Why does Dillard close by reiterating the image of the "coppers at the roots of trees"? Does the ending help you visualize and understand her meaning?

4. Compare the word order in the first sentence of paragraph 3 with that in the first sentence of paragraph 4. Explain the differences in structure.

5. What is meant by nature's "grand nonchalance" (par. 3)? Check the allusion in the last line of that paragraph: "a dancer who . . . flings away her seven veils." Does it help to know the allusion, or is the image sufficiently clear without that knowledge? Explain.

6. *Dillard's prose is poetic in ways other than the use of analogy.*
   a. *Point out examples of the use of sensory words to produce vivid pictures.*
   b. *Point out at least two examples of* alliteration *(the repetition of initial consonant sounds).*

7. *Words to learn and use:* compulsion *(par. 1);* tremulous, rueful *(par. 2);* nonchalance *(par. 3);* diehards *(par. 4).*

Generating Ideas

1. *You undoubtedly have found "hidden pennies," gifts of beauty or magic provided by nature. Write a paper that conveys some glimpses of beauty that you have experienced, those you have found either in nature or in your more everyday existence.*

2. *J. B. Priestley, an English essayist and novelist, has written a collection of essays entitled* Delight. *Each essay is a bit of praise, commemorating some delightful happening or discovery. Look up Priestley's volume and write about a delight or delights that you have experienced. If you can employ an analogy, all the better.*

3. *Write a paper in which you use an analogy comparing the idea of retrieving lost memories with one of the following situations or objects.*

   A photograph album of family memories, places visited or past friendships
   A trunk in the attic as a storehouse for tradition
   A jewel box in which old treasures are stored
   A cabinet of curios as a place for unexplainable occurrences
   A cupboard of broken dishes or a box of glass bits representing lost glories or unrealized hopes
   An old notebook of forgotten or neglected ideas
   An art gallery of grotesque portraits or a wax museum of strange figures out of the past
   A stamp collection representing forgotten but important events in shaping a nation or culture

Barry Lopez

Barry Lopez (b. 1945) is a free-lance writer and photographer. He grew up in New York and was educated at Notre Dame, but he now lives at the edge of the Willamette Forest in Oregon. He has published numerous articles and pictures, many of them in periodicals devoted to nature and conservation. His first book was *Desert Notes: Reflections in the Eye of a Raven* (1975). In 1978 he published *Of Wolves and Men*. Based on years of research and loving observation, this book provides fascinatingly original but thoroughly documented insights into animal life and into the relationship between people and nature. Two more books have followed: the first is a folk tale, *Giving Birth to Thunder, Sleeping with His Daughter: Coyote Builds North America* (1978); the second is a book of fiction, *River Notes: The Dance of the Heron* (1979). In "My Horse," which first appeared in the *North American Review*, Lopez describes his attachment to his truck and gives the reader a colorful glimpse into the life of a modern-day vagabond.

My Horse

1   It is curious that Indian warriors on the northern plains in the nineteenth century, who were almost entirely dependent on the horse for mobility and status, never gave their horses names. If you borrowed a man's horse and went off raiding for other horses, however, or if you lost your mount in battle and then jumped on mine and counted coup on an enemy—well, those horses would have to be shared with the man whose horse you borrowed, and that coup would be mine, not yours. Because even if I gave him no name, he was my horse.

2   If you were a Crow warrior and I a young Teton Sioux out after a warrior's identity and we came over a small hill somewhere in the Montana prairie and surprised each other, I could tell a lot about you by looking at your horse.

3   Your horse might have feathers tied in his mane, or in his tail, or a medicine bag tied around his neck. If I knew enough about the Crow, and had looked at you closely, I might make some sense of the decoration, even guess who you were if you were well-known. If you had painted your horse I could tell even more, because we both decorated our horses with signs that meant the same things. Your white handprints high on his flanks would tell me you had killed

an enemy in a hand-to-hand fight. Small horizontal lines stacked on your horse's foreleg, or across his nose, would tell me how many times you had counted coup. Horse hoof marks on your horse's rump, or three-sided boxes, would tell me how many times you had stolen horses. If there was a bright red square on your horse's neck I would know you were leading a war party and that there were probably others out there in the coulees behind you.

You might be painted all over as blue as the sky and covered with white dots, with your horse painted the same way. Maybe hailstorms were your power—or if I chased you a hailstorm might come down and hide you. There might be lightning bolts on the horse's legs and flanks, and I would wonder if you had lightning power, or a slow horse. There might be white circles around your horse's eyes to help him see better.

Or you might be like Crazy Horse, with no decoration, no marks on your horse to tell me anything, only a small lightning bolt on your cheek, a piece of turquoise tied behind your ear.

You might have scalps dangling from your rein.

I could tell something about you by your horse. All this would come to me in a few seconds. I might decide this was my moment and shout my war cry—*Hoka hey!* Or I might decide you were like the grizzly bear: I would raise my weapon to you in salute and go my way, to see you again when I was older.

I do not own a horse. I am attached to a truck, however, and I have come to think of it in a similar way. It has no name; it never occurred to me to give it a name. It has little decoration; neither of us is partial to decoration. I have a piece of turquoise in the truck because I had heard once that some of the southwestern tribes tied a small piece of turquoise in a horse's hock to keep him from stumbling. I like the idea. I also hang sage in the truck when I go on a long trip. But inside, the truck doesn't look much different from others that look just like it on the outside. I like it that way. Because I like my privacy.

For two years in Wyoming I worked on a ranch wrangling horses. The horse I rode when I had to have a good horse was a quarter horse and his name was Coke High. The name came with him. At first I thought he'd been named for the soft drink. I'd known stranger names given to horses by whites. Years later I wondered if some deviate Wyoming cowboy wise to cocaine had not named him. Now I think he was probably named after a rancher, an historical figure of the region. I never asked the people who owned him for fear of spoiling the spirit of my inquiry.

10   We were running over a hundred horses on this ranch. They all had names. After a few weeks I knew all the horses and the names too. You had to. No one knew how to talk about the animals or put them in order or tell the wranglers what to do unless they were using the names—Princess, Big Red, Shoshone, Clay.

11   My truck is named Dodge. The name came with it. I don't know if it was named after the town or the verb or the man who invented it. I like it for a name. Perfectly anonymous, like Rex for a dog, or Old Paint. You can't tell anything with a name like that.

12   The truck is a van. I call it a truck because it's not a car and because "van" is a suburban sort of consumer word, like "oxford loafer," and I don't like the sound of it. On the outside it looks like any other Dodge Sportsman 300. It's a dirty tan color. There are a few body dents, but it's never been in a wreck. I tore the antenna off against a tree on a pinched mountain road. A boy in Midland, Texas, rocked one of my rear view mirrors off. A logging truck in Oregon squeeze-fired a piece of debris off the road and shattered my windshield. The oil pan and gas tank are pug-faced from high-centering on bad roads. (I remember a horse I rode for a while named Targhee whose hocks were scarred from tangles in barbed wire when he was a colt and who spooked a lot in high grass, but these were not like "dents." They were more like bad tires.)

13   I like to travel. I go mostly in the winter and mostly on two-lane roads. I've driven the truck from Key West to Vancouver, British Columbia, and from Yuma to Long Island over the past four years. I used to ride Coke High only about five miles every morning when we were rounding up horses. Hard miles of twisting and turning. About six hundred miles a year. Then I'd turn him out and

ride another horse for the rest of the day. That's what was nice about having a remuda. You could do all you had to do and not take it all out on your best horse. Three car family.

My truck came with a lot of seats in it and I've never really known what to do with them. Sometimes I put the seats in and go somewhere with a lot of people, but most of the time I leave them out. I like riding around with that empty cavern of space behind my head. I know it's something with a history to it, that there's truth in it, because I always rode a horse the same way—with empty saddle bags. In case I found something. The possibility of finding something is half the reason for being on the road.

The value of anything comes to me in its use. If I am not using something it is of no value to me and I give it away. I wasn't always that way. I used to keep everything I owned—just in case. I feel good about the truck because it gets used. A lot. To haul hay and firewood and lumber and rocks and garbage and animals. Other people have used it to haul furniture and freezers and dirt and recycled newspapers. And to move from one house to another. When I lend it for things like that I don't look to get anything back but some gas (if we're going to be friends). But if you go way out in the country to a dump and pick up the things you can still find out there (once a load of cedar shingles we sold for $175 to an architect) I expect you to leave some of those things around my place when you come back—if I need them.

When I think back, maybe the nicest thing I ever put in that truck was timber wolves. It was a long night's drive from Oregon up into British Columbia. We were all very quiet about it; it was like moving clouds across the desert.

Sometimes something won't fit in the truck and I think about improving it—building a different door system, for example. I am forever going to add better gauges on the dash and a pair of driving lamps and a sunroof, but I never get around to doing any of it. I remember I wanted to improve Coke High once too, especially the way he bolted like a greyhound through patches of cottonwood on a river flat. But all I could do with him was to try to rein him out of it. Or hug his back.

18   Sometimes, road-stoned in a blur of country like southwestern Wyoming or North Dakota, I talk to the truck. It's like wandering on the high plains under a summer sun, on plains where, George Catlin wrote, you were "out of sight of land." I say what I am thinking out loud, or point at things along the road. It's a crazy, sun-stroked sort of activity, a sure sign it's time to pull over, to go for a walk, to make a fire and have some tea, to lie in the shade of the truck.

19   I've always wanted to pat the truck. It's basic to the relationship. But it never works.

20   I remember when I was on the ranch, just at sunrise, after I'd saddled Coke High, I'd be huddled down in my jacket smoking a cigarette and looking down into the valley, along the river where the other horses had spent the night. I'd turn to Coke and run my hand down his neck and slap-pat him on the shoulder to say I was coming up. It made a bond, an agreement we started the day with.

21   I've thought about that a lot with the truck, because we've gone out together at sunrise on so many mornings. I've even fumbled around trying to do it. But metal won't give.

22   The truck's personality is mostly an expression of two ideas: "with-you" and "alone." When Coke High was "with-you" he and I were the same animal. We could have cut a rooster out of a flock of chickens, we were so in tune. It's the same with the truck: rolling through Kentucky on a hilly two-lane road, three in the morning under a full moon and no traffic. Picture it. You roll like water.

23   There are other times when you are with each other but there's no connection at all. Coke got that way when he was bored and we'd fight each other about which way to go around a tree. When the truck gets like that—"alone"—it's because it feels its Detroit fat-ass design dragging at its heart and making a fool out of it.

24   I can think back over more than a hundred nights I've slept in the truck, sat in it with a lamp burning, bundled up in a parka, reading a book. It was always comfortable. A good place to wait out a storm. Like sleeping inside a buffalo.

The truck will go past 100,000 miles soon. I'll rebuild the 25 engine and put a different transmission in it. I can tell from magazine advertisements that I'll never get another one like it. Because every year they take more of the heart out of them. One thing that makes a farmer or a rancher go sour is a truck that isn't worth a shit. The reason you see so many old pickups in ranch country is because these are the only ones with any heart. You can count on them. The weekend rancher runs around in a new pickup with too much engine and not enough transmission and with the wrong sort of tires because he can afford anything, even the worst. A lot of them have names for their pickups too.

My truck has broken down, in out of the way places at 26 the worst of times. I've walked away and screamed the foulness out of my system and gotten the tools out. I had to fix a water pump in a blizzard in the Panamint Mountains in California once. It took all day with the Coleman stove burning under the engine block to keep my hands from freezing. We drifted into Beatty, Nevada, that night with it jury-rigged together with—I swear—baling wire, and we were melting snow as we went and pouring it in to compensate for the leaks.

There is a dent next to the door on the driver's side I put 27 there one sweltering night in Miami. I had gone to the airport to meet my wife, whom I hadn't seen in a month. My hands were so swollen with poison ivy blisters I had to drive with my wrists. I had shut the door and was locking it when the window fell off its runners and slid down inside the door. I couldn't leave the truck unlocked because I had too much inside I didn't want to lose. So I just kicked the truck a blow in the side and went to work on the window. I hate to admit kicking the truck. It's like kicking a dog, which I've never done.

Coke High and I had an accident once. We hit a badger 28 hole at a full gallop. I landed on my back and blacked out. When I came to, Coke High was about a hundred yards away. He stayed a hundred yards away for six miles, all the way back to the ranch.

I want to tell you about carrying those wolves, because it 29 was a fine thing. There were ten of them. We had four in the truck with us in crates and six in a trailer. It was a five hundred mile trip. We went at night for the cool air and because there wouldn't be as much traffic. I could feel from the way the truck rolled along that its heart was in the trip. It liked the wolves inside it, the sweet odor that came from the crates. I could feel that same tireless wolf-lope developing in its wheels; it was like you might never have to stop for gas, ever again.

30   The truck gets very self-focused when it works like this; its heart is strong and it's good to be around it. It's good to be *with* it. You get the same feeling when you pull someone out of a ditch. Coke High and I pulled a Volkswagen out of the mud once, but Coke didn't like doing it very much. Speed, not strength, was his center. When the guy who owned the car thanked us and tried to pat Coke, the horse snorted and swung away, trying to preserve his distance, which is something a horse spends a lot of time on.

31   So does the truck.

32   Being distant lets the truck get its heart up. The truck has been cold and alone in Montana at 38 below zero. It's climbed horrible, eroded roads in Idaho. It's been burdened beyond overloading, and made it anyway, I've asked it to do these things because they build heart, and without heart all you have is a machine. You have nothing. I don't think people in Detroit know anything at all about heart. That's why everything they build dies so young.

33   One time in Arizona the truck and I came through one of the worst storms I've ever been in, an outrageous, angry blizzard. But we went down the road, right through it. You couldn't explain our getting through by the sort of tires I had on the truck, or the fact that I had chains on, or was a good driver, or had a lot of weight over my drive wheels or a good engine, because it was more than this. It was a contest between the truck and the blizzard—and the truck wouldn't quit. I could have gone to sleep and the truck would have just torn a road down Interstate 40 on its own. It scared the hell out of me; but it gave me heart, too.

34   We came off the Mogollon Rim that night and out of the storm and headed south for Phoenix. I pulled off the road to sleep for a few hours, but before I did I got out of the truck.

It was raining. Warm rain. I tied a short piece of red avalanche cord into the grill. I left it there for a long time, like an eagle feather on a horse's tail. It flapped and spun in the wind. I could hear it ticking against the grill when I drove.

When I have to leave that truck I will just raise up my left 35 arm—*Hoka hey!*—and walk away.

Discussing Content and Form

1. Many people have thought of a car as possessing a personality and other human characteristics. What is your reaction to Lopez' comparison of his truck to a horse? Discuss the effectiveness of the analogy.

2. What special effect is produced by describing the Indian horses before mentioning the truck? What would be lost if the introductory paragraphs revealed the eventual purpose of the essay?

3. Lopez compares the truck to his own horse only after stating the analogy clearly. What is the essential difference in the way Lopez uses the two parts of the comparison—that to the Indian horses and that to his own horse?

4. Comment on the exactness and the vividness of the details. Do any of them seem superfluous? Why or why not?

5. Which details provide some insights into Lopez as a person? For instance, what is revealed by his statement, "I go mostly in winter and mostly on two-lane roads" (par. 13)? By the kinds of cargo that he carries in the truck? By his acting as his own repairman? Point out other statements that reveal his philosophy or life-style.

6. What does the writer mean when he says that his truck has "heart" (par. 25)? Why do some vehicles, such as the trucks of the weekend ranchers who "can afford anything, even the worst," lack heart as Lopez defines it?

7. Lopez only once (par. 18) refers to an authority or another writer—George Catlin (1796-1872), an American artist and writer who lived with Indians in the Midwest and in Central and South America. Which details in the essay might be derived from knowing the works of an artist-writer such as Catlin?

Considering Special Techniques

1. In a sentence or two, try to characterize the style of this essay. Then consider these specific questions:
    a. What elements help make the essay easy or smooth reading?
    b. What elements contribute to a sense of informality? Could you label the style "conversational"? Why or why not?

2. In the first few paragraphs, Lopez poses some "possibilities," e.g., "If you borrowed a man's horse" (par. 1); "If you were a Crow warrior and I a young Teton Sioux" (par. 2). How does the use of such hypothetical situations involve the reader in the essay?

3. What is the effect of the single-sentence paragraph (6): "You might have scalps dangling from your rein"?

4. What is the effect of introducing the Indian war cry "Hoka hey" at the end of the imaginative description in paragraph 7? Why (or why not) does this cry then make an effective ending (par. 35)? Why is it advantageous for a writer to anticipate what he or she will use as an ending?

5. Lopez' style is marked by the use of specific and vivid details. Examine several of these. Consider, for instance, what is gained by his use of place names. What would be lost if he said in paragraph 13, "I like to travel widely and have seen much of the country in the last few years"?

6. Consider the following sentence fragments that Lopez uses and draw some conclusions about their effectiveness:
    "I like it that way. Because I like my privacy." (par. 8)
    "You could do all you had to do and not take it all out on your best horse. Three car family." (par. 13)
    ". . .I always rode a horse the same way—with empty saddle bags. In case I found something." (par. 14)
Find still other fragments and speculate about the writer's reasons for using them where he does.

7. Lopez uses some words that are peculiar to a locale or a type of work. What is the effect of these technical or slang words: high-centering, spooked (par. 12); remuda (par. 13); road-stoned (par. 18)?

Generating Ideas

1. *Choose an object (car, bicycle, boat, piece of sports equipment, cabin, musical instrument, art object, heirloom, etc.) or an animal to which you have had a particular attachment. Use an analogy to explain that association, to clarify its meaning.*

2. *Lopez includes in his essay several memorable ideas, bits of philosophy summarized in quotable form. Use one of these (or another of your choice) as a starter for a paper:*

"The possibility of finding something is half the reason for being on the road." (par. 14)

"The value of anything comes to me in its use." (par. 15)

"The weekend rancher runs around in a new pickup . . . because he can afford anything, even the worst." (par. 25) (You may adapt this to fit other occupations, of course.)

"I don't think people in Detroit know anything at all about heart. That's why everything they build dies so young." (par. 32)

3. *Define "heart" as you might find it in things other than a truck or a horse; be sure to illustrate with one or more examples.*

4. *We often hear that America is built on waste, that we do not cherish objects that have lost their initial value. Using Lopez' feeling for his truck as well as other examples, prove that this philosophy is changing.*

5. *If you liked Lopez' description of the Indian feeling for the horse, look up* Of Wolves and Men *and discover some of the traditional beliefs that Indians held concerning wolves. Lopez states: "One of the problems that comes with trying to take a wider view of animals is that most of us have cut ourselves off from them conceptually. We do not think of ourselves as part of the animal kingdom. Indians did" (p. 98). In the book you will find many possible subjects for papers and discussion, but you might consider especially writing about some phase of human life by drawing an analogy between a human trait or habit and some animal characteristic.*

8

CAUSE AND EFFECT: ANALYZING REASONS AND RESULTS

One of the first questions we ask as children is "why?" "Why does it snow?" "Why did that team win the game?" We probe for causes, wanting this action or that thought explained. And we also want to know about effects: "Will connecting these wires make the motor work?" "Will putting in more money help win the election?"

A great deal of writing in your academic work requires the analysis of causes and effects. You may be asked in a history class to explain the reasons why the United States Senate failed to support President Wilson's dream of the League of Nations; you may be required in sociology to analyze the effects of a busing policy in the city schools; or in biology you may have to report on the cause/effect relationships between certain substances and the diseased respiratory systems of a group of rats. Similarly, in the business or professional world, you may be asked to issue a bulletin on the causes of a rise in coffee prices; or you may have to report on your search for causal relationships between asbestos and lung disease.

Whatever the subject or investigative task, writing based on cause/effect analysis requires careful observation and research. Analysis must be precise and well-founded in facts; often it requires experiment and proof. The "why" questions must get at fundamental causes, the true ones, and not stop with the merely superficial. Faulty analysis of causes results in false or careless inferences, in relating effects to causes that are inaccurate or only partial. For instance, from seeing one accident involving a Volkswagen you cannot infer that all small cars are dangerous. If a quarterback is injured, the team will not necessarily lose. The driver may have been at fault; the effect might be to make the team play harder. If writing based on cause/effect analysis is to be clear and convincing, it must show the logical relationships between the causes and the effects under discussion.

In the following paragraph the key phrase "two simple reasons" immediately points to the writer's purpose and his method of analyzing the causes of suburban sprawl, which he has described previously:

> Suburbia got that way for two simple reasons: first, because the developers who built it are, fundamentally, no different from manufacturers of any other mass-produced product: they standardize the product, package it, arrange for rapid distribution and easy financing, and sell it off the shelf as fast as they can. And, second, because the federal government, through FHA and other agencies set up to cope with the serious housing shortages that arose after World War II, has imposed a bureaucratic strait jacket on the design of most new houses, on the placement of these houses on individual lots, on landscaping, on street-planning, and on just about everything else that gives Suburbia its "wasteland" appearance. As Senator Harrison Williams, of New Jersey, put it recently: "The Federal Government, directly and indirectly, through the laws it writes, the programs it enacts and the regulations it issues, has contributed more than its share to the ugliness of our landscape."—Peter Blake, *God's Own Junkyard*

Cause/effect analysis, like other methods of exposition, may extend beyond the paragraph and become a dominant method for a longer unit. The complexity of the form increases, of course, in dealing with interrelated forces or ideas. But the presentation of causes and effects must always be based on the careful examination of evidence and must show clearly all inner connections.

Here is another paragraph that shows causes and effects. Again, the first sentence signals the writer's purpose and method:

> There have been a great many forces that have helped to shape the American household and the buildings that have kept it dry and warm and in some cases embellished it. The process of our domestication (some people might call it our becoming civilized, others our being tamed) has in some respects been slowed and in others hastened by our inability to stay put either physically or socially. Our mobility has revealed itself in our tastes in architecture, in our manners in the living room, and in the uses and characters of our parlors and dining rooms and kitchens. So, of course, has the wastefulness in which a nation overly rich in natural resources can indulge. So, too, has the inventiveness that has made our houses into museums of gadgets which replace servants that we have been, at least theoretically, rather embarrassed as good democrats to employ. Our beliefs in equality and our flouting of them have shaped our houses as surely as have our plentiful forests, our fascination with technology, and the surges of immigration of inexpensive labor from countries less fortunate than our own.—Russell Lynes, *The Domesticated Americans*

In writing to explain causes and effects, certain words serve as keys to the content and provide convenient links. The two sample paragraphs contain words such as "because" and "reasons," and phrases such as "has contributed"and "forces that . . . shape." A paragraph concerning effects might have phrases such as "several results" or "possible effects are. . . ." But both causes and effects can be stated without the use of such clues. In this selection almost every sentence indicates an interlocking cause/effect relationship:

> As the world daily grows larger, more complex, and more impersonal, man, more than ever, seeks the security of things. To fill in the void both around and within himself, man craves possessions to give his life an identifiable and pleasing shape. Paradoxically, however, by investing inanimate objects with power and significance, the individual, like

Lear, often diminishes himself. By seeking—whatever the cost—to be possessor, man often becomes, in turn, possessed. Or, as Ralph Waldo Emerson once lamented, "Things are in the saddle / And ride mankind."—Cynthia Golomb Dettelback, *In the Driver's Seat: The Automobile in American Literature and Popular Culture*

Here are four effects of the impersonal world on the modern individual: the search for security, the possession of objects, the diminishment of the self, and the possession by objects. The paragraph forms a kind of chain link, with each sentence providing the link to the next, for example: the "complex" and "impersonal"world causes "man" [to seek] "the security of things"; the desire "to fill in the void" [causes craving for] "possessions."

As in other methods of developing paragraphs and essays, the material should be narrowed and focused. The causes should truly fit the effect being analyzed. A paper based on cause/effect analysis avoids oversimplifications and mere suppositions. It contains well-reasoned inferences supported by concrete evidence. And it contains words and phrases that clearly and logically connect one idea to the next.

Carll Tucker

Carll Tucker (b. 1951) is a graduate of Yale University, where he was a Scholar of the House and Phi Beta Kappa. He became the editor of *Saturday Review* magazine in 1977, a position in which he succeeded the longtime editor, Norman Cousins. Before joining *Saturday Review*, Tucker had been a book columnist and theater critic for the *Village Voice*, a free-lance writer whose work appeared in the *New York Times Magazine*, the *New York Times Arts and Leisure* section, and the *New Republic*. From 1969-73, he wrote a weekly column for *Patent Trader* newspaper in Mt. Kisco, New York, and in the summers of 1973 and 1974, he served as director of the Poets in Person program at the Spoleto Festival in Italy.

Tucker's popular columns, "The Back Door," appear in each issue of *Saturday Review*. "Fear of Dearth," one of these essays, not only represents his amusingly philosophical style of comment but also reveals that one of his favorite pastimes is tennis.

Fear of Dearth

1

Statement of personal dislike for jogging (par. 1)

I hate jogging. Every dawn, as I thud around New York City's Central Park reservoir, I am reminded of how much I hate it. It's so tedious. Some claim jogging is thought conducive; others insist the scenery relieves the monotony. For me, the pace is wrong for contemplation of either ideas or vistas. While jogging, all I can think about is jogging—or nothing. One advantage of jogging around a reservoir is that there's no dry shortcut home.

2

Apparent dislike on part of fellow-joggers (par. 2)

From the listless looks of some fellow trotters, I gather I am not alone in my unenthusiasm: Bill-paying, it seems, would be about as diverting. Nonetheless, we continue to jog; more, we continue to *choose* to jog. From a practically infinite array of opportunities, we select one that we don't enjoy and can't wait to have done with. Why?

3

Some possible reasons why people jog (par. 3)

For any trend, there are as many reasons as there are participants. This person runs to lower his blood pressure. That person runs to escape the telephone or a cranky spouse or a filthy household. Another person runs to avoid doing anything else, to dodge a decision about how to lead his life or a realization that his life is leading nowhere. Each of us has his carrot and stick. In my case, the stick is my slackening physical condition, which keeps me from beating opponents at tennis whom I overwhelmed two years ago. My carrot is to win.

Beyond these disparate reasons, however, lies a deeper cause. It is no accident that now, in the last third of the 20th century, personal fitness and health have suddenly become a popular obsession. True, modern man likes to feel good, but that hardly distinguishes him from his predecessors.

With zany myopia, economists like to claim that the deeper cause of everything is economic. Delightfully, there seems no marketplace explanation for jogging. True, jogging is cheap, but then not jogging is cheaper. And the scant and skimpy equipment which jogging demands must make it a marketer's least favored form of recreation.

Some scout-masterish philosophers argue that the appeal of jogging and other body-maintenance programs is the discipline they afford. We live in a world in which individuals have fewer and fewer obligations. The work week has shrunk. Weekend worship is less compulsory. Technology gives us more free time. Satisfactorily filling free time requires imagination and effort. Freedom is a wide and risky river; it can drown the person who does not know how to swim across it. The more obligations one takes on, the more time one occupies, the less threat freedom poses. Jogging can become an instant obligation. For a portion of his day, the jogger is not his own man; he is obedient to a regimen he has accepted.

Theologists may take the argument one step further. It is our modern irreligion, our

4
Suggestion of deeper reasons (par. 4)

5
Economic reasons for jogging (par. 5)

6
Philosophical-psychological reasons (par. 6)

7
Theological reason (par. 7)

lack of confidence in any hereafter, that makes us anxious to stretch our mortal stay as long as possible. We run, as the saying goes, for our lives, hounded by the suspicion that these are the only lives we are likely to enjoy.

8

Acknowledgement of all views as plausible (par. 8)

All of these theorists seem to me more or less right. As the growth of cults and charismatic religions and the resurgence of enthusiasm for the military draft suggest, we do crave commitment. And who can doubt, watching so many middle-aged and older persons torturing themselves in the name of fitness, that we are unreconciled to death, more so perhaps than any generation in modern memory?

9

Suggestion of "real" reason: fear of dearth—depletion of resources (par. 9)

But I have a hunch there's a further explanation of our obsession with exercise. I suspect that what motivates us even more than a fear of death is a fear of dearth. Our era is the first to anticipate the eventual depletion of all natural resources. We see wilderness shrinking; rivers losing their capacity to sustain life; the air, even the stratosphere, being loaded with potentially deadly junk. We see the irreplaceable being squandered, and in the depths of our consciousness we are fearful that we are creating an uninhabitable world. We feel more or less helpless and yet, at the same time, desirous to protect what resources we can. We recycle soda bottles and restore old buildings and protect our nearest natural resource—our physical health—in the almost superstitious hope that such small gestures will help save an earth that we are blighting. Jogging becomes a sort of penance for our sins of gluttony, greed, and waste. Like a hairshirt or a bed of nails, the more one hates it, the more virtuous it makes one feel.

10

Conclusion: statement of personal reason for jogging (par. 10)

That is why *we* jog. Why *I* jog is to win at tennis.

Discussing Content and Form

1. Why does Tucker hate jogging? Why, then, does he do it?

2. What causes Tucker to think his fellow joggers share his dislike for the exercise?

3. The single word "Why?" at the end of the second paragraph obligates the writer to follow through with an answer to his question. Show that the balance of the essay is actually predicted in that single word.

4. Tucker first deals with a variety of individual reasons for jogging, and then turns to three groups of people who might have their own explanations for the craze for this form of exercise.

   a. How many individual reasons does Tucker give in paragraph 3? Does he presume to give them all? Why or why not?

   b. Identify the groups for whom Tucker invents theories or answers to the initial "Why?" Discuss the reasons assigned to each group. Why do you think the groups are treated in the order they are?

   c. In paragraph 8 Tucker says that all three groups may be "more or less right." Then he reinforces the theories of only two of the groups. Why do you think that he omitted the economic reasons (par. 5) from the summary?

5. The thesis of the essay—that the reason for jogging is "fear of dearth" rather than "fear of death"—is withheld until paragraph 9. What is the effect of building to this point rather than stating it at the outset? Why is the final reason offered only as a "hunch"?

6. By examining paragraphs 3-9, show that the reasons for jogging are presented in a pattern of increasing seriousness. What, then, is the effect of the addition of the personal reason in paragraph 10?

Considering Special Techniques

1. Discuss the value of the title "Fear of Dearth" as a way of conveying or emphasizing the message, and a way of catching interest.

2. A beginning and ending often "tie up" or enclose the material as a whole. Show that paragraphs 1 and 10 in this essay serve as a frame for what goes between.

    a. *The opening and closing paragraphs differ in tone from parts of the essay. Does the mixture of tones succeed? Explain your answer.*

    b. *Midway through the analysis Tucker first introduces his personal reason—beating his opponents at tennis (par. 3). How does the mention of his reason at that point help eventually to unify the essay?*

3. *Study these sentences as models for using the semicolon to combine closely related ideas. Consider especially any differences you can discover in the relationship between the combined thoughts. For instance, are they related to show contrast, cause and effect, or for some other reason?*

    "Some claim jogging is thought conducive; others insist the scenery relieves the monotony." (par. 1)
    "Nonetheless, we continue to jog; more, we continue to choose to jog." (par. 2)
    "Freedom is a wide and risky river; it can drown the person who does not know how to swim across it." (par. 6)
    "For a portion of his day, the jogger is not his own man; he is obedient to a regimen he has accepted." (par. 6)

4. *Just as this essay may be divided into various causes for taking up jogging, so may some of the paragraphs be divided into subordinate reasons for a main cause. From a diagram of the structure and links within a unified paragraph, you may discover ways of ordering your own ideas and making them coherent. A diagram of paragraph 6 might follow this pattern:*

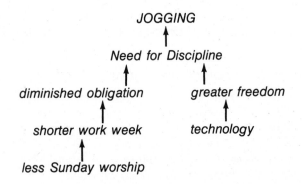

Note that the arrows lead from cause to effect. Make a similar diagram of one of the other paragraphs and explain how the organization represents logical and coherent thinking.

5. *Words to learn and use:* conducive *(par. 1);* diverting *(par. 2);* disparate *(par. 4);* myopia *(par. 5);* regimen *(par. 6);* charismatic, resurgence *(par. 8);* depletion, stratosphere, penance *(par. 9).*

6. *Explain the reference to "a hairshirt or a bed of nails" (par. 9). Why are penances or tortures thought of as a way of attaining virtue?*

Generating Ideas

1. Analyze the causes for a current fashion in physical recreation such as bicycling, cross-country skiing, karate, disco or some other form of dancing, racquetball, etc. Or analyze causes for the popularity of some game such as chess, backgammon, or bridge. Follow Tucker's pattern of probing various reasons for the general interest and, if you wish, differentiate those general reasons from any personal involvement you may have.

2. The suggestion that we have depleted natural resources and must now "fear dearth" is very grim. Write a thoughtful paper in which you consider the effects of the depletion of important resources. Most obvious perhaps are energy resources, but you might also write about depletion of soil through erosion or overuse, scarcity of some food or of food in general, imbalance caused by destruction of some form of wildlife, or the reduction of land area for agriculture caused by overbuilding of highways and spread of cities.

3. Tucker says that "Freedom is a wide and risky river; it can drown the person who does not know how to swim across it" (par. 6). Use his statement as a starter for a paper on the effects of freedom. You might agree with the idea that too much free time has disastrous results, or you might take an opposing stand and show the resulting values of having more leisure time to spend.

4. Is it true that we "crave commitment" as Tucker says in paragraph 8? Write a paper in which you analyze the reasons for making a commitment and/or the effects of finding a worthwhile commitment in a vocation or avocation.

5. A considerable amount of research has been done on the effects of television; certainly the "ratings" that television

networks covet are the products of research to discover what people watch and, by implication, what causes them to make the choices they do. Write a cause/effect paper dealing with some aspect of television watching. Narrow your topic to causes or effects as you wish and set some limits on your material. For instance, assessments of high school students' reading reveal that young people often choose a book because of a television production; you might write on the effects of television viewing on reading choices and habits. Or you might explore (by means of a few interviews) the effects of television watching during meals; does watching discourage conversation or merely give people more to talk about? If you are very ambitious, undertake some reading of published research in order to find a topic or to develop one.

Russell Lynes

Russell Lynes (b. 1910) was educated at Yale and has held positions in
publishing and served on the boards of many educational funds and
museums. He has written extensively about American culture and art and
the social forces that shape the national tastes, subjects on which he has
also lectured widely. His best-known books include *Highbrow, Lowbrow,
Middlebrow* (1949), *The Tastemakers* (1954), *The Domesticated Americans*
(1963), and *Confessions of a Dilettante* (1963). In "The Movers," from *The
Domesticated Americans*, he comments on American mobility and the effect
it has on national life. Lynes' detached and intelligent observations always
have the capacity to provoke further thought.

The Movers

On a winter afternoon in 1842, Charles Dickens, who had a
marked talent for setting the teeth of Americans on edge,
took a train from Boston, a city of which he had generally
approved, to Worcester, a matter of fifty odd miles. There
was a quality about the landscape that he saw from the
windows of the train that surprised and amused him. "All
the buildings," he wrote in his *American Notes*, "looked as if
they had been built and painted that morning and could be
taken down on Monday with very little trouble." Dickens,
of course, was used to stone houses in the English
landscape, houses that looked as though they were as
permanent as the hills about them. A New England village
where "every house is the whitest of white" and where
"the clean cardboard colonnades had no more perspective
than a bridge on a Chinese tea cup" made him wonder if
Americans ever intended to settle down. Not only did the
houses look impermanent; they looked unprivate.
". . . those slightly built wooden dwellings," he noted,
"behind which the sun was setting with a brilliant lustre,
could be so looked through and through, that the idea of
any inhabitant being able to hide himself from the public
gaze, or have any secrets from the public eye, was not
entertainable for a moment."

One of the reasons why Mr. Dickens got under the skin
of so many Americans was that his observations were so

frequently and so uncomfortably accurate. It was easy enough to explain, of course, that Americans built of wood rather than of stone because wood was so cheap and so available, but that did not explain either the disregard for privacy or why, as Dickens noted of the suburbs around Boston, American houses looked to be "sprinkled and dropped about in all directions, without seeming to have any root at all in the ground." Indeed, it appeared to him as though "the whole affair could be taken up piecemeal like a child's toy, and crammed into a little box." It was something more than white clapboards that gave America a here-today-gone-tomorrow look. It was more than just the newness of the houses and the fresh white paint, the meadows, "rank, and rough, and wild." It was something in the American character that, though Dickens did not define it, he seemed to discern: a restlessness, an urge to move on, a sense of there being unlimited space to be used or wasted, an unwillingness, in spite of all protestations to the contrary, to put down permanent roots.

3   The truth of the matter is that ours is a society as mobile as wheels, ambition, almost unlimited expanses of land, and an itch to sample the grass in the next pasture can make us. To move is as natural to the American as maintaining roots is to the European. Our restlessness and mobility are in our metaphors. In England a man *stands* for Parliament; in America he *runs* for the Senate. The American prides himself on his "get up and go." We think of progress as "covering ground" and we admire the man who "makes it under his own steam." The bright young man of promise is "a young man who's going places." The failure in our society is the man (or the institution, for that matter) who "stands still." The most famous exhortation in the American vernacular is "Go west, young man." We sing: "Where do we go from here, boys? Where do we go from here?" and "Don't Fence Me In," "How You Gonna Keep 'em Down on the Farm?" and "It's a Long, Long Trail."

4   There is more truth than humor for the American in the aphorism "Home is where you hang your hat." It is part of our mythology, rather than of our history or of our longest memories, that the American homestead is the symbol of

family continuity and stability and the stronghold of democratic institutions. We associate the homestead with the virtues of family unity and solidarity, the sacrifices that the family makes for its members, the peace and reassurance of the hearth, and the sharing of pleasures and tragedies. No legend, no nostalgia, is without some basis in fact, but enduring homesteads have been few in our history compared with the vast number of transitory homes, pickings-up and puttings-down, homes that were expected to be only stepping stones to something better. Our romanticized notion of the homestead reflects actuality about as accurately as a cheerful Currier and Ives print reflects nineteenth-century life on a farm. Americans are nomadic.

It is not possible to understand the relationship between the American and his house, which he is more likely to regard as a piece of equipment than as an institution, without considering the conflict that has been in progress for more than a century and a half between foot-loose Americans and those who have tried to get them to settle down and put permanent roots into the community. Some of the pressures that have kept us moving have been practical ones, some have been romantic. Sometimes our motives have been greed, sometimes escape, sometimes hope, sometimes despair, and sometimes merely the restlessness of boredom or loneliness. We have moved in order to avoid the snapping of an economic trap sprung by a failing industry or worn-out soil; we have moved because someone a long way off needed our skills and because nobody at home any longer did. We have moved because the character of neighborhoods changed and we no longer felt at home in them. We have moved because of divorce or because our children had been fledged. We have moved because of our social aspirations or because of our loss or gain in financial status. We have moved for the fun of it, because we got tired of the view from the terrace, because of another child in the family, or because we wanted a house with a picture window. We have moved for no reason at all, except for the sake of moving.

Discussing Content and Form

1. Summarize Dickens' description of the American scene (pars. 1 and 2). Is it still accurate? Explain.

2. One of the assumptions underlying Dickens' and Lynes' observations is that our houses reflect the character of the people who live in them. Do both writers build a strong enough case for this assumption? Explain.

3. In paragraph 3, Lynes gives examples of several metaphors that express American restlessness. Identify other popular metaphors that show the opposite tendency—a love of home and stability. Consider, for example, such song lines as "Over the river and through the woods, to Grandmother's house we go."

4. What commonly-held belief does Lynes refute in paragraph 4? Why is this refutation essential to his overall purpose?

5. How many separate reasons for moving does Lynes give in paragraph 5?

6. What is the effect of his conclusion that "We have moved for no reason at all, except for the sake of moving"? In what way does that statement relate to the assertions about the American character?

Considering Special Techniques

1. Notice the development in paragraph 5, the section that deals most clearly with why Americans move.
   a. Find several words that signal the fact that the structure is a list of reasons.
   b. How does the structure of several of the sentences reflect the logical relationship between cause and effect?

2. In what ways is the use of Dickens' observations an effective opener? Does it serve to do anything besides catch interest? Explain.

3. There are some subtle internal links between paragraphs in this selection.
   a. What relationships exist between the images in the Dickens description (par. 1) and the images of the homestead (par. 4)?
   b. Explain why Lynes refers to the nineteenth-century prints by Currier and Ives (par. 4).

4. *Words to learn and use:* protestations *(par. 2);* aphorism, transitory, nomadic *(par. 4);* aspirations *(par. 5).*

Generating Ideas

1. The noted historian Frederick Jackson Turner advanced the theory that the American character was shaped by the presence of a frontier, and that American life and character would change when the frontier vanished. Consider Turner's theory (look up more about it if you can) and write an essay on the vanishing American dream or the necessary changes in the pioneer spirit.

2. Huckleberry Finn, at the end of Mark Twain's novel that bears his name, turns his back on society and says that he is "going to strike out for the territory ahead of the rest." Write a paper explaining the reasons why you or some person or persons you know want to strike out for new territories.

3. Communities are sometimes classified as traditional or mobile, depending on whether they are places where families stay put or where there is constant migration in and out. Write a paper in which you analyze the community where you have lived most of your life. Into which type does it fall? What are the reasons for its stability or its constant change? How does the nature of the community affect attitudes and values, education, and social life? If you have lived in both types of communities, you might show why one differs from the other.

4. Use one of these topics to develop a paper by cause/effect:

    a. Why do people look for roots? Analyze some reasons for such things as visits to ancestral homes or countries, the collection and preservation of family heirlooms, the craze for antiques, or research into genealogy.

    b. Every year tourists visit restored villages such as Williamsburg in Virginia, Sturbridge in Massachusetts, and Greenfield Village outside Detroit. Account for this interest. Does it lie in a need to identify more strongly with our heritage or does it stem from mere curiosity?

5. Some people sentimentalize their childhood homes while others reject them. Account for one or the other of these attitudes by citing examples from your reading or from life.

Susan Schiefelbein

Susan Schiefelbein, a senior editor at the *Saturday Review*, writes on science, medicine, and the environment. Her articles have appeared in the *Washington Post*, the *Chicago Tribune*, and the *Congressional Record*. A winner of the Newswomen's Club of New York Front Page Award, she has also coauthored a series of articles on the ocean with Jacques Cousteau. She is at present working on a book about biological research into the regeneration of limbs. "Return of the Native," from a special *Saturday Review* issue on rural America, reveals her marvelous ability to make research both clear and interesting.

Return of the Native

LADY in a (theater) box: "Is there any culture. . .in Grover's Corners?"
MR. WEBB: "Well, ma'am, there ain't much. . . .Maybe this is the place to tell you that we've got a lot of pleasures of a kind here: we like the sun comin' up over the mountain in the morning, and we all notice a good deal about the birds . . . and we watch the change of seasons. . . ."

Our Town

1   For the first time in 50 years, more Americans are moving to small towns than to cities. In the three decades prior to 1970, nine million people left small towns and moved to urban areas; but in three short years after 1970, 1.5 million left metropolitan areas behind and headed for homes in small towns. Clearly, the once magical attractions of cosmopolitan life—the arts, the sophistication, the promise of success—no longer have the allure of those simple country "pleasures of a kind" so dear to Mr. Webb.

2   This trend is far too significant to be dismissed—along with organic gardens and communes—as nothing but a stale leftover from the Sixties. True, people who are moving from city to country are younger—by about 17 years—than those who are staying put; but statistics also show that they earn about $1,500 more annually, they have higher-status jobs, and they have on the average two years more education than their cohorts who have chosen to remain in urban areas. Nor are movers simply spilling over from city

to suburb: People are heading for small towns that are independent of cities. Although some of these areas are within commuting distance of cities and suburbs, the most spectacular growth is taking place in towns far from urban centers.

What is most important about this trend, however, is   3
not so much the types of people and towns involved as the fact that the shift represents an abrupt and dramatic break with the American tradition of urban expansion. For an entire century, people have abandoned the rustic amenities of country living in favor of urban sophistication and convenience. By the Sixties, city life seemed so important to our culture that the President's Commission on Rural Poverty called its report "The People Left Behind." Indeed they were: Some 200 counties had lost more than half their population to cities, and hundreds of others had dwindled almost as dramatically.

In the sociological literature, country folk have seemed   4
not so much "the people left behind" as the people entirely forgotten—as evidenced by the titles that line library shelves: *The Urbanization of America; The Making of Urban America; The Urban Prospect.* Even Robert and Helen Lynd's classic *Middletown* (1929) and *Middletown in Transition* (1937)—both recognized as being among the most valuable records on an American community ever written—deal not with a small town but with a small city—Muncie, Indiana, thinly disguised. During the 10 years in which the Lynds scrutinized "Middletown," its population grew from 36,000 to 50,000.

But even though the Lynds dealt with a middling-big   5
town, they said a lot about small ones in between the lines. In *Middletown*, rural America slowly became an anachronism as the town began to pulse with life, thanks to a natural gas boom and the advent of the auto and radio. Then in *Transition* the Lynds began to note the many admirable qualities of life Middletown's people had sacrificed in their rush to urbanization. " 'Progress'; 'growing' wealth and power; 'bigger and better' everything—these are some of the symbols that live daily in the skins of Middletown folk," the Lynds wrote. "People tend to lose each other. . . . One 'lives in' a town, 'makes one's

money there,'. . . rather than necessarily being an integral part of the town."

6   Despite the isolation that characterized city life, however, decades passed and the small-town exodus and concurrent urban explosion continued. People examined their options and chose to buck cosmopolitan problems rather than wrestle with rural ones.

7   The choice was not altogether irrational. The problems that plague small towns remain serious even today. Health facilities are the worst of the lot: In 1970 there were half as many doctors per 100,000 people in nonmetropolitan areas as there were in metropolitan areas. Chronic disease and infant mortality have far higher incidence in small towns, and old people who live in them have so many health problems—and find it so difficult to reach a doctor—that life for many of them ranges from the unpleasant to the unbearable.

8   Income is another problem. Nonmetropolitan residents earn only three fourths as much as city dwellers, and the difference is not wholly made up, as one might expect, in the lower cost of living. Worse, jobs are scarce: Should a factory close down outside a small town, there isn't another one a few blocks away to soak up the unemployed. Twice as many of the nation's poor live in nonmetropolitan areas as in cities. Finally, people who live in rural areas are less educated, and their attitudes are often very fundamental and conservative—partly because, sociologists say, they don't have the city dweller's exposure to many different ideas. As a result, small-town people may appear naïve or narrow-minded to city dwellers who are considering a move to the country.

9   Why then, with all the problems and after all these years, are so many city people now moving to small towns? Some reasons are obvious: Industries and businesses are moving to small towns, so more jobs are available. Better communications and transportation make for easier access to the city's benefits. The crime rates in cities have soared to such heights that many people are simply afraid to stay; the incidence of aggressive assault is twice as high in cities as in small towns, and the rate of robberies is 13 times as high. Another factor is pollution. Too many cities have taken

shortcuts in their race to profits, refusing to spend the money necessary to make their products or produce their energy in a safe, clean way. The environmental mess is no longer just a rallying point for people who are enamored of causes; statistics show that many of the people who are fleeing cities have lung and heart diseases caused by pollution and are too sick to take any more chances.

Sociological theories tell us more about the move to small towns than do any of the random factual or statistical explanations. In an article published in *The Geographical Review*, Wilbur Zelinsky hypothesizes that the more progressive a society becomes, the less the people flock toward traditional symbols of progress. As a society advances, he writes, economic features are not as important to them as human values, pleasures, and physical surroundings. 10

Another theory about the country's magnetic pull is developed with elaborate detail and admirable expertise in an issue of *The Annals of the American Academy* devoted to the "New Rural America" (January 1977). The numerous sociologists who contributed to this issue suggest that Americans have never wanted to live in the city at all; that the economic factor did not influence their choice—it *forced* their choice. Now that many Americans have achieved financial well-being, the *Annals* symposium suggests, they are concentrating on other needs—and are fulfilling these needs by moving to small towns. This theory is supported by Angus Campbell, whose studies show that although urban dwellers are satisfied with the specifics of life—hospitals, garbage collection, and so forth—they usually are not happy about life in toto. Rural people, on the other hand, are satisfied more with the whole of their life than with any of its parts. Another telling statistic from the *Annals* report: Six out of ten city dwellers want to move from the metropolitan areas; but nine out of ten small town-people wouldn't trade their life for any other. 11

Because the urban exodus of recent years began so suddenly, the sociological analysis of small-town living is currently more an art than a science. Besides examining the changing attitudes and values of Americans, sociologists have yet to address themselves to other pressing questions 12 raised by the new preference for small towns: How can they avoid the problems that plague the cities? How, for instance, can they cope with the population influx? Who should assume the high cost of providing services for rural areas? Few minorities move to small towns; how can villages avoid being characterized as racially and socially exclusive?

13   Social scientists will, for some time to come, be writing and publishing furiously on these topics. In the meantime, the Americans who have left the urban rat race and settled down in the countryside can finally concentrate, not on earning a living, but on savoring life itself.

STAGE MANAGER: "And this is Mrs. Webb's garden. Just like Mrs. Gibbs's, only it's got a lot of sunflowers, too. Right here's a big butternut tree. . . ." He looks at the audience for a minute. "Nice town, y'know what I mean?"

Discussing Content and Form

1. Sociologists devote considerable attention to demography, the study of statistics of populations, their growth and size, movement and concentration. What change in demographic patterns is the stated subject of this essay? How many paragraphs explain a past trend? Why is this background necessary to understanding the current shift?

2. Why does Schiefelbein assert that the present trend is not "a stale leftover from the Sixties" (par. 2)? What special significance does she attach to the age of persons now returning to small towns? In what ways does the current trend differ from the spread of cities to "suburbia" (par. 2)?

3. Why does the movement to small towns represent an "abrupt and dramatic break with the American tradition of urban expansion" (par. 3)? What problems still plague small towns?

4. List and discuss the reasons given for the exodus from cities. Consider any you might add. What essential distinction does Schiefelbein make between reasons that are observable and those that are theoretical? Why is such a distinction important in an analysis of causes?

5. Why are small town people more satisfied with "the

whole of their life" in spite of their many problems (par. 11)?

6. *In paragraphs 3-5 and 10-11 Schiefelbein cites several sociological studies and articles dealing with the topic she is considering. In what way is the mention of these sources important to the content of her article? What does she predict about future writing on similar subjects?*

Considering Special Techniques

1. *The quotations that Schiefelbein uses to introduce and close her article are from Thornton Wilder's* Our Town, *a play about life in Grover's Corners, New Hampshire, between 1901 and 1913. Some people might consider the play, now often used as a high school theater production, somewhat sentimental, but it has enjoyed wide popularity ever since it was first staged in New York in 1938.*
   a. *Discuss the value of opening and closing with the quotations. To what extent are the quotations effective even if a reader does not know the play itself?*
   b. *How do the quotations contribute to tone? What point in the content do they help reinforce? What, if anything, do they contribute to organization?*

2. *The references to sociological literature and government documents are part of the content of the essay, but they are also an important technique to lend strength to the writer's thesis. Note the number and variety of cited authorities. Why is it important to give the dates of these materials? What is the value of listing the titles in paragraph 4? What is achieved by labeling the Lynd studies "classic" and summarizing them more fully (pars. 4 and 5)?*

3. *Analyze the structure of paragraph 9, which presents a series of causes in smoothly linked sentences.*
   a. *What is the effect of the initial question? of the colon after the second sentence?*
   b. *Count the "reasons" and determine which of them are stated in single sentences and which are given further elaboration.*
   c. *Find the transition sentence that announces the final reason in the list. Why is it logical to leave the longest (the most fully developed) of the analyzed causes until last?*

4. *Go through the entire essay to discover some of the smooth links that give coherence between sentences and*

between paragraphs. Classify these transitional devices under several headings; here is an example of each for a start:
   a. *Linking words and phrases: "Finally" and "As a result" in paragraph 8.*
   b. *Repetition of words or phrases: "This trend" in the opening sentences of both paragraphs 2 and 3.*
   c. *Different forms of the same word: "chose" at the end of paragraph 6 links with "choice" at the start of paragraph 7.*
   d. *Echo words or phrases, linking the idea with different words: "Middletown" in paragraph 4 and "middling-big town" in paragraph 5.*
   e. *Time words that signal sequence: "For an entire century" and "By the Sixties" in paragraph 3.*

   5. *Words to learn and use:* metropolitan *and* cosmopolitan *(par. 1), explain any difference in the meaning of the two words;* amenities *(par. 3);* anachronism *(par. 5);* exodus, concurrent *(par. 6);* hypothesizes *(par. 10);* magnetic, symposium *(par. 11).*

Generating Ideas

   1. *Using your experience with living in a city, in a "middling-big" town, or in a small town or rural area, discuss the reasons why one might want to live there or why one might want to leave. You may make your essay entirely personal, writing from your own viewpoint about a specific town or city; or you may discuss reasons why people in general should come, stay, or leave the place you choose to write about.*

   2. *States and regions often vie with each other to attract industrial development, business growth. Imagine that you are employed as a researcher to help some business of your choice find a new location. Do some research on an area and write a proposal-paper setting forth the reasons for the move to the region you wish to suggest. Consider such factors as economic and environmental advantages, availability of manpower, educational, cultural and recreational opportunities for employees, and overall quality of living.*

   3. *Find an advertisement that invites people to settle in a particular area. For instance, find an ad for retirement in a town in the "Sunbelt," or an ad for jobs in Australia. After some investigation (do some library research or talk to people who have lived or visited in the area), write a paper setting*

forth the reasons why one should respond to the ads either positively or negatively.

4. Schiefelbein's essay examines some of the causes both for an earlier trend, the move to the city (par. 7), and for a new trend, the movement to the small town. Similarly, there are current changes in the choice of majors by college students, with a marked trend away from the liberal arts (majors in English, history, languages, philosophy, etc.) toward the business-oriented subjects. Choose one of the areas that is at present especially attractive and write a paper explaining the reasons for that appeal. Titles such as these may be suggestions:
"To Law School, To Law School"
"Women Flock to the M.B.A."
"The Lure of the Computer Sciences"
Or account for the lack of interest in some other field by writing on a topic such as "Forgotten Languages" or "Where Have All the English Majors Gone?"

5. Many courses you study in college will require that you analyze causes and effects, one or the other or both, related to various topics. For instance, in history classes you may be asked to study the effect of the early failure of the Maginot Line on the events of World War II, or to analyze the causes for one of the great nineteenth-century migrations to the United States and the subsequent effect of that migration on the U.S. labor market; or in an economics course you may need to analyze the rise or fall of interest rates or the effect of interest rates on the housing market. From one of the courses in which you are enrolled, choose a subject for a paper developed by analyzing reasons for some trend or event, for setting forth the effects that grow out of some action or event, or for dealing with both causes and effects of a happening, attitude, change, etc.

E. M. Forster

Edward Morgan Forster (1879-1970) was a British novelist, essayist, and short-story writer. Educated at King's College, Cambridge, he continued to live there and in the village of Abinger, which he used as the setting for *Abinger Harvest* (1936). He was associated with the famous Bloomsbury Group, the artistic and literary circle among whose best-known members were Virginia and Leonard Woolf, Lytton Strachey, Roger Fry, and Vanessa and Clive Bell. Forster's most widely read novel is *A Passage to India* (1924), a work in which he lays bare the prejudices and injustices of English rulers in colonial India. Among his other great works are *Howard's End* (1910), set in the country house where he grew up, and *Where Angels Fear to Tread* (1905) and *A Room with a View* (1908), both set in Italy, where he often traveled and lived for periods of time. After his early novels, he turned much of his attention to essays and literary criticism. "My Wood" is a delightfully personal and provocative essay which treats the human desire for more and more property.

My Wood

1   A few years ago I wrote a book which dealt in part with the difficulties of the English in India. Feeling that they would have had no difficulties in India themselves, the Americans read the book freely. The more they read it the better it made them feel, and a cheque to the author was the result. I bought a wood with the cheque. It is not a large wood—it contains scarcely any trees, and it is intersected, blast it, by a public footpath. Still, it is the first property that I have owned, so it is right that other people should participate in my shame, and should ask themselves, in accents that will vary in horror, this very important question: What is the effect of property upon the character? Don't let's touch economics; the effect of private ownership upon the community as a whole is another question—a more important question, perhaps, but another one. Let's keep to psychology. If you own things, what's their effect on you? What's the effect on me of my wood?

2   In the first place, it makes me feel heavy. Property does have this effect. Property produces men of weight, and it was a man of weight who failed to get into the Kingdom of Heaven. He was not wicked, that unfortunate millionaire in the parable, he was only stout; he stuck out in front, not

to mention behind, and as he wedged himself this way and that in the crystalline entrance and bruised his well-fed flanks, he saw beneath him a comparatively slim camel passing through the eye of a needle and being woven into the robe of God. The Gospels all through couple stoutness and slowness. They point out what is perfectly obvious, yet seldom realized: that if you have a lot of things you cannot move about a lot, that furniture requires dusting, dusters require servants, servants require insurance stamps, and the whole tangle of them makes you think twice before you accept an invitation to dinner or go for a bathe in the Jordan. Sometimes the Gospels proceed further and say with Tolstoy that property is sinful; they approach the difficult ground of asceticism here, where I cannot follow them. But as to the immediate effects of property on people, they just show straightforward logic. It produces men of weight. Men of weight cannot, by definition, move like the lightning from the East unto the West, and the ascent of a fourteen-stone bishop into a pulpit is thus the exact antithesis of the coming of the Son of Man. My wood makes me feel heavy.

In the second place, it makes me feel it ought to be 3 larger.

The other day I heard a twig snap in it. I was annoyed at 4 first, for I thought that someone was blackberrying, and depreciating the value of the undergrowth. On coming nearer, I saw it was not a man who had trodden on the twig and snapped it, but a bird, and I felt pleased. My bird. The bird was not equally pleased. Ignoring the relation between us, it took fright as soon as it saw the shape of my face, and flew straight over the boundary hedge into a field, the property of Mrs. Henessy, where it sat down with a loud squawk. It had become Mrs. Henessy's bird. Something seemed grossly amiss here, something that would not have occurred had the wood been larger. I could not afford to buy Mrs. Henessy out, I dared not murder her, and limitations of this sort beset me on every side. Ahab did not want that vineyard—he only needed it to round off his property, preparatory to plotting a new curve—and all the land around my wood was become necessary to me in order to round off the wood. A boundary protects. But—poor little thing—the boundary ought in its turn to be protected. Noises on the edge of it. Children throw stones. A little more, and then a little more, until we reach the sea. Happy Canute! Happier Alexander! And after all, why should even the world be the limit of possession? A rocket containing a Union Jack, will, it is hoped, be shortly fired at the moon. Mars. Sirius. Beyond which. . .But these immensities ended by saddening me. I could not suppose that my wood was the destined nucleus of universal dominion—it is so very small and contains no mineral wealth beyond the blackberries. Nor was I comforted when Mrs. Henessy's bird took alarm for the second time and flew clean away from us all, under the belief that it belonged to itself.

5   In the third place, property makes its owner feel that he ought to do something to it. Yet he isn't sure what. A restlessness comes over him, a vague sense that he has a personality to express—the same sense which, without any vagueness, leads the artist to an act of creation. Sometimes I think I will cut down such trees as remain in the wood, at other times I want to fill up the gaps between them with new trees. Both impulses are pretentious and empty. They are not honest movements towards money-making or beauty. They spring from a foolish desire to express myself and from an inability to enjoy what I have got. Creation, property, enjoyment form a sinister trinity in the human mind. Creation and enjoyment are both very good, yet they are often unattainable without a material basis, and at such moments property pushes itself in as a substitute, saying, "Accept me instead—I'm good enough for all three." It is not enough. It is, as Shakespeare said of lust, "The expense of spirit in a waste of shame": it is "Before, a joy proposed; behind, a dream." Yet we don't know how to shun it. It is forced on us by our economic system as the alternative to starvation. It is also forced on us by an internal defect in the soul, by the feeling that in property may lie the germs of self-development and of exquisite or heroic deeds. Our life on earth is, and ought to be, material and carnal. But we have not yet learned to manage our materialism and carnality properly; they are still entangled with the desire

for ownership, where (in the words of Dante) "Possession is one with loss."

And this brings us to our fourth and final point: the blackberries.

6

Blackberries are not plentiful in this meagre grove, but they are easily seen from the public footpath which traverses it, and all too easily gathered. Foxgloves, too—people will pull up the foxgloves, and ladies of an educational tendency even grub for toad stools to show them on the Monday in class. Other ladies, less educated, roll down the bracken in the arms of their gentlemen friends. There is a paper, there are tins. Pray, does my wood belong to me or doesn't it? And, if it does, should I not own it best by allowing no one else to walk there? There is a wood near Lyme Regis, also cursed by a public footpath, where the owner has not hesitated on this point. He has built high stone walls each side of the path, and has spanned it by bridges, so that the public circulate like termites while he gorges on the blackberries unseen. He really does own his wood, this able chap. Dives in Hell did pretty well, but the gulf dividing him from Lazarus could be traversed by vision, and nothing traverses it here. And perhaps I shall come to this in time. I shall wall in and fence out until I really taste the sweets of property. Enormously stout, endlessly avaricious, pseudo-creative, intensely selfish, I shall weave upon my forehead the quadruple crown of possession until those nasty Bolshies come and take it off again and thrust me aside into the outer darkness.

7

Discussing Content and Form

1. The book that "caused" Forster to buy his wood was A Passage to India, *first published in 1924. According to this essay, what, then, were the major effects on his character of buying the piece of property?*

2. Why do you think Forster limited his consideration to psychological effects, those pertaining to character, and ruled out economic matters? In your mind, is this limitation a good choice? Why or why not?

3. In paragraph 2 Forster refers to one of the parables from the Bible, a story in which Christ admonishes that it is harder for a rich man to enter heaven than it is for a camel to go through the eye of a needle (Matt. 19: 23-26). Go on through the essay and find other instances of Forster's way of suggesting that riches can be a deterrent to "gaining heaven."

    a. Check on Tolstoy's ideas concerning wealth and discuss them.

    b. Explain the line, "the ascent of a fourteen-stone bishop into a pulpit is thus the exact antithesis of the coming of the Son of Man" (par. 2).

    c. Look up the story of Dives and Lazarus (par. 7) and explain the relationship of that parable to Forster's fear of selfishness.

4. In paragraph 2 Forster names the result—the "weight" of his property; in paragraph 4 he never does name a trait of character outright. What, then, is the effect that he sustains from the incident of Mrs. Henessy's bird? What is the significance of his identification with Canute and Alexander the Great?

5. How does property lead to both walling in and fencing out (par. 7)? Discuss the four qualities Forster names in the last sentence of the final paragraph. Relate each of those four qualities to the paragraphs that they summarize.

6. Overall, would you say that this essay is humorous, serious, or a combination of the two? Defend your answer by citing evidence from the essay.

Considering Special Techniques

1. A writer must always decide how much of the pattern of an essay to announce, how much "skeletal structure" to make obvious.

    a. Identify the marking words and phrases that let you know exactly what the outline of Forster's essay is.

    b. What is the probable reason for setting the second announcement and the final one off as single sentences—paragraphs 3 and 6?

    c. Forster's ideas here are rather subtle. Why, then, do you think he chose to make the structure so apparent? Decide whether you think his choice was a good one and defend your answer.

2. Point out features in Forster's style that make this essay conversational and personal. You might begin with the phrase

"blast it" from paragraph 1, or with the use of the personal pronouns. Go on through the essay and find similar features that help develop the conversational tone.

3. Just as the overall structure of the essay shows cause and effects, so several sentences also show that relationship. For instance, see paragraph 2:

> *". . . if you have a lot of things you cannot move about a lot, . . . furniture requires dusting, dusters require servants, servants require insurance stamps, and the whole tangle of them makes you think twice. . . . "*

Find other illustrations of the cause/effect relationships expressed in single sentences or in short units within paragraphs.

4. Forster makes some interesting shifts in using personal pronouns. Much of the time he talks about himself—"I" and "me" and "my" figure prominently and serve as the viewpoint central to the essay.

> *a. Find examples of the inclusion of the reader as a "you," either directly expressed or implied. Is there a person implied in the questions of paragraph 1? What is the effect of "Don't let's" and "Let's" in that paragraph?*
>
> *b. Decide why Forster shifts to third person at the opening of paragraph 5—"In the third place, property makes its owner feel that he ought to do something," etc. How does the use of "he" there differ from that in the incidents or stories that serve as illustrations?*
>
> *c. Who are the "we" and "our" referred to in the last half of paragraph 5?*

Draw some conclusions about the clarity or lack of it caused by this variety of pronouns. Is there a risk involved in such shifts? Explain your answer.

5. Go through the essay and note the frequent use of the dash, a mark little used in formal writing but quite common in conversational styles such as Forster's. Determine how the dash is used to give emphasis or to show a short break in thought, and to enclose an interpolated element within a sentence.

6. Words to learn and use: parable, crystalline, asceticism, antithesis (par. 2); carnal, carnality (par. 5); traverses, avaricious (par. 7). Note the words that mark Forster as a British writer: his spelling of "cheque" (par. 1); measuring weight as "stone" (par. 2); "chap" (par. 7).

Generating Ideas

1. Examine an essay you have written recently and write a short analysis of the ways you clarified your system of outlining. Or compare the evidence of your structure to that of Forster in "My Wood." Summarize by drawing some conclusions about the value of being obvious or subtle in handling structure.

2. Have you ever been the recipient of a gift or the winner of some prize or honor that you feel may have changed your attitude or even your character? Write a paper in which you explain the effects of some event of that nature in your life.

3. We often hear the phrase, "Since he has . . . , it has gone to his head." Such statements are made about people who inherit money, about winners of Olympic gold medals, about bonus-baby athletes, about people who are elected or promoted in office, etc. Write an essay in which you discuss some public figure who you think has been changed by achievement or honor; analyze the cause and effect relationship you observe.

4. Several of Forster's ideas are expressed in single sentences which might serve as topics for themes. Consider one of these as a topic from which you can frame a thesis of your own:

"Creation, property, enjoyment form a sinister trinity in the human mind." (par. 5)

". . . we have not yet learned to manage our materialism and carnality properly. . . ." (par. 5)

"'Possession is one with loss.'"—Forster quotes from Dante. (par. 5)

"Pray, does my wood belong to me or doesn't it? And, if it does, should I not own it best by allowing no one else to walk there?" (par. 7)

5. In Walden, Henry David Thoreau (see p. 17) speaks at length on the problems that come with ownership of property. In the chapter entitled "Where I Live, and What I Lived For," he tells of the time when he almost bought the "Hollowell farm" that particularly attracted him. The owner's wife changed her mind and refused to sell to Thoreau, but from the experience he learned a lesson for he "retained the landscape" and lost the work. He could go on enjoying the vista of the farm, a yield that he could carry off "without a wheelbarrow." His final conclusion about property: "It makes but little difference whether you are committed to a farm or the county jail."

    a. Write a paper arguing for or against Thoreau's conclusion. Is property too much responsibility, too much work, to be worth it? If you consider such a stand "sour grapes" from one who has no property, write from that standpoint.

    b. Or apply the philosophy to some object in your experience. For instance, have you ever purchased a car and found that it made life more complicated than ever? Have you coveted a television set for your room and found that it dominated your life too fully? Have you ever bought some piece of clothing that proved to need too much care to be serviceable? Add other ideas of your own.

    6. Do some research on some person of wealth, either a living person or someone from the past; write a paper discussing the effects, as these appear from evidence you gather, of property on that person's life or on family life. You should, of course, consider what appear to be both rewards and drawbacks of great wealth.

Enid Nemy

Enid Nemy was born in Winnipeg, Canada, and educated at United
College in Winnipeg and at the University of Manitoba. After extensive
experience in journalism in her native country, where she was a reporter
for the *Montreal Standard* and the *Montreal Herald* as well as an editor for
the *Canadian Press* and a writer and broadcaster for the Canadian
Broadcasting Corporation, she joined the staff of the *New York Times* in
1963. There she writes on a variety of subjects, covering everything from
interviews with prominent men and women to feature stories on topics as
diverse as human frailties and parties. She has won an award from the
New York Newspaper Women's Club and a Front Page Award from the
New York Newspaper Guild. Her column "New Yorkers, Etc.," appearing
each Wednesday in the *Living* section of the *Times*, takes in the glitter,
activities, diversions, foibles and interests of the city's trend setters. The
essay that follows, from that column, shows Miss Nemy's ability to treat a
human foible both lightly and thoughtfully.

Someone Else's Always Looks Better

1   The other day, a young woman who is no slouch in the way
of looks, mentioned that she had the names and addresses
of 24 hairdressers buried at the bottom of her handbag.

2   "Whenever I see a hairdo I like, I always ask who did it
because I intend to rush over there and have them try the
same style on me," she said.

3   "Of course," she added, "I never do because by the time
I get around to thinking of it again, I've seen another one I
like."

4   It was pointed out that she had just recently changed
her own hair style, and that she looked terrific. Why, she
was asked, did she want yet another new look?

5   "Someone else's always looks better," she said.

6   Too true. Someone else's always does look better, and it
needn't be hair. Someone else's pants fit better, scarves
look smarter, wrist watch looks marvelous, jewelry is just
right, sport jacket is snappier and necktie is what neckties
should be.

7   Not everyone else's. No. Just some. And the some don't
belong to any one category.

8   It's easy enough to understand styles that filter down

from well-known personalities. Madame Pompadour at one time favored a puffy front roll and we're still living with pompadour hair styles in various parts of the country. Jacqueline Onassis, who was then Jacqueline Kennedy, must have shuddered when she saw versions of her pill box hat on thousands of unlikely heads, and Gloria Steinem may have had a similar reaction when her aviator glasses appeared on every second or third bespectacled face.

Recently, an executive who runs a major international company dictated a letter to his shirtmaker. He wanted epaulets added to the dozen shirts he had just ordered. He had never had epaulets before, but he had seen them on a shirt of a fellow exerciser at his health club. 9

"It wasn't that I hadn't seen them before," he said. "But I just thought that the fellow looked good. His shirt looked better than mine." 10

What isn't quite so easy to understand is why most of us, even men and women who consider themselves basically secure, are not infrequently given to self-doubts about something we were happy with only moments earlier. The watch just acquired at a horrifying price isn't as handsome as the one on the wrist of the woman at the next table. Or, assuming the watch is still O.K., how gauche to wear it on one wrist and skinny bracelets on the other, when they could be combined, as the woman across the way has done. Why does the other person always think of these things? And just who was that person who first tied a scarf around the handle of her handbag? Not us. 11

Some of these earth-shattering ideas are as trivial and ephemeral as the Hula-Hoop, but that isn't the point. We think they're right at the time, for a time, and suddenly the sedate scarf at the neck looks klutzy. It doesn't matter a bit that it makes more sense to tie a scarf at the neck than on a handbag. Sense has always been way down on the totem pole when it comes to almost anything, including the way we see ourselves. Including the way we see others, and the way we react to the things they do. 12

The apartment has just been painted. Breathe a sigh of relief as the painter goes out the door. The place is 13 gorgeous, pure and white, and the paintings look great. A few weeks later, there's a party in an apartment with glossy chocolate brown walls. What style! What sophistication! Those brown walls are terrific. We're still happy, but maybe not quite as . . . well, maybe not even so happy . . . darn it, we shouldn't have rushed into white.

14   While on the subject of apartments, why is it that after years of yearning after an uncluttered look, when all the knickknacks, objet and tsatskes have finally gone to the thrift shop, a walk into a dwelling with scarcely an inch of breathing space brings forth qualms, doubts, regrets. Somehow, all that stuff and nonsense seems warm and homey and lived in.

15   It's downright frustrating. There's only small comfort in knowing that the malady is almost universal.

Discussing Content and Form

1. *Enid Nemy declares that people in general want what others have, that the desire for attributes and possessions belonging to others is a universal "malady." Find several instances where she asks "why" this malady is so pervasive. What answers to the "why" does she suggest? Can you offer still other reasons why people want what others have?*

2. *To what extent do you think Nemy suggests that people are envious or jealous? How (and why) does she avoid saying that the desire to be like others is necessarily wrong or right?*

3. *Why do popular figures have a strong influence upon styles? Why is their influence a more understandable cause than some others?*

4. *Nemy says that it is hard to understand the desire in "men and women who consider themselves basically secure" (par. 11). Why might this be true? Why does she dismiss "sense" as an influence in human wishes?*

5. *Which of the examples Nemy describes have you yourself experienced? What do you think causes such desires on your part?*

Considering Special Techniques

1. *Although Nemy employs the short paragraphs characteristic of journalistic writing, she develops some*

paragraphs more fully than others. What is the effect of interspersing the short and the long paragraphs?

a. What is the method of development in paragraphs 8 and 11?
b. Examine paragraphs 5 through 8 as a block; show how this unit builds by stating a condition and then progressing to a possible cause for that condition.
c. Notice the links—both words and phrases— that make the connection between paragraphs; for instance, how does the first sentence of paragraph 11 link by reference and pattern to the first sentence in paragraph 8? Identify other methods of linking that you find in the essay.

2. Nemy assumes from observation that certain conditions (the universal desire for what others have) exist, and then she speculates about why this is true. Examine the direct use of "why" as it occurs throughout the essay:

"Why, she was asked, did she want yet another new look?" (par. 4)
"What isn't quite so easy to understand is why most of us. . . ." (par. 11)
"Why does the other person always think of these things?" (par. 11)
". . .why is it that after years of yearning after an uncluttered look. . . . " (par. 14)

What is gained by posing such questions even though they are not answered completely?

3. Writers use various devices or strategies to create the effect of conversation, an informality in style. Note these features of Nemy's informal style and point out examples other than those listed:

a. use of dialogue in paragraphs 2, 3, 5, and approximation of dialogue in paragraph 13: "What style! What sophistication! . . . We're still happy, but maybe not quite as . . . well, . . ."
b. use of contractions: "it's," "we're," "needn't," etc.
c. use of words and phrases customarily found in speech rather than in writing: "O.K." (par. 11); "klutzy" (par. 12).
d. use of short sentences and sentence fragments: "Too true" (par. 6); "Not everyone else's. No. Just some" (par. 7); "Including the way we see others, and the way we react to the things they do" (par. 12).

4. What are epaulets (par. 9)? In what sense are styles and tastes, as Nemy says, "ephemeral" (par. 12)? When is somebody or some action "gauche" (par. 11)? How would you explain "objet and tsatskes" (par. 14)? Even if you do not know these words, can you guess at their meaning from context?

Generating Ideas

1. Write a paper giving your explanation for the notion that what others have is better, easier, or in some way more desirable—that "pastures are always greener over the fence." You might both speculate on causes and advance reasons that you believe are plausible.

2. Write a paper using one of these titles, all of which suggest a cause/effect relationship:
"The Rush to Change Causes Regrets"
"Style Is Constantly Whimsical"
"Why We Fall Prey to Designers"
(or substitute Advertisers, Salesmen, etc.)
"Dissatisfaction—a General Malaise"
"Why Humans Too Follow the Herd"
"The Effects of Trend Setters"
"Easy to Want, Hard to Get"

3. Choose some style or craze and analyze the reasons for its popularity. For example, what are the reasons for the almost universal popularity of jeans? for the mass purchase of skateboards or roller skates? for the trend toward down-filled jackets?

4. Analyze the effects of the envy and jealousy that sometimes are part of "wanting what others have." What are the effects, for instance, on happiness? on patterns of spending? on personality? Narrow your paper as necessary and use examples to prove the points you make.

5. Argue the point that style is whimsical, therefore not explainable.

6. Write a paper explaining why one can safely say, as Nemy does, "Sense has always been way down on the totem pole" (par. 12).

9

DEFINITION: MAKING MEANINGS CLEAR

"There's glory for you!" says Humpty Dumpty to Alice in Lewis Carroll's *Through the Looking Glass,* and Alice says, "I don't know what you mean by 'glory.'" "Of course you don't—till I tell you. I meant 'there's a nice knock-down argument for you!'" "But 'glory' doesn't mean 'a nice knock-down argument,'" objects Alice.

Alice's and Humpty's disagreement over a definition results from a situation in which a word means one thing to one person and something else to the other. All of us ask for definitions, and we all have to give them. And many of the problems arise over the words most difficult to define— abstract ones like *glory, love, democracy,* and the like.

It is fairly easy to make concrete words clear, those whose meaning can be demonstrated by reference to actual objects and experiences. You ask the service-station attendant, "What do you mean, trouble with the generator?" He points to the mechanism, explains its function, and describes the trouble.

For most words, whether abstract or concrete, you check a dictionary. Friends tell you that they have been sailing in a sloop. A dictionary tells you a sloop is a "single-masted, fore-and-aft-rigged sailing boat with a short standing bowsprit or none at all." You may have to look up *bowsprit*, too. You will understand more clearly if you look at pictures of a sloop and compare it to other sailing vessels such as a ketch or a schooner, noting the differences in the masts and sails the three carry. And you will know that you, your friends, and others who use the term *sloop* will be talking about the same thing.

Synonyms often help to clarify meanings. If you look up *lucrative*, you find that a dictionary gives only synonyms in explanation: "Producing wealth, profitable." Here there is only one meaning. Across the page you see *lukewarm*, with two: "1) mildly warm; tepid. 2) lacking in enthusiasm; indifferent." And if you were confronted with the word in a piece of writing, you would then determine the more appropriate meaning from the context.

Misunderstandings may arise unless the context is established, and this is particularly true when words, unlike those we have been considering, do not have clear and precise referents, but are abstract, like *glory*, or *love*, or *democracy*. Such words are used to explain unfamiliar objects, to generalize about unshared experiences, to present new concepts. An abstract word has a general area of meaning within which different definitions are possible. For instance, a teacher might say, "She is a creative student," meaning that she brings insight and imagination to her work. But someone might limit *creative* to the more restricted and literal notion of creative *doing*. Some illustrations would then be needed to enlarge the word's circle of meaning to include creative *thinking*.

In a formal, or logical, definition, the writer draws a circle of meaning, and invites the reader to share in understanding the extent and limits of the term defined. Such a definition first places the term in a class, sometimes called the *genus*, and then gives the characteristics, or *differentia*, which distinguish it from other items in the same class:

term	genus	differentia
sloop	sailing boat	single-masted
		fore-and-aft-rigged
		short standing bowsprit
		or no bowsprit

Logical definition is particularly well-suited for factual or scientific terms. In writing exposition it is often helpful to see the parts of the logical definition and relate them to your wider purpose. Suppose, for instance, you are writing a paper on the history of several kinds of sailing vessels. Your introductory paragraphs might incorporate logical defini- tions of *sloop, ketch,* and *schooner* before you begin to trace their development. (You will find an expanded logical definition in the selection "Ethology" in this chapter.)

Notice how logical definition is used in this opening paragraph of an essay that examines the nature of a university:

> If I were asked to describe as briefly and popularly as I could, what a University was, I should draw my answer from its ancient designation of a *Studium Generale,* or "School of Universal Learning." This description implies the assem- blage of strangers from all parts in one spot—*from all parts;* else, how will you find professors and students for every department of knowledge? and *in one spot;* else, how can there be any school at all? Accordingly, in its simple and rudimental form, it is a school of knowledge of every kind, consisting of teachers and learners from every quarter. Many things are requisite to complete and satisfy the idea embodied in this description; but such as this a University seems to be in its essence, a place for the communication and circulation of thought, by means of personal intercourse, through a wide extent of country.—John Henry Newman, "What Is a University?"

Newman places the university in a wider class: "School of Universal Learning." He then examines what this designa- tion means in terms of particular characteristics, picking up the idea of universality and the central location implied by the word *school.* The rest of the essay extends the definition by explaining, among other things, how a university functions.

Another kind of definition is the one based on a word's etymology. An etymological definition traces the deriva- tion of a word back to its original meaning in order to shed light on its present meaning. *Democracy,* for example, is better understood when one knows that it is derived from *demos*, the Greek word for "common people." But it should be remembered that the meanings of many other words have changed radically over a period of time. *Romantic*, for instance, is now used in ways totally unrelated to its original meaning. (You will find useful etymological definitions in "Ballet," p. 275, and in "Ethology," p. 281.)

Writing definition, obviously, involves other methods of development. Definitions can be supported by giving illustrations, by clarifying the unfamiliar through the familiar. Comparison may be used to explain how one term resembles or differs from another. For instance, to explain the meaning of the word *antique* one might first establish criteria such as age and authenticity, then cite examples fulfilling them, and then contrast genuine antiques with reproductions or with items that are merely old. Another method is to trace origins or causes to explain the nature of something like *naturalism* in literature or the *dada* movement in art. How did the trend start? What influenced it? What effect did it have on later writers and artists?

Just as definition can involve other methods of development, definition itself is essential to almost every other kind of exposition. In writing essay answers, in giving a report or speech, in writing a research paper, you are expected to define your terms. Definition may be the whole or a part; it may be the central purpose or a step toward another goal; it may be as short as a single sentence or as long as a series of paragraphs of examples, comparisons, causes; it may be instructional and informative, personal and philosophical. Above all, it must be clear.

In the following informal definition, the writer uses several methods of development to suggest a core meaning from which a logical definition may be derived:

> The metaphor is something more than an amusing literary device; it is a continual play of wit, an illuminating *double entendre*, a nimble magic, in which writer and reader conspire to escape reality. Perhaps "escape" is the wrong word—the play of metaphor acts to enrich reality, even to heighten it. The average reader enjoys its intensification so much that he cannot help employing it. "My heart leaps," he says,

knowing quite well that it contracts and expands quietly within the pericardium. Or, he declares still more mendaciously, but earnestly, "my heart stood still." Even while he scorns poetry, the ordinary man helps himself to its properties and symbols; his daily life is unthinkable without metaphor. Having slept "like a log," he gets up in the morning "fresh as a daisy" or "fit as a fiddle"; he "wolfs down" breakfast, "hungry as a bear," with his wife, who has a "tongue like vinegar," but "a heart of gold." He gets into his car, which "eats up the miles," steps on the gas, and, as it "purrs" along through the "hum" of traffic, he reaches his office where he is "as busy as a one-armed paper hanger with hives." Life, for the average man, is not "a bed of roses," his competitor is "sly as a fox" and his own clerks are "slow as molasses in January." But "the day's grind" is finally done, and though it is "raining cats and dogs," he arrives home "happy as a lark."—Louis Untermeyer, "The Metaphor"

Writing definition, of course, involves a knowledge of the reader it is intended for. Untermeyer clarifies the meaning of *metaphor* by the use of examples taken from everyday speech and life. But if he were explaining the term for a scholarly audience, he would probably put his explanation in more formal language and would describe how metaphor operates in literature, as the writer of this definition does:

Metaphor: An implied analogy which imaginatively identifies one object with another and ascribes to the first one or more of the qualities of the second or invests the first with emotional or imaginative qualities associated with the second. It is one of the tropes; that is, one of the principal devices by which poetic "turns" on the meaning of words are achieved. I.A. Richards' distinction between the *tenor* and the *vehicle* of a metaphor has been widely accepted and is very useful. The *tenor* is the idea being expressed or the subject of the comparison; the *vehicle* is the image by which this idea is conveyed or the subject communicated.—C. Hugh Holman, *A Handbook to Literature*

It is not surprising that the examples that follow this definition come from literary works rather than from

Margot Fonteyn

Dame Margot Fonteyn (b. 1919) is perhaps more written about than she is known as a writer, for she is the Prima Ballerina and President of the Royal Academy of Dancing in London. After her debut as a snowflake in the Christmas production of *The Nutcracker* with the Vic-Wells Ballet in 1934, she fast rose to stardom. Her dancing partnership with Rudolf Nureyev during the 1960s brought them both international recognition. Married to Roberto de Arias, she tells the story of her life in *Margot Fonteyn*, published in 1976. *A Dancer's World* (1979), a clear explanation and history of dance, is the source of the definition given here.

Ballet

Ballet is a word that can cause some confusion when one is talking of dance. It is used in various contexts to mean different things. It originates from *ballo* in Italian and *bal* in French, meaning dance in the sense of "a dance" or "a ball"; that is to say, a social occasion at which people dance. The Italian word *balletto* was used in the sixteenth century for a series of social dances usually performed by, but not limited to, couples.

1
Placement of ballet in class *(genus):* dance
Derivation of term ballet (etymology) (par. 1)

In the sixteenth and seventeenth centuries, some of these social occasions became so elaborate that they included entertainments of music, poetry, and dance, somewhat like a lavish cabaret at a private party performed by the host and his friends. In France, this entertainment came to be called a *ballet*. When these entertainments moved from the great halls of royal palaces into real theatres, the dance element was developed and eventually separated from the speech or poetry. It retained the name *ballet*. So, first of all, ballet means a stage performance of dance. It can be any kind of dance.

2
Historical development of ballet (par. 2)

When ballet first moved into the professional theatre, it began to evolve a system of technique based quite simply on the social

3
Special techniques and costumes for ballet *(differentia)* (par. 3)

dances of the day. These social or ballroom dances were complicated; every respectable young man and woman spent a considerable amount of time perfecting the many difficult steps and learning the formation of each dance. For ease and grace, it was necessary to turn the feet out toward the side—as a fencer does in order to move rapidly in any direction with utmost control. In the theatre, it was only a question of elaborating these same steps with more intricate footwork, and adding more leaps and jumps and turns. Lo and behold! There was the style or technique of dancing that we now call ballet. So it is really nothing more than a legitimate development of the minuet and other eighteenth-century social dances. What makes it seem so far removed from everyday life is the footwear. Whereas ballroom, tap, jazz, and folk dancing can be done in normal shoes or boots, and modern dance is done in bare feet, only ballet dancers and gymnasts wear close-fitting little slippers with soft soles and no heels; and the women's toeshoes could be regarded as almost freakish if one were not accustomed to them.

Popularity of ballet costume (par. 4)

4 But as more of the workaday clothes of dancers and athletes, such as tights, leotards, track suits, and so forth, are adapted for casual fashion wear, so ballet becomes less and less remote from everyday life—almost back to where it started!

Differentiation by national labels and training (par. 5)

5 Another confusion is caused by references to Russian ballet, English ballet, American ballet, and so on. It is sometimes hard to know what is meant. People ask me which training is best, but in fact all ballet training is basically the same. There are, however, big differences in detail, and choice is a matter of personal taste. English training produces an effect of effortlessness; American training develops speed and agility. The expression "Russian

ballet method" does not have any precise meaning. Before the Russian Revolution the style of training in Moscow differed from that in St. Petersburg: Moscow dancers were more flamboyant; St. Petersburg dancers were softer. Soviet Russian training, which is different again in style, now accentuates high leaps and strength. Both the Leningrad and the Moscow schools have evolved and moved closer to each other but still retain individual characteristics. In spite of all these variations in detail, the technique is standard and universal. It presents no problems for ballet dancers of one nationality to perform in the ballet company of any other country.

"Classical ballet" is another confusing term. These days it is sometimes used to mean the type of training that we call ballet, and it is also applied to those ballets created in Russia during the late nineteenth century that are performed, either complete or in excerpts, in versions that are more or less related to their original productions. *Swan Lake, The Nutcracker, The Sleeping Beauty, Don Quixote, La Bayadère,* and *Le Corsaire* are the ones seen most frequently outside Russia, and only the first four of those are shown in their entirety. (*Giselle,* a French ballet, dates from an earlier period, the 1840s, and is classified as a "romantic" ballet. *Coppélia* is a French *demicaractère* ballet, dating from 1870, that can now be called "a classic.")

6
Explanation and examples of classical and romantic ballet (par. 6)

Discussing Content and Form

1. How has the term ballet *narrowed in meaning over the centuries? What special techniques now distinguish it from other forms of dance?*

2. Why are ballet costumes often adopted for casual wear? What single part of the costume is exclusively the dancer's?

3. From what languages is the term ballet *derived? In what country were the first ballets performed? Which country, judging from emphasis in the essay, seems to have contributed most to the development?*

4. In what feature does ballet training differ from country to country? Why is it possible for dancers to perform internationally?

5. Explain Fonteyn's distinction between "classical" and "romantic" ballet. (Coppélia she calls demi-caractère, or semi-character, because it is a dance of dolls—the coppélia are the creation of Dr. Coppelius, a toymaker. It is known for a mixture of styles because some of the dolls dance stiff-legged while still retaining character form.)

Considering Special Techniques

1. As the marginal gloss indicates, Fonteyn follows conventional methods of definition in her explanation of ballet.
   a. Show that her method is effective and clear by considering especially her use of etymology and the various differentia that distinguish ballet from other dance forms.
   b. Of what special value is the historical tracing in paragraph 2?

2. Note the balanced sentence patterns that help place one type of ballet against another in paragraph 5:
   "English training produces an effect of effortlessness; American training develops speed and agility. . . . Soviet Russian training . . . now accentuates high leaps and strength."
   "Before the Russian Revolution the style of training in Moscow differed from that in St. Petersburg: Moscow dancers were more flamboyant; St. Petersburg dancers were softer."
Explain the use of semicolons in the two sentence groups. Explain also the use of the colon in the second sentence. Why is the semicolon especially likely to occur in sentences of comparison or contrast like these?

3. Repetition of words—either exact repetition or of slightly changed forms of the same word—is another way of achieving unity both in entire essays or in single paragraphs.
   a. Notice Fonteyn's use of the word confusion in sentence 1. Show that the use of this word or another form of it helps link the paragraphs and ideas of the essay.

b. Point out the echo for the phrase "differences in detail" that helps unify the various contrasts discussed in paragraph 5.

4. Fonteyn twice uses the exclamation point:
"Lo and behold!" (par. 3)
". . . almost back to where it started!"(par. 4)
What is the effect of the exclamatory sentence in an essay of this kind? Why do you think writers seldom use exclamation points?

5. Writers often cite examples of the idea, object, or term they are seeking to define. What special value do the examples in paragraph 6 lend to the defining of classical ballet?

6. Words to learn and use: contexts (par. 1); lavish, cabaret (par. 2); legitimate (par. 3); flamboyant, accentuates (par. 5).

Generating Ideas

1. Choose some particular form of dance—one that is either currently popular or has been a fad of the past—and explain it by showing how it differs from other forms and how it developed, and by citing examples of music created for it or of dancers who made it popular. A few suggestions: the twist, the Charleston, disco, jive, boogey-woogey.

2. As viewers, listeners, or readers, people outside an artistic circle often need to understand some term that is unfamiliar to them. Choose a term from painting, sculpture, music, dance, drama, or literature and define it clearly enough to give information to a novice in the field. For instance, you might explain gouache or tempera (art); sonata or scherzo (music); flashback or chiaroscuro (as techniques in drama or film); aria or mezzo soprano (opera); cinquain or haiku (poetry). Add other terms as you wish.

3. Choose a term that has undergone changes in meaning over the years; trace the changes as you define the various meanings, Some suggestions: capsule, cockpit, computer, picket, pillbox, strike, tank, truck.

4. Write a paper about the value or the danger in using slang. Develop the paper partly by defining some slang terms that may be short-lived, misinterpreted, or highly effective. You might interview some older person to gather slang terms from a former time.

5. *You and a friend have just overheard one of the following statements; your friend asks that you explain what the speaker means. Write a paragraph or two giving a clear explanation.*

   "He gives good service as a maitre-d'."
   "What awful kitsch."
   "His speech is often epigrammatic."
   "She uses countless malapropisms."
   "He accused him of philistinism."
   "He is a member of the Savoyards."

6. *Papers of definition, like others that you write, should make a central point, carry a thesis or message. The following topics suggest a "stand" that will necessitate definition of a term or terms at the outset; choose one of these as a subject for a paper or devise a similar topic of your own:*

   The pleasures of being a dilettante
   The benefits (or evils) of philanthropy
   Romance as a worthy (or unworthy) goal
   One man's hero is another's villain
   Politics rely on pettifoggery
   The advantages (or dangers) of faculty tenure

7. *Most sports have a special terminology which participants and viewers learn. Choose a sport that you know well and explain its special terms to a novice. For instance, you might write about the vocabulary of hockey, of figure skating, of tennis, of football, of soccer, etc.*

Sally Carrighar

Sally Carrighar was born in Cleveland, Ohio, and attended Vassar College. After serving as a scriptwriter for films and radio, she became a free-lance writer in 1937. Her first books, *One Day on Beetle Rock* (1944) and *One Day at Teton Marsh* (1947), reflect her love of the American West. In the 1950's she spent some time in Alaska, and from that experience wrote *Icebound Summer* (1952) and *Wild Voice of the North* (1959). Her autobiography, *Home to the Wilderness* (1973), is a poignant account of her unhappy childhood and her search for a satisfying vocation. The clear and careful definition in "Ethology" (editor's title) is taken from *Wild Heritage* (1965), perhaps her best-known book. Its thesis is that we learn about ourselves from observing the behavior of animals in their natural surroundings.

Ethology

By . . . the 1920's and 1930's, there was a new generation   1
of biologists and many were ready to listen. While some of them have preferred to do their work in laboratories, others have gone out of doors, to make a real science of animal observation. They call themselves, these co-operating indoor and outdoor men, ethologists, and it is largely due to their efforts that we now have a reliable body of knowledge about our animal forebears.

For laymen ethology is probably the most interesting of   2
the biological sciences for the very reason that it concerns animals in their normal activities and therefore, if we wish, we can assess the possible dangers and advantages in our own behavioral roots. Ethology also is interesting methodologically because it combines in new ways very scrupulous field observations with experimentation in laboratories.

The field workers have had some handicaps in winning   3
respect for themselves. For a long time they were considered as little better than amateur animal-watchers— certainly not scientists, since their facts were not gained by experimental procedures: they could not conform to the hard-and-fast rule that a problem set up and solved by one scientist must be tested by other scientists, under identical conditions and reaching identical results. Of course many

situations in the lives of animals simply cannot be rehearsed and controlled in this way. The fall flocking of wild free birds can't be, or the homing of animals over long distances, or even details of spontaneous family relationships. Since these never can be reproduced in a laboratory, are they then not worth knowing about?

4   The ethologists who choose field work have got themselves out of this impasse by greatly refining the techniques of observing. At the start of a project all the animals to be studied are live-trapped, marked individually, and released. Motion pictures, often in color, provide permanent records of their subsequent activities. Recording of the animals' voices by electrical sound equipment is considered essential, and the most meticulous notes are kept of all that occurs. With this material other biologists, far from the scene, later can verify the reports. Moreover, two field observers often go out together, checking each other's observations right there in the field.

5   Ethology, the word, is derived from the Greek *ethos*, meaning the characteristic traits or features which distinguish a group—any particular group of people or, in biology, a group of animals such as a species. Ethologists have the intention, as William H. Thorpe explains, of studying "the whole sequence of acts which constitute an animal's behavior." In abridged dictionaries ethology is sometimes defined simply as "the objective study of animal behavior," and ethologists do emphasize their wish to eliminate myths.

6   Perhaps the most original aspect of ethology is the way that field observation is combined with experimentation in laboratories. Although the flocking of birds cannot be studied indoors, many other significant actions of animals that are seen only infrequently in the field, or seen only as hints, may be followed up later with indoor tests. Likewise investigations made first in laboratories can be checked by observations of animals ranging free in their normal environments.

7   Suppose that a field man, watching marked individuals, notes that an infant animal, *a*, is nursed by a female, *B*, known not to be its mother. Later he sees other instances of such maternal generosity. Is this willingness on the

female's part a case of inherited behavior, or has it been picked up as one of the social customs of the species; that is, is it *learned*? Does it mean that all the adult females of this species feel some responsibility for the young, and if so, is such a tendency innate, or could behavior like that be acquired?

Elephant mothers are among those which give milk to   8 offspring not their own. A group of elephants cannot very well be confined in a laboratory; but if the field worker is concerned with a species of smaller animals, he can bring newborn young into captivity, raise them and mate them there, and then note the behavior of the new mothers. Since they never have seen other females nursing young, their actions will be innate, inherited. And if it does turn out that one of these females will nurse any young that come to her, it will further have to be determined whether she recognizes her own. That question too can be answered in the laboratory; it is an easy problem for an experimental psychologist. By such techniques it has been found, for example, that in the species of small brown bats called *Myotis myotis* the mothers do know their own young and likewise will nurse any hungry infant regardless of blood relationship. This maternal behavior could have been observed in a colony of animals kept for generations indoors, but since the habitat there is artificial, the only way to know whether the behavior is normal to the species was to observe it first in animals living free in their natural world. Only by such a combination of laboratory and field work can instincts and acquired characteristics be distinguished. The value of knowledge like that is so great that the wonder is why such cooperation had not developed much earlier.

Discussing Content and Form

1. Carrighar follows the conventional methods of defining in her explanation of the work of the ethologist.
   a. Where does she place ethology in a class?
   b. How do her examples of the work of the ethologist differentiate that field from the larger class?
   c. What does she say is the most distinguishing feature of ethology?

2. *Show how Carrighar successfully answers the question she asks in paragraph 3: "Since these [facts about animal life] never can be reproduced in a laboratory, are they then not worth knowing about?"*

3. *The writer says that the work of the ethologist is interesting to laymen. What in the selection serves to make the subject interesting to the reader?*

4. *Find phrases and statements that show how the observations of ethologists have special implications for human life.*

5. *Why is it important that a newly developed scientific field affirm both its usefulness and its objectivity as a science? Where does Carrighar establish the fact that ethology has accomplished this?*

Considering Special Techniques

1. *Why do you think Carrighar places the etymological definition where she does? What is gained by giving the derivation as well as referring to the more limited statement from the abridged dictionary?*

2. *A major problem in writing scientific articles for the general public is achieving clarity. What features of Carrighar's style make this selection both clear and easy to read?*

   a. *Note the details that clarify the methods used by the ethologist (par. 4). What would be lost if the writer had said merely, "the ethologists developed better scientific techniques"?*

   b. *What point is made clear through the details concerning flocking birds (pars. 3 and 6) and elephant mothers (par. 8)?*

   c. *Why do you think the writer does not use more scientific terminology? Point out places where careful use of restatement helps make an idea clearer: for instance, "that is, is it learned?" (par. 7).*

3. *Carrighar several times poses questions that a reader might ask and that serve as links or introductions in her chain of ideas. The question at the end of paragraph 3, for instance, leads logically to the next paragraph. Find other such linking questions.*

4. *Words to learn and use:* scrupulous *(par. 2);* impasse, meticulous *(par. 4);* innate *(par. 7).*

Generating Ideas

1. *Choose one of the following branches of science or technology as the subject for an explanatory paper that requires definition as part of its development:*

seismology	thermodynamics	meteorology
genetics	oceanography	limnology
paleontology	(human) oncology	aerospace studies
radiology	anesthesiology	
cartography	geophysics	

2. *Many words from the sciences and technology have interesting derivations, some of them from Greek and Latin. Write an extended definition of one of these words; include one or several examples to show how the word is used. Here are some suggestions:*

cellular	laser	chronometer
radioisotopes	microwave	aerolite
neurosis	algorithms	computer language
psychochemistry	biofeedback	systemic
phoneme	astronaut (cosmonaut)	hydrofoil

3. *Do some reading and write a report about the work of a particular scientist or group of scientists who study animal behavior. For instance, some interesting research has been done by ethologists who band butterflies to study their patterns of migration.*

4. *Write a paper about some human trait such as intelligence over which exists the "inherited" versus "learned" controversy. You may need to look up some factual material to support your conclusions.*

Robert Pirsig

Robert Pirsig (b. 1928), a former college teacher and technical writer, says that he started "about 7000" writing projects in the four years he took to produce *Zen and the Art of Motorcycle Maintenance*. Published in 1974, it became an extraordinarily popular success. Pirsig's account of a motorcycle journey his narrator takes with his son combines elements of fiction and autobiography with philosophical musings. Each day the narrator presents a "Chautauqua," a lecture in which he not only gives instructions in motorcycle maintenance but also teaches values and attitudes. "Gumption" (editor's title), one of the Chautauquas, defines a quality needed for accomplishing important tasks, from maintaining a motorcycle to writing a book.

Gumption

1   I like the word "gumption" because it's so homely and so forlorn and so out of style it looks as if it needs a friend and isn't likely to reject anyone who comes along. It's an old Scottish word, once used a lot by pioneers, but which, like "kin," seems to have all but dropped out of use. I like it also because it describes exactly what happens to someone who connects with Quality. He gets filled with gumption.

2   The Greeks called it *enthousiasmos*, the root of "enthusiasm," which means literally "filled with *theos*," or God, or Quality. See how that fits?

3   A person filled with gumption doesn't sit around dissipating and stewing about things. He's at the front of the train of his own awareness, watching to see what's up the track and meeting it when it comes. That's gumption. . . .

4   The gumption-filling process occurs when one is quiet long enough to see and hear and feel the real universe, not just one's own stale opinions about it. But it's nothing exotic. That's why I like the word.

5   You see it often in people who return from long, quiet fishing trips. Often they're a little defensive about having put so much time to "no account" because there's no intellectual justification for what they've been doing. But the returned fisherman usually has a peculiar abundance of gumption, usually for the very same things he was sick to

death of a few weeks before. He hasn't been wasting time. It's only our limited cultural viewpoint that makes it seem so.

If you're going to repair a motorcycle, an adequate 6 supply of gumption is the first and most important tool. If you haven't got that you might as well gather up all the other tools and put them away, because they won't do you any good.

Gumption is the psychic gasoline that keeps the whole 7 thing going. If you haven't got it there's no way the motorcycle can possibly be fixed. But if you *have* got it and know how to keep it there's absolutely no way in this whole world that motorcycle can *keep* from getting fixed. It's bound to happen. Therefore the thing that must be monitored at all times and preserved before anything else is the gumption.

This paramount importance of gumption solves a 8 problem of format of this Chautauqua. The problem has been how to get off the generalities. If the Chautauqua gets into the actual details of fixing one individual machine the chances are overwhelming that it won't be your make and model and the information will be not only useless but dangerous, since information that fixes one model can sometimes wreck another. For detailed information of an objective sort, a separate shop manual for the specific make and model of machine must be used. In addition, a general shop manual such as *Audel's Automotive Guide* fills in the gaps.

But there's another kind of detail that no shop manual 9 goes into but that is common to all machines and can be given here. This is the detail of the Quality relationship, the gumption relationship, between the machine and the mechanic, which is just as intricate as the machine itself. Throughout the process of fixing the machine things always come up, low-quality things, from a dusted knuckle to an accidentally ruined "irreplaceable" assembly. These drain off gumption, destroy enthusiasm and leave you so discouraged you want to forget the whole business. I call these things "gumption traps."

There are hundreds of different kinds of gumption 10

traps, maybe thousands, maybe millions. I have no way of knowing how many I don't know. I know it *seems* as though I've stumbled into every kind of gumption trap imaginable. What keeps me from thinking I've hit them all is that with every job I discover more. Motorcycle maintenance gets frustrating. Angering. Infuriating. That's what makes it interesting. . . .

11   What I have in mind now is a catalog of "Gumption Traps I Have Known." I want to start a whole new academic field, gumptionology, in which these traps are sorted, classified, structured into hierarchies and interrelated for the edification of future generations and the benefit of all mankind.

12   *Gumptionology 101—An examination of affective, cognitive and psychomotor blocks in the perception of Quality relationships—3 cr, VII, MWF.* I'd like to see that in a college catalog somewhere.

13   In traditional maintenance gumption is considered something you're born with or have acquired as a result of good upbringing. It's a fixed commodity. From the lack of information about how one acquires this gumption one might assume that a person without any gumption is a hopeless case.

14   In nondualistic maintenance gumption isn't a fixed commodity. It's variable, a reservoir of good spirits that can be added to or subtracted from. Since it's a result of the perception of Quality, a gumption trap, consequently, can be defined as anything that causes one to lose sight of Quality, and thus lose one's enthusiasm for what one is doing. As one might guess from a definition as broad as this, the field is enormous and only a beginning sketch can be attempted here.

15   As far as I can see there are two main types of gumption traps. The first type is those in which you're thrown off the Quality track by conditions that arise from external circumstances, and I call these "setbacks." The second type is traps in which you're thrown off the Quality track by conditions that are primarily within yourself. These I don't have any generic name for—"hang-ups," I suppose. . . .

Discussing Content and Form

1. Pirsig explains the word gumption *by describing the actions of people who possess the attribute and by relating it to a synonym,* enthusiasm. *List some other possible synonyms. What do you think Pirsig means when he says that "someone who connects with Quality" is filled with gumption (par. 1)?*

2. Where does Pirsig describe what gumption is not? *Why is the negative definition effective here?*

3. What examples of gumption does the selection give? Why is it "the first and most important tool" in the maintenance job? Explain how this statement might relate to all fields of work.

4. In paragraph 8, why does the narrator find it a problem "to get off the generalities"? Explain how gumption helps him solve this problem.

5. What are "gumption traps"? Why are they particularly likely to occur in any sort of maintenance work?

6. In the proposal for "Gumptionology 101" (par. 12), Pirsig classifies the traps as "affective, cognitive, and psychomotor blocks." After checking the meanings of these words, explain how deterrents to good work can be of these three kinds.

7. Why does the "traditionalist" believe gumption is "a fixed commodity" (par. 13)? What then is the "nondualistic" view (par. 14)? To which attitude do you subscribe—that gumption is fixed or that it is attainable?

8. How do you think Pirsig would answer someone who says, "I can't do it because I wasn't born smart or brought up right"?

Considering Special Techniques

1. The tone of this selection is at once informal and serious, personal and philosophical. Find words and phrases that contribute to this mixed tone. Paragraph 5, for example, contains the informal "no account" and "sick to death," along with more formal phrases such as "intellectual justification" and "limited cultural viewpoint." Which of the two types seem to dominate the selection?

2. A definition often involves a word's etymology, but Pirsig uses this technique differently by tracing the derivation of a synonym rather than that of the word being defined. Why do you think he gives the derivation of enthusiasm, but not of gumption *(par. 2)? (Check the derivation of* gumption.)

3. Discuss how the following metaphors help clarify Pirsig's definition:

"He's at the front of the train of his own awareness, watching to see what's up the track and meeting it when it comes." (par. 3)

". . . gumption is the first and most important tool." (par. 6)

"Gumption is the psychic gasoline that keeps the whole thing going." (par. 7)

"It's variable, a reservoir of good spirits that can be added to or subtracted from." (par. 14)

4. What is the purpose of capitalizing the word Quality?

5. Connotations—the overtones of meaning, rather than the literal meaning or denotation—surrounding a word are very important in conveying emotions or arousing responses from readers. What connotations do you think gumption has for most people? In associating gumption with kin (par. 1), how does Pirsig suggest the connotations of both words?

6. In the following phrases, analyze the connotations of the italicized words; then substitute some synonyms for them and comment on any changes in meaning that result:

"it's nothing *exotic"* (par. 4). What is the effect of substituting flashy or unusual for exotic?

"paramount *importance"* (par. 8). Try first or chief instead of paramount.

"I've *stumbled into* every kind of gumption trap" (par. 10). Substitute fallen or experienced for stumbled.

Do the same thing with other examples in the selection.

7. Read paragraph 10 aloud. How do the sentence structure and arrangement of sentences give the effect that the writer is talking or thinking aloud?

Generating Ideas

1. Use Pirsig's catalogue description for a new college course in Gumptionology 101 as a model for a projected course that you would like to see taught. Create your own course description and then explain what you would put into the syllabus and the method you would use to teach the course.

2. *Do you believe that perseverance is inborn or determined by early training and thus cannot be acquired in later life? Or do you believe that the individual can develop a personal reservoir of strength that might be called gumption? Write a paper that discusses these two views, using specifics from your experiences or from those of other people to support your stand.*

3. *Choose a desirable or undesirable character trait and write a definition of it. Here are some suggestions:*

common sense	nobility	poise
persistence	integrity	egoism
gregariousness	courage	self-assurance
aspiration	generosity	abrasiveness
sense of humor	imagination	shyness
taste (bad or good)	modesty (immodesty)	good breeding
ambition	self-control	humility

4. *Define* Quality *and explain how you think it is possible to "connect" with it. You might consider whether it too may be a word that is "out of style [and] looks as if it needs a friend" (par. 1).*

5. *Slang phrases or labels often require definition. Choose some term currently used to describe an action or person and explain it to someone who is unfamiliar with it. Here are a few examples:*

"He's kooky—by that I mean. . . ."
"When I say something is weird, I just mean. . . ."
"That's far-out—really far-out. . . ."
"When someone is off the wall, he's. . . ."

Occasionally a word takes on so many meanings, covers so much, that it becomes almost meaningless—for example, fantastic *and* terrific. *Write a paper about such words; you may define them, classify them, or trace their popularity and decline.*

Laurie Lee

Laurie Lee (b. 1914) is a poet and essayist who lives in London. During World War II, he was a documentary film maker and publications editor for the British Ministry of Information. For six years following the war, he served as a film scriptwriter. In addition to several collections of poems, he has written two autobiographical accounts, *Cider with Rosie* (1959) and *As I Walked Out One Midsummer Morning* (1969), and a volume of personal reflections, *I Can't Stay Long* (1975). All of these have a congenial tone and lively style that are evident in "Charm," an essay taken from the latter book.

Charm

1   Charm is the ultimate weapon, the supreme seduction, against which there are few defences. If you've got it, you need almost nothing else, neither money, looks, nor pedigree. It's a gift, only given to give away, and the more used the more there is. It is also a climate of behaviour set for perpetual summer and thermostatically controlled by taste and tact.

2   True charm is an aura, an invisible musk in the air; if you see it working, the spell is broken. At its worst, it is the charm of the charity duchess, like being struck in the face with a bunch of tulips; at its best, it is a smooth and painless injection which raises the blood to a genial fever. Most powerful of all, it is obsessive, direct, person-to-person, forsaking all others. Never attempt to ask for whom the charm-bells ring; if they toll for anyone, they must toll for you.

3   As to the ingredients of charm, there is no fixed formula; they vary intuitively between man and woman. A whole range of mysteries goes into the cauldron, but the magic remains the same. In some cases, perhaps, the hand of the charmer is lighter, more discreet, less overwhelming, but the experience it offers must be absolute—one cannot be "almost" or "partly" charmed.

4   Charm in a woman is probably more exacting than in a man, requiring a wider array of subtleties. It is a light in the face, a receptive stance, an air of exclusive welcome, an almost impossibly sustained note of satisfaction in one's

company, and regret without fuss at parting. A woman with charm finds no man dull, doesn't have to pretend to ignore his dullness; indeed, in her presence he becomes not just a different person but the person he most wants to be. Such a woman gives life to his deep-held fantasies and suddenly makes them possible, not so much by flattering him as adding the necessary conviction to his long suspicion that he is king.

Of those women who have most successfully charmed me in the past, I remember chiefly their eyes and voices. That swimming way of looking, as though they were crushing wine, their tone of voice, and their silences. The magic of that look showed no distraction, nor any wish to be with anyone else. Their voices were furred with comfort, like plumped-up cushions, intimate and enveloping. Then the listening eyes, supreme charm in a woman, betraying no concern with any other world than this, warmly wrapping one round with total attention and turning one's lightest words to gold. Looking back, I don't pretend that I was in any way responsible; theirs was a charm to charm all men, and must have continued to exist, like the flower in the desert, when there was nobody there to see it.

A woman's charm needn't always cater to such extremes of indulgence—though no man will complain if it does. At the least, she spreads round her that particular glow of well-being for which any man will want to seek her out, and by making full use of her nature, celebrates the fact of his maleness and so gives him an extra shot of life. Her charm lies also in the air of timeless maternalism, that calm and pacifying presence, which can dispel a man's moments of frustration and anger and salvage his failures of will.

Charm in a man, I suppose, is his ability to capture the complicity of a woman by a single-minded acknowledgment of her uniqueness. Here again it is a question of being totally absorbed, of forgetting that anyone else exists—but *really* forgetting, for nothing more fatally betrays than the suggestion of a wandering eye. Silent devotion is fine, but seldom enough; it is what a man says that counts, the bold declarations, the flights of fancy, the uncovering of secret virtues. Praise can be a jewel, but the gift must be personal, the only one of its kind in the world; while flattery itself will never be thought excessive so long as there's no suspicion that it's been said before.

8   A man's charm strikes deepest when a woman's imagination is engaged, with herself as the starting point; when she is made a part of some divine extravaganza, or mystic debauch, in which she feels herself both the inspirer and ravished victim. A man is charmed through his eyes, a woman by what she hears, so no man need be too anxious about his age. As wizened Voltaire once said: "Give me a few minutes to talk away my face and I can seduce the Queen of France."

9   No man, even so, will wish to talk a woman to death; there is also room for the confessional priest, a role of unstinted patience and dedication to the cause, together with a modest suspension of judgment. "You may have sinned, but you couldn't help it, you were made for love. . . . You have been wronged, you have suffered too much. . . ." If man has this quality, it is as much a solace to a woman as his power to dilate her with praise and passion.

10   But charm, after all, isn't exclusively sexual, it comes in a variety of cooler flavours. Most children have it—till they are told they have it—and so do old people with nothing to lose; animals, too, of course, and a few outdoor insects, and certain sea-creatures if they can claim to be mammals— seals, whales, and dolphins, but not egg-laying fish (you never saw a fish in a circus). With children and smaller animals it is often in the shape of the head and in the chaste unaccusing stare; with young girls and ponies, a certain stumbling awkwardness, a leggy inability to control their bodies. The sullen narcissism of adolescents, product of over-anxiety, can also offer a ponderous kind of charm. But all these are passive, and appeal to the emotions simply by capturing one's protective instinct.

11   Real charm is dynamic, an enveloping spell which mysteriously enslaves the senses. It is an inner light, fed on reservoirs of benevolence which well up like a thermal spring. It is unconscious, often nothing but the wish to please, and cannot be turned on and off at will. Which would seem to cancel the claims of some of the notorious charmers of the past—Casanova, Lawrence of Arabia, Rubirosa—whose talent, we suspect, wasn't charm at all so

much as a compulsive need to seduce. Others, more recent, had larger successes through being less specific in their targets—Nehru, for instance, and Yehudi Menuhin, Churchill, and the early Beatles. As for the women—Cleopatra, Mata Hari, Madame du Barry—each one endowed with superb physical equipment; were they charmers, too?—in a sense they must have been, though they laid much calculated waste behind them.

You recognize charm by the feeling you get in its 12 presence. You know who has it. But can you get it, too? Properly, you can't, because it's a quickness of spirit, an originality of touch you have to be born with. Or it's something that grows naturally out of another quality, like the simple desire to make people happy. Certainly, charm is not a question of learning palpable tricks, like wrinkling your nose, or having a laugh in your voice, or gaily tossing your hair out of your dancing eyes and twisting your mouth into succulent love-knots. Such signs, to the nervous, are ominous warnings which may well send him streaking for cover. On the other hand, there is an antenna, a built-in awareness of others, which most people have, and which care can nourish.

But in a study of charm, what else does one look for? 13 Apart from the ability to listen—rarest of all human virtues and most difficult to sustain without vagueness—apart from warmth, sensitivity, and the power to please, what else is there visible? A generosity, I suppose, which makes no demands, a transaction which strikes no bargains, which doesn't hold itself back till you've filled up a test-card making it clear that you're worth the trouble. Charm can't withhold, but spends itself willingly on young and old alike, on the poor, the ugly, the dim, the boring, on the last fat man in the corner. It reveals itself also in a sense of ease, in casual but perfect manners, and often in a physical grace which springs less from an accident of youth than from a confident serenity of mind. Any person with this is more than just a popular fellow, he is also a social healer.

Charm, in the abstract, has something of the quality of 14 music: radiance, balance, and harmony. One encounters it unexpectedly in odd corners of life with a shock of brief, inexplicable ravishment: in a massed flight of birds, a string of running horses, an arrangement of clouds on the sea; wooded islands, Tanagra figures, old balconies in Spain, the line of a sports car holding a corner, in the writings of Proust and Jane Austen, the paintings of Renoir and Fragonard, the poetry of Herrick, the sound of lute and guitar. . . . Thickets of leaves can have it, bare arms interlocking, suds of rain racing under a bridge, and such simplicities as waking after a sleep of nightmares to see sunlight bouncing off the ceiling. The effect of these, like many others, is to restore one's place in the world; to reassure, as it were, one's relationship with things, and to bring order to the wilderness.

15   But charm, in the end, is flesh and blood, a most potent act of behaviour, the laying down of a carpet by one person for another to give his existence a moment of honour. Much is deployed in the weaponry of human dealings: stealth, aggression, blackmail, lust, the urge to possess, devour, and destroy. Charm is the rarest, least used, and most invincible of powers, which can capture with a single glance. It is close to love in that it moves without force, bearing gifts like the growth of daylight. It snares completely, but is never punitive, it disarms by being itself disarmed, strikes without wounds, wins wars without casualties—though not, of course, without victims. He who would fall in the battle, let him fall to charm, and he will never be humbled, or know the taste of defeat.

16   In the armoury of man, charm is the enchanted dart, light and subtle as a hummingbird. But it is deceptive in one thing—like a sense of humour, if you think you've got it, you probably haven't.

Discussing Content and Form

1. Does Lee say that charm is one thing or many things? Explain why a definition of such a quality as charm is of necessity very complex.

2. Art and literary critics disagree over whether a quality such as "meaning" resides in the work of art or exists only in the viewer's or reader's response. Does Lee think charm is entirely in the charmer? Explain. Find statements that indicate the importance of the respondent, the one who is being charmed.

3. This essay has a clear plan; make a gloss or outline of the essay by paragraphs and then group together those paragraphs which constitute each major section.

4. Why does Lee say that "one cannot be 'almost' or 'partly' charmed"?

5. Discuss the differences Lee sees between charm in a woman and in a man. Why do you think he remembers "eyes and voices" in the women who have charmed him? What are "listening eyes" (par. 5)?

6. What role does Lee say physical features play in female and male charm? How much of charm is sexual? Find phrases to support your answers. Discuss the statement, "A man is charmed through his eyes, a woman by what she hears, so no man need be too anxious about his age" (par. 8).

7. Lee mentions other kinds of charm in paragraph 10. What is the significance of this addition?

8. What is Lee's answer to the crucial question of whether charm can be acquired (par. 12)?

9. What is gained by discussing "charm in the abstract" (par. 14)? Why, after that section, does Lee say, "But charm, in the end, is flesh and blood" (par. 15)?

Considering Special Techniques

1. Lee uses many images in developing his definition.
   a. Note the unifying imagery of charm as a "weapon." Compare the images in the first sentence of the essay with those in the last two paragraphs. How many words in the concluding section carry the "weapon" image?
   b. Discuss the following images and find others which have "picture-making power."
   "It [charm] is also a climate of behaviour set for perpetual summer and thermostatically controlled by taste and tact." (par. 1)
   "That swimming way of looking, as though they were crushing wine . . . . " (par. 5)
   "Their voices were furred with comfort, like plumped-up cushions . . . . " (par. 5)
   "the line of a sports car holding a corner" (par. 14)

2. In defining charm, the essayist offers several seeming contradictions. What makes statements like the following provocative? In what way are they paradoxical?

"It's a gift, only given to give away, and the more used the more there is." (par. 1)

"if you see it working, the spell is broken." (par. 2)

"one cannot be 'almost' or 'partly' charmed." (par. 3)

"Most children have it—till they are told they have it. . . ." (par. 10)

3. Explain the method of development Lee uses in paragraphs 11, 13, and 14.

4. Explain if you can the literary allusion Lee uses in paragraph 2: "Never attempt to ask for whom the charm-bells ring; if they toll for anyone, they must toll for you." What is the relationship of the allusion to Lee's statement that by recognizing that someone possesses charm, we admit to being charmed?

5. Words to learn and use: seduction (par. 1); genial (par. 2); maternalism (par. 6); extravaganza, wizened (par. 8); unstinted, solace (par. 9); narcissism (par. 10); thermal, compulsive (par. 11); palpable, ominous (par. 12); inexplicable, ravishment (par. 14); deployed, invincible, punitive (par. 15).

Generating Ideas

1. During the next few days, jot down questions that you hear which necessitate an answer in the form of a definition, for example, "How do you define success, anyhow? Not the way I define it, I'll bet!" Or pose some questions for yourself and write paragraph-length answers for at least two of them.

2. Everyone has experienced charm, sometimes to the point of being obsessed with another person or with some object or place. Consider someone or something that has exerted power over you and write a definition using that experience as part of the extended development.

3. Choose a popular term that expresses extreme attraction of one person for another (e.g., charisma, sex appeal, machismo, spark) and write a paper that defines the term and then explains (seriously or humorously) the course of its influence in a particular situation. For example, you may choose charisma and show how the word applies (or fails to apply) to a specific politician or movie star.

4. In his play What Every Woman Knows, Sir James Barrie

provides this description of female charm: "If you have it, you
don't need to have anything else; and if you don't have it, it
doesn't much matter what else you have. Some women, the
few, have charm for all; and most have charm for one. But
some have charm for none."

    a. Write a descriptive paper in which you portray
       someone (real or imaginary) who has either "charm
       for all" or "charm for none." Show the difference the
       abundance or the deficiency makes in the life of your
       character.

    b. Check a book of quotations to find some other
       definition or comment about charm; then use that
       quotation as a starter for a paper written in a form
       of your choice.

5. There has been a great deal of recent legal controversy
over such terms as censorship and pornography. Do some
careful research and write a paper in which you define one of
these terms or some other that must be interpreted legally:
obscenity, invasion of privacy, civil rights, pollution. Or write a
paper defining some term used as a label for a crime:
misdemeanor, felony, fraud, larceny (petty or grand), rape,
arson.

10

CLASSIFICATION AND DIVISION:
SORTING IT OUT

In everyday life we sift, sort, group and divide items and ideas in order to arrive at patterns and meanings. A traveler, for instance, may arrange slides of a trip in various ways, depending upon the purpose for showing them. At times the slides may tell a story, tracing the sequence of a trip in a chronological arrangement similar to that of a narrative or a process paper. But at other times, slides might be grouped according to their subjects—cathedral pictures, for example, divided from those of mountain scenery or the seashore. Such classifications and divisions make it possible to convey certain impressions or conclusions that would not be immediately apparent from a sequential or random arrangement.

Classification and division go hand in hand, and it is difficult and perhaps unnecessary to draw a line between them, for the same general principles of organizing apply to both. Classification is essential in all types of thought and in all types of work. Scientists constantly divide and classify. The medical researcher isolates various kinds of drugs, separating them into groups in order to study such things as potential curative effects or possible reactions each group might cause. An agricultural biologist studies classes of plants, determining which grow best in certain soils, after, perhaps, already dividing soils overall into various subclasses or types.

Writers also use classification and division as one of the methods for finding structural patterns for transferring thoughts into expository writing. The method actually begins by comparing the facts, items, or ideas that are to be considered. From the comparison it is possible to identify a common characteristic or characteristics among the items. This characteristic, or commonality, furnishes a principle by which the items can be divided into groups and conveniently labeled, thus making it possible to get a handle on the subject.

The writer of this paragraph uses one principle to divide his subject:

> But what is a virus? Nobody knows. The term is difficult to define. We can say that most of the infectious diseases may be roughly classified under three headings according to the nature of the causal parasite: (1) the protozoal diseases, such as malaria and amoebic dysentery, which are caused by the invasion of microscopic animals; (2) the bacterial diseases, such as tuberculosis, meningitis, and the thousand and one infections which are spread by cocci, bacilli, spirilla, and other microscopic plants; and (3) the virus diseases, whose agent is neither like any of the little animals we know nor yet like any of the little plants, but appears to be of an entirely different order of organization. A few years ago the viruses were commonly known as the filter-passers, but this term ceased to be significant when it was found that certain bacteria could also pass through the fine pores of a porcelain filter and that some of these bacteria are as small as some of the viruses; i.e., the virus of smallpox.—George W. Gray, "The Problem of Influenza," *Harper's*

Gray classifies infectious diseases according to "the nature of the causal parasite," and labels the classes protozoal, bacterial, and virus. These labels serve as markers for the divisions in the paragraph. The number of items in a class may vary, of course, from only one or two to many.

Not all classification is this simple or directly announced, but no matter how complex the material or numerous the items, the grouping should be governed by one principle. Even when that principle is not named specifically, the reader should be able to see the relationships between items in a group. All the items should fit within the group where they are placed; that is, they should have the characteristics identified for that group. If there is overlapping or blurring, that group itself will need to be identified as one where items merge or fuse. This paragraph about the forms and variations of snow crystals reveals a more subtle handling of classification:

> In a single snowfall lasting an hour and a half several types of snow may fall from the sky. For ten or fifteen minutes the clouds may send down nothing but curtains of stellar crystals. Then the stars will become mixed with a few plates and a goodly quantity of asymmetrical crystals. Toward the end of the storm, most of the snow may be slender needles, mingled with brief showers of bouncing gravel. If you have the patience and an explorer's wardrobe—complete with warm long underwear—for making an extensive census of visitors from a January storm, you may be rewarded with the acquaintance of a few spatial dendrites and capped columns that managed to slip into the snow.—Corydon Bell, *The Wonder of Snow*

Although Bell says that he will treat "several types of snow," he does not announce the basis for his classification nor does he use numbers to designate his classes. Instead he employs transitional words and phrases to achieve a smooth coherence among his items.

There are several points to remember about a piece of writing that is structured around classification and division:

1. There should be a logical purpose for the system chosen. For instance, one way to divide various enjoyable novels is to group them according to the elements that make them pleasurable reading. Perhaps one group appeals because of its colorful characters; another because of the suspense or mystery in the plots; and a third because of its powerful and haunting themes.

2. The principle of classification should be consistent. In the classification of novels according to their appeal, for example, it would be inconsistent to include a group of novels that have been made into movies, or a class labeled "Novels written before 1900." To be sure, some of the enjoyable novels may have been made into movies, and that fact may be mentioned; but introducing this class violates the consistency and logic of the system and the outline of the paper.

3. The system of dividing and classifying should not be too rigid. One section of a paper may require more extensive development than another. In his famous *Screwtape Letters*, C.S. Lewis divides "the causes of human laughter into Joy, Fun, the Joke Proper, and Flippancy." His analyses of Joy, Fun, and Flippancy each require only a single paragraph, but the Joke Proper takes two, considerably longer, paragraphs. The system chosen should not be confining, but should provide the freedom to emphasize and expand any of the groups.

In the essays that follow, both dividing and classifying are used to handle numerous specifics. Like other patterns of development, classification is a method of conveying in an orderly and clear way the materials selected from close observation.

James Austin

Dr. James Austin was educated at Brown University and Harvard Medical School. After that he specialized in neurology at Boston City Hospital and at the Neurological Institute of Columbia Presbyterian Hospital in New York, and he has been involved in brain research for some two decades. For the past ten years he has been Professor and Chairman of the Department of Neurology at the University of Colorado Medical School, where his work won him the American Association of Neuropathologists' Prize. Dr. Austin has published many articles in medical journals and a book, entitled *Chase, Chance and Creativity, The Lucky Art of Novelty* (1978). "How to Make Your Luck Work for You" is an article first published in *Executive Health Report* and later reprinted in *House and Garden*.

How to Make Your Luck Work for You

1

Introduction: three
paragraph block

Of course, we all get lucky sometimes. But there is something to be learned about the structure of chance that may improve your percentage. In the past, the role of sudden flashes of insight in the process of discovery has perhaps been over-emphasized. Much has also been said about the need for plodding, methodical work before and after these creative flashes. But I would like to present the case

Definition of chance to
include human
intervention (par. 1)

for chance. What is chance? Dictionaries define chance as something fortuitous that happens unpredictably and without discernible human intention. True, chance is capricious, but we needn't conclude that it is immune from human intervention. Indeed, chance plays several distinct roles when humans react creatively with one another and with their environment. I use the word "roles" in the plural because chance comes in four forms and for four different reasons. Of these, only one is "pure blind luck." The principles involved in chance affect everyone and it is time, perhaps, to examine them more carefully. If you are completely candid with yourself you will soon discover how much your luck hinges on contingencies. Every now and then, when you happen to combine boldness and skill, you may be able to exploit a few of the lucky situations that arise. But skill alone will not be enough, for much of the novelty in creativity is decided only when you are bold enough to thrust at chance. "Behold the turtle, he makes progress only when he sticks his neck out," my neurology teacher at Columbia, Professor Houston Merritt, used to say. We, too, will only lurch forward if we stick our necks out to look around, and chance the consequences. Our self-mobilization to seek out and confront new situations is a powerful agent in creative discovery. We all need adventure, and our adventurous impulses may appear in some other form—dreams, for example—if not channeled into our work. For me, research is the essence of adventure. Being a neurologist raised in the conventional work ethic, I still believe that success in research comes from being hard-working, persistent, curious, imaginative, intuitive, and enthusiastic. But it still turns out that many of the lucky breaks in our laboratory are decided by extracurricular activities, by those pivotal events that come only when we have reached out in a spirit of adventure and jousted at chance. Once when we at the lab were trying to identify peculiar microscopic particles in a rare form of heredi- tary epilepsy called Lafora's disease, my dog, Tom, led us to the answer. Tom developed an inflammation of his lymph glands from wear- ing a new bell around his neck. After surgery, some of the diseased tissue was studied under a microscope. Curiously, some external tissue showed up as round spherules, first thought to be a fungus but later identified as starch. It got there, we concluded after much discussion, via

Discovery of solution to Lafora's disease (par. 1)

the starch dusted on the surgical gloves used for the operation. What struck us coincidentally, though, was that the starch spherules looked like the Lafora bodies we were studying! Tests confirmed our hypothesis, and within a few weeks we knew that Lafora bodies, like starch, were essentially made up of many sugar units linked together in a long chain to form a polymer.

2

In my view, this discovery was a typical case of Chance IV, the variety of chance that favors people with distinctive hobbies and activities (my dog Tom and I go hunting in thick cover, which was the reason I took the precaution of tying the bell around his neck).

3

Each of the four kinds of chance depends on a distinct kind of motor exploratory activity and special kind of sensory receptivity. Personality traits also influence them.

4

CHANCE I is the pure blind luck that comes with no effort on your part. In a bridge game, for example, it's "in the cards" for you to receive a hand of 13 spades, but statisticians tell us this will occur once in 635 billion deals. You will ultimately draw this lucky hand, but it may involve a longer wait than most of us have time for. Chance I is completely impersonal. You can't influence it. Personality traits only enter in the other forms of chance.

5

To evoke CHANCE II you will need a persistent curiosity about many things coupled with an energetic willingness to experiment and explore. Chance II is the kind of luck Charles Kettering, the automotive engineer, had in mind when he said: "Keep on going and the chances are you will stumble on something, perhaps when you are least expecting it. I have never heard of anyone stumbling on something sitting down." Consistent motion is what distinguishes Chance II. Its premise is that un-luck runs out if you persist. An element of the chase is also implicit in Chance II, but action is your primary goal, not results. The action is restless, driving, and occurs through your basic need to release energy rather than conscious intellectual effort. Of course, if you move around in more likely areas, Chance II may influence your results more fruitfully. In searching for orchids, for instance, you wouldn't go tramping around the desert. But still the principle here is press on. Action "stirs up the pot," brings in random ideas that will collide and stick together in fresh combinations. Keep on going, and the number of collisions between events is likely to increase.

In Chance I and II, the unique role of the individual is either lacking or minimal. In CHANCE III the individual needs discernment. Louis Pasteur characterized Chance III when he said: "Chance favors only the prepared mind." Sir Alexander Fleming gave us the classic example of this principle with his extraordinarily lucky break, the discovery of penicillin. He was at work in the laboratory when his mental sequences went something like this: (1) I see that a mold has fallen by accident into my culture dish. (2) The staphylococcal colonies residing near it failed to grow. (3) Therefore, the mold must have secreted something that killed the bacteria. (4) This reminds me of a similar experience I had once before. (Previously he had isolated lysozyme present in mucus and tears, which also killed bacteria but had proved too weak to be of medical use.) (5) If I could separate this new "something" from the mold, it could be used to kill staphylococci that cause human infections.

The discovery of the cause of puerperal sepsis by Ignaz Semmelweis marks another example of Chance III. One day in 1847, a male

6
Third division: Chance III—affected by discernment, insight (par. 6 and 7)
Illustration: Fleming (par. 6)

7
Second illustration: Semmelweis (par. 7)

laboratory assistant contracted a skin infection from infected pathological material. The infection spread and the man died. When the autopsy was performed, Semmelweis saw how closely this fatal disease resembled maternal "childbed fever." Suddenly he realized that when obstetricians (who in those days used nonsterile equipment) went directly from a room where one mother lay sick or dying to the delivery room, where another mother was giving birth, they were spreading the disease. Semmelweis was severely attacked for his conclusions but years later it was proved the disease was contagious, as he had predicted, and streptococci were shown to be the bacterial cause.

8

Summary of first three kinds of chance (par. 8)

One word evokes the quality of the operations involved in the first three kinds of chance. It is serendipity, coined by Horace Walpole in 1754, who used it with reference to the legendary tales of the Three Princes of Serendip. These princes quite unexpectedly encountered instances of good fortune on their travels. As the stories go, they ran into good luck by accident (Chance I), general exploratory behavior (Chance II), or sagacity (Chance III).

9

Fourth division: Chance IV—affected by wide-ranging interests (pars. 9 and 10)

If Chance II is concerned with personal sensory receptivity, its counterpart CHANCE IV is involved with personal motor behavior— *individualized action.* The English Prime Minister Benjamin Disraeli summed up the principle underlying Chance IV when he noted: "We make our fortunes and we call them fate." Disraeli, the practical politician, appreciated that by our actions we forge our own destinies, at least to some degree. The fourth element in good luck requires an active (but unintentional), subtle, personal prompting. Chance IV is the kind of luck that develops during a probing action with a distinctive personal flavor. It comes to you because of who you are and how you behave. It is as personal as your signature. Being highly personal, it is not easily understood by someone else the first time around. Neurologists like me may be a little more comfortable with the concept because so much of the nervous system exists as anatomically separate sensory and motor divisions. Unlike Chance II, Chance IV connotes no generalized activity, as bees might have in the anonymity of a hive. Instead, like a highly personal hobby, it comprehends a kind of discrete behavioral performance. Chance II allows anyone to complete the happy by-product of luck by a kind of circular stirring of the pot. But the links of Chance IV can be drawn together and fused only by one quixotic rider cantering in on his own homemade hobby-horse, intercepting the fortuitous event at some odd angle. Chance IV resists straight logic and takes on the same eccentric, elusive quality as a mirage. It is difficult to come to grips with, for it recedes when pursued and advances as we step back. But we still accept a mirage when we see it, because we vaguely understand the basis for the phenomenon. To convey the quality underlying Chance IV, I have made up the term "altamirage." By my definition, it is a facility for encountering unexpected good luck as the result of highly individualized action. Like serendipity, it is a compound word, derived from mirage and Altamira, the cave in Spain unearthed when a hunting dog fell into it while searching for game. Later, an amateur archaeologist looking for flint chippings in the cave accidentally discovered the magnificent primitive cave paintings. Like a shimmering mirage, the event of Altamira took shape when a highly personalized quest interacted with the invisible principles of chance, which we know, yet cannot touch.

"altamirage" defined, illustrated (par. 9)

Term used to describe the quality involved	Good luck is the result of	Classification	Elements involved	Personality traits you need
Serendipity	An accident	Chance I	"Blind" luck. Chance happens, and nothing about it is directly attributable to you, the recipient.	None
	General exploratory behavior	Chance II	The Kettering Principle. Chance favors those in motion. Events are brought together to form "happy accidents" when you diffusely apply your energies in motions that are typically nonspecific.	Curiosity about many things, persistence, willingness to experiment and to explore.
	Sagacity	Chance III	The Pasteur Principle. Chance favors the prepared mind. Some special receptivity born from past experience permits you to discern a new fact or to perceive ideas in a new relationship.	A background of knowledge, based on your abilities to observe, remember, and quickly form significant new associations.
Altamirage	Personalized action	Chance IV	The Disraeli Principle. Chance favors the individualized action. Fortuitous events occur when you behave in ways that are highly distinctive of you as a person.	Distinctive hobbies, personal lifestyles, and activities peculiar to you as an individual especially when they operate in domains seemingly far removed from the area of the discovery.

Chance IV may favor you if you have distinctive if not eccentric hobbies, a personal lifestyle and motor behavior. The farther apart your personal activities are from the other areas you are involved with, the more strikingly novel will be the creative product when the two meet. There were almost infinite distances separating my dog Tom, a bell, a starch granule, and a Lafora body. Four such seemingly incongruous elements could be soldered together only when chance interacted with the lifestyle and hobby of one individual.

10
Link to story of dog Tom from par. 1 (par. 10)

TO SUM UP: Don't count on luck, but don't discount it either. Learn something about the structure of luck so that, at the very least, you don't do anything to discourage it. Especially in your activities beyond work will the varieties of chance operate, setting the stage for new friends, fresh options, discoveries, and novel perceptions prompted by actions uniquely yours. Remember: Chance I is anyone's luck. Chance II is anyone in motion's luck. Chance III is luck that comes from personal discernment. Chance IV is luck that flows from personalized actions.

11
Summary: all four types of chance (par. 11)

Discussing Content and Form

1. How does Austin's concept of chance expand on the dictionary definition? What specific element does he add?
   a. Which one from among the four types of chance could be included under the dictionary definition?
   b. Find several phrases from paragraph 1 that express the idea that "human intention" has some effect on luck.

2. Discuss the point that "self-mobilization . . . is a powerful agent in creative discovery" (par. 1).
   a. What is the relationship between that idea and the incident concerning Austin's dog, Tom?
   b. The story of Tom and the discoveries concerning Lafora's disease are an instance of Chance IV. Why do you think Austin introduced the story here and

followed it with the brief explanation of Chance IV in paragraph 2 rather than saving all the material about that kind of luck until last?

3. What personal qualities are necessary "to evoke Chance II"? What special quality helps in attaining Chance III? How do the incidents concerning Fleming and Semmelweis give evidence that these scientists possessed this special quality?

4. In what sense is serendipity involved in the first three types of chance?

5. What is the principle of division Austin uses as a basis for determining the four kinds of chance?

6. Austin's Chance IV is seemingly more accidental than either Chance II or Chance III, but it too is affected by individual action.

   a. What is meant by "the links of Chance IV can be drawn together and fused only by one quixotic rider cantering in on his own homemade hobby-horse, intercepting the fortuitous event at some odd angle" (par. 9)?
   b. How does the story of the Altamira and the word "altamirage" fit Austin's experience with Chance IV in the story about his dog, Tom?
   c. What logic is there behind relating the wideness (the range) of personal interests to the chance of experiencing an "altamirage"?

7. Using the marginal gloss, discuss the outline of this essay as it is evident in the paragraph divisions.

   a. What is the effect of the very long (three paragraphs) introduction?
   b. Why did Austin choose the order that he did for the various roles of chance?
   c. Why is so little space needed to develop Chance I? Why do you think Austin chose to give two illustrations and devote two paragraphs to developing Chance III?

8. What is your reaction to the admonishments—the personal suggestions to the reader—in paragraph 11? Does this direct address to "you" as a reader make an effective ending? Why or why not?

Considering Special Techniques

1. Writers often repeat an idea with different words both in order to achieve emphasis and to give variety. Note several

ways in which Austin says, "Luck is up to you." All of these
are from paragraph 1:
> "you may be able to exploit a few of the lucky
> situations. . . ."
> "when you are bold enough to thrust at chance."
> "We, too, will only lurch forward if we stick our necks out to
> look around. . . ."
> "Our self-mobilization to seek out and confront new situations
> is a powerful agent. . . ."
> "those pivotal events that come only when we have reached
> out in a spirit of adventure and jousted at chance. . . ."

Go on through the essay and find other examples of the
same idea expressed in different ways. To what extent does
this repetition build a thesis for the essay? Why does such an
idea about luck need reiteration if it is to be convincing?

2. Many of the paragraphs in the main part of this essay
(pars. 4-10) open with clear announcement of the division so
that the reader follows an outline of the writer's pattern.

    a. Why is the opening identification for each paragraph
       helpful in an essay of division?

    b. What is the special function of paragraph 3? of
       paragraph 8?

3. Choice of details and vocabulary often reveal much
about a writer, about the "voice" behind any piece of writing.
Although Austin announces clearly what his profession is,
show that both the illustrations he uses and his choice of
words are keys to the person behind this essay.

4. Comment on the way the story of the dog Tom is used
to unify the essay—to link beginning and end. Note other
methods of linking:

    a. How do the first two sentences in paragraph 1 link to
       the first two sentences in paragraph 11?

    b. How do the quotations cited to various "stirring"
       personalities link to each other? The first is from
       paragraph 1: "'Behold the turtle, he makes progress
       only when he sticks his neck out.'"

5. Words to learn and use: capricious, contingencies,
intuitive (par. 1); sensory (par. 3); implicit (par. 5); discernment
(par. 6); serendipity, sagacity (par. 8); anatomically, anonymity,
quixotic, fortuitous (par. 9); incongruous (par. 10). Learn also
any of the medical/scientific terms that are unfamiliar:
neurology, spherules, polymer (par. 1); staphylococcal,
lysozyme, mucus, (par. 6); puerperal sepsis, pathological,
streptococci, bacterial (par. 7).

Generating Ideas

1. Choose one of these subjects for a paper of classification, or find a similar topic of your own: ways to spend leisure time, methods of learning (some particular subject), ways of making friends, ways of keeping friends, weekend pleasures, ways to save money, ways to conserve fuel, enjoyable reading, currently popular films, current prime time television shows, newscasters, sportscasters, physical activities for health, sports offered by a certain school district or college, sports injuries, academic honors, types of assignments encountered in school.

2. Write a paper about several pieces of luck that you have had. You might develop the paper simply by using the evidences of luck as examples to show some central point (for instance, that you are a truly fortunate person), or you might classify the instances into some different types of luck or lucky situations.

3. Austin believes that personality traits—especially the trait of "doing something," of being actively involved—are important in helping "make luck happen." Show why (or why not) you think this point is valid.

4. Austin says "if you move around in more likely areas," you have a better opportunity to experience the luck he classifies as Chance II; if you have discernment (intelligence) to bring things together, you have a better opportunity for Chance III; and if you have wide-ranging interests, you are more likely to encounter the happy juxtapositions of Chance IV. Underlying all these ideas is the "work ethic" that he mentions in paragraph 1. Write a paper of your own to classify the kinds of work that you think might bring luck—or at least the opportunity for it.

5. Someone has said, "Be careful what you wish for—for you are sure to get it." Consider the statement: do people inevitably get what they really wish for because they then work for that goal?

Martin Luther King, Jr.

Martin Luther King, Jr. (1929-1968) was born in Atlanta, Georgia. He
earned a B.A. at Morehouse College, a B.D. at Crozer Theological
Seminary, and a Ph. D. at Boston University. After his ordination as a
minister, he served as pastor of the Dexter Avenue Baptist Church in
Montgomery, Alabama, where his involvement in the famous 1955-56 bus
boycott led him to form the Southern Christian Leadership Conference, an
organization dedicated to nonviolent action to better the condition of
blacks in America. After moving back to Atlanta in 1959, Dr. King became
increasingly recognized and respected as a national leader. He organized
many civil rights demonstrations, among them the "March on Washington"
in 1963, where he delivered his stirring "I Have a Dream" speech. He
opposed United States entrance into South Vietnam and the draft system,
which he felt was racially unjust. In 1964 he was awarded the prestigious
Nobel Peace Prize. He continued his opposition to all forms of
discrimination until the time of his murder by an assassin in April, 1968,
an event which shocked the nation.

Dr. King's speeches and books remain a legacy to a world still torn by
strife. The books include *Stride Toward Freedom* (1958), *Why We Can't
Wait* (1964), and *Where Do We Go from Here: Chaos or Community?* (1967).
His thoughtful classification in "The Ways of Meeting Oppression"
(editor's title) comes from this last book.

The Ways of Meeting Oppression

Oppressed people deal with their oppression in three   1
characteristic ways. One way is acquiescence: the oppressed resign themselves to their doom. They tacitly
adjust themselves to oppression, and thereby become
conditioned to it. In every movement toward freedom
some of the oppressed prefer to remain oppressed. Almost
2800 years ago Moses set out to lead the children of Israel
from the slavery of Egypt to the freedom of the promised
land. He soon discovered that slaves do not always
welcome their deliverers. They become accustomed to
being slaves. They would rather bear those ills they have,
as Shakespeare pointed out, than flee to others that they
know not of. They prefer the "fleshpots of Egypt" to the
ordeals of emancipation.

There is such a thing as the freedom of exhaustion.   2
Some people are so worn down by the yoke of oppression
that they give up. A few years ago in the slum areas of
Atlanta, a Negro guitarist used to sing almost daily: "Ben

down so long that down don't bother me." This is the type of negative freedom and resignation that often engulfs the life of the oppressed.

3   But this is not the way out. To accept passively an unjust system is to coöperate with that system; thereby the oppressed become as evil as the oppressor. Noncoöperation with evil is as much a moral obligation as is coöperation with good. The oppressed must never allow the conscience of the oppressor to slumber. Religion reminds every man that he is his brother's keeper. To accept injustice or segregation passively is to say to the oppressor that his actions are morally right. It is a way of allowing his conscience to fall asleep. At this moment the oppressed fails to be his brother's keeper. So acquiescence—while often the easier way—is not the moral way. It is the way of the coward. The Negro cannot win the respect of his oppressor by acquiescing; he merely increases the oppressor's arrogance and contempt. Acquiescence is interpreted as proof of the Negro's inferiority. The Negro cannot win the respect of the white people of the South or the peoples of the world if he is willing to sell the future of his children for his personal and immediate comfort and safety.

4   A second way that oppressed people sometimes deal with oppression is to resort to physical violence and corroding hatred. Violence often brings about momentary results. Nations have frequently won their independence in battle. But in spite of temporary victories, violence never brings permanent peace. It solves no social problem; it merely creates new and more complicated ones.

5   Violence as a way of achieving racial justice is both impractical and immoral. It is impractical because it is a descending spiral ending in destruction for all. The old law of an eye for an eye leaves everybody blind. It is immoral because it seeks to humiliate the opponent rather than win his understanding; it seeks to annihilate rather than to convert. Violence is immoral because it thrives on hatred rather than love. It destroys community and makes brotherhood impossible. It leaves society in monologue rather than dialogue. Violence ends by defeating itself. It creates bitterness in the survivors and brutality in the destroyers. A voice echoes through time saying to every

potential Peter, "Put up your sword." History is cluttered with the wreckage of nations that failed to follow this command.

If the American Negro and other victims of oppression 6 succumb to the temptation of using violence in the struggle for freedom, future generations will be the recipients of a desolate night of bitterness, and our chief legacy to them will be an endless reign of meaningless chaos. Violence is not the way.

The third way open to oppressed people in their quest 7 for freedom is the way of nonviolent resistance. Like the synthesis in Hegelian philosophy, the principle of nonviolent resistance seeks to reconcile the truths of two opposites—acquiescence and violence—while avoiding the extremes and immoralities of both. The nonviolent resister agrees with the person who acquiesces that one should not be physically aggressive toward his opponent; but he balances the equation by agreeing with the person of violence that evil must be resisted. He avoids the nonresistance of the former and the violent resistance of the latter. With nonviolent resistance, no individual or group need submit to any wrong, nor need anyone resort to violence in order to right a wrong.

It seems to me that this is the method that must guide 8 the actions of the Negro in the present crisis in race relations. Through nonviolent resistance the Negro will be able to rise to the noble height of opposing the unjust system while loving the perpetrators of the system. The Negro must work passionately and unrelentingly for full stature as a citizen, but he must not use inferior methods to gain it. He must never come to terms with falsehood, malice, hate, or destruction.

Nonviolent resistance makes it possible for the Negro to 9 remain in the South and struggle for his rights. The Negro's problem will not be solved by running away. He cannot listen to the glib suggestion of those who would urge him to migrate en masse to other sections of the country. By grasping his great opportunity in the South he can make a lasting contribution to the moral strength of the nation and set a sublime example of courage for generations yet unborn.

10   By nonviolent resistance, the Negro can also enlist all men of good will in his struggle for equality. The problem is not a purely racial one, with Negroes set against whites. In the end, it is not a struggle between people at all, but a tension between justice and injustice. Nonviolent resistance is not aimed against oppressors but against oppression. Under its banner consciences, not racial groups, are enlisted.

11   If the Negro is to achieve the goal of integration, he must organize himself into a militant and nonviolent mass movement. All three elements are indispensable. The movement for equality and justice can only be a success if it has both a mass and militant character; the barriers to be overcome require both. Nonviolence is an imperative in order to bring about ultimate community.

12   A mass movement of a militant quality that is not at the same time committed to nonviolence tends to generate conflict, which in turn breeds anarchy. The support of the participants and the sympathy of the uncommitted are both inhibited by the threat that bloodshed will engulf the community. This reaction in turn encourages the opposition to threaten and resort to force. When, however, the mass movement repudiates violence while moving resolutely toward its goal, its opponents are revealed as the instigators and practitioners of violence if it occurs. Then public support is magnetically attracted to the advocates of nonviolence, while those who employ violence are literally disarmed by overwhelming sentiment against their stand.

13   Only through a nonviolent approach can the fears of the white community be mitigated. A guilt-ridden white minority lives in fear that if the Negro should ever attain power, he would act without restraint or pity to revenge the injustices and brutality of the years. It is something like a parent who continually mistreats a son. One day that parent raises his hand to strike the son, only to discover that the son is now as tall as he is. The parent is suddenly afraid—fearful that the son will use his new physical power to repay his parent for all the blows of the past.

14   The Negro, once a helpless child, has now grown up politically, culturally, and economically. Many white men fear retaliation. The job of the Negro is to show them that

they have nothing to fear, that the Negro understands and forgives and is ready to forget the past. He must convince the white man that all he seeks is justice, *for both himself and the white man.* A mass movement exercising nonviolence is an object lesson in power under discipline, a demonstration to the white community that if such a movement attained a degree of strength, it would use its power creatively and not vengefully.

Nonviolence can touch men where the law cannot reach   15
them. When the law regulates behavior it plays an indirect part in molding public sentiment. The enforcement of the law is itself a form of peaceful persuasion. But the law needs help. The courts can order desegregation of the public schools. But what can be done to mitigate the fears, to disperse the hatred, violence, and irrationality gathered around school integration, to take the initiative out of the hands of racial demagogues, to release respect for the law? In the end, for laws to be obeyed, men must believe they are right.

Here nonviolence comes in as the ultimate form of   16
persuasion. It is the method which seeks to implement the just law by appealing to the conscience of the great decent majority who through blindness, fear, pride, or irrationality have allowed their consciences to sleep.

The nonviolent resisters can summarize their message   17
in the following simple terms: We will take direct action against injustice without waiting for other agencies to act. We will not obey unjust laws or submit to unjust practices. We will do this peacefully, openly, cheerfully because our aim is to persuade. We adopt the means of nonviolence because our end is a community at peace with itself. We will try to persuade with our words, but if our words fail, we will try to persuade with our acts. We will always be willing to talk and seek fair compromise, but we are ready to suffer when necessary and even risk our lives to become witnesses to the truth as we see it.

The way of nonviolence means a willingness to suffer   18
and sacrifice. It may mean going to jail. If such is the case the resister must be willing to fill the jail houses of the South. It may even mean physical death. But if physical death is the price that a man must pay to free his children

and his white brethren from a permanent death of the spirit, then nothing could be more redemptive.

Discussing Content and Form

1. King announces in the first sentence that there are three ways in which oppressed people may deal with oppression. Go through the selection and mark off the three divisions, each of which explains one of the ways.

2. What is King's major criticism of the "giving in," the acceptance that is the first way of meeting oppression? Mention any other examples in history of such resignation on the part of oppressed peoples.

3. What are King's objections to the second way? Prove, if you can, that his criticisms are borne out by historical evidence in other situations as well as in those he cites.

4. In what way does the third way incorporate (synthesize) both of the others without having their faults? In discussing nonviolence, King refers to Georg Friedrich Wilhelm Hegel (1770-1831), a German philosopher who believed that every thesis implies its own antithesis, and that conflict ends in a synthesis. Name the elements in this third way that represent a synthesis of the other two.

5. What are the projected results—the promise for eventual success—of nonviolence? Why is it the only possible way to an "ultimate community" (par. 11)?

6. What "direct action" does King urge his people to take? Why must nonviolence involve "willingness to suffer and sacrifice" (par. 18)?

Considering Special Techniques

1. A writer may give emphasis to an idea by position or proportion. Show that King achieves emphasis by both methods in developing his "third way."

2. As an ordained minister, King uses allusions to the Bible and to classical literature. Find four separate allusions to the Bible. Explain those that you know and use a concordance or index to look up the others.

> *a. If allusions are to be an effective technique, they must be apt, applicable to the situation they are intended to illuminate. Look up the story of Moses in the Old Testament Book of Exodus and explain the*

relationship it has to the present that King describes.
   b. Do the same for the reference to Shakespeare's
      Hamlet, *Act III, Sc. 1.*

   3. Note the announcing sentences with which King
introduces the main divisions of his essay. How does he vary
the structure of these sentences without sacrificing their
clarity as signals?

   4. Read a paragraph of this essay aloud and notice the
rhythm of the prose.
   a. How does the balance of phrases in these sentences
      from paragraph 3 make ideas forceful?
      "To accept passively an unjust system is to coöperate
         with that system. . . . "
      "To accept injustice or segregation passively is to say
         to the oppressor that his actions are morally right."
   b. How does repetition of the pattern of sentences in
      paragraph 5 help King accumulate a list of causes?
      How many of those sentences begin with "Violence
      . . . is . . . "? How many use a substitute "It" to refer
      to violence?
   c. Study the repetition that produces the rhythm in
      paragraph 17. How does that repetition and rhythm
      make the ideas forceful?
   d. Separate paragraph 17 into sentences, placing one
      sentence under another. Show how rhythm and
      repetition help make the ideas forceful.
From analysis of King's prose style in these and other
sections of the essay, draw some conclusions about the
relationship between content and form. What relationship do
you see between the prose style and the writer's
persuasiveness?

   5. *Words to learn and use:* tacitly, emancipation *(par. 1);*
acquiescence *(par. 3);* corroding *(par. 4);* recipients *(par. 6);*
synthesis *(par. 7);* perpetrators *(par. 8);* inhibited, repudiates
(par. 12); mitigated *(par. 13);* retaliation *(par. 14);* irrationality,
demagogues *(par. 15);* redemptive *(par. 18).*

Generating Ideas

   1. Write a paper explaining the various ways in which you
or others might deal with a personal problem such as one of
these: too much work, overeating, noisy neighbors, careless
roommates, general boredom, frustrating or dead-end jobs,
poor grades, inadequate study skills, lack of preparation in

some area, lack of friends, intrusions from unwanted acquaintances, shortness of money.

2. From one of your other courses, choose a question that requires an answer based on classification and create an outline of its structure. For instance, you might find a question like this in biology or environmental studies: "Controversy among farmers often arises over the control of various kinds of predators; discuss some suggested methods of dealing with this problem and determine which are most acceptable." Or, in sociology, you might be asked to discuss various types of welfare services and suggest better ways to deliver them. In constructing your outline, be aware that classification is not an end in itself, but is used to set forth some conclusions or a proposal as Martin Luther King, Jr., did in his essay.

3. Write a paper in which you employ a classification system to explain various ways of approaching some national problem. These areas should suggest a topic, although you should feel free to add others of your own:

> *The problems of educating everyone*
> *Various methods of taxation*
> *Ways of balancing a budget*
> *Methods for conserving energy or some other resource*
> *Methods for controlling the arms race*
> *Ways to meet the problem of youth unemployment*
> *Ways of controlling some kind of crime*
> *Ways of making air travel safer, or making automobile travel safer*

4. Attitudes toward a current event or social change may be classified or divided in order to arrive at a decision about where you stand. Write a paper exploring the divided opinions people hold about some subject similar to one of these:

> *Employing women in fire or police departments*
> *Drafting of women in the armed forces*
> *Grouping of students for educational purposes*
> *Giving grades in school subjects*
> *Regulating (controlling) the kinds of books that go into school libraries*

Shana Alexander

Shana Alexander (b. 1925), after graduating from Vassar College in 1945 and working as a writer and editor for various publications, served as a staff writer and columnist for *Life* magazine from 1954 to 1964. From 1972–1975 she was a columnist and contributing editor for *Newsweek*, and since 1974 she has been a regular commentator on "Point-Counterpoint," a featured section of the CBS television program "60 Minutes." Out of her observations of the contemporary social scene have come four books: *The Feminine Eye* (1970), *Shana Alexander's State-by-State Guide to Women's Rights* (1975), *Woman Talking* (1976), and *Anyone's Daughter* (1979). "The Fine Art of Marital Fighting," a slightly shortened version of an essay from *Woman Talking,* is a model of classification as well as a tongue-in-cheek account of various ways to handle marital strife.

The Fine Art of Marital Fighting

In the morning, his secretary quits; in the afternoon, his archrival at the office gets a promotion; when he gets home that evening he finds out his wife has put a dent in the new car. He drinks four martinis before dinner, and then calls his wife a lousy cook. She says how can he tell with all that gin in him, and he says she is getting as mean tempered as her stupid mother, and she says at least her mother wasn't stupid enough to marry a phony slob, by which time he is bellowing like an enraged moose, she is shrieking and hurling dishes, the baby is screaming, the dogs are yapping, the neighbors are pounding on the walls, and the cops are on their way. Suddenly a car screeches to the curb and a little man with a tape recorder under his arm hops out and dashes inside.

This scene is a recurrent dream of George R. Bach, Ph.D., a Los Angeles clinical psychologist and West Coast chairman of the American Academy of Psychotherapy. For him, it is not a nightmare but a rosy fantasy of things to come. His great ambition is to set up a Los Angeles Municipal Fight Center which any embattled husband or wife, regardless of race, creed, or hour of the night, could telephone and get a fair hearing. Trained marriage counselors would man the switchboards, referee the disputes, tape-record the hubub for analysis by dawn's

1

2

early light, and if necessary, dispatch a mobile referee on a house call.

3   It is Bach's dream to become that referee. He studies human aggression, and he loves his work. Over the last twenty-five years, he has professionally analyzed 23,000 marital fights, including, he figures, at least 2,500 of his own. Gifted marital gladiators in action thrill him as the sunset does the poet.

4   Unfortunately, his clinical practice yields so few sunsets that Bach feels the future of American family life is gravely threatened. He recently told a startled audience of newsmen and psychiatrists at the annual meeting of the Ortho-Psychiatric Association that a primary aim of psychotherapy and marriage counseling should be "to teach couples to have more, shorter, *more constructive* fights." Along with a growing number of his colleagues, he says, he has come to believe that proper training in "the fine art of marital fighting" would not only improve domestic tranquillity, it could reduce divorces by up to 90 per cent.

5   What dismays the doctor is not bloodshed per se; it is the native cowardice and abysmal crudity of American domestic fighting style. Most husbands and wives, he has found, will avail themselves of any sneaky excuse to avoid a fight in the first place. But if cornered, they begin clobbering away at one another like dull-witted Neanderthals. They are clumsy, weak-kneed, afflicted with poor aim, rotten timing, and no notion of counterpunching. What's more, they fight dirty. Their favorite weapons are the low blow and the rock-filled glove.

6   The cause of the shoddy, low estate of the marital fight game is a misunderstanding of aggression itself, says the fight doctor. "Research has established that people always dream, and *my* research has established that people are always to some degree angry. But today they are ashamed of this anger. To express hostile feelings toward a loved one is considered impolite, just as the expression of sexual feelings was considered impolite before Freud."

7   What Freud did for sex, Bach, in his own modest way, would like to do for anger, which is almost as basic a human impulse. "We must remove the shame from aggression,"

he exhorts in a soft, singsong German accent much like Peter Lorre's. "Don't repress your aggressions—program them!"

When primitive man lived in the jungle, surrounded by real, lethal enemies, the aggressive impulse is what kept him alive. For modern man, the problem gets complicated because he usually encounters only what the psychologist calls "intimate enemies"—wives, husbands, sweethearts, children, parents, friends, and others whom he sometimes would like to kill, but toward whom he nonetheless feels basic, underlying goodwill.   8

When he gets mad at one of these people, modern man tends to go to pieces. His jungle rage embarrasses, betrays, even terrifies him. "He forgets that real intimacy *demands* that there be fighting," Bach says. He fails to realize that "nonfighting is only appropriate between strangers—people who have nothing worth fighting about. When two people begin to really *care* about each other, they become emotionally vulnerable—and the battles start."   9

Listening to Bach enumerate the many destructive, "bad" fight styles is rather like strolling through a vast Stillman's gym of domestic discord. Over there, lolling about on the canvas, watching TV, walking out, sitting in a trancelike state, drinking beer, doing their nails, even falling asleep, are the "Withdrawal-Evaders," people who will not fight. These people, Bach says, are very sick. After counseling thousands of them, he is convinced that "falling asleep causes more divorces than any other single act."   10

And over *there*, viciously flailing, kicking, and throwing knives at one another, shouting obnoxious abuse, hitting below the belt, deliberately provoking anger, exchanging meaningless insults (You stink! *You* doublestink!)—simply needling or battering one another for the hell of it—are people indulging in "open noxious attack." They are the "Professional Ego-Smashers," and they are almost as sick—but not quite—as the first bunch.   11

An interesting subgroup here are the "Chain-Reactors," specialists in what Bach once characterized as "throwing in the kitchen sink from left field." A chain-reacting husband opens up by remarking, "Well, I see you burned the toast again this morning." When his   12 wife begins to make new toast, he continues, "And another thing . . . that no-good brother of yours hasn't had a job for two years." This sort of fight, says Bach, "usually pyramids to a Valhalla-type of total attack."

13   The third group of people are all smiling blandly and saying, "Yes, dear." But each one drags after him a huge gunnysack. These people are the "Pseudo-Accommodators," the ones who pretend to go along with the partner's point of view for the sake of momentary peace, but who never really mean it. The gunnysacks are full of grievances, reservations, doubts, secret contempt. Eventually the overloaded sacks burst open, making an awful mess.

14   The fourth group are "Carom Fighters," a sinister lot. They use noxious attack not directly against the partner but against some person, idea, activity, value, or object which the partner loves or stands for. They are a whiz at spoiling a good mood or wrecking a party, and when they *really* get mad, they can be extremely dangerous. Bach once made a study of one hundred intimate murders and discovered that two-thirds of the killers did not kill their partner, but instead destroyed someone whom the partner loved.

15   Even more destructive are the "Double Binders," people who set up warm expectations but make no attempt to fulfill them or, worse, deliver a rebuke instead of the promised reward. This nasty technique is known to some psychologists as the "mew phenomenon": "Kitty mews for milk. The mother cat mews back warmly to intimate that kitty should come and get it. But when the kitten nuzzles up for a drink, he gets slashed in the face with a sharp claw instead." In human terms, a wife says, for example, "I have nothing to wear." Her husband says, "Buy yourself a new dress—you deserve it." But when she comes home wearing the prize, he says, "What's that thing supposed to be, a paper bag with sleeves?"—adding, "Boy, do you look fat!"

16   The most irritating bad fighters, according to Bach, are the "Character Analysts," a pompous lot of stuffed shirts who love to explain to the mate what his or her real, subconscious, or hidden feelings are. This accomplishes nothing except to infuriate the mate by putting him on the defensive for being himself. This style of fighting is

common among lawyers, members of the professional classes, and especially, psychotherapists. It is presumptuous, highly alienating, and never in the least useful except in those rare partnerships in which husband and wife are equally addicted to a sick, sick game which Bach calls "Psychoanalytic Archaeology—the earlier, the farther back, the deeper, the better!"

In a far corner of Bach's marital gym are the "Gimmes," 17 overdemanding fighters who specialize in "overloading the system." They always want more; nothing is ever enough. New car, new house, more money, more love, more understanding—no matter what the specific demand, the partner never can satisfy it. It is a bottomless well.

Across from them are found the "Withholders," stingily 18 restraining affection, approval, recognition, material things, privileges—anything which could be provided with reasonable effort or concern and which would give pleasure or make life easier for the partner.

In a dark, scary back corner are the "Underminers," 19 who deliberately arouse or intensify emotional insecurities, reinforce moods of anxiety or depression, try to keep the partner on edge, threaten disaster, or continually harp on something the partner dreads. They may even wish it to happen.

The last group are the "Benedict Arnolds," who not 20 only fail to defend their partners against destructive, dangerous, and unfair situations, forces, people, and attacks but actually encourage such assaults from outsiders.

Husbands and wives who come to Psychologist Bach for 21 help invariably can identify themselves from the categories he lists. If they do not recognize themselves, at least they recognize their mate. Either way, most are desperate to know what can be done. Somewhere, they feel, there must be another, sunnier, marital gym, a vast Olympic Games perhaps, populated with nothing but agile, happy, bobbing, weaving, superbly muscled, and incredibly sportsmanlike gladiators.

Discussing Content and Form

1. What is the effect of treating marital fights as a sport, setting them in a "marital gym" and calling the psychotherapist a "referee"? Does Alexander treat the subject satirically or merely lightly? Explain.

2. A workable classification system must follow a single principle, and each item must fit into one of the classes or groups.
   a. What is the principle by which Alexander says Bach classifies marital fighters? Why is this system successful for her purpose?
   b. How many classes or groups of marital fighters does Alexander actually name? Why is the group in paragraph 12 a subgroup, rather than another major division?

3. What are " 'intimate enemies' " (par. 8)? Why, in Alexander's opinion, is it more difficult to handle aggressions with people who are closely related, even loved? What do you think of the statement that "'real intimacy demands that there be fighting'" (par. 9)?

4. Do you think that it would be possible for most husbands and wives to identify themselves from the categories listed here? Would other kinds of fights also fit some of the categories? Explain.

Considering Special Techniques

1. One notable feature of the essay is Alexander's ability to recreate scenes in a way that makes them come alive.
   a. Which details make the fighters and their fights especially vivid?
   b. What does the use of dialogue contribute? Note especially the imaginary exchange between a husband and wife in paragraph 15.
   c. Find several examples of colorful metaphors or similes: e.g., "like an enraged moose" (par. 1) and "marital gladiators" (par. 3). Analyze the analogy, or extended metaphor, explaining the "'mew phenomenon'" in paragraph 15.

2. Each of the various groups of fighters is clearly designated by an introductory phrase, starting with "Over there, lolling about on the canvas" in paragraph 10. Make a

list of these phrases and examine their similarities and
differences.

3. Alexander's lively style is achieved partly by sentences
which pile up parallel elements in rapid-fire succession; for
example:

". . . he is bellowing like an enraged moose, she is
shrieking and hurling dishes, the baby is screaming,
the dogs are yapping, the neighbors are pounding on
the walls, and the cops are on their way." (par. 1)
"They are clumsy, weak-kneed, afflicted with poor
aim, rotten timing, and no notion of counterpunching."
(par. 5)

Find several other sentences that contain the same
pattern.

4. How would you characterize the level of language in this
selection?

Generating Ideas

1. Write a paper in which you extend some of the
Bach-Alexander classifications to fighting in general. For
instance, are there children who are "Gimmes"? Parents who
are "Double Binders"? Do you have friends who are
"Pseudo-Accommodators"?

2. Write a paper classifying human relationships in some
way; before starting, work out a list of your groupings. One
method might classify human ties as those we are born to,
those we choose, and those forced on us by circumstance.
You may, of course, limit the area of relationships to be
classified.

3. One purpose of classification and division is to make the
whole group of which the classes are a part more readily
understood. Choose one subject from the list below and
divide it into several classes, making sure that your technique
leads to a generalization about the subject:

Types of academic courses
Career choices
Various purposes for reading
Kinds of reading material
Ways in which the public is kept informed about
current events: e.g., governmental agencies, the
media, public relations organizations

*Types of neighborhoods/shopping facilities/recreational
services in your city or area
Methods of travel/transportation
Current favorites in music, musicians, films, television
shows, etc.*

4. *Make a point about one of these subjects by using
classification and division as part of the development: kinds
of restaurants; advertisements; heroes or heroines in fiction;
types of parents; entertainers; television personalities.*

5. *Adapt one of these thesis sentences as the basis for a
classification paper:*

*"The tactics for getting good grades fall into several
distinct patterns."*

*"Part of my education has been achieved through
observation of the ways of getting ahead."*

*"Among my fellow workers I saw several methods of
fooling the boss."*

*"Coaches (basketball, football, etc.) may be classified
as parents, bosses, or very good friends."*

James Thurber

James Thurber (1894-1961) grew up in Columbus, Ohio, and graduated
from Ohio State University. After a start as a newspaperman, he began his
lifelong career with the *New Yorker* as a writer and cartoonist, an
association he commemorated in his book *The Years with Ross* (1959).
Many of his articles have been collected in *The Thurber Album* (1952) and
Thurber Country (1953), and his other books include *My Life and Hard
Times* (1933), *Fables for Our Times* (1940), and *My World and Welcome to
It!* (1942). All of his work displays a humorous and gently mocking view
of the human condition. "A Discussion of Feminine Types," in a slightly
longer form, first appeared in *Is Sex Necessary?* (1929), a book to which
E. B. White (p. 86) also contributed. In the essay Thurber treats what has
become a delicate subject with characteristically affectionate humor.

A Discussion of Feminine Types

In speaking of the weaker sex in this book, the authors   1
usually confine themselves to the generalization
"Woman," "women," and "the female." For the larger
discussions of sex, these comprehensive terms suffice. Yet
no examination of the pitiable problem of Man and Woman
would be complete without some effort to define a few of
the more important types of the female. One cannot say,
"Oh, well, you know how women are," and let it go at that.
Many truths apply, and many foibles are common, to the
whole sex, but the varieties of the female of the species are
as manifold as the varieties of the flower called the
cineraria.

Successfully to deal with a woman, a man must know   2
what type she is. There have been several methods of
classification, none of which I hold thoroughly satisfactory,
neither the glandular categories—the gonad, thyroid,
etc.—nor the astrological—Sagittarius, Virgo, Pisces, and
so on. One must be pretty expert to tell a good gonad when
he sees one. Personally, I know but very little about them,
nor if I had a vast knowledge would I know what to do with
it. It is even more difficult, and just as unimportant, to
arrive at a zodiacal classification, because that is altogether
dependent upon determining the year the woman was
born, and because, even if you should ascertain her date of

birth, the pishtosh of analysis and prediction which derives therefrom is a lot of mediæval guesswork. Or so it seems to me, and to Zaner, Blifil, Gorley, Peschkar, Rittenhouse, and Matthiessen.

3   Of much greater importance is a classification of females by actions. It comes out finally, the nature of a woman, in what she does—her little bag of tricks, as one might say.

4   A type of which one hears a great deal but which has never been very ably or scientifically analyzed, for the guidance of men, is the Quiet Type. How often one hears the warning, "Look out for the Quiet Type." Let us see if we should look out for it, and why.

5   The element of menace in the Quiet Type is commonly considered very great. Yet if one asks a man who professes knowledge of the type, why one should look out for it, one gets but a vague answer. "Just look out, that's all," he usually says. When I began my researches I was, in spite of myself, somewhat inhibited by an involuntary subscription to this legendary fear. I found it difficult to fight off a baseless alarm in the presence of a lady of subdued manner. Believing, however, that the best defense is an offense, I determined to carry the war, as it were, into the enemy's country. The first Quiet Type, or Q.T., that I isolated was a young woman whom I encountered at a Sunday tea party. She sat a little apart from the rest of the group in a great glazed chintz, I believe it was, chair. Her hands rested quietly on the chair arms. She kept her chin rather down than up, and had a way of lifting her gaze slowly, without disturbing the set of her chin. She moved but twice, once to put by a cup of tea and once to push back a stray lock from her forehead. I stole glances at her from time to time, trying to make them appear ingenuous and friendly rather than bold or suggestive, an achievement rendered somewhat troublesome by an unfortunate involuntary winking of the left eyelid to which I am unhappily subject.

6   I noted that her eyes, which were brown, had a demure light in them. She was dressed simply and was quite pretty. She spoke but once or twice, and then only when spoken to. In a chance shifting of the guests to an adjacent room to examine, I believe, some water colors, I was left quite alone

with her. Steeling myself for an ordeal to which I am unused—or was at the time—I moved directly to her side and grasped her hand. "Hallo, baby! Some fun—hah?" I said—a method of attack which I had devised in advance. She was obviously shocked, and instantly rose from her chair and followed the others into the next room. I never saw her again, nor have I been invited to that little home since. Now for some conclusions.

Patently, this particular Q.T., probably due to an individual variation, was not immediately dangerous in the sense that she would seize an opportunity, such as I offered her, to break up the home of, or at least commit some indiscretion with, a man who was obviously—I believe I may say—a dependable family man with the average off-hand attractions. Dr. White has criticized my methodology in this particular case, a criticism which I may say now, in all good humor, since the danger is past, once threatened to interpose insuperable obstacles, of a temperamental nature, in the way of this collaboration. It was his feeling that I might just as well have removed one of the type's shoes as approach her the way I did. I cannot hold with him there. Neither, I am gratified to say, can Zaner, but in fairness to White it is only just to add that Tithridge can.

However, the next Q.T. that I encountered I placed under observation more gradually. I used to see her riding on a Fifth Avenue bus, always at a certain hour. I took to riding on this bus also, and discreetly managed to sit next her on several occasions. She eventually noticed that I appeared to be cultivating her and eyed me quite candidly, with a look I could not at once decipher. I could now, but at that time I couldn't. I resolved to put the matter to her quite frankly, to tell her, in fine, that I was studying her type and that I wished to place her under closer observation. Therefore, one evening, I doffed my hat and began.

"Madam," I said, "I would greatly appreciate making a leisurely examination of you, at your convenience." She struck me with the palm of her hand, got up from her seat, and descended at the next even-numbered street—Thirty-sixth, I believe it was.

I may as well admit here and now that personally I enjoyed at no time any great success with Q.T.'s. I think one may go as far as to say that any scientific examination of the Quiet Type, as such, is out of the question. I know of no psychologist who has ever got one alone long enough to get anywhere. (Tithridge has averred that he began too late in life; Zaner that he does not concur in the major premise.) The Quiet Type is not amenable to the advances of scientific men when the advances are of a scientific nature, and also when they are of any other nature. Indeed, it is one of the unfortunate handicaps to psychological experimentation that many types of women do not lend themselves readily to purposeful study. As one woman said to me, "It all seems so mapped out, kind of. . . ."

11   In my very failures I made, I believe, certain significant findings in regard to the Quiet Type. It is not dangerous to men, but to a particular man. Apparently it lies in wait for some one individual and gets him. Being got by this special type, or even being laid in wait for, would seem to me in some cases not without its pleasurable compensations. Wherein, exactly, the menace lies, I have no means of knowing. I have my moments when I think I see what it is, but I have other moments when I think I don't.

12   The Buttonhole-twister Type is much easier to come at. A girl of this persuasion works quite openly. She has the curious habit of insinuating a finger, usually the little finger of the right hand, unless she be left-handed, into the lapel buttonhole of a gentleman, and twisting it. Usually, she picks out a man who is taller than herself and usually she gets him quite publicly, in parks, on street corners, and the like. Often, while twisting, she will place the toe of her right shoe on the ground, with the heel elevated, and will swing the heel slowly through an arc of about thirty or thirty-five degrees, back and forth. This manifestation is generally accompanied by a wistful, far-away look on the woman's face, and she but rarely gazes straight at the man. She invariably goes in for negative statements during the course of her small writhings, such as "It is not," "I am not," "I don't believe you do," and the like. This type is demonstrative in her affections and never lies in wait with any subtlety. She is likely to be restless and discontented with the married state, largely because she will want to go

somewhere that her husband does not want to go, or will not believe he has been to the places that he says he just came from. It is well to avoid this type.

A charming but altogether dangerous type is the 13 "Don't, dear" Type. By assuming a middle of the road, this way and that way, attitude toward a gentleman's advances, she will at once allure and repulse him. The man will thus be twice allured. He calls on her, and they sit in the porch swing, let us say. When he slips his arm around her, she will say in a low tone, "Don't, dear." No matter what he does, she will say, "Don't, dear." This type is a homemaker. Unless the man wants a home made for him within a very short time, it is better for him to observe the "don't" rather than the "dear," and depart. The type is common in the Middle West, particularly in university towns, or was some few years ago, at any rate. Any effort to classify modern university types would be difficult and confusing. They change from year to year, and vary with the region. I am told that one type has actually been known to get the man of her choice down and sit, as it were, side-saddle of him. I would not give even this brief mention, in passing, to college types of the female, were they not important because they so frequently divert a man from his career and tie him down before he has a chance to begin working, or even to say anything.

The rest of the types of American women, such as the 14 Outdoors, the Clinging Vine, and so on and so on, are too generally known to need any special comment here. If a man does not know one when he sees it, or cannot tell one from another, of these more common types, there is little that can be done for him. No man should contemplate marriage, or even mingle with women, unless he has a certain measure of intuition about these more obvious types. For example, if a man could not tell instantly that a woman was the sort that would keep him playing tennis, or riding horseback, all afternoon, and then expect him to ride back and forth all night on the ferry, no amount of description of the Outdoors Type would be of any avail.

There is, however, one phenomenal modern type, a 15 product of these strange post-war years, which will bear a brief analysis. This is the type represented by the girl who gets right down to a discussion of sex on the occasion of her first meeting with a man, but then goes on to betray a great deal of alarm and aversion to the married state. This is the "I-can't-go-through-with-it" Type. Many American virgins fall within this classification. Likewise it contains women who have had some strange and bitter experience about which they do a great deal of hinting but which they never clearly explain. If involved with, or even merely presented to, a woman of this type, no man in his right mind will do anything except reach for his hat. Science does not know what is the matter with these women, or whether anything is the matter. A lot of reasons have been advanced for girls acting in this incredible, dismayed manner—eleven reasons in all, I believe—but no one really knows very much about it. It may be their mothers' teaching, it may have been some early childhood experience, such as getting caught under a gate, or suffering a severe jolting up by being let fall when a boy jumped off the other end of a teeter-totter, or it may simply be a whim. We do not know. One thing is sure, they are never the Quiet Type. They talk your arm off.

Discussing Content and Form

1. The selection was first published in 1929, certainly with the intention of amusing the reader. Do changes in time and audience make it less humorous today? Explain.

2. How many classes or types of women does Thurber identify? What is his principle of classification?

3. If a method of classification is to be comprehensive, all of the subjects under consideration should fall into one of the classes. How does Thurber protect his system from the charge that he omits some women? Can all women be classified on the basis of Thurber's system? Why or why not?

4. Why does Thurber consider other methods of classification and reject them (par. 2)?

5. Make a list of Thurber's classes and discuss the order in which he presents them.
   a. Why does he give the most space to the Quiet Type?
   b. Why do you think he places the "I-can't-go-through-with-it" Type last?
   c. Analyze Thurber's use of transitions between his various types. Although he includes numerous details

*about each type, what transitions keep the essay
moving coherently? Comment on the effect of these
signals on the logic and the clarity of the selection.*

6. *Point out examples of Thurber's laughter at himself.
What does this self-deprecation contribute to the tone of the
essay?*

Considering Special Techniques

1. *Classification is frequently part of scientific writing. Point
out several methods that Thurber uses to give the impression
that his study is based on scientific investigation.*

    a. *What is the effect of the citation to authorities "Zaner,
Blifil, Gorley, Peschkar, Rittenhouse, and Matthiessen"
(par. 2)? Do these people need to be "real"? Why or
why not? "Dr. White" (par. 7) is E. B. White,
Thurber's collaborator on the book from which the
selection comes. What special humor is achieved
through recounting their supposed differences?*

    b. *In which incidents does Thurber attempt to give the
appearance that he is a scientific observer? Could
some of the humor in the essay be directed at
scientists as well as at the man-woman relationship?
Explain.*

2. *Thurber frequently uses lofty and elevated expressions to
convey some rather simple ideas. For example, his statement,
"I was . . . somewhat inhibited by an involuntary subscription
to this legendary fear" (par. 5), basically means that he was
afraid. Find examples of other such expressions and show
how they contribute to the overall humorous effect of the
selection.*

3. *Words to learn and use:* foibles *(par. 1);* gonad, thyroid,
astrological, zodiacal *(par. 2);* patently, insuperable,
collaboration *(par. 7);* amenable *(par. 10).*

Generating Ideas

1. *Write a paper based on a classification of "modern
university types" (par. 13), including both females and males.
Choose your own system for classifying.*

2. *Classify politicians or voters by using some system other
than the customary broad classes of* liberal *and* conservative.

3. *Choose some large group of persons to classify*

according to a system that is inclusive and clear, then write a humorous paper describing the characteristics of each group. Here are some suggestions: students, professors or teachers, parents, sales clerks, automobile drivers, heroes, popular singers, policemen, sports personalities. For example, you might classify automobile drivers by a system based on their attitudes toward bikers and pedestrians.

4. Thurber's reaction to the behavior of the Quiet Type might be called "fresh" or "forward." Think of other types of approaches to this kind of person and write a humorous essay of classification in which you give various examples of the "come-on" or "put-down."

5. Some words and incidents in Thurber's essay serve to date it. Write a critical reaction to that "datedness," showing why you find this characteristic appealing or objectionable. Be sure to use specifics from the essay to support your opinion. For instance, the porch swing (par. 13), once common in American homes, is now largely obsolete.

ARGUMENT AND PERSUASION:
MAKING A TELLING POINT

"My firm opinion is. . . ." "There is plenty of proof. . . ." "You must believe that. . . ." In writing as in speech we constantly state propositions, take stands on issues or actions, and back up views with argument in order to persuade someone to agree. The writers of many of the essays in this text not only give information but they also express opinions; and in the process of explaining their subjects they employ various methods, subtle or obvious, to win agreement. Thus expository writing often has an argumentative edge, for a writer may both explain and persuade. Similarly, the writer whose primary purpose is to persuade makes use of the expository techniques—arranging examples, comparing one thing to another, defining terms, tracing cause/effect relationships, and so on. But in persuasive writing, there are other methods used by the persuader that are worthy of special examination.

Consider some of the persuasive writing that occurs in daily life. One advertiser points out that a small car provides better gas mileage, while another hints that a large one gives its owner status. A political candidate hands out pamphlets explaining his proposals for cutting property taxes or building a downtown parking area. An editorialist denounces the city council for failing to extend bus service to the suburbs, or criticizes a President's cabinet appointments.

In every case the success of the persuasion depends on how well the writer reaches the intended audience. One of the writer's first requirements is to assess the interests and opinions of the reader, and then to decide on the kind of tone to employ in presenting the subject. Overdoing—"the hard sell"—may offend; belittling—"talking down"—may insult; emotional appeals—"loaded language"—may be detected and assumed false, even in a good cause. It is usually safest to regard the reader as an intelligent thinker who will best respond to well-considered proof and careful logic. And it is usually best to assume an attitude of mutual concern, writing as one who shares rather than browbeats or badgers.

A classic failure in persuading is exemplified by Dr. Stockmann, the main character of Henrik Ibsen's play *An Enemy of the People*. Dr. Stockmann is a medical officer who discovers that the baths from which his town makes a living are polluted and that the people who visit the town are being infected from the waters. Envisioning himself as a savior with a message for which he feels certain he will win acclaim, Stockmann rashly misjudges the narrowness of his audience and only offends them with his arrogance. Even though he is completely right in what he says, he fails to win their support.

Although tone is important, good persuasion ultimately rests firmly on sound knowledge, on a command of the facts on all sides of an issue. Sufficient information, whether gathered by direct observation or by up-to-date research, is essential not only for building a convincing case but also for anticipating and refuting possible counterarguments.

Persuasive writing uses two principal methods: (1) logical argument, and (2) appeal to the emotions. Satiric persuasion is sometimes considered a third method, but satire usually combines the other two. In "A Modest Proposal" (p. 389), Jonathan Swift uses both logic and emotion, so that the difference is one of tone rather than of method. In persuasion as in exposition, the methods overlap, and most persuasion involves both logical argument and emotional appeal.

Because it is very prevalent and familiar in everyday life, it may be easier to consider emotional persuasion first. Arousing a reader's emotions depends largely upon choosing words with strong connotations to elicit a desired response. The use of such language colors almost every controversial issue. Environmentalists, for example, call industrialists "polluters" or "profiteering destroyers of national wildlife," while industry labels some conservation groups "obstructionists who are destroying our national economy." Repetition, especially of such strong words and of rhythmic sentence patterns, also helps move an audience or reader. The charged language and the rhythmic sentences of this passage first stirred readers during the American Revolution:

> These are the times that try men's souls. The summer soldier and the sunshine patriot will in this crisis, shrink from the service of his country; but he that stands it NOW, deserves the love and thanks of man and woman. Tyranny, like hell, is not easily conquered; yet we have this consolation with us, that the harder the conflict, the more glorious the triumph. What we obtain too cheap, we esteem too lightly; 'tis dearness only that gives everything its value. Heaven knows how to put a proper price upon its goods; and it would be strange indeed, if so celestial an article as FREEDOM should not be highly rated. Britain, with an army to enforce her tyranny, has declared that she has a right (*not only to* TAX) but "to BIND *us in* ALL CASES WHATSOEVER," and if being *bound in that manner,* is not slavery, then is there not such a thing as slavery upon earth. Even the expression is impious, for so unlimited a power can belong only to God.—Tom Paine, *The Crisis*

While such appeals can be sincere and moving, and can be effective in achieving immediate goals, they can also be dangerous and inaccurate. There is nothing inherently good or bad about appealing to the emotions, yet conscientious writers and wary readers must recognize the method and judge for themselves.

Logical argument proceeds by two chief avenues of reasoning—*induction* and *deduction*. Although the two are separated here for the purpose of examination, they function together in most pieces of persuasive writing. Inductive reasoning involves considering a number of particulars (facts, examples, observed phenomena) to arrive at a general conclusion. For example, if seven students you know get failing or D grades in Physics 101, you conclude that the course is difficult. Or if several bicycle owners mention that they find the Motobecane great for touring, you may decide to buy that make of bicycle. The scientist constantly employs induction. For instance, Samuel Scudder in Chapter 1 tells how his teacher expected him to observe a preserved fish and to reach conclusions about it; and Sally Carrighar in Chapter 9 explains how the ethologist observes animal behavior to arrive at generalized conclusions.

If the induction is sound, the particulars lead logically to the generalization by an *inductive leap,* or step in the thinking process. If the particulars are too few or are not representative, the reasoning will be illogical and will lead to a *hasty generalization.* From visiting London during a week of sunny weather, you cannot logically conclude that all stories about British fog are false; because a French restaurant near you closes, you cannot assume that your town does not appreciate continental cuisine. Such hasty generalizations will not convince a thinking reader.

Put simply, deductive reasoning is characterized by the application of the general to the specific, by moving from a general statement to further instances, similar cases, or comparable situations. The logician refers to this type of reasoning as a *syllogism,* and reducing an argument to syllogistic form is a test of the logic behind it. Follow the reasoning behind these syllogisms:

Major premise: Students learn little in large classes.
Minor premise: Classes in this school are large.
Conclusion: Students in this school learn little.

Major premise: Drivers who have accidents pay
                higher insurance rates.

Minor premise: Tom recently had two accidents:
Conclusion: Tom's insurance rate will increase.

If an argument is to hold up, to appear logical, the premises must be valid. Further induction, achieved by gathering additional evidence, may be necessary to validate the premises. In this way, the two types of logical reasoning work together. For instance, the first syllogism above may be considered too broad and the major premise may seem invalid. But if it were supported by data gathered from tests given in large classes and in smaller ones, the premise would be valid and the logic convincing.

Notice how evidence from history serves as the basis for an inductive leap to the conclusion in this paragraph:

> If anything conclusive could be inferred from experience, without psychological analysis, it would be that the things which women are not allowed to do are the very ones for which they are peculiarly qualified; since their vocation for government has made its way, and become conspicuous, through the very few opportunities which have been given; while in the lines of distinction which apparently were freely open to them, they have by no means so eminently distinguished themselves. We know how small a number of reigning queens history presents, in comparison with that of kings. Of this smaller number a far larger proportion have shown talents for rule; though many of them have occupied the throne in difficult periods. It is remarkable, too, that they have, in a greater number of instances, been distinguished by merits the most opposite to the imaginary and conventional character of women: they have been as much remarked for the firmness and vigour of their rule, as for its intelligence. When, to queens and empresses, we add regents, and viceroys of provinces, the list of women who have been eminent rulers of mankind swells to a great length. This fact is so undeniable, that someone, long ago, tried to retort the argument, and turned the admitted truth into an additional insult, by saying that queens are better than kings, because under kings women govern, but under queens, men.—John Stuart Mill, *The Subjection of Women*

From Mill's "experience" of knowing about "a greater number of instances" in which women have ruled well in difficult times, he concludes that women are "peculiarly qualified" to govern. He might, of course, have named particular women who distinguished themselves as rulers, thereby making statements that were less abstract and more concrete, but the pattern of reasoning would remain the same. In contrast, this paragraph follows a deductive pattern:

> I shall not go back to the remote annals of antiquity to trace the history of women; it is sufficient to allow, that she has always been either a slave or a despot, and to remark, that each of these situations equally retards the progress of reason. The grand source of female folly and vice has ever appeared to me to arise from narrowness of mind; and the very constitution of civil governments has put almost insuperable obstacles in the way to prevent the cultivation of the female understanding; yet virtue can be built on no other foundation! The same obstacles are thrown in the way of the rich, and the same consequences ensue.—Mary Wollstonecraft, *Observations on the State of Degradation to Which Woman Is Reduced by Various Causes*

The reasoning in this paragraph might be represented by a syllogism:
Slavery and despotism equally retard the progress of reason.
Women have always been either slaves or despots.
Therefore, women have been prevented from cultivating their powers of reason.

Effective persuasive writing involves several stages of development: first, a thoughtful presentation of the writer's self, a careful analysis of the intended audience, and a considered choice of tone provide the foundation. Second, a thorough knowledge of particulars (the basis for induction) and sound deductive logic establish the reasonableness of the argument. Finally, a judicious use of emotional appeals helps move the reader. Although the same methods may be utilized to persuade for wrong causes as for right ones, the ethical sense of the persuader and the intelligent appraisal by the reader should, ideally at least, guard against persuasion for wrong purposes.

Howard Temin

Howard Temin (b. 1935) is Professor of Oncology at the University of Wisconsin-Madison. He was awarded the 1975 Nobel Prize in Medicine for his research into the genetic basis of cancer. Temin's work at McArdle Laboratories continues to point the way for further research into the causes and cures for cancer. He has consistently spoken for the elimination of cancer-producing agents from the environment, as he does in the following selection. "A Warning to Smokers," first presented as a speech to a Senate subcommittee, is one of several appeals that Temin has made in support of increased government regulation of research funding.

A Warning to Smokers

My point of view is that of a cancer researcher who has been working for the last 20 years with RNA viruses that cause cancer in chickens.

Since the early years of this century, it has been known that viruses cause cancer in chickens. In more recent years viruses have been shown to cause cancer not only in chickens, but also in mice, cats, and even in some primates. Therefore, it was a reasonable hypothesis that viruses might cause cancer in humans and that, if a human cancer virus existed, it could be prevented by a vaccine as so many other virus diseases have been prevented.

Experiments performed in recent years have led to an understanding of much of the genetic basis of how viruses cause cancer in animals, namely, by adding their genetic information to the DNA, that is, the genetic material, of the cell. With this understanding and the tools of molecular biology, it has been possible to look for viruses potentially preventable by vaccines that might cause human cancer. Unfortunately, I think we can now conclude that most human cancer is not caused by such viruses.

1
Statement of position
as researcher
(establishes speaker)
(par. 1)

2
Summary of earlier
hypothesis about
possible cause and
cure of cancer
(provides background)
(pars. 2–4)

3

4   Scientifically this conclusion is an advance, for science progresses by disproving hypotheses. But, in terms of preventive medicine, I believe this conclusion ends the hope for a vaccine that would prevent cancer caused by viruses.

Transition (par. 5)

5   Must we, therefore, give up hope of preventing cancer?

Presentation of currently accepted hypothesis and call for action (par. 6)

6   No. For in recent years, the hypothesis that chemicals and radiation probably cause cancer by mutation of the cell genome has been strongly supported. Furthermore, epidemiological evidence has shown that the incidence of human cancer is not the same in all parts of the world and in all population groups, but that the incidence of human cancer varies from country to country, region to region, and population group to population group depending on the nature of the environment. Therefore, there must be environmental features that play a determining role in the formation of human cancer. One of the most clearly established of these environmental features is smoking, especially cigaret smoking. Cigaret smokers not only have a much greater probability of developing lung cancer than do otherwise similar nonsmokers, but the smokers have a greater probability of dying from a number of other diseases. Therefore, our best present hope of preventing cancer does not appear to lie in a vaccine against viruses, but in removing or reducing the levels of chemical carcinogens from the environment.

Expression of main point: cigaret smoking is the greatest source of carcinogens (states proposition) (par. 7)

7   The single most important source of these carcinogens and the one which should be most easily removable is tobacco, probably especially the tars from tobacco. The American Cancer Society estimates that the life expectancy of a man of 25 who continually smokes 2 packs of

cigarets a day is 8 years less than that of a 25-year-old nonsmoker. Stopping cigaret smoking would have the greatest effect on increasing life expectancy, but, if that is not possible, reducing the level of tar from tobacco would at least serve to reduce the cancer risk of smokers. Therefore, if a tax based on the level of tar and nicotine in cigarets decreased the amount of exposure to tar, it would help to prevent some of the cancers which otherwise would be caused by smoking.

However, further research is still needed on cancer and other diseases both to help prevent those diseases that are not caused by smoking and to help cure those diseases that cannot be prevented. For example, we need to develop better therapies for cancer based upon an understanding of the differences in biochemistry and control of cell multiplication between cancer cells and normal cells. Comparison of virus-transformed cells and normal cells is one of the best systems to find such differences.

8
Call for better methods of cancer prevention (makes proposals) (pars. 8 and 9)

However, we must try even harder to prevent cancer before it starts, since so far it has been difficult to find many biochemical differences between cancer cells and normal cells that can be exploited in therapy. For prevention, we must devise better methods of testing for factors in the environment, including chemicals from industrial processes and possibly food additives, that can cause cancer, and after we find these factors we must try to remove them. In addition, we must try to understand more of the mechanisms by which chemicals and radiation cause cancer in the hope that such knowledge will make it easier for us to recognize these carcinogens and perhaps to devise means to prevent their action. However, when, as in the case of

9

smoking, we find that a carcinogen exists, we must act to prevent it from entering the environment.

10
Statement that
government should
take stronger stand on
smoking (par. 10)

From the point of view of a scientist engaged in cancer research, it is paradoxical that the U.S. people, through Congress, spend hundreds of millions of dollars a year for research to prevent and cure human cancer. But when we can say how to prevent much human cancer, namely, stop cigaret smoking, little or nothing is done to prevent this cancer. In fact, I believe the U.S. government even subsidizes the growing of tobacco. As I said at the Nobel festival banquet in Stockholm, I am outraged that this one major method available to prevent much human cancer, namely the cessation of cigaret smoking, is not more widely adopted.

11
Call for care in
government research
funding (par. 11)

I should also like to comment on a possible large increase in funding for biomedical and other health-related research. At present the U.S. system of support of biomedical research and the results of this research are the best in the world. Therefore, we must be careful before undertaking drastic changes in the way we fund biomedical research, and we should especially be careful to ensure that quality is stressed in all biomedical research. An excellent way to insure this quality is the system of peer review of grants used at NIH [National Institutes of Health]. Furthermore, although at a particular time we might wish to work on a particular problem in biomedical research or solve some health-related problems, if techniques and theoretical knowledge are not advanced enough to supply a proper foundation for the research, it may not be possible to approach such problems. Nature yields her secrets slowly, and only when a proper foundation of previous knowledge exists. Therefore, I wonder about the advisability of trying to spend rapidly much larger sums of money in this area. I suggest that a large and rapid increase in money is not warranted. More important is a mechanism for assurance of continuing support of good basic biomedical research and a good peer review system.

In conclusion, I feel that the support previously extended to cancer research by the U.S. people through the Congress indicates a concern with preventing this disease. Research indicates that the best present method available to prevent much cancer is to decrease smoking. I, therefore, support Congressional action to decrease smoking.

12
Recapitulation of previous views (par. 12)

Discussing Content and Form

1. Speakers and writers often establish their credentials—their "right to speak" on a subject—before beginning their main presentation, a convention that Temin follows in his first paragraph. What effect does his position as a scientist have on the tone, form, and content of the selection? What further personal qualifications does he mention after that paragraph?

2. Why do you think Temin dismisses the idea that cancer is caused by viruses before stating his own position?

3. Make a list of all the facts Temin presents in the order in which he presents them. Are his opinions and recommendations based logically on his facts? Explain.

4. Explain the statement, "science progresses by disproving hypotheses" (par. 4).

5. Is Temin's essay persuasive enough to convince you that cigaret smoking is a cause of cancer? If you are a smoker, is it persuasive enough to convince you to quit smoking? Why or why not?

Considering Special Techniques

1. Speakers and writers of persuasion must be especially sensitive to the audience they are addressing. How does the fact that this is a statement to a Senate subcommittee affect the tone, the form, and the content?

2. What is the effect of the single question paragraph (par. 5)? What is the effect of answering with the single word "No" (par. 6)?

3. Does Temin's use of scientific terms (DNA, cell genome, carcinogens, etc.) interfere with your understanding? Why or why not?

4. Restate paragraphs 6 and 7 in the form of syllogisms, and discuss the logic of Temin's deductive arguments.

5. Examine some of the phrases and words that Temin uses to indicate logical connections between ideas: e.g., "With this understanding" and "we can now conclude" (par. 3); and in paragraph 6 he uses "Furthermore" once and "Therefore" twice. Why are such links especially important in Temin's argument?

Generating Ideas

1. Write a persuasive paper using the material in Temin's report and designing it for the popular audience of a magazine such as Reader's Digest.

2. Write a persuasive paper in which you present your view that no-smoking areas in public buildings should (or should not) be strictly enforced. Direct the paper to a specific audience, for example, an alderman or city council.

3. Make a study of the amount of money the U.S. government has spent on subsidizing the tobacco industry over the last few years and write a paper in which you suggest how this money could have been used for such purposes as health-related research. Or, write a paper in which you show the political reasons behind the tobacco subsidy.

4. Write a paper using the following sentence from the selection as a thesis statement: "Nature yields her secrets slowly, and only when a proper foundation of previous knowledge exists." Support your statements by citing examples.

5. In the New Yorker, December 13, 1976, and December 20, 1976, Paul Brodeur in "A Reporter at Large," discusses the biological effects of long-term, low-level microwave radiation on radar technicians and microwave workers. Read these articles and write a paper presenting your opinion of the validity of Brodeur's arguments.

Norman Cousins

Norman Cousins (b. 1912) is one of the nation's most distinguished
journalists and editors. He began his career on the editorial staff of the
New York Evening Post, moved to *Current History*, and in 1940 became
executive editor of *Saturday Review*, the magazine with which he has been
associated in some capacity ever since, and where he now serves as
Chairman of the Editorial Board. Cousins' leadership on many
public-service groups and foundations has never deterred him from writing
prolifically. Among his many books are *The Good Inheritance: The
Democratic Chance* (1942), *Modern Man Is Obsolete* (1945), *Who Speaks for
Man?* (1952), *The Last Defense in a Nuclear Age* (1960), and an
autobiography, *Present Tense: An American Editor's Odyssey* (1968).
Recently his *Anatomy of an Illness* (1979) has become a best-seller and a
milestone in what is sometimes called a "holistic" view of medicine.
Cousins' personal experience with a serious illness led him to write the
book, for which the full title indicates the subject is illness "as Perceived
by the Patient: Reflections on Healing and Regeneration." Cousins' skill in
handling evidence and his brilliance of literary style make the section
entitled "Pain Is Not the Ultimate Enemy" a very forceful essay in itself.

Pain Is Not the Ultimate Enemy

Americans are probably the most pain-conscious people on
the face of the earth. For years we have had it drummed
into us—in print, on radio, over television, in everyday
conversation—that any hint of pain is to be banished as
though it were the ultimate evil. As a result, we are
becoming a nation of pill-grabbers and hypochondriacs,
escalating the slightest ache into a searing ordeal.

We know very little about pain and what we don't know
makes it hurt all the more. Indeed, no form of illiteracy in
the United States is so widespread or costly as ignorance
about pain—what it is, what causes it, how to deal with it
without panic. Almost everyone can rattle off the names of
at least a dozen drugs that can deaden pain from every
conceivable cause—all the way from headaches to hemor-
rhoids. There is far less knowledge about the fact that about
90 percent of pain is self-limiting, that it is not always an
indication of poor health, and that, most frequently, it is the
result of tension, stress, worry, idleness, boredom,
frustration, suppressed rage, insufficient sleep, overeating, poorly balanced diet, smoking, excessive drinking,

inadequate exercise, stale air, or any of the other abuses encountered by the human body in modern society.

3   The most ignored fact of all about pain is that the best way to eliminate it is to eliminate the abuse. Instead, many people reach almost instinctively for the painkillers—aspirins, barbiturates, codeines, tranquilizers, sleeping pills, and dozens of other analgesics or desensitizing drugs.

4   Most doctors are profoundly troubled over the extent to which the medical profession today is taking on the trappings of a pain-killing industry. Their offices are overloaded with people who are morbidly but mistakenly convinced that something dreadful is about to happen to them. It is all too evident that the campaign to get people to run to a doctor at the first sign of pain has boomeranged. Physicians find it difficult to give adequate attention to patients genuinely in need of expert diagnosis and treatment because their time is soaked up by people who have nothing wrong with them except a temporary indisposition or a psychogenic ache.

5   Patients tend to feel indignant and insulted if the physician tells them he can find no organic cause for the pain. They tend to interpret the term "psychogenic" to mean that they are complaining of nonexistent symptoms. They need to be educated about the fact that many forms of pain have no underlying physical cause but are the result, as mentioned earlier, of tension, stress, or hostile factors in the general environment. Sometimes a pain may be a manifestation of "conversion hysteria," as mentioned earlier, the name given by Jean Charcot to physical symptoms that have their origins in emotional disturbances.

6   Obviously, it is folly for an individual to ignore symptoms that could be a warning of a potentially serious illness. Some people are so terrified of getting bad news from a doctor that they allow their malaise to worsen, sometimes past the point of no return. Total neglect is not the answer to hypochondria. The only answer has to be increased education about the way the human body works, so that more people will be able to steer an intelligent course between promiscuous pill-popping and irresponsible disregard of genuine symptoms.

Of all forms of pain, none is more important for the   7
individual to understand than the "threshold" variety.
Almost everyone has a telltale ache that is triggered
whenever tension or fatigue reaches a certain point. It can
take the form of a migraine-type headache or a squeezing
pain deep in the abdomen or cramps or a pain in the lower
back or even pain in the joints. The individual who has
learned how to make the correlation between such
threshold pains and their cause doesn't panic when they
occur; he or she does something about relieving the stress
and tension. Then, if the pain persists despite the absence
of apparent cause, the individual will telephone the doctor.

If ignorance about the nature of pain is widespread,   8
ignorance about the way pain-killing drugs work is even
more so. What is not generally understood is that many of
the vaunted pain-killing drugs conceal the pain without
correcting the underlying condition. They deaden the
mechanism in the body that alerts the brain to the fact that
something may be wrong. The body can pay a high price for
suppression of pain without regard to its basic cause.

Professional athletes are sometimes severely disadvan-   9
taged by trainers whose job it is to keep them in action. The
more famous the athlete, the greater the risk that he or she
may be subjected to extreme medical measures when injury
strikes. The star baseball pitcher whose arm is sore because
of a torn muscle or tissue damage may need sustained rest
more than anything else. But his team is battling for a place
in the World Series; so the trainer or team doctor, called
upon to work his magic, reaches for a strong dose of
butazolidine or other powerful pain suppressants. Presto,
the pain disappears! The pitcher takes his place on the
mound and does superbly. That could be the last game,
however, in which he is able to throw a ball with full
strength. The drugs didn't repair the torn muscle or cause
the damaged tissue to heal. What they did was to mask the
pain, enabling the pitcher to throw hard, further damaging
the torn muscle. Little wonder that so many star athletes
are cut down in their prime, more the victims of
overzealous treatment of their injuries than of the injuries
themselves.

The king of all painkillers, of course, is aspirin. The U.S.   10

Food and Drug Administration permits aspirin to be sold without prescription, but the drug, contrary to popular belief, can be dangerous and, in sustained doses, potentially lethal. Aspirin is self-administered by more people than any other drug in the world. Some people are aspirin-poppers, taking ten or more a day. What they don't know is that the smallest dose can cause internal bleeding. Even more serious perhaps is the fact that aspirin is antagonistic to collagen, which has a key role in the formation of connective tissue. Since many forms of arthritis involve disintegration of the connective tissue, the steady use of aspirin can actually intensify the underlying arthritic condition.

11   The reason why aspirin is prescribed so widely for arthritic patients is that it has an antiinflammatory effect, apart from its pain-deadening characteristics. In recent years, however, medical researchers have suggested that the antiinflammatory value of aspirin may be offset by the harm it causes to the body's vital chemistry. Doctors J. Hirsh, D. Street, J.F. Cade, and H. Amy, in the March 1973 issue of the professional journal *Blood,* showed that aspirin impedes the interaction between "platelet release" and connective tissue. In the *Annals of Rheumatic Diseases,* also in March 1973, Dr. P.N. Sperryn reported a significant blood loss in patients who were on heavy daily doses of aspirin. (It is not unusual for patients suffering from serious rheumatoid arthritis to take as many as twenty-four aspirin tablets a day.)

12   Again, I call attention to the article in the May 8, 1971 issue of *Lancet,* the English medical journal. Dr. M.A. Sahud and Dr. R.J. Cohen stated that the systematic use of aspirin by rheumatoid patients produces abnormally low plasma-ascorbic-acid levels. The authors reported that aspirin blocks the "uptake of ascorbic acid into the blood platelets." Since vitamin C is essential in collagen formation, its depletion by aspirin would seem to run directly counter to the body's need to combat connective tissue breakdown in arthritic conditions. The *Lancet* article concludes that, at the very least, ascorbic acid should be administered along with aspirin to counteract its harmful effects.

Aspirin is not the only pain-killing drug, of course, that   13
is known to have dangerous side effects. Dr. Daphne A.
Roe, of Cornell University, at a medical meeting in New
York City in 1974, presented startling evidence of a wide
range of hazards associated with sedatives and other pain
suppressants. Some of these drugs seriously interfere with
the ability of the body to metabolize food properly,
producing malnutrition. In some instances, there is also the
danger of bone-marrow depression, interfering with the
ability of the body to replenish its blood supply.

Pain-killing drugs are among the greatest advances in   14
the history of medicine. Properly used, they can be a boon
in alleviating suffering and in treating disease. But their
indiscriminate and promiscuous use is making psychological cripples and chronic ailers out of millions of people. The
unremitting barrage of advertising for pain-killing drugs,
especially over television, has set the stage for a mass
anxiety neurosis. Almost from the moment children are old
enough to sit up-right in front of a television screen, they
are being indoctrinated into the hypochondriac's clamorous and morbid world. Little wonder so many people
fear pain more than death itself.

It might be a good idea if concerned physicians and   15
educators could get together to make knowledge about
pain an important part of the regular school curriculum. As
for the populace at large, perhaps some of the same
techniques used by public-service agencies to make people
cancer-conscious can be used to counteract the growing
terror of pain and illness in general. People ought to know
that nothing is more remarkable about the human body
than its recuperative drive, given a modicum of respect. If
our broadcasting stations cannot provide equal time for
responses to the pain-killing advertisements, they might at
least set aside a few minutes each day for common-sense
remarks on the subject of pain. As for the Food and Drug
Administration, it might be interesting to know why an
agency that has so energetically warned the American
people against taking vitamins without prescriptions is
doing so little to control over-the-counter sales each year of
billions of pain-killing pills, some of which can do more
harm than the pain they are supposed to suppress.

Discussing Content and Form

1. Cousins makes the assertion that "we are becoming a nation of pill-grabbers and hypochondriacs" (par. 1). Explain why (or why not) this is an acceptable premise from which to develop his argument. Cite any support that you find later in the essay to further strengthen this original statement.

2. Some persuasion is aimed at revealing a situation and winning agreement of opinion, while other persuasion is intended to move readers beyond mere consideration and to get them to take some action. In which category would you place this selection? Explain your answer.

3. Considering paragraph 1 as an introduction, divide the overall plan or structure of Cousins' argument into two major sections of development.
   a. How much of the essay deals with "ignorance about pain," first announced in paragraph 2?
   b. What is the second area of ignorance?
   c. What is the function then of the final paragraph?

4. How many specific areas of ignorance about pain does Cousins name? What facts does he introduce to support the statement "that about 90 percent of pain is self-limiting" (par. 2)?

5. What have been the boomeranging effects of the "campaign to get people to . . . a doctor" (par. 4)?

6. According to Cousins, what is an "intelligent course" in regard to pain? Discuss the last sentence in paragraph 6 as a possible thesis for the essay: "The only answer has to be increased education . . ." etc.

7. Cousins devotes three paragraphs (10, 11, and 12) to the discussion of aspirin. Why is it logical or necessary to give this much space to the one drug? What methods does he use to support his claims concerning the dangers of overuse of aspirin?

8. Cousins twice mentions the Food and Drug Administration. What seems to be his attitude toward that agency?

9. How does Cousins think the same agencies that have influenced Americans in their attitude toward pain and drugs can help to alleviate the problems they have caused?

Considering Special Techniques

1. The writer of persuasion must always consider how to approach or address the reader, the audience. What is the special value of using the first person "we" and of the inclusion of "almost everyone" in attacking "ignorance" and the widespread use of drugs?

2. Persuasion uses (and fuses) many methods of development. Cousins, for instance, explains through a cause/effect relationship in paragraph 1. What is the dominant method of developing paragraph 2? of paragraphs 4 and 5?

3. For the most part, Cousins depends upon logical reasoning and factual information to build his argument. For instance, his argument might be reduced to this syllogism:

Major premise: *Education is the corrective for ignorance.*
Minor premise: *We are ignorant about the nature of pain.*
Conclusion: *Therefore, we need education about pain.*

In writing an argument, however, the entire syllogism seldom appears. Rather, the reasoning is reduced to a shortened form of the syllogism called an enthymeme. The enthymeme may be constructed by beginning with the conclusion of the syllogism and adding the minor premise in a subordinate clause:

We need education about pain because we are ignorant concerning its nature and causes.

You may add to the pattern of reasoning by adding further clauses: second, third, and fourth reasons, as necessary. For instance, Cousins says we need education about pain because we are ignorant about its nature, because we tend to become hypochondriacs, because we run to the doctor unnecessarily, because we too often resort to drugs, etc.

Construct an enthymeme for two or three of the single paragraphs within Cousins' essay: for instance, you might begin with "We need to know more about aspirin because . . ." and add the clauses that complete that part of the argument.

4. What is the emotional value of the illustration concerning the "star baseball pitcher" in paragraph 9? What advantage is gained by not naming the player? Explain why the reader probably accepts the story as "fact" even without the actual names.

5. What is the persuasive power of the citation of authorities in paragraphs 11, 12, and 13? Why is Cousins careful to cite exact titles and dates? Draw some conclusions about the points to consider in choosing and using authority in persuasive writing.

6. Examine such sentences as these and explain how the tone of reasonableness strengthens the persuasion in this essay:

"Obviously, it is folly for an individual to ignore symptoms that could be a warning of a potentially serious illness." (par. 6) "Properly used, they can be a boon in alleviating suffering and in treating disease." (par. 14)

7. Words to learn and use: hypochondriacs (par. 1); barbiturates, analgesics (par. 3); psychogenic (par. 4); malaise (par. 6); collagen (par. 10); antiinflammatory (par. 11); metabolize (par. 13); indiscriminate, promiscuous, neurosis, clamorous (par. 14).

Generating Ideas

1. Write a persuasive paper advocating education in some other area where you think it is particularly needed. These problems are suggestions, but you can add other topics of your own:

The high rate of accidental death among young drivers
Teen-age pregnancies
Early marriage and divorce
School vandalism
Theft of bicycles, cars
Adolescent alcoholism
Sports accidents, dangers

2. Do some research and write a paper prersuading your reader of the merits or dangers of a particular drug or food. For instance, you might write about a health food, about vitamins or a particular vitamin, about foods that are thought to be cholesterol producing, about caffeine in coffee and tea, etc. You might even try finding other studies regarding the dangers or merits of aspirin and add something to the reports given by Cousins in this essay.

3. In paragraph 2 Cousins lists a number of causes that may result in poor health or in pain—tension, stress, worry, etc. Use one of the items from that list of fourteen possible

causes and write a paper in which you suggest ways for remedying or overcoming that particular difficulty. For instance, write an informative or a persuasive paper setting forth some ways to control stress or to improve habits of exercise.

4. Cousins' book Anatomy of an Illness, *from which this selection comes, is a remarkable account of how he recovered from a very serious illness. He moved from a hospital to a hotel; there he enjoyed a rather luxurious rest, took quantities of vitamin C, read for pleasure, and watched many old comedies which provided large doses of laughter. If you can, read the book and write a persuasive paper prescribing Cousins' way of returning to health for someone you know. Or write a paper setting forth ideas of your own concerning "the best ways to keep healthy" or "the best ways to get over an illness." Or try a third "best way" paper persuading someone of the meritorious effects of a particular type of vacation or change.*

5. Cousins says that we "have had it drummed into us—in print, on radio, over television, in everyday conversation—that any hint of pain is to be banished. . ." (par. 1). Of course, this is not the only thing that is "drummed into us." Choose some other adverse influence that you find pervasive in society today and write a paper persuading your reader of ways to counteract that strong influence.

Sydney J. Harris

Sydney J. Harris (b. 1917) came to the United States from England when he was five years old. He attended public schools in Chicago and the University of Chicago before starting his career with various newspapers in that city. Since 1941 he has been identified with the Chicago Daily News and with the syndicated column "Strictly Personal." Harris has had numerous awards and honorary degrees, and he has published several collections of his columns as well as other popular books. Best known are *Strictly Personal* (1953), *Last Things First* (1961), *For the Time Being* (1972), *Winners and Losers* (1973), and *The Best of Harris* (1975). In his columns Harris comments on every facet of American life, from the misuse of language to foreign relations. "Goal of Age: the Older, the Better" shows that he can take a rather unlikely stand on a subject that eventually affects everyone.

Goal of Age: The Older, the Better

1   We older folk like to prate a lot about the "duties" and "responsibilities" of young people, but have we ever thought of the obligation that is entailed upon us by growing older?

2   I don't mean the financial and social and family obligations, which we all accept and understand, but the obligation to become more appealing on the inside as we become less attractive on the outside.

3   An older person who gets all dried up and brittle and wrinkled and full of complaints is just a total drag, no matter how rich or influential he may be. Most people allow age to do awful things to them.

4   It seems to me that growing older imposes a duty upon us to get more like a peach on the inside as we get more like a prune on the outside; otherwise, what's the point of it all?

5   We have to get cuter and funnier and mellower and more tolerant and more perceptive and wiser, simply to compensate for the external ravages of the aging process. Instead, most older people allow themselves to become more rigid, more disapproving, more psychically constipated, more narrowly opinionated and more querulously self-centered as they pass from childhood to senescence without ever having arrived at maturity.

Actually, young people have a natural love and affinity   6
for oldsters who have maintained the spirit of youth within
themselves; what they reject and resent are old people who
have forgotten what it was to be young, who have
discarded their earlier stages of life instead of incorporating
them into the total personality at some deep and
permanent level.

Our desperate quest for youth must be turned inside   7
out; an older person who tries to look and act and dress like
a junior is simply an object of fun or pity. Youth is an
emanation from the inside, not a cosmetic application, and
it is the inner spirit of the person that youngsters respond
to, not the surface appearance.

Old people who feel alienated from the young tend to   8
blame the "changing times," when in reality it is their own
inability or unwillingness to deepen their perceptions and
broaden their sympathies. Most of us get worse as we get
older, when we should get better—we settle into our
individual deformations, instead of emerging from the
hard shell of self to meet the new world at least halfway.

There is no more delightful person in the world than an   9
octogenarian who is both childlike and wise, spirited and
supportive, more willing to learn than he is quick to advise.
Socrates began taking dancing lessons at seventy; most of
us just take dying lessons.

Discussing Content and Form

*1. Where does Harris first state his proposition? What
particular group of readers is he challenging? What is his
attitude toward that audience?*

*2. Is this essay deductive or inductive in its method of
persuading? Support your answer by referring to the essay
itself. If you consider it deductive, try writing a syllogism or
enthymeme (see p. 357) in summary of the argument.*

*3. What qualities does Harris recommend that people
cultivate as they grow older? What qualities does he think
young people like in "oldsters"? What makes some older
people feel alienated from the young?*

*4. What criticism does Harris make of people who try "to
look and act and dress like a junior"?*

5. Why (or why not) are you persuaded to agree with Harris' statements? Draw some conclusions about the possibility for winning agreement in persuasion that might be described as chiefly personal opinion.

Considering Special Techniques

1. As a newspaper columnist, Harris uses the shorter paragraphs characteristic of journalism. Which of his paragraphs are single sentences? Why are these shorter paragraphs suitable here whereas they might not be in developing many subjects in expository or persuasive writing?

2. Words such as rigid, psychically constipated, opinionated, querulously self-centered (par. 5) are emotive or charged. Why—or why not—might these words offend some readers? Find other examples of such strong language used to produce a reaction.

3. What is the effect of slang words and phrases such as "prate a lot" (par. 1) and "just a total drag" (par. 3)?

4. Find several sentences in which Harris employs the semicolon to weld two related ideas. Separate the elements he fuses in this way and consider why he made the choice he did.

5. Words to learn and use: entailed (par. 1); psychically, querulously, senescence (par. 5); affinity (par. 6); octogenarian (par. 9).

Generating Ideas

1. Gerontology—the study of aging—is more and more discussed, more and more an area for study and perhaps for future work. Write a persuasive paper in which you set forth the advantages of going into a field of work related to the process of aging.

2. With declining birth rates and increasingly effective health care, the population grows steadily older and entirely different problems must be faced by society in general. Write a persuasive paper about one of the problems faced by a society in which the median-age is steadily advancing. For instance, you might argue that it is good or bad to have segregated retirement communities where people are all relatively the same age. Or you might argue for or against setting a definite retirement age for all occupations or for

specified ones. You may need to do some research for facts to support your proposition.

3. We hear a great deal about the "desperate quest for youth" that Harris mentions. Write a persuasive paper on a subject related to that quest. For instance, you might persuade your readers that the "cosmetic application" of youth is actually desirable, even though it is not "from the inside" (par. 7). Or you might write a persuasive paper declaring that the expenditure for such a quest is either foolish or desirable.

4. Reverse Harris' comment in paragraph 8 to read "Young people who feel alienated from the old tend to blame . . ." and complete the statement with a reason of your own. Write a persuasive paper showing what should be done to help bring generations into better understanding.

Marya Mannes

Marya Mannes (b. 1905) was educated at private schools in New York City, and has lived in various European countries. In her autobiographical *Out of My Time* (1971) she tells the fascinating story of growing up as the child of artistic parents and of defining her role as a woman and as a writer. She has written novels, essays, satirical poems, and many articles. For some time she was a staff writer for the *Reporter*, and she has appeared widely as a lecturer and panelist.

Mannes has been described as a "questioner," and many of her essays and speeches question the myths and practices of government, business, and other institutions. "What's Wrong with Our Press?" was first delivered as a speech in 1960 to the Women's National Press Club, where Mannes appeared as a substitute for Eleanor Roosevelt. The speech, which is now part of the collection *But Will It Sell?* (1964), was printed by only a few newspapers and magazines at the time. But the comparison Mannes makes between television reporting and the news coverage by most newspapers is still a subject for discussion and controversy.

What's Wrong with Our Press?

1   Newspapers have two great advantages over television. They can be used by men as barriers against their wives. It is still the only effective screen against the morning features of the loved one, and, as such, performs a unique human service. The second advantage is that you can't line a garbage pail with a television set—it's usually the other way around.

2   But here are some interesting statistics from a little, and little known, survey by Mr. Roper called "The Public's Reaction to Television Following the Quiz Investigations." In it he asks everybody but me this question: Suppose you could continue to have only one of the following—radio, television, newspapers, or magazines—which would you prefer? Newspapers came in second: Forty-two per cent said if they could only have one, they would keep television. Thirty-two per cent said if they could only have one, they would keep newspapers.

3   Even so, newspaper people should be much happier than the magazine people, because only four per cent said they needed magazines, as against nineteen per cent for radio.

But listen to this. Mr. Roper asked these same harried 4
people: "If you get conflicting or different reports of the
same news story from radio, television, the magazines, and
the newspapers, which of the four versions would you be
most inclined to believe?" Thirty-two per cent believe
newspapers as against thirty per cent who believe
television. But then something really strange happens.
When Mr. Roper asked his guinea pigs *which* of these media
they would be least inclined to believe, the newspapers
topped the list. In a big way, too. Twenty-four per cent
don't believe newspapers as against nine per cent who
don't believe television. And though I'm as leery of certain
polls as anyone, this margin of credulity is too wide to be
discounted.

The fact is that although network television still allots 5
too little time to the vital service of informing the public, it
does a better job in that little time than the nation's press as
a whole. And when I speak of the nation's press as a whole,
I am *not* speaking of the five or six splendid newspapers—
and the one great newspaper—which serve the world as
models of responsible public information. I am speaking of
the local press which in hundreds of American communities is the *only* news available, aside from those recitals of
ticker tape that pass for radio news, and which defaults on
its obligations to the public.

Why do I think network TV does a better job of 6
informing than these papers? Well, let's get the partisan bit
over with. Television lives on advertising to an even greater
extent than newspapers, and since advertising is big
business, advertising is by nature Republican. Yet nowhere
in network newscasts or network commentaries on current
events have I encountered the intense partisanship, the
often rabid bias that colors the editorial pages of the
majority of newspapers in this country. Douglass Cater, in
his book *The Fourth Branch of Government*, confines himself
to only one pungent footnote on this subject. "I have
deliberately avoided," he writes, "getting into the pre-
dominantly one-party nature of newspaper ownership. It is
a fact of life." This particular fact of life is a shameful one:
that newspapers whose duty it is to inform the American
public give them only one side of the issues that affect them

profoundly—the Republican side. This is shameful not only for Democrats—they have survived it before and will survive it again—but for the maturity of our people. Some of the same papers which loudly extol the virtues of free enterprise and a free press are consistently failing to print the facts on which a people can form a balanced and independent opinion. That balanced and independent opinion is our only real security as a nation.

7   Now, very often, television coverage of news is superficial and inadequate. Very often the picture takes precedence over the point. But by and large the news reports and commentaries on CBS and NBC and ABC make every effort to present viewers with more than one aspect of an issue, either by letting opposing spokesmen have their say, or by outlining the positions held by both major parties on the subject involved.

8   Television also provides a wide range of opinion by setting up four or five experts and letting them knock each other down. What has the local press of this nature? Is it discharging its duty to diversity by printing snippets of opinion from unqualified readers? Is this exploring an issue?

9   Television may not have a Lippmann or a Reston, but then, what papers in America can claim an Eric Sevareid, a Walter Cronkite, a Huntley or a Brinkley, or—although he is invisible—an Edward Morgan?

10   Another thing. Among the leading commentators on television, you find no Pegler, no Winchell, no Fulton Lewis, Jr. Fortunately for the American public, television does not tolerate the kind of distortion of fact, the kind of partisan virulence and personal peeve, that many newspapers not only welcome but encourage. In its entertainment, television caters far too much to the lowest instincts of man, particularly the lust for violence and—at the opposite end of the spectrum—the urge to escape from reality into sedation. But there is one appetite it does not feed and which the partisan newspapers of the nation do: the appetite for hate—hate of whatever is different. I do not find on television the kind of editorials chronic in the New York tabloids as well as in many local papers across the

country where the techniques of demagoguery prevail: Rouse the Rabble by Routing Reason.

A newspaper has the right—the duty even—to assume 11 an attitude, to take a position. But it has an equally sacred right to explain that position in the light of the opposing one, to document that position, and to bolster it, not with emotion but with fact.

Here, of course, is where background information helps 12 the public to draw its conclusions. TV does a great deal of this in the form of documentaries, and you can of course say that they have the time and the money to do this and you haven't. Yet across this wide country, and with the exception of a handful of syndicated columns, I fail to find in any local paper any attempt, however minimal, to strengthen this muscle of digestion, without which news can neither nourish nor inform. It can only stuff. Between the opinions of the editor and the bare statements of the wire services there is nothing, nothing, that is, except a collection of snippets used as fillers between the ads and picked at random.

One of the greatest and most justified criticisms of 13 television has been that in appealing to the largest audience possible, it neglects minority audiences and minority tastes. This is still largely true. But there is, perhaps, one program a day and many, of course, on Sunday which an intelligent man or woman can enjoy and derive interest from. In my trips east or west or north or south, I pick up the local paper to find this enjoyment or interest—in vain. Now, surely there's something wrong here. Many of these places I've visited—and I'm sure this is true of the whole country—have college communities where highly intelligent and talented people live, whether they are teachers or doctors or lawyers or musicians or scientists. What is there for them in the paper, usually the only paper, of their town? What features are provided for these people? What stimulation? How many times have I heard them say: "If you want to see what a really bad paper is like, read our sheet." When a local paper has a monopoly in a region, as most of them do, why is it necessary to aim at the lowest common denominator?

14   I believe that over a period of decades newspapers have become a habit rather than a function. They have held their franchise so long that change has become inadmissible. I do not know, in fact, of any medium that has changed as little in the last twenty years as the daily press. And this resistance to change is the end of growth—which, in turn, marks the end of usefulness.

15   Change means trouble, change means work, change means cost. It is easier to print wire services dispatches than have a reporter on the beat. It is easier to buy syndicated columns than find—and train—local talent. It is easier to let the ads dictate the format than develop a format that elevates news above dogfood. It is easier to write editorial copy that appeals to emotion rather than reason. And in handling straight news, it is easier to assume the pious mantle of objectivity than to edit. To quote Eric Sevareid: "Our rigid formulae of so-called objectivity, beginning with the wire agency bulletins and reports—the warp and woof of what the papers print . . . our flat, one-dimensional handling of news, have given the lie the same prominence and impact that truth is given. They have elevated the influence of fools to that of wise men; the ignorant to the level of the learned; the evil to the level of the good." This featureless objectivity is nothing less than the editor's abdication of responsibility and is just as dangerous as the long and subtle processing of fact to fit a policy that characterizes certain weekly magazines. The one is dereliction; the other is deception. And both may provide a reason for the decline of public confidence in their press.

16   This is, to me a tragedy. I am a printed-word woman myself, and I still think the word was not only in the beginning but will be in the end. No picture can ever be an adequate substitute. The word will prevail; that is, if you, who are its guardians, treat it with the respect it deserves. For if you degrade and cheapen the word too long, the people will turn to the picture. They are beginning to turn to the picture now. Not in New York, maybe, not in Washington, D.C., or St. Louis, or two or three other cities, but in hundreds of towns across the country. Oh, they will buy your papers—to hold up at breakfast or to line the trash

can or to light a fire. But not to learn. And you may wake up one day to find you have lost the greatest power entrusted to men: to inform a free people.

Discussing Content and Form

1. Rhetoricians sometimes distinguish between persuasion and argument by saying that the former is intended to move an audience to action, while the latter is intended to win agreement, although most scholars recognize that it is difficult to define a precise line between the two. Compare Mannes' speech-essay with the speech by Howard Temin (p. 345). Are any of the differences that you can identify attributable to the fact that one speaker wishes to move to action while the other aims merely at winning agreement? Explain.

2. Where does Mannes first state the proposition which she wants to prove? What is the purpose of reporting the results of the Roper survey (pars. 2-4) before stating the proposition explicitly? How would you answer the questions in that survey?

3. Mannes is careful to set cautious limits for her opinions by excluding "five or six splendid newspapers" from her generalization (par. 5). Why is this caution necessary? Point out other examples of her care in setting limits around her argument by acknowledging weaknesses in TV.

4. Because Mannes' thesis requires proving one thing better than another, she makes extensive use of comparison and contrast. Make a list (beginning with paragraph 6) of the ways she says TV does a better job than newspapers do. Based on your experience, how many of these points are valid? Point out any that you think are less true or more true than they were in 1960, when the speech was written.

5. On what does Mannes base her charge that newspapers are more partisan and show more bias than TV does? On what does she base her charge that newspapers actually depend less on research and provide less background for discussing an issue than TV does?

6. Identify the names in paragraphs 9 and 10. Why does Mannes object to the appeal of "Pegler. . .Winchell. . .Fulton Lewis, Jr."? What is meant by the "techniques of demagoguery" (par. 10)? If you think any of her critical comments unjustified, explain your position.

7. Perhaps the most valuable message for a reader of this

essay comes in the form of Mannes' statements or implications about what constitutes good reporting—the qualities or standards that she commends in either TV or newspapers. Make a list of those requirements and discuss their value as guideposts for handling news in any medium.

Considering Special Techniques

1. *Tone is especially important in writing persuasion, especially in writing what Donald Davidson calls "an article of opinion," a class into which this essay could easily fit. How would you characterize the tone of this article? When it was first presented as a speech, very few newspapers and magazines printed it. Might the tone of the comments offend some groups other than the press? Explain.*
   a. *Point out elements of humor and informality in the article. What do these elements contribute?*
   b. *If you consider Mannes' tone harsh, account for the force of her opening sentences in the final paragraph: "This is, to me, a tragedy. I am a printed-word woman myself, and I still think the word was not only in the beginning but will be in the end."*

2. *To be convincing, a writer must be especially careful to choose appropriate words and phrases to show logical connections between points. Note these examples of well-chosen connectives: "But listen to this" (par. 4); "The fact is that" (par. 5); "Why do I think network TV does a better job" (par. 6). Find other phrases and sentences that help you follow Mannes' argument.*

3. *Writers often use statistics to support generalizations. Comment on the statistical evidence that Mannes cites in paragraphs 2-4.*

4. *Another device that lends weight to general statements is the "appeal to authority," a method Mannes uses in paragraph 15. What force does she gain by citing Eric Sevareid?*

5. *It is important for a persuader to establish himself or herself as "believable," as one who has a right to speak. Where do you find Mannes offering her "credentials"?*

6. *Mannes often uses a memorable or quotable phrase, one intended to provoke thought and to linger in the reader's mind. Find a few such phrases and discuss their special force. You might start with phrases like "duty to diversity"*

(par. 8), "partisan virulence and personal peeve" (par. 10), or a sentence such as this one from paragraph 15: "The one is dereliction; the other is deception."

7. Comment on the metaphors in these phrases: "I fail to find . . . any attempt . . . to strengthen this muscle of digestion, without which news can neither nourish nor inform" (par. 12); "'the wire agency bulletins and reports—the warp and woof of what the papers print'" (par. 15).

8. Words to learn and use: credulity *(par. 4);* partisan, pungent *(par. 6);* virulence, spectrum, sedation, tabloids *(par. 10);* abdication, dereliction *(par. 15).*

Generating Ideas

1. Write a paper comparing and contrasting the coverage offered by the newspaper and the television newscasts with which you are familiar. Come out with a convincing argument for believing one is better than the other, or that one is better in some areas than the other. For instance, you might show that television has a big advantage in presenting the weather, or some sports spectacular, but that newspapers do a better job of reporting a trial or the negotiations in a labor dispute or strike, thus proving Mannes partially wrong. Or you might follow reporting of some local political issue to determine how fairly and completely the two news services handle it.

2. The responsibility of the press is a frequently debated subject, and people other than Mannes have declared that there is a "decline of public confidence" (par. 15). The press is at times accused of revealing classified information, of misusing or slanting news to win political advantages, etc. On the other hand, the press is sometimes accused of withholding information that the public ought to have. Rather than treating the responsibility or action of the press as a whole, write a persuasive paper in which you cite illustrations of what you consider responsible or irresponsible journalism (newspaper or TV) related to a particular issue or in one particular instance.

3. Mannes says that "by and large the news reports and commentaries on CBS and NBC and ABC make every effort to present viewers with more than one aspect of an issue" (par. 7). Choose a recent and familiar documentary, news special, or interview program and write a persuasive review of it in order to convince your readers of its merit or its weaknesses in meeting such a requirement.

4. Use Mannes' statement "Change means trouble, change means work, change means cost" (par. 15) as the key idea for a paper dealing with some subject of your choice. For instance, how could you apply that statement to some change you think is needed in education or in your community? to developing energy saving cars or developing solar heat for homes?

5. Should home, church, or school be responsible for sex education or for education concerning alcohol, drug abuse, smoking as a health hazard, and driving safety? Choose one of these subjects and argue that one agency is better than another for teaching in that area. Pattern your essay after Mannes' argument of the advantages of TV over newspapers.

Lewis Thomas

Lewis Thomas (b. 1913) earned his M.D. at Harvard and has been Dean of
the Medical Schools at New York University-Bellevue and at Yale.
President of Memorial Sloan-Kettering Cancer Center in New York since
1972, he is recognized internationally for his medical research. As a writer,
Dr. Thomas has contributed to many scientific journals and published two
best-selling collections of essays, *The Lives of a Cell* (1974) and *Medusa and
the Snail* (1979). The first collection won him a National Book Award in
1975. In "Death in the Open," one of the essays from *The Lives of a Cell,*
Dr. Thomas gives a new perspective to society's attitudes toward death.

Death in the Open

Most of the dead animals you see on highways near the   1
cities are dogs, a few cats. Out in the countryside, the forms
and coloring of the dead are strange; these are the wild
creatures. Seen from a car window they appear as
fragments, evoking memories of woodchucks, badgers,
skunks, voles, snakes, sometimes the mysterious wreckage
of a deer.

It is always a queer shock, part a sudden upwelling of   2
grief, part unaccountable amazement. It is simply astounding to see an animal dead on a highway. The outrage
is more than just the location; it is the impropriety of such
visible death, anywhere. You do not expect to see dead
animals in the open. It is the nature of animals to die alone,
off somewhere, hidden. It is wrong to see them lying out on
the highway; it is wrong to see them anywhere.

Everything in the world dies, but we only know about it   3
as a kind of abstraction. If you stand in a meadow, at the
edge of a hillside, and look around carefully, almost
everything you can catch sight of is in the process of dying,
and most things will be dead long before you are. If it were
not for the constant renewal and replacement going on
before your eyes, the whole place would turn to stone and
sand under your feet.

There are some creatures that do not seem to die at all;   4
they simply vanish totally into their own progeny. Single
cells do this. The cell becomes two, then four, and so on,
and after a while the last trace is gone. It cannot be seen as

death; barring mutation, the descendants are simply the first cell, living all over again. The cycles of the slime mold have episodes that seem as conclusive as death, but the withered slug, with its stalk and fruiting body, is plainly the transient tissue of a developing animal; the free-swimming amebocytes use this organ collectively in order to produce more of themselves.

5   There are said to be a billion billion insects on the earth at any moment, most of them with very short life expectancies by our standards. Someone has estimated that there are 25 million assorted insects hanging in the air over every temperate square mile, in a column extending upward for thousands of feet, drifting through the layers of the atmosphere like plankton. They are dying steadily, some by being eaten, some just dropping in their tracks, tons of them around the earth, disintegrating as they die, invisibly.

6   Who ever sees dead birds, in anything like the huge numbers stipulated by the certainty of the death of all birds? A dead bird is an incongruity, more startling than an unexpected live bird, sure evidence to the human mind that something has gone wrong. Birds do their dying off somewhere, behind things, under things, never on the wing.

7   Animals seem to have an instinct for performing death alone, hidden. Even the largest, most conspicuous ones find ways to conceal themselves in time. If an elephant missteps and dies in an open place, the herd will not leave him there; the others will pick him up and carry the body from place to place, finally putting it down in some inexplicably suitable location. When elephants encounter the skeleton of an elephant out in the open, they methodically take up each of the bones and distribute them, in a ponderous ceremony, over neighboring acres.

8   It is a natural marvel. All of the life of the earth dies, all of the time, in the same volume as the new life that dazzles us each morning, each spring. All we see of this is the odd stump, the fly struggling on the porch floor of the summer house in October, the fragment on the highway. I have lived all my life with an embarrassment of squirrels in my backyard, they are all over the place, all year long, and I

have never seen, anywhere, a dead squirrel.

I suppose it is just as well. If the earth were otherwise, and all the dying were done in the open, with the dead there to be looked at, we would never have it out of our minds. We can forget about it much of the time, or think of it as an accident to be avoided, somehow. But it does make the process of dying seem more exceptional than it really is, and harder to engage in at the times when we must ourselves engage. 9

In our way, we conform as best we can to the rest of nature. The obituary pages tell us of the news that we are dying away, while the birth announcements in finer print, off at the side of the page, inform us of our replacements, but we get no grasp from this of the enormity of scale. There are 3 billion of us on the earth, and all 3 billion must be dead, on a schedule, within this lifetime. The vast mortality, involving something over 50 million of us each year, takes place in relative secrecy. We can only really know of the deaths in our households, or among our friends. These, detached in our minds from all the rest, we take to be unnatural events, anomalies, outrages. We speak of our own dead in low voices; struck down, we say, as though visible death can only occur for cause, by disease or violence, avoidably. We send off for flowers, grieve, make ceremonies, scatter bones, unaware of the rest of the 3 billion on the same schedule. All of that immense mass of flesh and bone and consciousness will disappear by absorption into the earth, without recognition by the transient survivors. 10

Less than a half century from now, our replacements will have more than doubled the numbers. It is hard to see how we can continue to keep the secret, with such multitudes doing the dying. We will have to give up the notion that death is catastrophe, or detestable, or avoidable, or even strange. We will need to learn more about the cycling of life in the rest of the system, and about our connection to the process. Everything that comes alive seems to be in trade for something that dies, cell for cell. There might be some comfort in the recognition of synchrony, in the formation that we all go down together, in the best of company. 11

Discussing Content and Form

1. This essay moves from a series of particulars to a general conclusion. What seems to be the writer's purpose? State the thesis of the essay in your own words.

2. Explain the following statement and relate it to the essay as a whole: "In our way, we conform as best we can to the rest of nature" (par. 10). How does Thomas say we conform?

3. How do you explain the fact that animals conceal their dying? How does their dying compare with that of human beings? Why does Thomas say that we regard death as unnatural?

4. Explain the conclusion that "There might be some comfort in the recognition of synchrony . . . " (par. 11).

5. Which details in the essay reveal that the writer is a scientist? Is he writing for an audience of scientists or for people in general? Explain.

Considering Special Techniques

1. This essay offers an example of the inductive *pattern, moving as it does from specific examples to a general conclusion. Why does Thomas offer such a wide range of examples from the world of nature? What is the effect of these?*

2. Writers sometimes use a catalogue *technique, accumulating specifics to achieve a particular effect. Notice the list in this sentence: "Seen from a car window they appear as fragments, evoking memories of woodchucks, badgers, skunks, voles, snakes, sometimes the mysterious wreckage of a deer" (par. 1). Point out other sentences that follow this pattern.*

3. Thomas uses many cumulative sentences *in which modifiers of various kinds are added after the main clause. Point out several sentences that follow this pattern and examine their effect on the style of the essay. Here are two examples:*

> *"It is the nature of animals to die alone, off somewhere, hidden." (par. 2)*
> *"They are dying steadily, some by being eaten, some just dropping in their tracks, tons of them around the earth, disintegrating as they die, invisibly." (par. 5)*

4. Thomas' reasoning involves the use of a very "strict"

analogy: that is, he draws conclusions or points out similarities between two examples that may be said to be from the same "class"—animal and human. Do you find the analogy between animal and human dying in any way offensive? Why do you think Thomas delayed the application to humanity until paragraph 9?

5. *Words to learn and use:* impropriety *(par. 2);* progeny, mutation, amebocytes *(par. 4);* plankton *(par. 5);* incongruity *(par. 6);* inexplicably *(par. 7);* enormity, anomalies *(par. 10);* synchrony *(par. 11).*

Generating Ideas

1. Thomas suggests that we should find "comfort in the recognition of synchrony," in the realization that death is part of a natural process. Defend or attack his belief in an essay of your own.

2. A great deal has been written recently about customs concerning death and dying. Write a persuasive paper defending or attacking those customs you may be familiar with.

3. Use one of these lines from Thomas as the key idea for a paper:
"Everything in the world dies, but we only know about it as a kind of abstraction." (par. 3)
"We will need to learn more about the cycling of life in the rest of the system, and about our connection to the process." (par. 11) (This sentence could be applied to characteristics or events other than death.)

4. Read at least two of these well-known poems and write a paper presenting the poets' attitudes toward death: John Donne, "Death Be Not Proud"; Emily Dickinson, "Because I Could Not Stop for Death"; John Crowe Ransom, "Janet Waking"; Dylan Thomas, "Do Not Go Gentle into That Good Night." Or read William Cullen Bryant's "Thanatopsis" and write a paper comparing the "comfort" expressed there to that suggested by Lewis Thomas.

James Baldwin

James Baldwin (b. 1924) has been called the "foremost literary spokesman for the American Negro." When he was just starting as a writer, he spent ten years in Paris, and he has travelled extensively throughout Europe. A lecturer on civil rights and a member of many national boards, Baldwin nevertheless has found time to write more than a dozen fine books and numerous articles and essays. Among the books are *Go Tell It on the Mountain* (1953), *Notes of a Native Son* (1955), *Giovanni's Room* (1958), *Nobody Knows My Name* (1960), *The Fire Next Time* (1963), *No Name in the Street* (1972), and *One Day When I Was Lost* (1973). "Unnameable Objects, Unspeakable Crimes" first appeared in *Ebony* magazine. In this often reprinted essay, Baldwin uses both logical and emotive techniques of persuasion.

Unnameable Objects, Unspeakable Crimes

1   I have often wondered, and it is not a pleasant wonder, just what white Americans talk about with one another. I wonder this because they do not, after all, seem to find very much to say to *me*, and I concluded long ago that they found the color of my skin inhibitory. This color seems to operate as a most disagreeable mirror, and a great deal of one's energy is expended in reassuring white Americans that they do not see what *they* see. This is utterly futile, of course, since *they do* see what *they* see. And what they see is an appallingly oppressive and bloody history, known all over the world. What they see is a disastrous, continuing, present, condition which menaces them, and for which they bear an inescapable responsibility. But since, in the main, they appear to lack the energy to change this condition, they would rather not be reminded of it. Does this mean that, in their conversations with one another, they merely make reassuring sounds? It scarcely seems possible, and yet, on the other hand, it seems all too likely.

2   Whatever they bring to one another, it is certainly not *freedom from guilt*.

3   The guilt remains, more deeply rooted, more securely lodged, than the oldest of old trees; and it can be unutterably exhausting to deal with people who, with a

really dazzling ingenuity, a tireless agility, are perpetually defending themselves against charges which one has not made.

One does not have to make them. The record is there for all to read. It resounds all over the world. It might as well be written in the sky.   4

One wishes that Americans, white Americans, would read, for their own sakes, this record, and stop defending themselves against it. Only then will they be enabled to change their lives. The fact that Americans, white Americans, have not yet been able to do this—to face their history, to change their lives—hideously menaces this country. Indeed, it menaces the entire world.   5

For history, as nearly no one seems to know, is not merely something to be read. And it does not refer merely, or even principally, to the past. On the contrary, the great force of history comes from the fact that we carry it within us, are unconsciously controlled by it in many ways, and history is literally *present* in all that we do. It could scarcely be otherwise, since it is to history that we owe our frames of reference, our identities, and our aspirations.   6

And it is with great pain and terror that one begins to realize this. In great pain and terror, one begins to assess the history which has placed one where one is, and formed one's point of view. In great pain and terror, because, thereafter, one enters into battle with that historical creation, oneself, and attempts to re-create oneself according to a principle more humane and more liberating; one begins the attempt to achieve a level of personal maturity and freedom which robs history of its tyrannical power, and also changes history.   7

But, obviously, I am speaking as an historical creation which has had bitterly to contest its history, to wrestle with it and finally accept it, in order to bring myself out of it. My point of view is certainly formed by my history and it is probable that only a creature despised by history finds history a questionable matter. On the other hand, people who imagine that history flatters them (as it does, indeed, since they wrote it) are impaled on their history like a butterfly on a pin and become incapable of seeing or changing themselves or the world.   8

9   This is the place in which, it seems to me, most white Americans find themselves. They are dimly, or vividly, aware that the history they have fed themselves is mainly a lie, but they do not know how to release themselves from it, and they suffer enormously from the resulting personal incoherence. This incoherence is heard nowhere more plainly than in those stammering, terrified dialogues white Americans sometimes entertain with that black conscience, the black man in America.

10   The nature of this stammering can be reduced to a plea: Do not blame *me*. I was not there. I did not do it. My history has nothing to do with Europe or the slave trade. Anyway, it was *your* chiefs who sold *you* to *me*. I was not present on the middle passage. I am not responsible for the textile mills of Manchester, or the cotton fields of Mississippi. Besides, consider how the English, too, suffered in those mills and in those awful cities! I, also, despise the governors of Southern states and the sheriffs of Southern counties; and I also want your child to have a decent education and rise as high as his capabilities will permit. I have nothing against you, *nothing!* What have *you* got against *me? What do you want?*

11   But, on the same day, in another gathering, and in the most private chamber of his heart always, he, the white man, remains proud of that history for which he does not wish to pay, and from which, materially, he has profited so much. On that same day, in another gathering, and in the most private chamber of the black man's heart always, he finds himself facing the terrible roster of the lost: the dead, black junkie; the defeated, black father; the unutterably weary, black mother; the unutterably ruined black girl. And one begins to suspect an awful thing: that people believe that they *deserve* their history and that when they operate on this belief, they perish. But they can scarcely avoid believing that they deserve it—one's short time on this earth is very mysterious and very dark and hard. I have known many black men and women and black boys and girls, who really believed that it was better to be white than black, whose lives were ruined or ended by this belief; and I myself carried the seeds of this destruction within me for a long time.

Now, if I, as a black man, profoundly believe that I 12
deserve my history and deserve to be treated as I am, then I
must also, fatally, believe that white people deserve their
history and deserve the power and glory which their
testimony and the evidence of my own senses assure me
that they have. And if black people fall into this trap, the
trap of believing that they deserve their fate, white people
fall into the yet more stunning and intricate trap of
believing that they deserve *their* fate, and their comparative
safety; and that black people, therefore, need only do as
white people have done to rise to where white people now
are. But this simply cannot be said, not only for reasons of
politeness or charity, but also because white people carry in
them a carefully muffled fear that black people long to do to
others what has been done to them. Moreover, the history
of white people has led them to a fearful, baffling place
where they have begun to lose touch with reality—to lose
touch, that is, with themselves—and where they certainly
are not happy. They do not know how this came about;
they do not dare examine how this came about. On the one
hand, they can scarcely dare to open a dialogue which
must, if it is honest, become a personal confession—a cry
for help and healing, which is really, I think, the basis of all
dialogues—and, on the other hand, the black man can
scarcely dare to open a dialogue which must, if it is honest,
become a personal confession which, fatally, contains an
accusation. And yet, if we cannot do this, each of us will
perish in those traps in which we have been struggling for
so long.

The American situation is very peculiar, and it may be 13
without precedent in the world. No curtain under heaven is
heavier than that curtain of guilt and lies behind which
Americans hide: it may prove to be yet more deadly to the
lives of human beings than that iron curtain of which we
speak so much—and know so little. The American curtain
is color. We have used this word, this concept, to justify
unspeakable crimes, not only in the past, but in the
present. One can measure very neatly the white American's distance from his conscience—from himself—by
observing the distance between himself and black people.
One has only to ask oneself who established this distance.

Who is this distance designed to protect? And from what is this distance designed to protect him?

14   I have seen this very vividly, for example, in the eyes of Southern law enforcement officers barring, let us say, the door to the courthouse. There they stand, comrades all, invested with the authority of the community, with helmets, with sticks, with guns, with cattle prods. Facing them are unarmed black people—or, more precisely, they are faced by a group of unarmed people arbitrarily called black, whose color really ranges from the Russian steppes to the Golden Horn, to Zanzibar. In a moment, because he can resolve the situation in no other way, this sheriff, this deputy, this honored American citizen, must begin to club these people down. Some of these people may be related to him by blood; they are assuredly related to the black Mammy of his memory, and the black playmates of his childhood. And for a moment, therefore, he seems nearly to be pleading with the people facing him not to force him to commit yet another crime and not to make yet deeper that ocean of blood in which his conscience is drenched, in which his manhood is perishing. The people do not go away, of course; once a people arise, they never go away, a fact which should be included in the Marine handbook; and the club rises, the blood comes down, and our crimes and our bitterness and our anguish are compounded. Or, one sees it in the eyes of rookie cops in Harlem, who are really among the most terrified people in the world, and who must pretend to themselves that the black mother, the black junkie, the black father, the black child are of a different human species than themselves. They can only deal with their lives and their duties by hiding behind the color curtain. This curtain, indeed, eventually becomes their principal justification for the lives they lead.

15   But it is not only on this level that one sees the extent of our disaster. Not so very long ago, I found myself in Montgomery, with many, many thousands, marching to the Capitol. Much has been written about this march—for example, the Confederate flag was flying from the Capitol dome; the Federalized National Guard, assigned to protect the marchers, wore Confederate flags on their jackets; if the late Mrs. Viola Liuzzo was avoiding the patrols on that

deadly stretch of road that night, she had far sharper eyesight than mine, for I did not see any. Well, there we were, marching to that mansion from which authority had fled. All along that road—I pray that my countrymen will hear me—old, black men and women, who have endured an unspeakable oppression for so long, waved and cheered and sang and wept. They could not march, but they had done something else: they had brought us to the place where we could march. How many of us, after all, were brought up on the white folks leavings, and how mighty a price those old men and women paid to bring those leavings home to us!

We reached the white section of town. There the businessmen stood, on balconies, jeering; there stood their maids, in back doors, silent, not daring to wave, but nodding. I watched a black, or rather, a beige-colored woman, standing in the street, watching us thoughtfully; she looked as though she probably held a clerical job in one of those buildings; proof, no doubt, to the jeering white businessmen that the South was making progress. This woman decided to join us, for when we reached the Capitol, I noticed that she was there. But, while we were still marching, through the white part of town, the watching, the waiting, the frightened part of town, we lifted our small American flags, and we faced those eyes—which could not face ours—and we sang. I was next to Harry Belafonte. From upstairs office windows, white American secretaries were leaning out of windows, jeering and mocking, and using the ancient Roman sentence of death: thumbs down. Then they saw Harry, who is my very dear friend and a beautiful cat, and who is also, in this most desperately schizophrenic of republics, a major, a reigning matinée idol. One does not need to be a student of Freud to understand what buried forces create a matinée idol, or what he represents to that public which batters down doors to watch him (one need only watch the rise and fall of American politicians. This is a sinister observation. And I mean it very seriously). The secretaries were legally white—it was on that basis that they lived their lives, from this principle that they took, collectively, their values; which is, as I have tried to indicate, an interesting spiritual

16

condition. But they were also young. In that ghastly town, they were certainly lonely. They could only, after all, look forward to an alliance, by and by, with one of the jeering businessmen; their boyfriends could only look forward to becoming one of them. And they were also female, a word, which, in the context of the color curtain, has suffered the same fate as the word, "male": it has become practically obscene. When the girls saw Harry Belafonte, a collision occurred in them so visible as to be at once hilarious and unutterably sad. At one moment, the thumbs were down, they were barricaded within their skins, at the next moment, those downturned thumbs flew to their mouths, their fingers pointed, their faces changed, and exactly like bobby-soxers, they oohed, and aahed and moaned. God knows what was happening in the minds and hearts of those girls. Perhaps they would like to be free.

17   The white man's guilt, which he pretends is due to the fact that the world is a place of many colors, has nothing to do with color. If one attempts to reduce his dilemma to its essence, it really does not have much to do with his crimes, except in the sense that he has locked himself into a place where he is doomed to continue repeating them. The great, unadmitted crime is what he has done to himself. A man is a man, a woman is a woman, and a child is a child. To deny these facts is to open the doors on a chaos deeper and deadlier, and, within the space of a man's lifetime, more timeless, more eternal, than the medieval vision of Hell. And we have arrived at this unspeakable blasphemy in order to acquire things, in order to make money. We cannot endure the things we acquire—the only reason we continually acquire them, like junkies on a hundred dollar a day habit—and our money exists mainly on paper. God help us on that day when the population demands to know what is behind the paper. But, beyond all this, it is terrifying to consider the precise nature of the things we buy with the flesh we sell.

18   In Henry James' novel *The Ambassadors* published not long before World War I, and not long before his death, he recounts the story of a middle-aged New Englander, assigned by his middle-aged bride-to-be—a widow—the task of rescuing from the flesh-pots of Paris her only son.

She wants him to come home to take over the direction of the family factory. In the event, it is the middle-aged New Englander— *The Ambassador*—who is seduced, not so much by Paris, as by a new and less utilitarian view of life. He counsels the young man to "live. Live all you can. It is a mistake not to." Which I translate as meaning "Trust life, and it will teach you, in joy and sorrow, all you need to know." Jazz musicians know this. Those old men and women who waved and sang and wept as we marched in Montgomery know this. White Americans, in the main, do not know this. They are still trapped in that factory to which, in Henry James' novel, the son returns. We never know what this factory produces, for James never tells us. He only conveys to us that the factory, at an unbelievable human expense, produces unnameable objects.

Discussing Content and Form

1. Explain in your own words Baldwin's key idea or thesis: "the great force of history comes from the fact that we carry it within us, are unconsciously controlled by it in many ways, and history is literally present in all that we do" (par. 6).
   a. In what way is every "self" a creation of history?
   b. Why does Baldwin say the failure to face history can lead only to disaster?
   c. What personal confrontation has Baldwin himself had with history?
   d. Why does he feel that it is wrong to believe a people (white or black) "deserve their history"?

2. What relationship exists between the inability of white Americans to talk to blacks—to hold honest dialogue—and the white feelings of guilt? Explain what Baldwin means by the "personal incoherence" (par. 9) that can lead only to stammering phrases such as "Do not blame me" (par. 10).

3. According to Baldwin, how has the "curtain of color" been used to "justify unspeakable crimes, not only in the past, but in the present" (par. 13)?
   a. How does Baldwin prove or develop this "crime of color" concept in paragraphs 15-16?
   b. The march to Montgomery that Baldwin speaks of occurred in 1963. Why (or why not) is this incident an effective illustration?

4. In paragraph 17 Baldwin explains what he thinks is the fundamental reason for the "unadmitted crimes" the white man has done the black. What is that reason?

Explain how Baldwin's statements here bear out what is sometimes called the "economic view of history." What is meant by the statement that "it is terrifying to consider the precise nature of the things we buy with the flesh we sell" (par. 17)?

5. Why does Baldwin say "once a people arise, they never go away" (par. 14)?

6. Explain the fascination of the matinée idol for the "legally white" secretaries. What is the "collision" that occurred in them? Why does Baldwin find their behavior both "hilarious and unutterably sad" (par. 16)?

7. In what ways does the final paragraph of the essay relate to the main ideas? Why does this final paragraph at first glance seem a shift or change of subject? How does being trapped in a factory making unnameable objects relate to being trapped by the forces of history?

Considering Special Techniques

1. Baldwin uses the failed dialogue—the lack of communication—as an introduction and as a central image throughout his essay. Locate the places where he returns to that image and discuss its effectiveness as a unifying device.

2. Baldwin's use of detail makes many of the incidents he cites very vivid, but those details also underscore ideas. For instance, consider the special significance of these details:

the Southern law enforcement officers barring the door to the courthouse (par. 14)

the anguish or fear in the eyes of rookie cops in Harlem (par. 14)

the Confederate flags (par. 15) and the small American flags (par. 16)

the old black people who could not march but "had done something else" (par. 15)

the "beige" secretary who watched and then later joined the marchers (par. 16)

the importance of Harry Belafonte (par. 16)

the "thumbs down" gesture changed to "thumbs flew to their mouths" (par. 16)

3. Baldwin uses many metaphors and similes, thus leading his reader, through the device of comparison, to see clearly and to think about meanings. Discuss the strength of these comparisons in particular; then find others that you think are forceful:

"color seems to operate as a most disagreeable mirror" (par. 1)

"guilt remains, more deeply rooted, more securely lodged, than the oldest of trees" (par. 3)

"impaled on their history like a butterfly on a pin" (par. 8)

4. Follow the logical argument Baldwin sets up in paragraph 12 by constructing a syllogism or an enthymeme (see p. 357) to represent his thinking.

5. Writers of persuasion choose emotive language to match their power of ideas. Discuss the effectiveness of such words and phrases as these and find others that affect you strongly:

"appallingly oppressive and bloody history" (par. 1)

"disastrous, continuing, present, condition which menaces them" (par. 1)

"great pain and terror" (par. 7)

"tyrannical power" (par. 7)

"stammering, terrified dialogues" (par. 9)

"stunning and intricate trap of believing" (par. 12)

6. Baldwin's title is especially interesting since only half of its meaning is apparent throughout the essay. What special force is gained from the title once the concluding paragraph with its images of the factory is in place? Why do you think Baldwin chose the order he did for the two parts of the title?

7. Words to learn and use: inhibitory, appallingly (par. 1); ingenuity (par. 3); resounds (par. 4); aspirations (par. 6); impaled (par. 8); incoherence (par. 9); roster, unutterably (par. 11); schizophrenic, reigning, sinister, obscene, hilarious (par. 16); dilemma, essence, blasphemy (par. 17).

Generating Ideas

1. Recall or reread George Orwell's essay "Marrakech" (p. 45), and write a paper comparing the ideas about the "color curtain" as these are developed by both Baldwin and Orwell.

2. Baldwin writes "A man is a man, a woman is a woman, and a child is a child" (par. 17). Write a paper in which you

consider the humanity of all individuals, whatever their race, social status, or economic condition. Write to persuade your reader of the importance of the "everyman" ideal, to convince your reader that all persons share certain rights as human beings. You might use as supporting examples various movements in history when mankind has fought for those "inalienable rights."

3. Do you know of persons who are trapped in a "factory" where they dedicate life to "unnameable objects"? Write a persuasive paper in which you show the value of breaking out of narrowness or blindness of some sort in order to achieve a greater freedom. For instance, consider how people sometimes are barricaded behind a prejudice, not necessarily a prejudice of race or class, but of any type. Or consider how people are sometimes trapped by the desire for things—objects that are not, in the long run, very important.

4. Write a paper in which you attempt to convince your reader about the importance of dialogue regarding some social or personal situation. Show, if you can, that people (individuals or groups, depending on your subject) often have misunderstandings because they do not communicate honestly.

5. Use one of these subject-titles for a paper suggested by Baldwin's discussion of the failure to face history:
"Get Rid of Guilt by Accepting It"
"Learning More about the Past Leads to Understanding"
"Knowing Good Traditions from Bad"
"When We Need to Break the Pattern"
"Inherited Notions and Taboos—Their Merit and Their Danger"

6. Write a short research paper about one or several of the important protests from the history of the struggle for civil rights, In order to write you might do some further reading about the life of James Baldwin or of Martin Luther King, Jr. (p. 315).

Jonathan Swift

Jonathan Swift (1667–1745), one of the greatest satirists in English literature, was the son of English parents residing in Ireland. Ordained as an Anglican clergyman, he eventually became Dean of St. Patrick's, Dublin, in 1713. During this time he began to write poetry, as well as religious and political satire, most notably *The Battle of the Books* (1704) and *A Tale of a Tub* (1704). In 1726 he published his best-known work, *Gulliver's Travels.* "A Modest Proposal" (1729), one of a series of pamphlets he wrote on the English oppression of the Irish, is one of the most bitter and outrageous satires in our language.

A Modest Proposal

For Preventing the Children of Poor People in Ireland from Being a Burden to Their Parents or Country, and for Making Them Beneficial to the Public

It is a melancholy object to those who walk through this great town or travel in the country, when they see the streets, the roads, and cabin doors, crowded with beggars of the female-sex, followed by three, four, or six children, all in rags and importuning every passenger for an alms. These mothers, instead of being able to work for their honest livelihood, are forced to employ all their time in strolling to beg sustenance for their helpless infants, who, as they grow up, either turn thieves for want of work, or leave their dear native country to fight for the Pretender in Spain, or sell themselves to the Barbadoes.

I think it is agreed by all parties that this prodigious number of children in the arms, or on the backs, or at the heels of their mothers, and frequently of their fathers, is in the present deplorable state of the kingdom a very great additional grievance; and therefore whoever could find out a fair, cheap, and easy method of making these children sound, useful members of the commonwealth would deserve so well of the public as to have his statue set up for a preserver of the nation.

But my intention is very far from being confined to

provide only for the children of professed beggars; it is of a much greater extent, and shall take in the whole number of infants at a certain age who are born of parents in effect as little able to support them as those who demand our charity in the streets.

4 As to my own part, having turned my thoughts for many years upon this important subject, and maturely weighed the several schemes of other projectors, I have always found them grossly mistaken in their computation. It is true, a child just dropped from its dam may be supported by her milk for a solar year, with little other nourishment; at most not above the value of two shillings, which the mother may certainly get, or the value in scraps, by her lawful occupation of begging; and it is exactly at one year old that I propose to provide for them in such a manner as instead of being a charge upon their parents or the parish, or wanting food and raiment for the rest of their lives, they shall on the contrary contribute to the feeding, and partly to the clothing, of many thousands.

5 There is likewise another great advantage in my scheme, that it will prevent those voluntary abortions, and that horrid practice of women murdering their bastard children, alas, too frequent among us, sacrificing the poor innocent babes, I doubt, more to avoid the expense than the shame, which would move tears and pity in the most savage and inhuman breast.

6 The number of souls in this kingdom being usually reckoned one million and a half, of these I calculate there may be about two hundred thousand couple whose wives are breeders; from which number I subtract thirty thousand couples who are able to maintain their own children, although I apprehend there cannot be so many under the present distresses of the kingdom; but this being granted, there will remain an hundred and seventy thousand breeders. I again subtract fifty thousand for those women who miscarry, or whose children die by accident or disease within the year. There only remain an hundred and twenty thousand children of poor parents annually born. The question therefore is, how this number shall be reared and provided for, which, as I have already said, under the present situation of affairs, is utterly impossible by all the

methods hitherto proposed. For we can neither employ them in handicraft or agriculture; we neither build houses (I mean in the country) nor cultivate land. They can very seldom pick up a livelihood by stealing till they arrive at six years old, except where they are of towardly parts; although I confess they learn the rudiments much earlier, during which time they can however be looked upon only as probationers, as I have been informed by a principal gentleman in the county of Cavan, who protested to me that he never knew above one or two instances under the age of six, even in a part of the kingdom so renowned for the quickest proficiency in that art.

I am assured by our merchants that a boy or a girl before 7 twelve years old is no salable commodity; and even when they come to this age they will not yield above three pounds, or three pounds and half a crown at most on the Exchange; which cannot turn to account either to the parents or the kingdom, the charge of nutriment and rags having been at least four times that value.

I shall now therefore humbly propose my own 8 thoughts, which I hope will not be liable to the least objection.

I have been assured by a very knowing American of my 9 acquaintance in London, that a young healthy child well nursed is at a year old a most delicious, nourishing, and wholesome food, whether stewed, roasted, baked, or boiled; and I make no doubt that it will equally serve in a fricassee or a ragout.

I do therefore humbly offer it to public consideration 10 that of the hundred and twenty thousand children, already computed, twenty thousand may be reserved for breed, whereof only one fourth part to be males, which is more than we allow to sheep, black cattle, or swine; and my reason is that these children are seldom the fruits of marriage, a circumstance not much regarded by our savages, therefore one male will be sufficient to serve four females. That the remaining hundred thousand may at a year old be offered in sale to the persons of quality and fortune through the kingdom, always advising the mother to let them suck plentifully in the last month, so as to render them plump and fat for a good table. A child will make two dishes at an entertainment for friends; and when the family dines alone, the fore or hind quarter will make a reasonable dish, and seasoned with a little pepper or salt will be very good boiled on the fourth day, especially in winter.

11   I have reckoned upon a medium that a child just born will weigh twelve pounds, and in a solar year if tolerably nursed increaseth to twenty-eight pounds.

12   I grant this food will be somewhat dear, and therefore very proper for landlords, who, as they have already devoured most of the parents, seem to have the best title to the children.

13   Infant's flesh will be in season throughout the year, but more plentiful in March, and a little before and after. For we are told by a grave author, an eminent French physician, that fish being a prolific diet, there are more children born in Roman Catholic countries about nine months after Lent than at any other season; therefore, reckoning a year after Lent, the markets will be more glutted than usual, because the number of popish infants is at least three to one in this kingdom; and therefore it will have one other collateral advantage, by lessening the number of Papists among us.

14   I have already computed the charge of nursing a beggar's child (in which list I reckon all cottagers, laborers, and four fifths of the farmers) to be about two shillings per annum, rags included; and I believe no gentleman would repine to give ten shillings for the carcass of a good fat child, which, as I have said, will make four dishes of excellent nutritive meat, when he hath only some particular friend or his own family to dine with him. Thus the squire will learn to be a good landlord, and grow popular among the tenants; the mother will have eight shillings net profit, and be fit for work till she produces another child.

15   Those who are more thrifty (as I must confess the times require) may flay the carcass; the skin of which artificially dressed will make admirable gloves for ladies, and summer boots for fine gentlemen.

16   As to our city of Dublin, shambles may be appointed for this purpose in the most convenient parts of it, and butchers we may be assured will not be wanting; although I rather recommend buying the children alive, and dressing them hot from the knife as we do roasting pigs.

A very worthy person, a true lover of his country, and   17
whose virtues I highly esteem, was lately pleased in
discoursing on this matter to offer a refinement upon my
scheme. He said that many gentlemen of this kingdom,
having of late destroyed their deer, he conceived that the
want of venison might be well supplied by the bodies of
young lads and maidens, not exceeding fourteen years of
age nor under twelve, so great a number of both sexes in
every county being now ready to starve for want of work
and service; and these to be disposed of by their parents, if
alive, or otherwise by their nearest relations. But with due
deference to so excellent a friend and so deserving a patriot,
I cannot be altogether in his sentiments; for as to the males,
my American acquaintance assured me from frequent
experience that their flesh was generally tough and lean,
like that of our schoolboys, by continual exercise, and their
taste disagreeable; and to fatten them would not answer the
charge. Then as to the females, it would, I think with
humble submission, be a loss to the public, because they
soon would become breeders themselves: and besides, it is
not improbable that some scrupulous people might be apt
to censure such a practice (although indeed very unjustly)
as a little bordering upon cruelty; which, I confess, hath
always been with me the strongest objection against any
project, how well soever intended.

But in order to justify my friend, he confessed that this   18
expedient was put into his head by the famous Psalmana-
zar, a native of the island Formosa, who came from thence
to London above twenty years ago, and in conversation
told my friend that in his country when any young person
happened to be put to death, the executioner sold the
carcass to persons of quality as a prime dainty; and that in
his time the body of a plump girl of fifteen, who was
crucified for an attempt to poison the emperor, was sold to
his Imperial Majesty's prime minister of state, and other
great mandarins of the court, in joints from the gibbet, at
four hundred crowns. Neither indeed can I deny that if the
same use were made of several plump young girls in this
town, who without one single groat to their fortunes
cannot stir abroad without a chair, and appear at the
playhouse and assemblies in foreign fineries which they

never will pay for, the kingdom would not be the worse.

19   Some persons of a desponding spirit are in great concern about that vast number of poor people who are aged, diseased, or maimed, and I have been desired to employ my thoughts what course may be taken to ease the nation of so grievous an encumbrance. But I am not in the least pain upon that matter, because it is very well known that they are every day dying and rotting by cold and famine, and filth and vermin, as fast as can be reasonably expected. And as to the younger laborers, they are now in almost as hopeful a condition. They cannot get work, and consequently pine away for want of nourishment to a degree that if at any time they are accidentally hired to common labor, they have not strength to perform it; and thus the country and themselves are happily delivered from the evils to come.

20   I have too long digressed, and therefore shall return to my subject. I think the advantages by the proposal which I have made are obvious and many, as well as of the highest importance.

21   For first, as I have already observed, it would greatly lessen the number of Papists, with whom we are yearly overrun, being the principal breeders of the nation as well as our most dangerous enemies; and who stay at home on purpose to deliver the kingdom to the Pretender, hoping to take their advantage by the absence of so many good Protestants, who have chosen rather to leave their country than to stay at home and pay tithes against their conscience to an Episcopal curate.

22   Secondly, the poorer tenants will have something valuable of their own, which by law may be made liable to distress, and help to pay their landlord's rent, their corn and cattle being already seized and money a thing unknown.

23   Thirdly, whereas the maintenance of an hundred thousand children, from two years old and upwards, cannot be computed at less than ten shillings a piece per annum, the nation's stock will be thereby increased fifty thousand pounds per annum, besides the profit of a new dish introduced to the tables of all gentlemen of fortune in the kingdom who have any refinement in taste. And the

money will circulate among ourselves, the goods being entirely of our own growth and manufacture.

Fourthly, the constant breeders, besides the gain of eight shillings sterling per annum by the sale of their children, will be rid of the charge of maintaining them after the first year.   24

Fifthly, this food would likewise bring great custom to taverns, where the vintners will certainly be so prudent as to procure the best receipts for dressing it to perfection, and consequently have their houses frequented by all the fine gentlemen, who justly value themselves upon their knowledge in good eating; and a skillful cook, who understands how to oblige his guests, will contrive to make it as expensive as they please.   25

Sixthly, this would be a great inducement to marriage, which all wise nations have either encouraged by rewards or enforced by laws and penalties. It would increase the care and tenderness of mothers toward their children, when they were sure of a settlement for life to the poor babes, provided in some sort by the public, to their annual profit instead of expense. We should see an honest emulation among the married women, which of them could bring the fattest child to the market. Men would become as fond of their wives during the time of their pregnancy as they are now of their mares in foal, their cows in calf, or sows when they are ready to farrow; nor offer to beat or kick them (as is too frequent a practice) for fear of a miscarriage.   26

Many other advantages might be enumerated. For instance, the addition of some thousand carcasses in our exportation of barreled beef, the propagation of swine's flesh, and improvement in the art of making good bacon, so much wanted among us by the great destruction of pigs, too frequent at our tables, which are no way comparable in taste or magnificence to a well-grown, fat, yearling child, which roasted whole will make a considerable figure at a lord mayor's feast or any other public entertainment. But this and many others I omit, being studious of brevity.   27

Supposing that one thousand families in this city would be constant customers for infants' flesh, besides others who might have it at merry meetings, particularly weddings and   28 christenings, I compute that Dublin would take off annually about twenty thousand carcasses, and the rest of the kingdom (where probably they will be sold somewhat cheaper) the remaining eighty thousand.

29   I can think of no one objection that will possibly be raised against this proposal, unless it should be urged that the number of people will be thereby much lessened in the kingdom. This I freely own, and it was indeed one principal design in offering it to the world. I desire the reader will observe, that I calculate my remedy for this one individual kingdom of Ireland and for no other that ever was, is, or I think ever can be upon earth. Therefore let no man talk to me of other expedients: of taxing our absentees at five shillings a pound: of using neither clothes nor household furniture except what is of our own growth and manufacture: of utterly rejecting the materials and instruments that promote foreign luxury: of curing the expensiveness of pride, vanity, idleness, and gaming in our women: of introducing a vein of parsimony, prudence, and temperance: of learning to love our country, in the want of which we differ even from Laplanders and the inhabitants of Topinamboo: of quitting our animosities and factions, nor acting any longer like the Jews, who were murdering one another at the very moment their city was taken: of being a little cautious not to sell our country and conscience for nothing: of teaching landlords to have at least one degree of mercy toward their tenants: lastly, of putting a spirit of honesty, industry, and skill into our shopkeepers; who, if a resolution could now be taken to buy only our native goods, would immediately unite to cheat and exact upon us in the price, the measure, and the goodness, nor could ever yet be brought to make one fair proposal of just dealing, though often and earnestly invited to it.

30   Therefore I repeat, let no man talk to me of these and the like expedients, till he hath at least some glimpse of hope that there will ever be some hearty and sincere attempt to put them in practice.

31   But as to myself, having been wearied out for many years with offering vain, idle, visionary thoughts, and at

length utterly despairing of success, I fortunately fell upon this proposal, which, as it is wholly new, so it hath something solid and real, of no expense and little trouble, full in our own power, and whereby we can incur no danger in disobliging England. For this kind of commodity will not bear exportation, the flesh being of too tender a consistence to admit a long continuance in salt, although perhaps I could name a country which would be glad to eat up our whole nation without it.

After all, I am not so violently bent upon my own opinion as to reject any offer proposed by wise men, which shall be found equally innocent, cheap, easy, and effectual. But before something of that kind shall be advanced in contradiction to my scheme, and offering a better, I desire the author or authors will be pleased maturely to consider two points. First, as things now stand, how they will be able to find food and raiment for an hundred thousand useless mouths and backs. And secondly, there being a round million of creatures in human figure throughout this kingdom, whose sole subsistence put into a common stock would leave them in debt two millions of pounds sterling, adding those who are beggars by profession to the bulk of farmers, cottagers, and laborers, with their wives and children who are beggars in effect; I desire those politicians who dislike my overture, and may perhaps be so bold to attempt an answer, that they will first ask the parents of these mortals whether they would not at this day think it a great happiness to have been sold for food at a year old in the manner I prescribe, and thereby have avoided such a perpetual scene of misfortunes as they have since gone through by the oppression of landlords, the impossibility of paying rent without money or trade, the want of common sustenance, with neither house nor clothes to cover them from the inclemencies of the weather, and the most inevitable prospect of entailing the like or greater miseries upon their breed forever.

I profess, in the sincerity of my heart, that I have not the least personal interest in endeavoring to promote this necessary work, having no other motive than the public good of my country, by advancing our trade, providing for infants, relieving the poor, and giving some pleasure to the rich. I have no children by which I can propose to get a single penny; the youngest being nine years old, and my wife past childbearing.

Discussing Content and Form

1. What is the premise behind Swift's essay?

2. List in order the arguments that Swift's speaker uses to support his proposal: the number of children, the futility of their prospects in life, etc.

3. List some of the ways Swift satirizes people's attitudes toward money. How does he show his attitude toward the English government? Who are the "landlords" referred to in paragraph 12?

4. Examine the organization of the essay by grouping all the paragraphs into sections and determining what the chief function of each section is:

    a. What is the special purpose of the first three paragraphs? Of the last three? What is the relationship between these two sections?

    b. Which paragraphs are given to the proposal itself? Which involve what might be called the practical matters of carrying it out? How many paragraphs deal with the advantages of the plan? How are these paragraphs introduced?

    c. It is common in argument to anticipate and answer possible counterarguments. Where do you find Swift's speaker answering objections to his proposal?

    d. How does the essay's organization contribute to the legalistic and formal tone of the monstrous proposal? What seems to be the connection between the organization and the irony behind the satire?

5. What can you tell about the religious attitudes in Ireland during Swift's time?

6. List some of Swift's criticisms of social conditions in Ireland. How do these conditions serve as background for the "proposal"? Where does Swift indicate what he thinks ought to be done about such conditions?

Considering Special Techniques

1. Swift's essay is, of course, satire—his method is sustained irony. Throughout the "proposal" his fictitious spokesman makes monstrous suggestions that are the opposite of what is really meant. The writer of irony must give sufficient clues so that the reader does not take the statements literally.

   a. When do you first detect the irony? What clues lead to the recognition?

   b. What qualities in the character of Swift's speaker make him seem a convincing advocate of the "proposal"? How does he establish himself? Does he seem modest? Well-informed? Reasonable?

   c. The language and details of the selection are made carefully appropriate to the fictitious speaker; discuss the irony in these statements and find others which seem to you especially outrageous:

   "Infant's flesh will be in season throughout the year. . . ." (par. 13)

   ". . . this would be a great inducement to marriage, which all wise nations have either encouraged by rewards or enforced by laws and penalties." (par. 26)

   "Men would become as fond of their wives during the time of their pregnancy as they are now of their mares in foal. . . ." (par. 26)

2. What is the effect of the comment that the "helpless infants" must become thieves, "or leave their . . . country to fight for the Pretender in Spain, or sell themselves to the Barbadoes" (par. 1)? What is the effect of the references to the American friend (pars. 9 and 17)?

3. What is the effect of referring to children and their parents as if they are animals: "a child just dropped from its dam" (par. 4); "an hundred seventy thousand breeders" (par. 6), etc.? Do you find it ironic to juxtapose this language with the references to the people as "souls"? Explain.

4. Words to learn and use: melancholy, importuning, sustenance (par. 1); prodigious, deplorable, grievance (par. 2); raiment (par. 4); apprehend, rudiments, proficiency (par. 6); nutriment (par. 7); eminent, collateral (par. 13); scrupulous (par. 17); expedient (par. 18); desponding, encumbrance (par. 19); vintners (par. 25); emulation (par. 26); exportation, propagation (par. 27); parsimony, animosities, factions (par. 29); effectual, inclemencies (par. 32).

Generating Ideas

1. From the essay, construct a mental picture of the person who is making the proposal. Then write a paper in which you describe his background, personality, and the attitudes and beliefs that may have led him to write as he does. Be sure that you use the essay itself for evidence to support your descriptive details.

2. Write a paper in which you discuss the language and style of the essay and show how they are related to the character who makes the proposal and to his purpose in the essay.

3. Write your own "modest" proposal for solving one or more of our present-day ills: unemployment, inflation, care of children and of the aged poor, export trade, or armament, for example.

Glossary of Techniques

Throughout this text the techniques of the various essayists are pointed out and defined in the material accompanying the essays. The following list of terms (with brief definitions) is intended to help students locate the fuller explanations and illustrations of techniques which they in turn may practice in their own writing. Numbers in parentheses indicate pages where those specific techniques are discussed.

Alliteration   The repetition of an initial consonant sound in a line of prose or poetry.   (221)

Allusion   A reference, usually brief, to a literary work or historical event, employed to clarify or reinforce some point in speech or writing.   (84, 103, 127, 133, 139, 161, 198, 209, 220, 253, 259–60, 320–21)

Analogy   A comparison linking an unfamiliar object or event with one likely to be familiar for the purpose of explaining the lesser known of the two. Explained as method of development, 211–14.   (94, 217, 220, 229)

Anecdote   A narrative incident, often used as story-illustration of a point or as an opening to lead to a point.   (52, 84, 102, 139, 197, 313)

Antithesis   A rhetorical device that contrasts ideas by placing them in parallel grammatical structures.   (149)

Audience   The readers whom the writer wishes to reach, to convince or persuade, in view of their presumed interests and opinions.   (76, 197, 340, 349, 357, 376)

Authority   Citing important, established, or widely-known studies or persons to strengthen the writer's position.   (253, 349, 358, 370)

Balanced Sentences   A device which juxtaposes two similar elements and therefore emphasizes the connection and sometimes produces evenness of rhythm.   (114, 161, 171, 182–83, 198, 278, 321)

Cause and Effect   The analysis of either causes and effects, or both, in order to explain the reasons and/or consequences of an event, opinion, or trend. Explained as method of development, 232–35.   (240–41, 246, 253, 261)

Characterization   Presentation of persons by the use of direct comment, reproduction of their actions and speech, and the comment of others.   (69–70, 156, 181)

Classification and Division   The management of items and ideas by arranging them into divisions or groups in accord with the writer's purpose and intended meaning. Explained as method of development, 300–3.   (312, 320, 328, 336)

Coherence   The use of devices to ensure that the reader perceives underlying connections. See also **connectives.**   (114)

Comparison and Contrast   The pointing out of likenesses and differences or both in order to carry intended meaning. Explained as method of development, 173–78.   (181–82, 189, 197, 204, 209)

Connectives (transitions)   The use of function words or phrases, echoes, repetition, and careful sequence in both sentences and longer units in order to link details, items of information, and ideas. Treated throughout text in introductions to chapters.   (114, 149, 155, 162, 209, 253–54, 267)

Connotation   The overtones or associations surrounding a word as opposed to its denotation, its literal or explicit meaning.   (23, 290)

Credentials (of speaker in persuasion)   A statement of the basis of the writer's "right to speak," his claim to authority.   (122, 349, 370)

Cumulative Sentence   A sentence pattern in which one or more modifying elements, coordinate or subordinate, are added to the main clause to create a complicated unit with various levels of meaning.   (94, 210, 376)

Deduction   The logical process of drawing conclusions by reasoning from the general to the specific. See **induction.**   (339–44, 350, 357)

Definition   The analysis of the essence or characteristics of a thing or idea by various means such as comparing it to others, either similar or dissimilar; citing examples; tracing etymology; or explaining function. Explained as method of development, 269–74. (277–78, 283, 289–90, 296, 311)

Description   The use of details to make the reader feel, hear, and see. Explained as method of development, 20–23. (28, 51, 53, 103, 208)

Details   The use of concretes, selected for the writer's purpose, ranging from objective (scientific) to subjective (personal). (21–23, 27–28, 34, 41, 42, 51, 52, 76, 103, 132, 208, 220, 229)

Dialogue   Written presentation of speech, quotation from person or persona, in order to reveal the speaker or carry the writer's message. (70, 84, 189, 267)

Diction   A writer's choice of words to convey exact meaning or a special effect. (Exactness: 28, 77, 94, 103, 127, 260–61, 399) (Sensory words: 28, 35, 42–43, 209, 221)

Direction of Movement   Arrangement of material in paragraphs or longer units to move from particulars to general, or from general to particulars. See also **thesis, topic sentence**. (103, 209, 376)

Dominant Impression   The chief impression (picture, feeling) often left unstated, created by descriptive writing. (21, 51)

Emotional Appeal   The use of emotive language, situations, persons, or incidents to win the reader's sympathy in persuasive writing. (340–41, 362, 370–71, 387, 398–99)

Emphasis   Showing the reader by position or proportion what is less important, what is more. (208-9, 303, 320)

Endings (conclusions)   The expression of completeness, convincing the reader that the final word has been said. (76, 93, 162, 197, 204, 209, 220, 230, 239, 253, 260, 386, 398)

Enthymeme   A syllogism shortened by omitting one of the premises or the conclusion. (357, 361, 387)

Euphemism   The substitution of a more agreeable term for one that is ordinarily considered offensive. (204)

Examples   The concrete support required to make a generalization convincing. Explained as method of development, 105–9. (113–14, 121, 126, 132–33, 171, 266, 279, 376)

Factual Evidence   The use of verifiable facts, often statistics, to prove or develop an argument. (133, 349, 370)

Figurative Language   Use of words in a non-literal sense, a change or extension of the word's meaning. See **metaphor, simile, understatement**. (220)

Fragment A deliberately incomplete sentence structure, often used for special effect. (35, 70, 230)

Generalization The overall conclusion, expressed (usually) or implied, to which the writer has come on the topic treated. (41–42, 51, 105–9, 339–44)

Humor Lightness of tone, real or apparent, to make a point or strengthen an impression. (42, 76–77, 114, 122, 133, 260, 337, 370)

Images (imagery) Use of words or phrases to evoke sense impressions. (35, 52, 77, 140, 297)

Induction (inductive development) The logical process of arriving at a conclusion by reasoning from particulars (collected evidence, observations) to the general. (342–45, 376)

Inference A conclusion drawn from evidence. (1–2, 3–7, 42) (Distinguished from implication, 42)

Irony Use of incongruity in speech, actions, situations, or characters, usually to create humor or to achieve a striking or memorable effect. (52, 76, 113, 220, 260, 399)

  verbal irony A twist in expression, using words or phrases to convey a different (often opposite) meaning from the apparent or literal one. Saying one thing, meaning another. (133–34, 204, 399)

Levels of Language Words primarily drawn from the vocabulary of a particular group of speakers or writers, or from a particular social level.

  informal language Language drawn from speech or informal discourse, not usually found in formal writing. (84, 103, 127, 155, 260–61)

  jargon Language, often peculiar to a single profession or trade, that is so overworked or vague that it has little real meaning. (183)

  scientific language Words customarily found in writing about science, specialized language. (35, 209, 284, 350)

Metaphor A figure of speech that implies, rather than states, a likeness between two apparently unlike things. Extensively defined, 272–73. Related to analogy, 211–14. (34–35, 70, 209–10, 246, 290, 328, 371, 387)

Narration Telling a story, recounting actions and events from the writer's experience or that of someone else (or created from imagination). Narration is often used in expository writing to help carry a message, rather than for the sake of the story itself. Explained as method of development, 55–59. (69, 93, 102–3)

Objective Looking at material and selecting for writing from an outside viewpoint, without the writer's intrusion of personal feeling or bias. (28, 34, 171)

Observation An indispensable technique fundamental to all writing, whether it be personal or transactional, fictional or expository. (3–7, 9–11, 12–14, 42, 51)

Openings (introductions) A prediction, even a guarantee, that what follows will be deserving of the reader's attention. (83–84, 93, 114, 139, 220, 229–30, 246, 253)

Organization The pattern or plan a writer chooses, obvious or subtle, to give order to his concept. See introductions and marginal guides for first selections in each chapter. (28, 52–53, 102–3, 121, 126, 133, 155, 170, 198, 240, 260–61)

Paradox Presentation of two items that are contradictory, seemingly impossible together, to provoke thought. (298)

Paragraph The divisions, normally indicated by indentation and ranging from single sentences to groups of related sentences, within a longer piece of discourse. (As divisions related to larger organization: 114, 133, 171, 198, 261) (Internal organization: 93–94, 126) (Journalistic paragraph: 266–67, 362) (Single sentence and transitional: 52, 76, 84, 198, 230, 350)

Parallelism (in sentence) Laying stress on similarity of meaning by using similar structures. (321, 329)

Person (point of view) The grammatical choice of person speaking, spoken to, and spoken about in any piece of writing. Pronouns (first, second, third persons) indicate the point of view most obviously. (28, 53, 58, 113, 115, 121, 171, 261)

Persuasion Writing in order to win agreement or to move to action; also called argument. (339–44, plus examples following in final chapter.)

Premise The starting point or points (the initial concept) on which an argument can be built; the first two statements in a syllogism. (342–43, 356–57)

Process Tracing steps, usually chronologically, in an operation or event, scientific or historical, or in giving instructions. Explained as method of development, 142–45. (148, 155, 162, 170, 278)

Punctuation The mechanical, not necessarily logical, graphic system by which meaning is built into sentences. In text questions, attention is called to those marks that are used to give variety to style. (Colon: 253, 278) (Dash: 76, 140, 162, 261) (Exclamation mark: 279) (Semi-colon: 161–62, 182–83, 240, 278) (Quotations, italics: 183)

Refutation The anticipation and counteraction of arguments that might be used against the writer's or speaker's position on an issue. (349, 369, 398)

Repetition The practice of restating words or phrases for one of several purposes. (For clarity: 284) (For coherence and unity: 220, 278. See also **connectives**) (For emphasis, as motif: 52, 171, 312–13, 386)

Rhetorical Question A question asked in order to lead the reader's thoughts, not intended to be answered. (84, 162)

Satire A critical attack, humorous or serious or both, upon a condition or person in order to point out need for change. (42–43, 76–77, 83, 132, 328, 398–99)

Simile (See also figurative language) A stated comparison, using *like* or *as*, between things or ideas. (35, 53, 70, 77, 209–10)

Style The overall effect of the way a writer writes, affected by many elements such as diction, point of view, number and kind of details, sentence structure, and general tone. (189, 230, 321)

Syllogism A method of describing the process of a deductive argument, reducing the reasoning to major and minor premises and conclusion. (342–43, 350, 357, 387)

Synonyms Words with approximately the same meaning, chosen by writers for variety and exactness of expression. (204, 270, 289–90)

Tense The time element in verbs which writers must respect and manipulate to arrange events and ideas clearly; tense sequence is especially important in narration and in process tracing. (58–59, 76–77, 94, 144, 170–71)

Thesis The *sine qua non*, the concept, expressed or understood, underlying writing. (41, 121, 138, 161, 196–97, 208, 220, 239, 260, 369, 385, others) (Implied thesis: 132, 209)

Title, significance and effectiveness   Possibly, but not necessarily, an encapsulated thesis.   (43, 76, 139, 239)

Tone   The attitude, evident in the writing, in regard to audience, material, and the writer himself or herself; closely allied to voice.   (84, 113, 133–34, 149, 160–61, 171, 260–61, 337) (In persuasion: 340–41, 358, 370, 398)

Topic Sentence   The controlling or central sentence in a paragraph, usually the sentence at the highest level of generalization around which the specifics of the paragraph may be organized.   (106, 133, 313)

Understatement   A deliberate minimizing or playing down of something, usually to create a humorous effect.   (156)